Flint Daggers in Prehistoric Europe

edited by

Catherine J. Frieman and Berit Valentin Eriksen

Oxbow Books
Oxford & Philadelphia

Published in the United Kingdom in 2015 by
OXBOW BOOKS
10 Hythe Bridge Street, Oxford OX1 2EW

and in the United States by
OXBOW BOOKS
1950 Lawrence Road, Havertown, PA 19083

Hardcover Edition: ISBN 978–1–78570-018–7
Digital Edition: ISBN 978–1-78570-019-4

A CIP record for this book is available from the British Library

Library of Congress Cataloging-in-Publication Data

Flint daggers in prehistoric Europe / edited by Catherine J. Frieman and Berit Valentin Eriksen. -- Hardcover edition.
    pages cm
 Includes bibliographical references and index.
 ISBN 978-1-78570-018-7 (hardback)
 1. Weapons, Prehistoric--Europe. 2. Daggers--Europe. 3. Stone age--Europe. 4. Europe--Antiquities. I. Frieman, Catherine, 1982- editor, author. II. Eriksen, Berit Valentin, editor, author.
 GN799.W3F55 2015
 936--dc23
                        2015031209

Printed in the United Kingdom by Gomer Press

For a complete list of Oxbow titles, please contact:

UNITED KINGDOM
Oxbow Books
Telephone (01865) 241249, Fax (01865) 794449
Email: oxbow@oxbowbooks.com
www.oxbowbooks.com

UNITED STATES OF AMERICA
Oxbow Books
Telephone (800) 791-9354, Fax (610) 853-9146
Email: queries@casemateacademic.com
www.casemateacademic.com/oxbow

Oxbow Books is part of the Casemate Group

Front cover: Two type IV flint daggers with fishtail shaped hilt. Holstein-Rathlou collection, Moesgaard Museum, Denmark. Photo Rógvi N. Johansen, foto/medie Moesgaard, on a background showing a 'cache' of reproduction flint daggers made by Pete Bostrom (copyright Pete Bostrom, Lithic Casting Lab. Inc. reproduced by permission)
Back cover: Experimental daggers (taken from Van Gijn, *Flint in Focus. Lithic Biographies in the Neolithic and Bronze Age*, p. 191)

CONTENTS

CONTRIBUTORS

ERIK DRENTH

Erik Drenth graduated in 1988 from the State University of Groningen after having written an MA thesis about the social organisation of the Single Grave Culture in the Netherlands. Subsequently, he was employed by the State Service for Archaeological Investigations in the Netherlands. There, he was as a specialist in prehistory involved in the development of a computerised national archaeological database. As a prehistorian and quality manager, respectively, Drenth participated in project teams directing large-scale investigations in the central and southern Netherlands. At present, he works as a senior archaeologist and specialist in flint and prehistoric pottery in the Dutch archaeological firm ArcheoMedia.

BERIT VALENTIN ERIKSEN

Berit Valentin Eriksen is research director at the Centre for Baltic and Scandinavian Archaeology (ZBSA). She lectures on Palaeolithic and Mesolithic archaeology as a privatdozent at the University of Kiel and as a Professor II at the University of Bergen. She is also a specialist in flint technology and particularly interested in the use of lithics in the Bronze Age societies of Scandinavia.

CATHERINE J. FRIEMAN

Catherine Frieman is a lecturer in European archaeology at the Australian National University. She first wrote about flint daggers as an undergraduate and went on to study the fishtail daggers of Late Neolithic Scandinavia as part of her University of Oxford DPhil research into the process of metal adoption in Europe. Aside from flint daggers, her research interests include the nature of archaeological inquiry, innovation, skeuomorphism, and the beginning of the metal ages, as well as Neolithic and Bronze Age beads and personal ornamentation.

CAROLYN GRAVES-BROWN

Carolyn Graves-Brown gained a BA Hons. in archaeology from Durham University in 1983. She has curated collections in several museums and, in 1997, took up her present post as curator of the Egypt Centre, the Museum of Egyptian Antiquities at Swansea University. This sparked an interest in Egyptian Dynastic lithics. In 2011, she gained a PhD as a part-time student at the Institute of Archaeology, University College London for her thesis on 'The Ideological Significance of Flint in Dynastic Egypt'. She is a member of the Lithics Study Society and now lives with her husband and two greyhounds in Llanelli.

WITOLD GRUŻDŻ

Witold Grużdż is a PhD student in the department of History and Social Science at the Cardinal Stefan Wyszyński University in Warsaw (Poland). His research focuses on bifacial technology during the 3rd and 2nd millennia BC in one of the flint-rich regions in southeastern Poland. He is the author of two peer-reviewed papers on Swiderian and Magdalenian blade debitage techniques.

DENIS GUILBEAU

Denis Guilbeau completed a PhD in 2010 on specialised lithic production during the Neolithic and the Eneolithic in Italy. He is a specialist in flint knapping techniques and their social implications. His main areas of study cover the central (Italy) and eastern (western Turkey) Mediterranean basin during the Neolithic and the Chalcolithic.

EWEN IHUEL

Ewen Ihuel's work on the circulation of Grand-Pressigny flint in Brittany (France) was published in 2004. He completed a PhD in 2008 which was supervised by Catherine Perlès at the University of Nanterre on the circulation of flint daggers and blades in the western part of France. Since 2007, he has worked in the archaeological office of the Dordogne department council.

Nicole Mallet

Nicole Mallet is a French archaeologist, interested in the geological and petrographical aspects of flint. She completed a PhD in 1992 about the diffusion of Grand-Pressigny flint in the eastern part of France (Jura) and western Switzerland. She is a member of two archaeological societies (BAMGP and CEDP) and has led several excavation since 1970. Currently, she manages a research program focused on the diffusion of Grand-Pressigny material in Western Europe.

Witold Migal

Witold Migal works in the State Archaeological Museum in Warsaw (Poland). His research is focused on lithic technology and experimental archaeology. He initiated and supervised the project "Documentation of flint mines with use of non-invasive methods". He is the author of numerous papers on late flint industries and flint mining.

Jacques Pelegrin

Jacques Pelegrin is research director for CNRS and manages the UMR 7055 "Préhistoire et technologie". He is specialist in lithic technology, including both archaeological and experimental approaches. He has studied the Grand-Pressigny technology for more than 25 years.

Antonín Přichystal

Prof. RNDr. Antonín Přichystal, DSc (born 1950) graduated in geology from the J. E. Purkyně University in Brno. He carried out post-graduate studies at the Charles University in Prague. For about 35 years, he has collaborated with archaeologists from Central Europe in determining raw materials used for the production of stone artefacts. Presently, as professor at the Institute of Geological Sciences of the Masaryk University in Brno, he works on the issue of stone raw materials used in prehistoric times, especially regarding their petrographic determination. As a visiting professor, he has also lectured at the Silesian University in Opava.

Katarzyna Pyżewicz

Katarzyna Pyżewicz is a lecturer at the Institute of Prehistory at the Adam Mickiewicz University in Poznań (Poland). She is interested in the applications of use-wear analysis on Late Palaeolithic and Mesolithic lithic materials from the Polish Lowlands as well as the flint materials obtained from experimental archaeology. She is also a participant in an interdisciplinary research project aimed at reconstructing the past landscape around Poznań. She has taken part in excavations in Sandomierska Upland, Pomerania, Great Poland and Lubusz Land.

Lubomír Šebela

PhDr. Lubomír Šebela, CSc. (born 1953) graduated in 1977 in archaeology and history from the J. E. Purkyně University in Brno (now the Masaryk University), and became a professional prehistorian. From 1981, he was an employee of the Archaeological Institute of the Academy of Sciences of the Czech Republic in Brno. His major interest is the Eneolithic and the Early Bronze Age in Central Europe. In recent years, he has focused on lithic chipped industries of these periods. He frequently collaborates with Antonín Přichystal (the Masaryk University in Brno) who is responsible for petrographic expertise in their joint projects.

Shinya Shoda

Shinya Shoda is a Japanese archaeologist whose research interests include the development of production systems in areas of northeast Asia that are peripheral to the Chinese Central Plains. He holds a PhD in archaeology from Chungnam National University, with a dissertation, *Production and Society in the South Korean Bronze Age*, published in Korea (2009). His studies have recently become more multi-disciplinary, based on his interests especially in metallurgy and plant-use, as well as diet and cookery. He co-authored *The Archaeology of Pottery Firing* (2007), *The Archaeology of Cooking* (2008), and *AMS Dating and Archaeology* (2012).

Daniel Steiniger

Daniel Steiniger studied Prehistoric Archaeology, Geology and Mineralogy in Freiburg i.B. (Germany) and Basel (Switzerland). His PhD thesis focused on different topics in Chalcolithic Italy. He builds reconstructions of ancient dry stone walls and is engaged in archaeometallurgical experiments, especially copper smelting from polymetallic ores. He is a specialist in mining archaeology and has participated in excavations in this field throughout Europe, the Near East and Central Asia. He has worked at several Departments of the Landesamt für Denkmalpflege (in Baden-Württemberg and Sachsen-Anhalt) and was recently engaged in a research project entitled "Early mining in central Italy" at the German Archaeological Institute (Dep. Rome).

Annelou van Gijn

Annelou van Gijn is Professor of Archaeological Material Culture and Artefact Studies at Leiden University. She is interested in the biographies of objects and the transformations these undergo when moving between cultural contexts. She specialises in microwear studies of flint, stone, bone and antler artefacts and is currently directing an experimental reconstruction of a Neolithic house.

JEANETTE VARBERG

Jeanette Varberg is a curator at the New Moesgaard Museum, Aarhus, Denmark and responsible for the Bronze Age exhibition opening in 2014. She is an archaeologist interested in the transformation of society, social identities, gender, warfare and prehistoric religion in the Nordic Late Neolithic and Bronze Age.

CHRISTIAN VERJUX

Christian Verjux works for the ministry for culture in the archaeological office of the Centre region (Orléans). He has studied a pressignan workshop in la Guerche (1991) and, since 2006, he has managed the excavation of extensive knapping workshops at la Guerche, Bergeresse.

THOMAS ZIMMERMANN

Thomas Zimmerman graduated from the University of Regensburg, where he completed his studies in Pre- and Protohistory, European Ethnology and Classical Archaeology. For his PhD project, he was based in the Römisch-Germanisches Zentralmuseum Mainz, studying Copper Age burials with daggers in their technological and social dimensions, as part of the Early Elites Research Cluster. He is currently Assistant Professor and Acting Chair at the Department of Archaeology at Bilkent University, Ankara. His research interests include science in archaeology, early metallurgy, the emergence of elites in 3rd millennium Asia Minor and the history of archaeological methodology.

FOREWORD

For more than a century flint daggers have been among the most closely studied and most heavily published later prehistoric lithic tools. It is well established that they are found across Europe and beyond, and that many were widely circulated over many generations. Yet, few researchers have attempted to discuss the entirety of the flint dagger phenomenon. The purpose of the present volume is to bring together papers offering a glimpse into the regional variability and socio-technical complexity of flint daggers and flint dagger production. It focuses on the typology, chronology, technology, functionality and meaning of flint and other lithic daggers produced primarily in Europe, but also in the Eastern Mediterranean and East Asia, in prehistory. In this way, the volume brings together papers on flint daggers by scholars working in myriad national and archaeological research traditions and provides a comprehensive overview of the state of knowledge concerning various flint dagger corpora as well as potential avenues for future research across national, regional and disciplinary boundaries.

It consists of the proceedings of a session dedicated to *Flint Daggers in Europe and Beyond* that was held at the 2011 meeting of the European Association of Archaeology meeting in Oslo, Norway. The aim of the session was to bring together researchers from across Europe working on flint dagger assemblages in order to spark discussion; to encourage them to begin looking at regionally bounded artefact types in a broader technological, chronological and social lens; and to develop a research agenda for the future of flint dagger studies. The original group of papers presented in Oslo have been further enriched by papers from authors who were not able to participate in the session.

We would like to thank all the contributors for their participation in the original session and publication project and for their patience throughout the process. Several colleagues and peers have been invaluable sounding boards for the development of this volume and of some of the ideas presented within it, particular thanks go to Alan Saville and Hugo Anderson-Whymark. Julie Gardiner and Clare Litt at Oxbow are also heartily thanked for their enthusiasm and patience. Finally we acknowledge the generous sponsorship provided by the Centre for Baltic and Scandinavian Archaeology, Foundation Schleswig-Holstein State Museums, Schloss Gottorf.

Catherine J. Frieman
Berit Valentin Eriksen

INTRODUCTION. FLINT DAGGERS: A HISTORICAL, TYPOLOGICAL AND METHODOLOGICAL PRIMER

Catherine J. Frieman & Berit V. Eriksen

Even before the discipline of archaeology was fully developed, ancient lithic implements held great fascination for the people who discovered them. Historic sources tell us that stone tools were sometimes thought to be elf-shot or thunder stones, and they were supposed to have curative or preservative properties (Davidson 1960; Goodrum 2008; Johanson 2009). Famously, excavations at Roman temple sites in Gaul and Britain have revealed votive deposits of stone tools, such as polished stone axes dating to the Neolithic or Palaeolithic handaxes (Adkins & Adkins 1985; Turner & Wymer 1987). In regions where they were produced, flint daggers also appear to have been incorporated into ritual activities which greatly postdate their primary period of production and circulation (Johanson 2009:159f). For example, Stensköld (2006) describes a find from Ullstorp bog in Scania, southern Sweden, which consisted of a Neolithic flint dagger embedded in a Viking period horse's skull. Evidently, the dagger, which probably dates to ca 2200–2000 BC, had been collected before being used to kill the horse sometime during the 10th–11th centuries AD, with the result that the skull and flint were deposited together in a bog.

With the formalisation of antiquarian activities into the discipline of archaeology, lithic implements became crucial items for delineating period, and later cultural, boundaries. From Frere's famous letter suggesting that a flint handaxe from Hoxne, Suffolk, England dated to a period before written history to Thomsen's development of a chronological system for the prehistoric world divided into three ages – one of stone, one of bronze and one of iron – stone tools were central to the discovery and classification of the past (Rowley-Conwy 2007; Schnapp 1996; Trigger 2006). Simple typologies, based on gross morphology and analogy to historical or non-western tools, were developed to prop up

these chronological systems and, eventually, to distinguish between contemporary groups with different tool kits. Flint daggers were first identified as part of these campaigns of ordering and classifying the past. In Scandinavia, where much of this early typological work developed, they were so numerous that a separate 'Dagger Age' was suggested to exist between the Stone Age and the Bronze Age (Lomborg 1973; Müller 1902). Around Europe, catalogues of flint daggers were compiled in the early twentieth century (e.g. Hue 1910; Müller 1902; Smith 1919); and it was widely agreed that these tools were likely to have been weapons wielded by men at the end of the Neolithic or beginning of the Bronze Age. Their similarity of form to apparently contemporary blades in copper and copper alloy prompted archaeologists to suggest they were, in fact, copies of more valuable metal forms. As debitage studies and technological analyses began to dominate lithic research in the later 20th century, the study of flint daggers stalled, leaving the interpretations developed by antiquarians and early archaeologists more or less unchanged.

While early archaeologists found flint daggers fascinating because they were typologically and chronologically distinct, more recent research has also highlighted the specialised production processes developed to produce them and the extreme distances across which they were exchanged. That they are – and presumably were – frequently beautiful objects made from eye-catching raw materials is also significant as they appear to have been produced largely during a period of social and technological transition which saw the manipulation and display of a variety of new tools and ornaments made from novel materials with new textures and colours.

The last several decades have seen a renewed interest in flint daggers as new methodologies, new interpretative frameworks and new data about the past have been brought to bear on the question of what purpose they served, how they were made, where they circulated and why they appear alongside similarly shaped daggers in other materials, notably metal. Yet, these studies have rarely looked beyond a single variety of flint dagger or a reasonably bounded region (although see Zimmermann 2007). Thus, their development over space and time has never been fully explored; and we are left with the rather unsatisfying idea that the thousands of prehistoric flint daggers are all copies of metal daggers in spite of their different morphologies, deposition locales and, potentially, uses. In this chapter, we will discuss the identification and interpretation of lithic daggers and their regional variation in order to introduce the themes of this volume and the contributions made by the individual papers collected in it.

Understanding lithic daggers

Clearly, the first question that must be answered by a book about flint daggers is what actually constitutes a *flint dagger* and whether the terminology itself creates useful typological or archaeological categories. We class a number of different types of lithic implement as flint (or lithic) daggers. In Europe, the vast majority of these objects are produced from flint sources, many of them of very high quality, but their forms vary considerably from region to region and period to period. Outside Europe, we are faced with an even wider variety of raw materials, object morphologies, apparent functions and deposition locales.

The daggers discussed in this volume are flat and plano-convex, bifacially worked and unifacially worked, knapped and ground or polished, totally unretouched, beautifully pressure flaked and heavily resharpened; some consist of a blade with a small hafting tang while others have carefully shaped handles in addition to the blade end. Zimmermann (this volume) suggests a broad definition for daggers as double-edged knives with a pointed tip that are less than 35cm long; yet this definition excludes the curved Egyptian psS-kf (Graves-Brown, this volume) and, lacking a minimum length, would not allow flint daggers to be distinguished from other doubled-edged pointed implements, such as projectile points. At the same time, typological classifications of northern Italian flint implements are hazy enough that the blade found with the ice mummy in the Similaun Alps might have been determined to be a projectile point based on its diminutive length if not for the organic hafting (cf. Guilbeau, this volume). Perhaps the only definition we can rely on is the broadest possible: a double-edged blade, usually with a pointed tip, designed to be held and wielded in the hand (rather than hafted on a longer handle). Even this definition becomes problematic when we accept that some of these objects may have had

shifting functions over the course of their use-life which would have affected how they were hafted, wielded and resharpened (see Grużdź *et al.*, this volume).

Thus, any definition of a flint dagger must include the object's function at some level, but functional definitions are just as difficult, as there is so little information available to us as to the day to day use of flint daggers. A dagger in the modern sense is a weapon designed for close-proximity combat or self defense; due to its use in historic weapons assemblages, it has associations with maleness and martiality. Double-edged knives, however, play different sorts of roles in different social contexts. In some cultures, they are neither a weapon nor a tool; but a potent symbol of manhood (Camman 1977); in others, they are ritual objects used in sacred body modification, such as circumcision (e.g. Silverman 2006:125ff). The few functional analyses of flint daggers, carried out through microanalysis of wear traces, are inconsistent in their results but point to a variety of possible physical functions. A similar variety of final deposition locations paints an equally complex picture. Despite the traditional focus on flint daggers found in funerary assemblages, most flint daggers are in fact not found with burials. While the majority, unsurprisingly, are stray finds with no archaeological context, many also derive from settlement contexts, from caches or hoards and from ambiguous contexts which might indicate ritualised deposition, for example in rivers and bogs (Stensköld 2004; Frieman 2014). Essentially, we are still only beginning to understand how flint daggers were used, whether they had a single use over the course of their use life or were adapted for different tasks and how these uses affected their final form and deposition locale. Essentially, though archaeologists call many different implements with similar morphologies flint daggers, we cannot assume that these objects served similar functions or carried identical meanings, even if we accept that they were widely recognised as potent tools for identity creation and display (cf. Varberg, this volume).

In the end, we are left more or less where we began: a *flint dagger* is an archaeological classification of a sort of hand-held tool with two edges and (usually) a point which could have been produced through one of a variety of *chaînes opératoires*, could have had one or more of a variety of physical functions from items of display, to weaponry, to kitchen or ceremonial knife or butchery tool. Ultimately, understanding what flint daggers were, and concomitantly, why they were valued enough to be produced and reproduced over a considerable geographic area and long period of time, relies on our understanding of the variety within the flint dagger assemblage. Instead of focussing on determining a single meaning for all flint daggers (e.g. Skak-Nielsen 2009), we need to return to the local scale and focus on understanding how different people in different places and in different times made, used and deposited the objects we collectively term flint daggers.

Only through synthesising this information will answers emerge to the broader questions we want to ask.

Interpreting lithic daggers

Flint daggers have been studied from a variety of perspectives, often as part of research trying to answer the major questions of the day. Thus, until the last several decades, the vast majority of archaeological writing about flint daggers was either typological or chronological in nature as they were ideal type finds for the transition from Neolithic to Bronze Age society, since they appeared to be the stone version of metal objects which were thought to replace them. Over the course of the early 20th century, typologies of flint daggers were developed and refined in a number of European regions, but not all clusters of flint daggers received detailed attention. While books were written about flint daggers from France, Germany and Scandinavia, a single 10-page article was accepted as the definitive statement on British flint daggers until the 1980s. This focus on typology and chronology, and particularly the formal relationship of flint and metal daggers in these typo-chronological schemas, crucially shaped the dialogue which would occur around flint daggers well into the present day. As the discipline of archaeology developed, separate worlds of research grew around lithic and metal objects. Flint daggers sat – and continue to sit – uneasily between these worlds.

With the turn to technological analysis in the mid–20th century, lithic specialists have developed sophisticated analytical and interpretative methodologies to discuss the manufacture and use of stone tools. Technological studies of flint tools have often followed the French *chaîne opératoire* approach introduced by Leroi-Gourhan (1964, 1965) and focussed on analysing the knapping sequences of unifacially and bifacially worked long blades, often through experimental knapping programmes (Apel 2001; Callahan 2006; Kelterborn 1984; Nunn 2006a, 2006b; Pelegrin 2002; Stafford 1998, 2003). Again, as with the production of typologies, knapping sequences were only developed in detail for a few of the corpora of flint daggers in circulation, generally the most numerous and eye-catching, including the French (see Ihuel *et al.*, this volume) and Scandinavian types. Elsewhere, such as in the Italian peninsula, dynamic technological studies of flint daggers are just now being carried out (e.g. Guilbeau, this volume), even though technological aspects, including resharpening, have obvious implications for typological classification (Mottes 2001).

In response to the discovery and investigation of several flint extraction sites in the 20th century, the sources of flint used for tool production became a major focus of investigation. In particular, flint mining and raw material procurement has been the subject of several international conferences and conference proceedings. World famous sites of prehistoric flint mining such as Krzemionki Opatowskie in Poland, Grimes Graves and Cissbury in Great Britain, Rijckholt-St. Geertruid in Holland and, not least, the World Heritage Site of Spiennes in Belgium represent the oldest industrial monuments in Europe and, since their discovery in the late 19th and early 20th centuries also sparked an interest in large scale production strategies. Unquestionably, the industrial scale mass production of axes and blade blanks throughout the Neolithic at these prominent sites must have required a well-established infrastructural support. This is certainly also the case with respect to the industrial scale production of daggers and dagger blanks from the Grand-Pressigny extraction site in France (Ihuel *et al.*, this volume). The Grand-Pressigny daggers were produced for export and distributed through Europe wide networks. However, even in regions (e.g. the island of Rügen in Northern Germany) where good quality flint for dagger production was widely available, and only distributed apparently at a more regional scale, there would appear to have been some degree of local control regarding access to raw materials during the Late Neolithic (Rassmann 2000).

Moreover, investigations of production strategies at large scale flint extraction sites (mines) as well as small scale production sites (workshops) evidence the differing technological preferences of certain raw materials. It is well known that the colour and origin of lithic raw materials used to produce Neolithic ground-stone axes affected the value and deposition of the finished pieces (e.g. Bradley & Edmonds 1993; Pétrequin *et al.* 2012). Increasing numbers of microscopic and technological studies of flints used in later prehistory seem to indicate a similar preference for specific raw materials in different flint dagger production centres, perhaps due to their accessibility, to their desirable physical properties or to more culturally specific perceptions of their value (Graves-Brown, this volume). Certainly, research on Scandinavian lithic sources has made clear that different flint types were consciously chosen for the production of axes or daggers, because of the physical properties of the respective flint types (Högberg & Olausson 2007). Moreover, microscopic analyses of flint are widening our knowledge about where flint daggers were being produced and by whom (e.g. Přichystal & Šebela, this volume), highlighting the presence of smaller flint dagger production centres at the periphery of the better-known flint dagger circulation networks. These investigations are closely tied to more technological perspectives on flint daggers, especially as regards questions of technological specialisation and skilled knapping traditions.

As production technology came to dominate discussions of flint daggers, the significance of their complex manufacture processes became another key point in understanding their value and place in prehistoric society. As numerous technological studies have emphasised, producing a flint dagger – particularly one of the large, elaborate examples – required both know-how, the experiential knowledge of flint flaking and knapping sequences, also including motor skills acquired through years of training, and considerable technological knowledge, that is, the cognitive understanding of what sort of raw material, techniques and knapping trajectories would lead to a successfully completed flint dagger (Pelegrin 1990). Clearly, strategies had been put in place to communicate the knowledge of flint dagger production from generation to generation and to give knappers time and guidance to develop the required know-how as well. Many lithic specialists now believe that formal apprenticeship systems were in place in many flint dagger producing regions to allow for the passing on of these skills (Apel 2008; Högberg *et al.* 2001). Moreover, this model also implies the presence of recognised and highly experienced experts whose skills were valued and cultivated, perhaps by aggrandising elites looking for special tools, technologies and materials to use in displays of status and as trade goods (Apel 2000, 2001; Apel & Knutsson 2006; Earle 2004; Olausson 2008). These technological perspectives on flint daggers obviously diverged from earlier concerns about the relationship between similarly shaped flint and metal tools, but they did not lose sight of their contemporaneity. The flourishing of elaborate lithic production sequences in the third millennium BC, and the production of dagger-shaped lithic implements in particular, were frequently linked to a desire on the part of marginal groups to access lucrative metal exchange networks or acquire valued metal objects (e.g. Earle 2004). In this framework, knappers developed such specialised production processes because they were in competition with metallurgists in an emerging prestige-goods economy based around metal objects. Alternatively, it has been proposed that early metallurgy and elaborate lithic production sequences emerged from of a newly developed interest in specialised production processes and the objects derived from them (Frieman 2012a, 2012b). Finally, an even more direct relationship has been hinted at based on technological studies of Scandinavian type III and IV fishtail daggers. According to Stafford (1998:242) "pressure flakers tipped with copper or soft bronze are ideal" for manufacturing the punched 'stitching' on the handle of these dagger types. It is even argued "that the detailed stitching present on the handles of some type IV daggers could not have been done without the aid of metal tools" (ibid.).

Over the years, many interpretative frameworks have been proposed for understanding why flint daggers were produced, valued and widely circulated. Among the earliest and most long-standing interpretations for their appearance – and one that transcends Europe (see Shoda, this volume; Shoda & Frieman 2010) – is that they were intentional copies, that is *skeuomorphs* (Frieman 2010, 2012b), of metal daggers. The rarity of metal, the allure of its unique physical properties (e.g. recyclability, malleability, ductility,

lustre) and its central role in continent-spanning exchange networks were believed to contribute to its high value in prehistoric society. Contact with this novel material and with the emerging elites who used access to it to bolster their social position has been suggested to have caused innovation in other materials, such as the production of new elaborate lithic tool types (Earle 2004; Strahm 1961–1962). This picture of metal rapidly replacing stone as the preferred tool type is becoming harder to defend as more data becomes available for the slow and punctuated adoption of metal and metallurgy (Roberts & Frieman 2013); but a real relationship does seem to exist between flint and metal daggers – though whether the lithic tools copy metal, the metal tools copy flint (e.g. Karimali 2010; Steiniger, this volume) or both draw from a similar pool of ideas about technology, morphology and weapon shapes (Frieman 2012a) is yet to be resolved.

However, as numerous lithics specialists have made clear, the presence of flint daggers in funerary assemblages from across Europe (and beyond!) indicates that these implements are more than just knock-off copies of more desirable metal objects. Flint daggers are found in burials dating to the final Neolithic or beginning of the Bronze Age from Italy to Scandinavia. They are incorporated into locally significant rites, but often accompany single inhumations (although not always). These burials, when they contain material other than the deceased and a flint dagger, tend to include material deriving from the Bell Beaker funerary sphere, such as Beaker ceramics, flint arrowheads, beads or buttons and lithic tools, including wrist-guards, shafthole axes and cushion stones (Barfield 2001; Frieman 2014; Salanova 2007; Sarauw 2007; Siemann 2003; Van Gijn 2010a). In Britain, a number are also associated with bone or antler spatulae, a somewhat curious tool type thought to be linked either to leather working or, perhaps more tellingly, pressure flaking (Olsen in Duncan 2005; Harding 2011; Harding & Olsen 1989). While skeletal analyses are only rarely available, these burials are almost invariably described as male. These associations, as well as broader interpretations of the Bell Beaker funerary rite and its social context, have led to the widely accepted suggestion that flint (and metal) daggers were, in fact, both weapons used in personal combat (or self-defence: see Varberg, this volume) and prestige goods linked to a specifically masculine identity built on one's status as a warrior (Heyd 2007; Vandkilde 2001). As such, flint daggers are frequently interpreted not just as an indicator of gender, but also as indicating a certain amount of prestige or power which accrued to the man who possessed them. Certainly, this pattern seems to find a parallel in northeast Asia, where lithic daggers are found with male burials of often apparently high prestige (Shoda, this volume). Moreover, they seem to have served as markers to indicate affiliation with the wider Bell Beaker community and, perhaps with specific communities or trading partners within it (Frieman 2014; Honegger & de Montmollin 2010;

Sarauw 2008). In recent years, the more technological approaches discussed above have been drawn into this interpretative framework to suggest that flint daggers were prestigious status markers not just because they drew on the symbolism of weapons and warriors, but also because their specialised production was controlled, at least somewhat, by aggrandising elites (Earle 2004), giving them value within the prestige goods economy hypothesised to characterise Beaker period Europe.

While the flint daggers from funerary contexts loom large in the literature, most flint daggers were not recovered from such contexts and cannot be so easily fit into narratives of personal identity and status. It is evident that, in many parts of the world, flint daggers played a role in ceremonial and ritual contexts quite separate from the domains of daily life or the burial sphere. In Egypt, where narrative art and descriptive texts exist, some pressure flaked flint knives have been interpreted as forming part of ritual tool kits used to animate mummies and statues, while others had more mundane functions in the domestic or military sphere (Graves-Brown, this volume). Other flint daggers have been suggested to have been used in scarification (Stensköld 2004) or sacrificial rites (Skak-Nielsen 2009) before being discarded away from settlement contexts. Recent re-evaluations of the dagger assemblages in the Netherlands (Van Gijn, this volume) and in Britain (Frieman, this volume) have demonstrated that a not insignificant number of flint daggers in these regions were recovered from watery contexts, perhaps indicating their use as votive deposits. Where functional analyses have been carried out, both Dutch and British flint daggers show traces of usewear consistent only with being repeatedly placed in and withdrawn from organic sheathes (Grace 1990; Green *et al.* 1982; Van Gijn 2010a, 2010b).

Although the prevailing interpretative framework still persists in linking the value of flint daggers to the value of metal and metal daggers, the long period over which they were produced and the wide geographic area over which they were distributed suggests that flint daggers had a distinct value of their own. Drenth (this volume) suggests that some Scandinavian flint daggers were prestige goods used in gift giving between communities. Certainly, the immense area over which Scandinavian daggers are found, from Norway (Solberg 1994) to Iberia (Suárez Otero 1998), and the evidence for the exchange of broken dagger fragments (e.g Peiler 1999) suggest that, even divorced from local contexts of production and significance and lacking a fully dagger-like morphology, these pieces retained value. In some cases, the value might have accrued to them because of the rare and visually striking raw materials from which many were made. For example there is no source of high quality flint in the Netherlands, so a large flint tool would have been an exotic and obviously foreign object (Drenth, this volume; Van Gijn, this volume). In others, the quality

of workmanship, even of a broken piece, may have been prized as evidence of skilled and specialised production (Frieman 2012b). However, the sheer persistence of the flint dagger form and its links to exchange and trade suggest that they also served the valuable purpose of signifying shared identities across ethnic or language boundaries: dagger bearing people were people who valued trade contacts, long distance exchange and, perhaps, certain forms of exchange as well (Varberg, this volume; Frieman 2012a).

The Dagger Age

The production and use of flint daggers was a widespread phenomenon which lasted a considerable period of time. While some early archaeologists posited a 'Dagger Age' between the Neolithic and Bronze Age, flint daggers were produced through much of the European Neolithic and continued in use alongside metal in many areas. Their origins are particularly fuzzy. The earliest European flint daggers appear to date to the mid- to late 4th millennium BC, with the well-known dagger industries in France and Scandinavia developing several centuries later in the mid to late 3rd millennium BC. Their appearance largely mirrors the earliest presence of copper blades in central and northern Europe, but not west-central France where the Grand-Pressigny blades developed (Ihuel *et al.*, this volume). The latter examples, like daggers in southern Italy (Steiniger, this volume), seem to develop organically out of pre-existing lithic industries (Ihuel 2004); although, in most regions, research into the technological development of flint daggers and the pre-existing technologies out of which they developed is still emerging. In fact, in many regions which later developed flint dagger industries lithic implements can be identified which may have been early dagger-like forms, for example the mid 4th millennium BC so-called 'flint halberds' from the Baltic zone which are somewhat plano-convex, bifacially worked double-edged blades with a pointed tip (Ebbesen 1992; Klassen 2000: 260f). Zimmerman (this volume, 2007) suggests that there may be an earlier form of flint dagger which was produced in the Eastern Mediterranean during the Pre-pottery Neolithic. Certainly, the small number of flint daggers from Çatalhöyük which demonstrate a very refined pressure flaking technique implies a connection between Europe and the Eastern Mediterranean; but these are highly anomalous pieces with no clear parallel or predecessors in Anatolia and a surprisingly early date of early 7th millennium BC, based on their stratigraphic contexts (Zimmermann, this volume). Aside from these Anatolian examples, the earliest dagger variants outside Europe do seem to coincide with the social changes linked to the adoption of metallurgy (e.g. Shoda, this volume), even if an imitative relationship between flint or lithic and metal objects can be identified.

However, a tight focus on the origin of flint daggers also

disregards the presence of daggers in other materials, not just metal but also organic materials such as bone, antler and wood; although these are usually dated as contemporary to or more recent than the earliest lithic daggers. At least one bone dagger, contemporary with metal and flint examples, is known from Spilamberto, a north Italian Late Neolithic cemetery (Bagolini 1981:130; Barfield & Chippendale 1997). A small number have also been recovered from waterlogged contexts in Britain where they are dated to the early 2nd millennium BC, due to perceived morphological similarities to specific types of metal daggers (ApSimon 1954–1955; Gerloff 1975; Smith 1920). The extremely fortunate preservation of these pieces hints at the wider circulation of daggers in materials other than stone and metal, a suggestion that perhaps finds a parallel in the flat axe, another widely circulated lithic object type, made from wood and preserved in a waterlogged context in Robenhausen, Switzerland (Strahm 1995:18). Just as wooden models such as this one might have served as templates for clay-moulds so that identical metal artefacts could be cast, full-sized, three-dimensional models are highly valued by modern flint knappers who benefit from having an exemplar to handle while making identical copies of ancient flint daggers (Callahan pers. comm.; Nunn pers. comm.).

The frequent associations between a dagger-like form, funerary contexts and associated grave-goods linked to apparently male and martial spheres has led a rather universalised interpretation of flint daggers in prehistoric society (see above). Yet, decades of detailed analysis of specific assemblages of flint daggers tend to undermine these broad interpretations and suggest a variety of local uses for and meanings applied to these implements. Even when specific pieces are typologically similar (or even identical), such as is the example of the plano-convex Grand-Pressigny daggers (Ihuel *et al.*, this volume), the archaeological evidence points to the primacy of localised functions and meanings, only some of which relate to funerary or ritual contexts. Moreover, many attempts at interpreting flint daggers fail to take into account that many – if not most – were obviously resharpened, and that their function could have changed over the course of their uselife. Even the dagger form itself, could be a product of a single phase in the implement's life, as demonstrated by Gruźdź *et al.* (this volume) who note that the Volhynian implements they examined had gloss consistent with their use as sickles either prior to being reshaped into daggers or subsequent to their dagger phase of use. Moreover, although we know that certain types of flint daggers, such as the French blade daggers, were produced and circulated over generations if not centuries, archaeologists have rarely had to grapple with the period of time an individual dagger remained in use. Observations by Van Gijn (this volume) and others suggest that, in many parts of Europe, daggers were sheathed and

curated, suggesting a long period of use. Similarly, many of the Grand-Pressigny daggers were heavily resharpened over the course of their uselives, presumably to retain them as functional tools for the myriad tasks to which they were suited (Ihuel *et al.*, this volume).

Flint daggers in prehistoric Europe and beyond

A key element which colours our understanding of the flint daggers, their chronology, function and connectedness are the different national traditions of research which have affected not just the questions asked of these implements, but also the methodologies applied to investigate them. It is well known that, within Europe and beyond, the discipline of archaeology has developed differently due to historical contexts, political structures and available materials and sites (Trigger 2006). As briefly outlined above, lithics research has also followed different trajectories in different countries. Previous research often suffered from the 'pretty piece syndrome' with the main focus being on establishing a typochronological sorting of artefacts. However, in recent years the dynamic technological approach aiming at a contextual *chaîne opératoire* analysis has pervaded the discipline even with respect to flint working in metal-using societies (Eriksen 2010).

In terms of flint dagger studies, the result of these varying histories of research is that very different information is available about flint daggers in different regions. For example, the long tradition of lithics research in France means that Grand-Pressigny daggers are very well understood technologically and archaeologically; while, by contrast, a long-standing lack of interest in Metal Age lithics in Britain means that the British flint daggers have languished largely unstudied for most of the last century. We are still struggling to align regional typochronologies of flint daggers with radiocarbon dates and then to correlate those dates across the broad swathes of Europe over which some of the dagger varieties are found (see for example the disparities in dating Scandinavian type flint daggers in Bloemers 1968; Lomborg 1973; Rasmussen 1990; Vandkilde *et al.* 1996). Similarly, our understanding of the raw materials from which flint daggers were made is well advanced in some areas, while it remains a research desideratum in others. Furthermore, like archaeologists studying many other key prehistoric innovations, flint dagger specialists have paid particular attention to the origin of flint daggers, but very little to when they ceased to circulate. Consequently, the later history of flint daggers, comprising the period after the main production areas ceased to be centres of flint dagger manufacture but during which numerous flint daggers remained in circulation, is almost entirely obscured.

This volume presents the first multi-regional overview of the entire flint dagger phenomenon. It brings together recent and ongoing research on largely contemporary material from the Eastern Mediterranean to Scandinavia and sets it alongside case studies of similar implements from Early Neolithic Anatolia and Early Bronze Age northeast Asia. In scope, the volume aims to serve as the foundation for the development of regional and continental sequences of dagger production and use. Moreover, it brings together research rarely published in a common language and never previously published together to allow the interpretative and methodological frameworks in which flint dagger research is currently being carried out to be compared and contrasted. Consequently, a major goal of the volume is not just to highlight the wealth of exciting research into flint daggers currently being carried out, but also to make visible the gaps in our knowledge. The authors included in this volume bring a wealth of experience and knowledge to bear in interpreting the flint daggers within their region of speciality, but each paper approaches flint daggers from a distinctly different perspective and uses wholly dissimilar methodologies to study them. Although flint daggers have been a focus of archaeological investigation for over a century, as the papers included in this volume demonstrate, there are still many questions to ask of these singularly beautiful implements and many ways of learning about them.

References

Adkins, L. & Adkins, R. 1985. Neolithic axes from Roman sites in Britain. *Oxford Journal of Archaeology* 4 (1): 69–76.

Apel, J. 2000. Flint daggers and technological knowledge. Production and consumption during LN1. In: D.S. Olausson & H. Vandkilde (eds.), *Form, Function & Context: material culture studies in Scandinavian archaeology.* Acta archaeologica Lundensia, series in 8°, No. 31. Stockholm: Almqvist and Wiksell. 135–154.

Apel, J. 2001. *Daggers, Knowledge and Power: The Social Aspects of Flint-Dagger Technology in Scandinavia 2350–1500 cal BC.* Coast to Coast-book 3. Uppsala: Department of Archaeology and Ancient History, Uppsala University.

Apel, J. 2008. Knowledge, Know-how and raw material – the production of late neolithic flint daggers in Scandinavia. *Journal of Archaeological Method and Theory* 15 (1): 91–111.

Apel, J. & Knutsson, K. eds. 2006. *Skilled production and social reproduction. Aspects of traditional stone-tool technologies. Proceedings of a symposium in Uppsala, August 20–24, 2003.* Stone Studies 2. Uppsala: Societas Archaeologica Upsaliensis and the Department of Archaeology and Ancient History, Uppsala University.

ApSimon, A. M. 1954–1955. A decorated bronze dagger of Arreton Down type from the Thames near Bourne End. *Berkshire Archaeological Journal* 54: 119–122.

Bagolini, B. 1981. *Il neolitico e l'Eta del Rame: ricerca a Spilamberto e S. Cesario, 1977–1980.* Bologna: Cassa di Risparmio di Vignola.

Barfield, L. 2001. Beaker lithics in northern Italy. In: F. Nicolis (ed.), *Bell Beakers Today: Pottery, People, Culture, Symbols in Prehistoric Europe. Proceedings of the International Colloquium, Riva del Garda (Trento, Italy) 11–16 May 1998.* Trento, Italy: Provincia Autonoma di Trento Servizio Beni Culturali Ufficio Beni Archeologici. 507–518.

Barfield, L. & Chippendale, C. 1997. Meaning in the later prehistoric rock-engravings of Mont Bégo, Alpes-Maritimes, France. *Proceedings of The Prehistoric Society* 63: 103–128.

Bloemers, J. H. F. 1968. Flintdolche vom scandinavischen Typus in den Niederlanden. *Berichten van de Rijksdienst voor het Oudheidkundig Bodemonderzoek* 18: 47–110.

Bradley, R. & Edmonds, M. R. 1993. *Interpreting the Axe Trade: Production and Exchange in Neolithic Britain, New Studies in Archaeology.* Cambridge: Cambridge University Press.

Callahan, E. 2006. Neolithic Danish daggers: An experimental peek. In: J. Apel & K. Knutsson (eds.), *Skilled Production and Social Reproduction. Aspects of Traditional Stone-Tool Technologies. Proceedings of a Symposium in Uppsala, August 20–24, 2003.* Stone Studies 2. Uppsala: Societas Archaeologica Upsaliensis and the Department of Archaeology and Ancient History, Uppsala University. 115–129.

Camman, S. V. R. 1977. The cult of the Jambiya: dagger wearing in Yemen. *Expedition* 19 (2): 27–34.

Davidson, T. 1960. The cure of elf-disease in animals. *Journal of the history of medicine and allied sciences* 15 (3): 282–291.

Duncan, H. 2005. Bone artefacts. In: I. Roberts & J. Prudhoe (eds.), *Ferrybridge Henge: the Ritual Landscape. Archaeological Investigations at the Site of the Holmfield Interchange of the A1 Motorway.* Leeds: Archaeological Services WYAS. 163–165.

Earle, T. 2004. Culture matters in the Neolithic transition and emergence of hierarchy in Thy, Denmark: Distinguished lecture. *American Anthropology* 106: 111–125.

Ebbesen, K. 1992. Tragtbægerkulturens dolkstave (The halberds of the Funnel Beaker Culture). *Aarbøger for nordisk Oldkyndighed og Historie*: 103–136.

Eriksen, B. V. ed. 2010. *Lithic Technology in Metal Using Societies.* Aarhus: Jutland Archaeological Society.

Frieman, C. J. 2010. Imitation, identity and communication: The presence and problems of skeuomorphs in the Metal Ages. In: Eriksen (ed.) 2010: 33–44.

Frieman, C. J. 2012a. Flint daggers, copper daggers and technological innovation in Late Neolithic Scandinavia. *European Journal of Archaeology* 15 (3): 440–464.

Frieman, C. J. 2012b. *Innovation and imitation: stone skeuomorphs of metal from 4th–2nd millennia BC northwest Europe.* Oxford: Archaeopress.

Frieman, C. J. 2014. Double edged blades: Revisting the Early Bronze Age flint daggers of Great Britain and Ireland. *Proceedings of the Prehistoric Society* 80: 33–65.

Gerloff, S. 1975. *The Early Bronze Age Daggers in Great Britain and a Reconsideration of the Wessex Culture.* Prähistorische Bronzefunde 6, 2. Munich: Prähistorische Bronzefunde.

Goodrum, M. R. 2008. Questioning thunderstones and arrowheads: The problem of recognizing and interpreting stone artifacts in the seventeenth century. *Early Science and Medicine* 13 (5): 482–508.

Grace, R. 1990. The limitations and applications of usewear data. *Aun* 14: 9–14.

Green, H. S., Houlder, C. H. & Keeley, L. H. 1982. A flint dagger from Ffair Rhos, Ceredigion, Dyfed, Wales. *Proceedings of the Prehistoric Society* 48: 492–495.

Harding, P. 2011. Spatula. In: A. Fitzpatrick (ed.), *The Amesbury Archer and the Boscombe Bowmen: Bell Beaker Burials on Boscombe Down, Amesbury, Wiltshire.* Salisbury: Wessex Archaeology. 158–159.

Harding, P. & Olsen, S. 1989. Flint and the burial group in 1017 with a note on the antler spatulae. In: P. J. Fasham, D. E. Farwell & R. J. B. Whinney (eds.), *The Archaeological Site at Easton Lane, Winchester.* Winchester: Hampshire Field Club & Wessex Archaeology. 99–107.

Heyd, V. 2007. Families, prestige goods, warriors and complex societies: Beaker groups in the 3rd millennium cal BC. *Proceedings of the Prehistoric Society* 73: 327–380.

Högberg, A., Apel, J., Knutsson, K., Olausson, D. S. & Rudebeck, E. 2001. The spread of flint axes and daggers in Neolithic Scandinavia. *Památky Archeologické* 92 (2): 193–221.

Högberg, A. & Olausson, D. 2007. *Scandinavian Flint – an Archaeological Perspective.* Aarhus: Aarhus University Press.

Honegger, M. & de Montmollin, P. 2010. Flint daggers of the Late Neolithic in the Northern Alpine area. In: Eriksen (ed.) 2010: 129–142.

Hue, E. 1910. Distribution géographique de l'industrie en silex du Grand-Pressigny. In: *Actes du VIe Congrès Préhistorique de France, Tours 1910.* Paris: Société Préhistorique Français. 386–436.

Ihuel, E. 2004. *La diffusion du silex du Grand-Pressigny dans le massif armoricain au Néolithique.* Paris: Comité des travaux historiques et scientifiques.

Johanson, K. 2009. The changing meaning of 'Thunderbolts'. *Folklore* 42: 129–174.

Karimali, E. 2010. Lithic and metal tools in the Bronze Age Agean: A parallel relationship. In: Eriksen (ed.) 2010: 157–167.

Kelterborn, P. 1984. Towards replicating Egyptian predynastic flint knives. *Journal of Archaeological Science* 11 (6): 433–453.

Klassen, L. 2000. *Frühes Kupfer im Norden: Untersuchungen zu Chronologie, Herkunft und Bedeutung der Kupferfunde der Nordgruppe der Trichterbecherkultur.* Jutland Archaeological Society publications 36. Højbjerg, Århus: Moesgård Museum and Jutland Archaeological Society; Aarhus University Press.

Leroi-Gourhan, A. 1964. *Le geste et la parole.* Vol. 1, *Sciences d'aujourd'hui.* Paris: A. Michel.

Leroi-Gourhan, A. 1965. *Le geste et la parole.* Vol. 2, *Sciences d'aujourd'hui.* Paris: A. Michel.

Lomborg, E. 1973. *Die Flintdolche Dänemarks: Studien über Chronologie und Kulturbeziehungen des südskandinavischen Spätneolithikums.* Nordiske fortidsminder. Serie B-in quarto; bd. 1. København: Universitetsforlaget i kommission hos H.H.J. Lynge.

Mottes, E. 2001. Bell Beakers and beyond: flint daggers of northern Italy between technology and typology. In: F. Nicolis (ed.), *Bell Beakers Today: Pottery, People, Culture, Symbols in Prehistoric Europe. Proceedings of the International Colloquium, Riva del Garda (Trento, Italy) 11–16 May 1998.* Trento, Italy: Provincia Autonoma di Trento Servizio Beni Culturali Ufficio Beni Archeologici. 519–545.

Müller, S. 1902. *Flintdolkene i den nordiske Stenalder.* Nordiske Fortidsminder I, 5. Copenhagen: Gyldendal.

Nunn, G. R. 2006a. *Replicating the type 1C Neolithic Danish*

dagger: Advanced flintknapping with Greg Nunn.* Castle Valley, Utah: Paleo Technologies.

Nunn, G. R. 2006b. Using the Jutland type IC Neolithic Danish Dagger as a model to replicate parallel, edge-to-edge pressure flaking. In: Apel & Knutsson (eds.) 2006: 81–113.

Olausson, D. 2008. Does practice make perfect? Craft expertise as a factor in aggrandizer strategies. *Journal of Archaeological Method and Theory* 15 (1): 28–50.

Peiler, F. 1999. Ein nordischer Flintdolch aus Falkenstein in Niederösterreich. *Archäologie Österreichs* 10 (2): 45–48.

Pelegrin, J. 1990. Prehistoric lithic technology: some aspects of research. *Archaeological Review from Cambridge* 9 (1): 116–125.

Pelegrin, J. 2002. La production des grandes lames de silex du Grand-Pressigny. In: J. Guilaine (ed.), *Matériaux, productions, circulations, du Néolithique à l'Âge du Bronze.* Paris: Errance. 125–141.

Pétrequin, P., Cassen, S., Errera, M., Klassen, L., Sheridan, A. & Pétrequin, A.-M. (eds.) 2012. *JADE. Grandes haches alpines du Néolithique européen, Ve au IVe millénaires av. J.-C.* Besançon, France: Presses Universitaires de Franche-Comté.

Rasmussen, L. W. 1990. Dolkproduktion og -distribution i senneolitikum. *Hikuin* 16: 31–42.

Rassmann, K. 2000. Die Nutzung baltischen Feuerstein an der Schwelle zur Bronzezeit – Krise oder Konjunktur der Feuersteinverarbeitung? *Bericht der Römisch-Germanischen Kommission* 81: 5–36.

Roberts, B. W. & Frieman, C. J. 2013. Early metallurgy in western and northern Europe. In: C. Fowler, J. Harding & D. Hofmann (eds.), *The Oxford Handbook of Neolithic Europe.* Oxford: Oxford University Press. 27–39.

Rowley-Conwy, P. 2007. *From Genesis to Prehistory: the Archaeological Three Age System and its Contested Reception in Denmark, Britain, and Ireland.* Oxford Studies in the History of Archaeology. Oxford: Oxford University Press.

Salanova, L. 2007. Les sépultures campaniformes: lecture sociale. In: J. Guilaine (ed.), *Le chalcolithique et la construction des inégalités.* Paris: Errance. 213–228.

Sarauw, T. 2007. Male symbols or warrior identities? The 'archery burials' of the Danish Bell Beaker Culture. *Journal of Anthropological Archaeology* 26 (1): 65–87.

Sarauw, T. 2008. Danish Bell Beaker Pottery and flint daggers – the display of social identities. *European Journal of Archaeology* 11 (1): 23–47.

Schnapp, A. 1996. *The Discovery of the Past: the Origins of Archaeology.* London: British Museum Press.

Shoda, S. & Frieman, C. J. 2010. Comparative study of the adoption of metallurgy in northeast Asia and northwest Europe Focusing on weapon-shaped bronze and stone tools [in Japanese]. In: S. Shoda, T. Kishimoto & S. Arai (eds.), *Program and Abstracts of the 3rd International Conference of the Society for the History of Asian Casting Technology.* Tokyo: Society for the History of Asian Casting Technology. 79–80.

Siemann, C. 2003. *Flintdolche Norddeutschlands in ihrem grabrituellen Umfeld.* Universitätsforschungen zur prähistorischen Archäologie 97. Bonn: Habelt.

Silverman, E. K. 2006. *From Abraham to America: A History of Jewish Circumcision.* Lanham, MD: Rowman and Littlefield.

Skak-Nielsen, N.V. 2009. Flint and metal daggers in Scandinavia and other parts of Europe. A re-interpretation of their function in the Late Neolithic and Early Copper and Bronze Age *Antiquity* 83 (320): 349–358.

Smith, R. 1919. [The chronology of flint daggers]. *Proceedings of the Antiquaries of London* 32 (1): 6–22.

Smith, R. 1920. Specimens from the Layton Collection, in Brentford Public Library. *Archaeologia* 69: 1–30.

Solberg, B. 1994. Exchange and the role of import to western Norway in the Late Neolithic and Early Bronze Age. *Norwegian Archaeology Review* 27 (2): 111–126.

Stafford, M. D. 1998. In search of Hindsgavl: Experiments in the production of Neolithic Danish flint daggers. *Antiquity* 72 (276): 338–349.

Stafford, M. D. 2003. The parallel-flaked flint daggers of late Neolithic Denmark: an experimental perspective. *Journal of Archaeological Science* 30: 1537–1550.

Stensköld, E. 2004. *Att berätta en senneolitisk historia. Sten och metall i södra Sverige 2350–1700 f. Kr.*, Stockholm Studies in Archaeology 34. Stockholm: Stockholm University.

Stensköld, E. 2006. Flying daggers, horse whisperers and a midwinter sacrifice. Creating the past during the Viking Age and early Middle Ages. *Current Swedish Archaeology* 14: 199–219.

Strahm, C. 1961–1962. Geschäftete Dolchklingen des Spätneolithikums. *Jahrbuch des Bernischen historischen Museums in Bern* 41/42: 447–478.

Strahm, C. 1995. Die Anfänge der Metallurgie in Mitteleuropa. *Helvetia archaeologica* 25: 2–39.

Suárez Otero, J. 1998. El puñal de sílex nórdico de Cela: una revisión. *Gallaecia* 17: 137–150.

Trigger, B. G. 2006. *A History of Archaeological Thought.* Cambridge: Cambridge University Press (2nd ed.).

Turner, R. & Wymer, J. 1987. An assemblage of Palaeolithic hand-axes from the Roman religious complex at Ivy Chimneys, Witham, Essex. *Antiquaries Journal* 67 (1): 43–60.

Van Gijn, A. 2010a. *Flint in Focus: Lithic biographies in the Neolithic and Bronze Age.* Leiden: Sidestone.

Van Gijn, A. 2010b. Not at all obsolete! The use of flint in the Bronze Age Netherlands. In: Eriksen (ed.) 2010: 45–60.

Vandkilde, H. 2001. Beaker representation in the Danish Late Neolithic. In: F. Nicolis (ed.), *Bell Beakers Today: Pottery, People, Culture, Symbols in Prehistoric Europe. Proceedings of the International Colloquium, Riva del Garda (Trento, Italy) 11–16 May 1998.* Trento, Italy: Provincia Autonoma di Trento Servizio Beni Culturali Ufficio Beni Archeologici. 333–360.

Vandkilde, H., Rahbek, U. & Rasmussen, K. L. 1996. Radiocarbon dating and the chronology of Bronze Age southern Scandinavia. *Acta Archaeologica* 67: 183–198.

Zimmermann, T. 2007. *Die ältesten kupferzeitlichen Bestattungen mit Dolchbeigabe: archäologische Untersuchungen in ausgewählten Modellregionen Alteuropas.* Mainz: Verlag des Römisch-Germanischen Zentralmuseums.

LITHIC DAGGERS IN THE ANCIENT NEAR EAST – WHENCE AND WHITHER?

Thomas Zimmermann

This contribution considers and reassess the presently available evidence for identifiable double-edged, short shafted flint dagger blades mainly from Anatolian contexts, starting with the earliest examples, as found in Pre-Pottery Neolithic contexts, to the dagger blades of Later Neolithic provenance. Moreover, especial attention is paid to issues such as conspicuous raw material use, use and wear traces, and the function of daggers as status-enhancing items. Finally, attention is drawn to the (potential lack of any) interactions between flint knappers and metalworkers, which are so beautifully documented in Europe, but much more difficult to identify in the Near East.

> "Is this a dagger I see before me? The handle toward my hand?
> Come, let me clutch thee..."
>
> (William Shakespeare, *Macbeth*, Act II, scene 1)

It would probably be slightly over the top to label archaeology as an academic discipline that is largely obsessed with the quest for "firsts" in a history only populated by Homo sapiens, the predominant mammal species; but there might be some basis to the statement. To trace back and identify decisive innovations in a diachronic perspective of human history can without a doubt tell us a lot about the adoption, rejection and eventual transfer of certain technological applications that eventually triggered much more profound cultural changes. Well-known examples of this process would encompass the iconic wheeled vehicle, pottery production and extractive metallurgy. Furthermore, when it comes to artefacts purposely made with aggressive intent, the dagger might be considered to be one of the earliest clearly identifiable weapons for face-to-face close combat. Yet, it is also a weapon often stigmatised as a, literally, 'backstabbing' blade, handled by dubious individuals for devious attacks – "et tu, Bruté?"

In general terms, a dagger blade, regardless of whatever raw material it is made from, is characterised through having two sharpened edges which clearly distinguish this implement from the single-edged knife. However, there is no agreement on what specific maximum length of such a double-edged blade would make it a long dagger rather than a short sword, an entirely different class of weapon. With regard to metal examples, suggestions for what should be considered the maximum length of a dagger range from about 25cm to 50cm, with Brockhaus' 1837 edition of his *Encyclopaedia* defining double-edge bladed weapons in the 35–55cm range as being too large to be daggers but not quite swords (cf. Zimmermann 2007a:5f). In fact, there are few (though telling) examples of double-edged blades from the Chalcolithic period onwards which were undoubtedly used as stabbing weapons rather than merely as multifunctional cutting tools (Zimmermann 2007a:7f).

Be that as it may, the subject here is the identification of those artefacts of stone that might be classed as dagger blades. As it is, stone daggers hold a very special place in the study of European prehistory. Thanks to their abundant occurrence, especially as regards the 2nd millennium BC examples from Scandinavia, when they demonstrate a breathtaking competition between traditional flint-smiths and the 'novel' metal-smiths, a vast number of special studies have been published on their typology, distribution and consumption (e.g., Trnka 1991; Stafford 1998; Rassmann 2000; Apel 2001; Siemann 2003). Unfortunately, until recently, the same was not the case with regard to Anatolia. The main reason for this neglect is that lithic daggers are still a rather exotic item among the versatile range of flint and obsidian objects from prehistoric contexts in the region. Even so, they are occasionally found (Fig. 1.1).

From a chronological point of view, Klaus Schmidt has suggested that the earliest examples of what might be identified as purpose-made dagger blades are represented by a series of flint points from sites in south-east Turkey and Upper Mesopotamia that are dated to the Pre Pottery Neolithic (PPN) era, approximately the 10th to the second half of the 9th millennia BC (Schmidt 1998). As he stressed in his article, the particular points he has identified as what might be dagger blades could be differentiated as an implement group quite separate from the more usual symmetrical, roughly leaf-shaped projectile points, such as arrow- or javelin-heads because of their size, weight, and shape (Schmidt 1998: 682). The examples he listed were mainly from south-east Turkey and included several fragments of broken-off tangs from the (already inundated) PPN site of Nevalı Çori together with complete – and presumably slightly older, hence early PPNA – examples from Göbekli Tepe and from nearby Gürcütepe. For Upper Mesopotamia at large, he also suggested as dagger blades a series of large, leaf-shaped flint blades from Mureybet, northern Syria, and a point fragment from Nemrik 9, Northern Iraq (Kozłowski 1994: 162; Schmidt 1998: 684f) (Fig. 1.2).

However, although Schmidt's arguments for identifying these finds as daggers are entirely persuasive, we nonetheless should note that his identifications are based on typological factors. That is to say, a consideration and analysis of their relative weight, length, the dimension of the tang, and the steep shape of the blade's tip, all combine – in Schmidt's opinion – to exclude their possible use as points for medium or long range projectile weapons. Rather, he sees their morphology as suggesting their likely function as the points of weapons with short shafts that were primarily used for cutting and stabbing: in other words, as daggers. In truth, although Schmidt's arguments from the typological and functional analysis of these items are, in themselves, convincing, what might be of use here would be the macroscopic and microscopic use and wear analyses of the finds in question, with the objective of identifying traces that would verify or contradict their identification as dagger blades. That said, it is also clear that the comparably small number of pieces currently identified as possible dagger blades together with the absence of reliable use and wear studies would perhaps preclude such a positive identification one way or the other.

Consequently, in the absence of such analysis we might, for the time being, accept Schmidt's hypothesis on the original function of these objects as daggers; and even emphasise other factors of note relevant to this interpretation. For example, we might usefully focus on a large presumed dagger blade from a burial at PPN Nevalı Çori (Schmidt 1998: 682f) (Fig. 1.3). The blade weighs nearly 54 gr (Fig. 1.3), rather on the heavy side for a throwing or thrusting weapon, and it was found directly beneath a separated skull situated amidst at least three disarticulated burials; although the blade was (apparently) not related to the decapitation process involving the separation of this skull from its parent body (Schmidt 1998: 682f). The special treatment of skulls as a distinctive funeral ritual is, of course, a well-known phenomenon in the Early Neolithic of the Ancient Near East; but, in this case, as the large blade in question was directly associated with the skull of one specific individual rather than being randomly placed in the burial, one is tempted to interpret it as a status-enhancing burial gift, so perhaps more likely to be an exotic item such as a dagger rather than a more common projectile point.

Yet, strangely enough, this apparent PPN tradition of producing large, heavy double-edged flint blades that might well have functioned as dagger blades is seemingly not continued in the later stages of the Pre-Pottery Neolithic (late phase "B"), coinciding with the mid to late 9th millennium BC (Schmidt 1998: 685f). For a comprehensive survey of published flint and obsidian blades from the Near Eastern Pre-Pottery and Early Pottery Neolithic contexts has not identified any items that could possibly have been intended for use as short range, double-edged stabbing tools. This particular situation makes the daggers from Neolithic Çatalhöyük, located in the Konya plain, South Central Anatolia, even more unusual in the sense that they would seem to materialise all of a sudden, lacking any clear connection, both in shape and technique to the identifiable daggers of the early PPN. Still, what we have here are, without any doubt, daggers (Fig. 1.4). Of the several examples found at the Neolithic "supersite", a site that has been controversially debated ever since the illustrious James Mellaart first scratched its surface in 1957 (e.g., Mellaart 1967; Hassan 1997; Hodder 1998a, 1998b, 2000, 2006) , the best known example was that associated with an intramural burial in layer VI, house 29, corresponding to approximately 6750 BC. Its bone handle in the shape of a curled snake is attached to a perfectly symmetrical blade with flawlessly exercised parallel pressure-flaked retouch on its dorsal surface, and a carefully serrated double edge. Moreover, the "fine grained tabular flint" (Conolly 1999: 41) used for this blade (it is currently unclear whether it was also used for the others) is, most likely, a raw material imported from elsewhere, since no resources of translucent, honey-yellow flint are yet known from the vicinity of Çatalhöyük. Here, obsidian from central and eastern Anatolia was the predominant raw material in all levels, with only a small percentage of flint items recorded (Carter *et al.* 2005; Carter

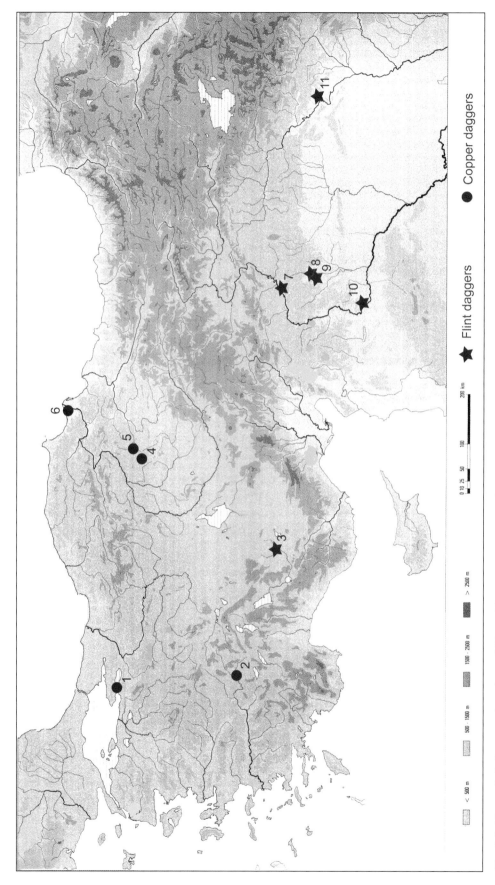

Fig. 1.1. *Map with findspots in Anatolia and Upper Mesopotamia mentioned in the text: 1) Ilıpınar; 2) Beycesultan; 3) Çatalhöyük; 4) Çamlıbel Tarlası; 5) Alaca Höyük and Kalınkaya; 6) İkiztepe; 7) Nevalı Çori; 8) Göbekli Tepe; 9) Gürcütepe; 10) Mureybet (Syria); 11) Nemrik (Iraq).*

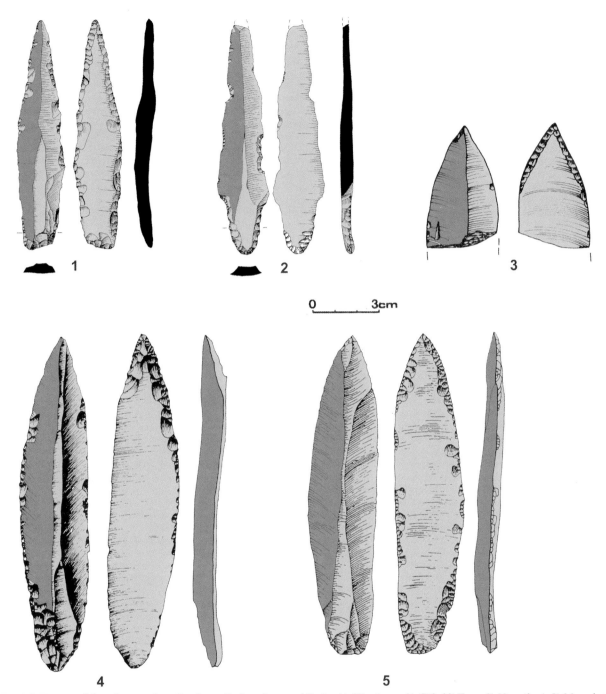

Fig. 1.2. Presumed flint daggers from Southeast Turkey, Iraq and Syria: 1) Gürcütepe; 2) Göbekli Tepe; 3) Nemrik; 4–5) Mureybet (after Schmidt 1998 and Kozłowoski 1994).

2011). More to the point, this example, the best known of the daggers found during Mellaart's campaigns at Çatalhöyük, needs to be considered alongside a group of at least eight other blades, mainly from funerary contexts, which retain the same stylistic and technological details. This group includes a fragment interpreted as originally having been a dagger tang which was repeatedly reworked until, in its final form,

it ended up as some kind of cutting or scraping tool (Fig. 1.4.8). To these examples we might add the fruits of the more recent campaigns at the site, including an exquisite dagger with a handle in the shape of a boar's head from "space 89", again associated with an intramural inhumation (Stevanovic & Tringham 1998; Hodder 2006: 246).

These fine daggers, with their distinctive technology and

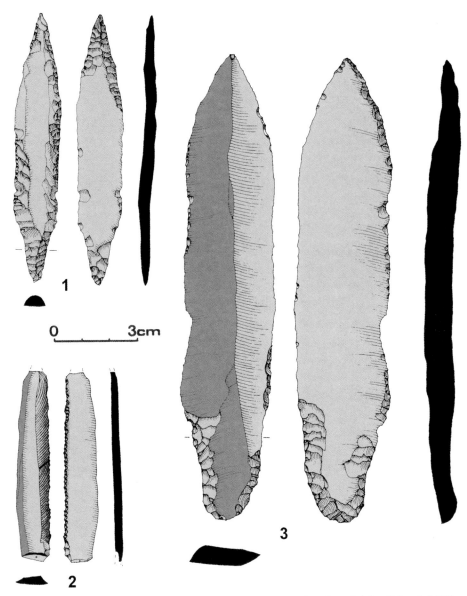

Fig. 1.3. Nevalı Çori: Lithic items associated with one secondary burial (after Schmidt 1998).

finish, with a parallel "Egyptian" [*sic*!] unifacial retouch and a polished ventral side makes these items easily distinguishable from the numerous leaf-shaped blades, presumably spearheads with bifacial retouch, recovered from Çatalhöyük (Bialor 1962; Mellaart 1963: 75, 101) (Fig. 1.4.6 & 1.4.7). However, although their excellent finish is clear testimony to a high level of craftsmanship, they remain unique in the sense that there is absolutely no material to compare them with from the immediate or wider vicinity or time period. Their exclusive association – at least if we only consider complete items – with burials strongly points to their function as status-enhancing objects, a view strengthened by the knowledge that the preparation of such fine daggers, with their parallel retouch, serrated edges and, in some cases, elaborately carved handles, is clearly more time- and energy-consuming even for a skilled knapper than producing a conventional bifacial blade. For the time being, no further observations concerning use and wear of the dagger blades has been reported; although, *if* the reworked fragment published by Conolly (1999: Fig.1.4.8) does indeed represent what was originally a dagger tang, then we might consider that such elaborate objects were not only manufactured for display or funerary gifts, but also saw active use.

What is surprising in many ways, though, is that no such excellence in lithic craftsmanship was ever again achieved in Anatolia. The production of clearly identifiable lithic daggers seems to begin, peak and end with the Early Pottery

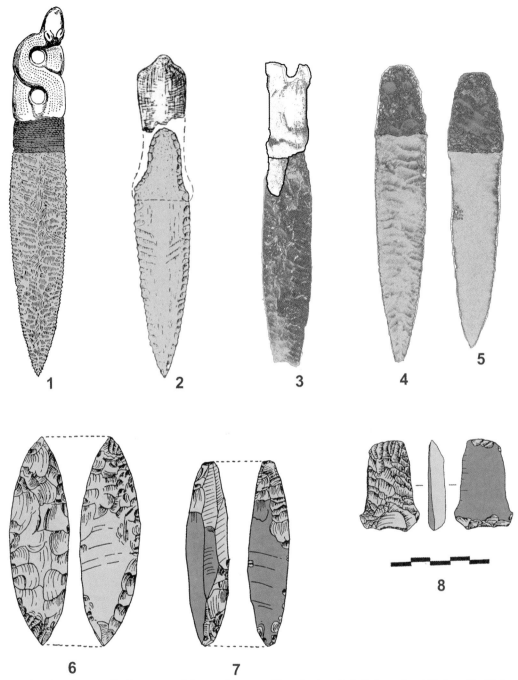

Fig. 1.4. Çatalhöyük: Flint daggers (1–5), presumed dagger fragment (8) and points (6 & 7) (spearheads?) from Neolithic contexts (after Mellaart 1964 [1–2], Hodder 2006 [3], Mellaart 1967 [4–5], Bialor 1962 [6–7] and Conolly 1999 [8]) – not to same scale.

Neolithic period at Çatalhöyük. From this period onwards, lithic products are more or less carefully worked utilitarian devices, lacking any of the material or technical qualities which would set them apart as status-enhancing objects. Only the (much later) flint and quartzite leaf-shaped points from Late Chalcolithic Central Anatolian sites like Alaca Höyük (Schoop 2005:41) or Kalınkaya (second half of the 4th millennium BC) (Fig. 1.5) retain something approaching the same elaborate treatment. However, their small size excludes a function as a short-range stabbing or cutting device. Indeed, from a wider perspective, the only Near Eastern items that could technically compete in terms of craftsmanship with the flint daggers from Çatalhöyük are the magnificent large flint knifes and daggers with carved

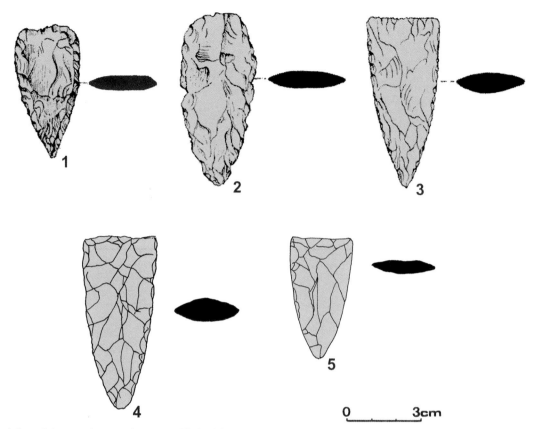

Fig. 1.5. Leaf shaped (quarzite) points from Late Chalcolithic contexts at Alaca Höyük (1–3) and Kalınkaya (4–5) – after Schoop 2005 (1–3); 4 & 5 drawn by Ben Claasz Coockson – drawings 1-4 approximate scale: 1:3.

ivory handles from 4th millennium BC Pre-Dynastic Egypt (Naqada I–II) (Bénédite 1918; Kaiser 1985; Baumgartel 1960; Graves-Brown, this volume). During the course of Naqada II, these knives and daggers were replaced by a distinctively smaller version (Baumgartel 1960: 38) (Fig. 1.6). As an aside, we should note that such convergent developments are by no means indicators for a genetic relationship between any Neolithic Anatolian community and later Predynastic Egypt. Furthermore, in passing, we should remember the unique flint dagger with "Egyptian retouch" found in a burial of unknown date at Discio, Southern Italy (Gervasio 1915: 174f), which might be technically identical to genuine Upper Egyptian dagger and knife blades due to its raw material's surface texture (Barfield 1981: 28).

This overview of the available evidence regarding confirmed flint daggers in the Ancient Near East leaves us with a strange picture made up of a series of finds that are very much dispersed in terms of time and space and which seem to lack any clearly defined forerunners that would allow for a typological grouping, evolutionary development or traceable chronological trajectory. Furthermore, the situation becomes even more disturbing when one tries to evaluate the development of lithic dagger production in

the region vis-à-vis the spread of metal dagger blades. In continental Europe, these two working traditions can be nicely paralleled from the late 3rd through the first half of the 2nd millennia BC (Rassmann 2000). The ever-growing utilisation of copper-based metallurgy provoked flint knappers to rise to previously unseen heights in preparing lithic tools and weapons, but only for a comparatively short time. The spread of the sword as the new iconic sign of rank and status from *ca.* 1600 BC resulted in the steady demise of the established flint industry (Rassmann 2000:31). In light of this trajectory, we can position the lithic "composite sword" from Åtte, Denmark (Müller-Karpe 1974; recently, Zich 2004) as representative of both the apogee and impracticability of challenging a fully-fledged and versatile bronze industry with weapons made from siliceous stone.

However, for the Near East in general and Anatolia in particular, the picture is somewhat different. The earliest identifiable metal daggers are found in Late Chalcolithic contexts dated to the second half of the 4th millennium BC. These earliest daggers comprise a single triangular example from Çamlıbel Tarlası (near Hattusha-Boğazköy, Çorum province) (Schoop 2009: 64) and a fragment from the Chalcolithic levels of Beycesultan (Lloyd & Mellaart 1962: 280f; Zimmermann 2004–2005: 256), complemented

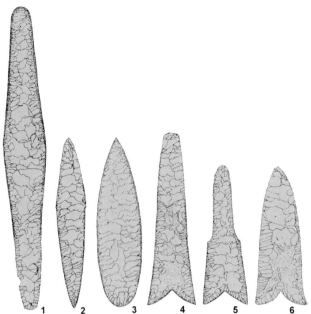

Fig. 1.6. Flint daggers and "knives" from predynastic Naqada necropolis, Egypt (after Müller-Karpe 1968) – scale unknown.

millennium (Rahmstorf 2006; Efe 2007) might have made demands for a competitive lithic industry obsolete.

By way of conclusion, the examples from Çatalhöyük still remain awkwardly isolated from the overall lithic traditions of the Ancient Near East in terms of their date and technology. Any material that pre- or postdates these outstanding daggers cannot be directly connected to them; however, it must be remembered that our knowledge about obsidian greatly exceeds our understanding of flint deposits and their local uses (Carter *et al.* 2005; archaeological and archaeometrical obsidian studies are rather abundant, cf. Oddone *et al.* 1997; Balkan-Atlı *et al.* 1999; Carter 2011 with bibliography). Comprehensive archaeometric analysis of flint artefacts and raw material resources might shed a different light on the whence and whither of these exceptional items. Even so, from a general perspective, the relative scarcity of easily identifiable lithic daggers still obstructs a better diachronic understanding of their social value and practical function. Nevertheless, any new addition to the meagre corpus of Near Eastern lithic daggers might well topple our current impression and literally add a fresh new layer to the patchy picture we currently rely on.

Acknowledgements

This contribution is a revised and enlarged version of a paper I delivered in the "Prehistoric flint daggers in Europe (and beyond?)" workshop, organised by Catherine Frieman and Berit Valentin Eriksen at the 17th annual meeting of the EAA in Oslo 2011. I am grateful to the organisers for their kind invitation, their encouragement and their stoic patience to realise a distinguished, comprehensive volume on this particular issue. I am likewise indebted to my Bilkent colleague Julian Bennett for proofreading the manuscript.

by a series of arsenical copper daggers from the Late Chalcolithic cemetery of Ilıpınar in northwest Turkey (Begemann *et al.* 1994; Roodenberg 2001). These early metal daggers, especially the rhombic, unriveted blades from Ilıpınar, are likely to represent – as a reversal of the *Ex Oriente Lux* paradigm – the influence of early, simple, double-edged items from southeastern European Copper Age contexts (Zimmermann 2007a: 121f). In addition, we should note that, with regard to the Black Sea littoral, the still much-debated stratigraphy of İkiztepe might be interpreted as providing metal daggers of 4th millennium date (Zimmermann 2004–2005; 2007b). However, it is not until the Early Bronze Age, from the 4th to the 3rd millennia BC, that the metal dagger becomes the regular, if not indispensable, companion of (exclusively male?) burials throughout Anatolia and the Near East.

The fact remains that there is absolutely no evidence that the various flint types or obsidian were ever considered to be materials valuable or workable enough to produce fine close-combat weapons. Lithic objects securely or tentatively dated to the 4th or 3rd millennia BC largely serve simple utilitarian purposes that hardly go beyond simple cutting, scraping or drilling activities, with no tendency to be transformed into something even mildly elaborate. The neatly retouched leaf shaped points from Central Anatolian Late Chalcolithic sites discussed above might be a notable exception, but they were definitely not intended to serve as stabbing tools. Secure access to relatively abundant copper sources and, for a broad zone stretching from northwest Turkey to Upper Mesopotamia, to the much sought-after tin in the 3rd

References

Apel, J. 2001. *Daggers, Knowledge and Power. The Social Aspects of Flint-Dagger Technology in Scandinavia 2350–1500*. Coast to Coast-book 3. Uppsala: Department of Archaeology and Ancient History, Uppsala University.

Balkan-Atlı, N., Binder, D. & Cauvin, M. C. 1999. Obsidian sources, workshops, and trade in central Anatolia. In: M. Özdoğan & N. Başgelen (eds.), *Neolithic in Turkey the Cradle of Civilization. New Discoveries*. Istanbul: Arkeoloji ve Sanat Yayınları. 133–145.

Barfield, L. H. 1981. Patterns of North Italian Trade 5.000–2.000 b.c. In: G. Barker & R. Hodges (eds.), *Archaeology and Italian Society. Prehistory, Roman and Medieval Studies*. Papers in Italian Archaeology II. Oxford: British Archaeological Reports International Series 102. 27–51.

Baumgartel, E. J. 1960. *The Cultures of Prehistoric Egypt II*. London: Oxford University Press.

Begemann, F., Pernicka, E. & Schmitt-Strecker, S. 1994. Metal finds from Ilıpınar and the advent of arsenical copper. *Anatolica* 20: 203–219.

Bénédite, G. 1918. The Carnarvon Ivory. *The Journal of Egyptian Archaeology* 5: 1–15, 225–241.

Bialor, P. A. 1962. The chipped stone industry of Çatal Höyük. *Anatolian Studies* 12: 67–110.

Carter, T. 2011. A true gift of mother earth: the use and significance of obsidian at Çatalhöyük. *Anatolian Studies* 61: 1–19.

Carter, T., Conolly, J. & Spasojević, A. 2005. The chipped stone. In: I. Hodder (ed.), *Changing Materialities at Çatalhöyük. Reports from the 1995–1999 Seasons*. Cambridge: Cambridge University Press. 221–283, 467–533.

Conolly, J. 1999. *The Çatalhöyük Flint and Obsidian Industry. Technology and Typology in Context*. BAR international series 787. Oxford: Archaeopress.

Efe, T. 2007. The theories of the 'Great Caravan Route' between Cilicia and Troy: the Early Bronze Age III period in inland western Anatolia. *Anatolian Studies* 57: 47–64.

Gervasio, M. 1915. *I dolmen e la civiltà del Bronzo nelle Puglie*. Bari s.n.

Hassan, F. 1997. Beyond the surface: comments on Hodder's 'reflexive excavation methodology'. *Antiquity* 71: 1020–1025.

Hodder, I. 1998a. Whose rationality? A response to F. Hassan. *Antiquity* 72: 21–27.

Hodder, I. 1998b. The past as passion and play: Çatalhöyük as a site of conflict in the construction of multiple pasts. In: L. Meskell (ed.), *Archaeology Under Fire: Nationalism, Politics and Heritage in the Eastern Mediterranean and Middle East*. London: Routledge. 124–139.

Hodder, I. ed. 2000. *Towards Reflexive Method in Archaeology: The Example at Çatalhöyük*. Ankara: British Institute of Archaeology at Ankara Monograph.

Hodder, I. 2006. *Çatalhöyük. The Leopard's Tale. Revealing the Mysteries of Turkey's Ancient 'Town'*. London: Thames & Hudson.

Kaiser, W. 1985. Zur Südausdehnung der vorgeschichtlichen Deltakulturen und zur frühen Entwicklung Oberägyptens. *Mitteilungen des Deutschen Archäologischen Instituts, Abteilung Kairo* 41: 61–87.

Kozłowski, S. K. 1994. Chipped Neolithic Industries at the Eastern Wing of the Fertile Crescent. (Synthesis Contribution). In: H. G. Gebel & S. K. Kozłowski (eds.), *Neolithic Chipped Stone Industries of the Fertile Crescent*. Berlin: Ex Oriente. 143–171.

Lloyd, S. & Mellaart, J. 1962. *Beycesultan Vol. I. The Chalcolithic and Early Bronze Age Levels*. London: British Institute of Archaeology at Ankara.

Mellaart, J. 1963. Excavations at Çatal Höyük, 1962. Second preliminary report. *Anatolian Studies* 13: 42–103.

Mellaart, J. 1964. Excavations at Çatal Höyük, 1963. Third preliminary report. *Anatolian Studies* 13: 39–119.

Mellaart, J. 1967. *Çatal Hüyük. A Neolithic Town in Anatolia*. New York: MacGraw-Hill.

Müller-Karpe, H. 1968. *Handbuch der Vorgeschichte. Band II Jungsteinzeit*. München: C. H. Beck.

Müller-Karpe, H. 1974. *Handbuch der Vorgeschichte Band IV. Bronzezeit. Dritter Teilband Tafeln*. München: C. H. Beck.

Oddone, M., Yegingil, Z., Bigazzi, G., Ercan, T. & Özdoğan, M. 1997. Chemical characterisations of Anatolian obsidians by instrumental and epithermal neutron activation analysis. *Journal of Radioanalytical and Nuclear Chemistry* 224 (1–2): 27–38

Rahmstorf, L. 2006. Zur Ausbreitung vorderasiatischer Innovationen in der frühbronzezeitlichen Ägäis. *Praehistorische Zeitschrift* 81: 49–96.

Rassmann, K. 2000. Vortrag zur Jahressitzung der Römisch-Germanischen Kommission. Die Nutzung baltischen Feuersteins an der Schwelle zur Bronzezeit – Krise oder Konjunktur der Feuersteinverarbeitung? *Berichte der Römisch-Germanischen Kommission* 81: 5–36.

Roodenberg, J. 2001. A Late Chalcolithic Cemetery at Ilıpınar in Northwestern Anatolia. In: R. M. Böhmer & J. Maran (eds.), *Lux Orientis. Archäologie zwischen Asien und Europa. Festschrift Harald Hauptmann zum 65. Geburtstag*. Rahden/Westfalen: Verlag Marie Leidorf. 351–355.

Schmidt, K. 1998. Frühneolithische Silexdolche. In: G. Arsebük, M. J. Mellink & W. Schirmer (eds.), *Light on Top of the Black Hill. Studies Presented to Halet Çambel*. Istanbul: Ege Yayınları. 681–692.

Schoop, U. 2005. *Das anatolische Chalkolithikum. Eine chronologische Untersuchung zur vorbronzezeitlichen Kultursequenz im nördlichen Zentralanatolien und den angrenzenden Gebieten*. Remshalden: Verlag Berhard Albert Greiner.

Schoop, U. 2009. Ausgrabungen in Çamlıbel Tarlası 2008. In: A. Schachner, Die Ausgrabungen in Boğazköy-Hattuša 2008. *Archäologischer Anzeiger* 2009(1): 56–72.

Siemann, C. 2003. *Flintdolche Norddeutschlands in ihrem grabrituellen Umfeld*. Universitätsforschungen zur prähistorischen Archäologie Band 97. Bonn: Habelt.

Stafford, M. 1998. In search of Hindsgavl: experiments in the production of Neolithic Danish flint daggers. *Antiquity* 72: 338–349.

Stevanovic, M. & Tringham, R. 1998. The BACH 1 Area. *Çatalhöyük Archive Report* 1998. http://catal.arch.cam.ac.uk/catal/Archive_rep98/stevanovic98.html.

Trnka, G. 1991. Nordische Flintdolche in Österreich. *Archäologie Österreichs* 2(2): 4–10.

Zich, B. 2004. Vom Dolch zum Schwert. In: H. Meller (ed.), *Der geschmiedete Himmel. Die weite Welt im Herzen Europas vor 3600 Jahren*. Stuttgart: Konrad Theiss. 132–133.

Zimmermann, T. 2004–2005. Early daggers in Anatolia – A necessary reappraisal. *ANODOS* 4–5: 251–262.

Zimmermann, T. 2007a. *Die ältesten kupferzeitlichen Bestattungen mit Dolchbeigabe. Archäologische Untersuchungen in ausgewählten Modellregionen Alteuropas*. Monographien des Römisch-Germanischen Zentralmuseums Band 71. Mainz: Römisch-Germanisches Zentralmuseum.

Zimmermann, T. 2007b. Anatolia and the Balkans, once again – Ring-shaped idols from Western Asia and a critical reassessment of some "Early Bronze Age"-items from İkiztepe, Turkey. *Oxford Journal of Archaeology* 26: 25–33.

2

DAGGER-LIKE FLINT IMPLEMENTS
IN BRONZE AGE EGYPT

Carolyn Graves-Brown

The paper begins with a summary of the morphology and contexts of flint dagger-like tools of Dynastic Egypt and shows that all dagger-like tools were more than utilitarian. It is drawn from sections of the author's doctoral thesis. Those tools considered are: bifacial knives, the ritual tool known as the psS-kf *and particularly large projectile points. The second part of the paper incorporates textual evidence supporting the idea that flint tools were ideologically significant. The study shows that flint was not only practically important but was also linked with the gods, specifically the sun-god Re, and the northern night sky. Flint was both protective and creational and thus an important weapon against the enemies of the sun-god and a tool to encourage rebirth.*

Introduction

In popular thought, Egypt is often considered innovative, yet it continued to produce high quality flint work later than elsewhere in the Near East (Tillmann 1998). Of Dynastic Period (*ca.* 3100BC–30 BC) tools, bifacial flint knives are perhaps the best known, but other forms include: blades (sickle blades, borers, drills, chisels, razors), bracelets, axeheads, picks, arrowheads, burnishers, etc. Excitingly, we also have iconographic and textual evidence.

Here, I discuss only dagger-like tools: knives, large projectile points and the ritual implement known as the *psS-kf*. While all three are included because their bifacial characteristics and parallel faces give them commonality, I concentrate upon one type: the large projectile points which are particularly frequent on military sites. These are all too often ignored in studies of Egyptian weaponry and are frequently mistaken for daggers. It will be shown that flint weaponry, in certain circumstances, could be more effective than metal. A study of the three types of tool shows that flint items were more than functional. If we expand the evidence to include text it can be seen that flint was considered a perfect weapon of the sun-god and thus that the material may have been also employed in weaponry for religious purposes.

Definitions

I know of no clearly provenanced Dynastic Period tools which could be justifiably defined as daggers in the narrow sense of parallel-sided, close-combat weapons, and none are listed in studies of Egyptian daggers (e.g. Petschel 2011). However, various tools could be categorised as 'dagger-like', in that they are bifacial, have two long cutting edges and have a point at one end. Large projectile points are particularly dagger-like in having parallel edges, and indeed are often mistaken for such. The period under study is from about 3000 BC to 700 BC, a period roughly equating to the Bronze Age (Table 2.1). I use the term 'flint' to mean sedimentary, siliceous rocks usually worked by knapping. I have chosen this term rather than 'chert' because the term 'flint' is traditionally used by English-speaking archaeologists working on Old World material; because, among archaeologists, 'chert' is often thought of as low grade and, yet, Egyptian material is high grade; and because the ancient Egyptians probably used only one term, *ds*, to refer to 'flint' and 'chert' so I feel no need to distinguish between the two.

Table 2.1. Chronology of the Egyptian Bronze Age. The period from the 3100 BC to 30 BC, shaded grey, is generally considered the Dynastic Period.

Period	Calendar date (BC)	Technological and social development
Predynastic	5500–3100	Early use of copper
Early Dynastic	3100–2686	State formation
Old Kingdom	2686–2181	Copper commonly used
First Intermediate Period	2181–2055	
Middle Kingdom	2055–1650	
Second Intermediate Period	1650–1550	
New Kingdom	1550–1069	
Third Intermediate Period	1069–747	Iron smelting *ca.* 700 BC
Late Period	747–332	
Ptolemaic Period	332–30	
Roman Period	30 BC–AD 395	

Background

There were three watersheds in the decline of flint tools: *ca.* 2500 BC, *ca.* 1200 BC, and *ca.* 600 BC (Graves-Brown 2011: vol. 1, chp. 3). After *ca.* 2500 BC, there were few really high quality items, though flint continued to be used everyday up until *ca.* 1200 BC. After this date, flint was mainly used for expedient tools. After *ca.* 600 BC, it was uncommon, though not unknown.

Possible Predynastic flint daggers are documented (Gilbert 2004: 42f, fig. 5.9), though some are plausibly misidentified and could be projectile points or knives. The same problem arises with several so-called Dynastic daggers. So, for example, while bifacial tools from the fort of Buhen, without hafting evidence, have been claimed as daggers (Emery *et al.* 1979: 116ff, pl. 102), hafting evidence from very similar types at Mirgissa (Vila 1970), clearly shows these were large projectile points. There is a flint dagger in the British Museum with remains of a wooden haft and leather sheath (EA22816; Petschel 2011: 352). While this has been catalogued as Middle Kingdom, the date is questionable as no provenance is known and the piece has not been radio-carbon dated. While the form of EA22816 is similar to some Dynastic metal daggers, for example Petrie Museum UC40673, it is also close to some metal Predynastic daggers, for example the silver and ivory dagger from El-Amrah (Cairo Museum 35158; Randall-MacIver & Mace 1902: 23, 40, pl. 6.1 & 6.2; Petschel 2011: 350).

While I know of no flint Dynastic daggers, metal Dynastic daggers are neither rare nor common and appear to have been personal weapons rather than military issue (Vila 1970: 91; Petschel 2011). Gilbert (2004: 43) suggests that daggers were usually manufactured of metal, as flint would tend to break when twisted.

Dagger-like tools

This overview is based upon a more detailed typology (Graves-Brown 2011: vol. 2, appx 1) which used the datasets of flint tools from British museums, published sources and my own work on flint from the New Kingdom site of Amarna. Three forms may be said to be similar to daggers: flint knives, the psS-kf and large projectile points; of the three the latter is the most dagger-like in form. I begin with knives and the psS-kf.

Knives

Bifacial knives are perhaps the most familiar of Egyptian flint tools, largely as they are reasonably common, are often aesthetically pleasing and are depicted on tomb walls in cattle slaughter rituals. Such knives were perhaps also familiar throughout the ancient world. They have been found throughout the Levant, for example from Early Bronze I Erani (Rosen 1988). Others were transported to Byblos (Dunand 1954) and Knossos (Cadogan 1966: fig.1), both cited in Tillmann (1992: 198f).

Sub-forms[1]

While Egyptian flint knives may be bifacial or unifacial, only the bifacial types are close to dagger shapes. Bifacial knives have two, long asymmetric edges one of which is used for cutting, and a point at one or both ends end. They tend to measure between 10cm and 16cm in length, though the Early Dynastic Period includes several oversize (probably ritual) examples (Graves-Brown 2011: vol. 1, section 3.3.4.4.) (Fig. 2.1).

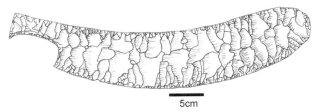

Fig. 2.1. Bifacial knife with cut-out handle from Abydos. After Hikade 1999:fig. 4.

5cm

There is no evidence that flint knives copied the shape of metal ones. Predynastic flint knives were rhomboidal, fishtail, crescentic or comma-shaped and occasionally have gold or ivory handles. The earliest metal examples date to the Early Dynastic Period, are tanged and have parallel edges. It is later metal knives which are, like the flint forms, more crescentic; whether copying flint forms or otherwise cannot be proven.

Generally, Dynastic Egyptian knives move from the comma-shaped with concave back, to the straight- or even convex-backed knives. Some Early Dynastic types have cut-out handles (see Fig. 2.1). Wooden handles (e.g. Berlin Ägyptisches Museum 18999; Scharff 1931: 53, pl. 4.65) are rare. Later types may have handles manufactured from cord wrapped around one end of the blade (e.g. Spurrell 1891: pl. 13.6 from a house at Middle Kingdom Lahun). Flint knives were common until at least the New Kingdom and the latest example of which I am aware comes from the site of Third Intermediate Period site of el-Ashmunein (Spencer 1993: 31, 33, pls 27, 29).

Generally, Predynastic to Early Dynastic forms show the greatest knapping skill, using pressure flaking to produce long blades of narrow width. The ripple-flaked knife is probably the most well known, though there are others. Generally, at this date, knapping is extremely regular and the edges of some almost look as though they were drawn with a ruler (e.g. Pitt-Rivers Museum 1901.40.24.9 and 1901.40.42.10). Additionally, flake scars are shallower and smaller than later examples. After the Early Dynastic Period, knives cease to exhibit the same kind of care and skill. However, it is noticeable that the large, finely made types come from Early Dynastic royal tombs and that even in the Early Dynastic there are rough examples. It could be then, that the apparent decline is due to a decrease in royal tombs rather than a general reduction in highly skilled knapping.

One particular type of Early Dynastic knife has a concave back (Fig. 2.1) and cut-out handle and is finely knapped, though not as finely made as the ripple-flaked type. The fine knapping, together with the fact that this type is often oversized, ritually broken or found as one of a pair (Graves-Brown 2011: vol.1, section 5.2.4.5), suggests some ritual significance.

Manufacture

Flint is ubiquitous in Egypt as far south as Hierakonpolis (for more information on quarries and mines see James Harrell's web site[2]). Flint quarries are known and flint was also obtained as a by-product of rock-cut tomb construction. Manufacturing sites are hard to identify. It seems that knives were usually produced away from use-sites. In the Early Dynastic, temple sites were associated with knife manufacture (Holmes 1992) suggesting royal control. A large number of undated roughout knives have been found at Wadi el-Sheik, a major quarry source for knives, suggesting manufacture also took place near quarry sites. Quarries would have been controlled by the king.

At least some knives were made on the tabular flint commonly found in Egypt (e.g. M5386 A and B from Abydos). It is possible that most were manufactured from this, though cortex removal makes proof impossible. Other pieces may have been made on large flakes removed from large cores. Flaking scars suggest that early examples were finished by pressure flaking, but those from the later Old Kingdom onwards could have been made using a soft hammer.

The aesthetically pleasing Predynastic and Early Dynastic ripple-flaked forms (Midnant-Reynes & Tixier 1981; Kelterborn 1984) in particular, have been subject to replication exercises. These have shown that such fine examples take about 17 hours to manufacture by modern knappers. However, replication never proves that the ancients used a particular technique. Depictions of flint knife manufacture in tombs at Middle Kingdom Beni Hasan (Fig. 2.2) are difficult for modern knappers to understand which has led to the claim that ancient artists had a poor understanding of knapping. However, work by Marquardt Lund (demonstration at Egypt Centre Conference May 2010, now online; Lund 2015) has shown a possible method which correlates with the Beni Hasan scenes. Lund used a wooden percussion tool of around 30cm long, tipped with copper which was held vertically by the knapper and grasped in the hand as one might hold a pencil. The flint to be knapped was held freehand in the left hand and flakes knocked off the core away from the knapper's body. Such work highlights the danger of assuming that ancient and modern knappers used the same tool types and techniques. One might assume that similar techniques were used for all bifacial Egyptian forms.

Dating and function

Flint knives are extremely common on Egyptian sites until the New Kingdom. Although Eggebrecht (1973: 114) states that, from the New Kingdom, knives are manufactured of metal, archaeology has uncovered many New Kingdom flint examples. Indeed, as stated above, at least one flint

Fig. 2.2. Manufacture of flint knives depicted in Middle Kingdom tombs at Beni Hasan. After Griffith 1896: plate 15.

knife is known from a Third Intermediate Period context. Iconographic evidence for the flint knife is most apparent in the Old Kingdom but continues until the Middle Kingdom. Textual evidence for the specifically *flint* knife, largely of a religious nature, begins in the Middle Kingdom but seems particularly salient in the New Kingdom and continues until the Graeco-Roman Period. Presumably, before the Middle Kingdom the ancient Egyptians did not find it necessary to specify that a knife was flint, as most were.

There is no evidence that knives were ever used as weapons in Egypt. Traditionally, Egyptologists have tended to view flint knives as primarily used for ritual cattle slaughter taking place at internments. While those specifically studying lithics understand that flint knives were used in everyday contexts, I have noticed that it is still commonly believed by Egyptologists who are not specialists of lithics that flint knives were largely ceremonial. It is clear that they were also used for other purposes, including, the cutting of plant material.

Although flint knives are commonly associated with ritual slaughter, archaeological examples of flint knives in slaughter contexts are rare. One exception comes from Early Dynastic Helwan, where a flint knife was found in a magazine in a layer of ox bones and two other flint knives

were found in a cross shape at the bottom of the structure (Saad 1951: 10f, pl. 7–8).

Flint knives, at least until the end of the Old Kingdom, are more usually found in burial and temple contexts (Schmidt 1992: 87; Tillmann 1992) – sites usually classified as ritual (as shown below in later periods formal flint knives are common on domestic sites). Old Kingdom-Second Intermediate Period 'Ayn-Asīl however, is more clearly domestic, yet has produced flint knives; though, as Midant-Reynes (1998: 44) states, there is a far smaller percentage of knives from this site than at others. Miller (1985) believes that stone knives found at New Kingdom Karnak were used for temple butchery. But, such context-derived conclusions alone are imprecise. Temples were engaged in what we would classify as secular activity, such as running large farming estates, so these contexts do not prove ritual use.

Cattle slaughter scenes are shown on tomb walls of the elite. Very often, the knife sharpening motif occurs alongside motifs depicting the dispatch of the unfortunate beast (Fig. 2.3). But were the tools shown metal, not stone? Some Egyptologists even deny the use of flint knives in the Old Kingdom. For example, in the Old Kingdom *mastaba* of Hetepka, 'sparks are seen falling from sharpened knives,

Fig. 2.3. Knife sharpening scene from an Old Kingdom tomb (redrawn after Montet 1910: fig. 2).

indicating that they are of metal' (Martin 1979: 12). Martin makes no admission that 'sparks' may be flint spalls.

Close investigation of tool sharpening scenes (probably of ritual significance in their own right; Graves-Brown 2011) and, in particular, of how implements therein are held, suggest that, up to the Middle Kingdom, but not thereafter, the flint knife was the normal slaughter implement. For example the Old Kingdom tomb of princess Idut at Saqqara shows the striking tool held in the *right* hand and the knife in the *left* hand, as one would expect for a re-sharpening stone (illustrated in Houlihan 1996: fig. 14) and similar scenes are found in many other Old Kingdom tombs. Compare this with the New Kingdom knife sharpening scene from the tomb of Khaemwese where the whetstone is held in the right hand (Martin 1991: fig. 124), or the 25th Dynasty scenes from the tomb of Mentuemhat at Thebes (Fig. 2.4). However, since flint knives are known from New Kingdom contexts, I would not be sure that they were *never* used in ritual slaughter. A New Kingdom flint knife depicted in the tomb of Tetiky (Davies 1925: pl. 3, after Carnarvon *et al.* 1912: pl. 6) is shown with a roughened texture resembling flint, rather than the smooth surface of metal.

These formal bifacial tools were probably used in killing the animal (slaughter) rather than hacking up the carcass (butchery). It is likely that large flakes roughly made and soon discarded would have been used in actual cattle butchery. So, for example, the tools associated with the butchery of cattle at Panhesy's Great Aten Temple House at Amarna, are expedient type tools (Graves-Brown 2009).

Knives are not confined to cutting flesh. For example, the late Old Kingdom, crescent-shaped bifacial 'knife' with denticulated back, from 'Ayn-Asīl, is probably a 'sickle' (Midant-Reynes 1998: 35, pl. 37; Roubet 1982: pl. 43). Predynastic knives, without denticulation have been found with silica gloss (Christensen & Walter 1992: 493). Early Dynastic Manchester Museum M5383A, a standard knife form, has gloss which looks to the eye to be sickle gloss. Tillmann (1992: fig. 76) shows a blade of the Old Kingdom from Tell el-Dabʿa with sickle gloss. The piece is broken but has the appearance of a traditional straight-backed knife. Silica gloss can also be produced through friction with wood (Jensen 1993). Egyptian flint does not easily develop a gloss (Holmes 1987). Werschkun (2007: 158) reports use-wear on some Old Kingdom Giza bifacial knives consistent with woodworking.

While there is no evidence that knives were used as weapons, there is conceivably some overlap in use between the more dagger-like projectile points and knives, particularly on military sites. My study of the Middle Kingdom site of Kahun, a site which housed laypeople and priests concerned

Fig. 2.4. Knife sharpening scene from Mentuemhat at Thebes. Courtesy of Saint Louis Art Museum, Museum Purchase 1.1958.1.

with the cult of the dead, showed that, in British museums, of 534 extant flint tools, 158 were probable knife fragments. Yet, from Buhen, a military site, I found only one knife fragment (DUROM 1964.106) in over 330 pieces, and that from an unreliable context (Graves-Brown 2011: vol 1, section 5.2.1). It could well be then that, on military sites, large projectile points substituted for knives (symmetrical implements are used as knives in Egypt; Petschel 2011: 267ff).

PsS-kf

There has been much discussion of this bifurcated bifacial and symmetrical implement (Fig. 2.5), sometimes called a lance, sometimes a knife. This was clearly a ritual implement.

Morphology and dating

The morphological definition of the *psS-kf* knife depends on where one draws the line between these Dynastic items and the fishtailed knives of Predynastic periods. It is generally believed that the *psS-kf*, literally in ancient Egyptian 'split' or 'split flint' derives from the Predynastic fishtail knife. 'Forked knife', 'fishtail knife' and '*psS-kf*' are terms often used interchangeably. However, Hikade (2003) makes a strong case that the association is more presumed than real.

Generally, the Dynastic *psS-kf* is a polished, bifacial tool with squared-off handle and bifurcated blade. It usually measures between 10cm and 20cm in length. Most examples are polished, though some unpolished forms occur (van Walsem 1978: 227f, figs. 1.1, 1.8 and 1.22). The *psS-kf* proper (as opposed to the amuletic version) is not usually found in isolation but as part of a set of instruments. In tombs, these objects were placed in a limestone slab with recesses cut therein to hold the objects. Not all *psS-kf* are of flint, despite the fact that the *kf* part of the name is believed to mean 'flint.' In fact, the flint *psS-kf* is rare after the Early Dynastic Period, and van Walsem (1978: 231) records only one example from the late Old Kingdom. Other examples of limestone or alabaster continue into the Middle Kingdom and later.

Early Dynastic amuletic flint *psS-kf* are also known (e.g. British Museum EA37279; Petrie 1902: 24 and pl. 51, 22; Spencer 1980: 101 (no.755), pl. 79; Roth 1992: 136ff; Fig. 2.5). Later amuletic *psS-kf* are known in other materials (Roth 1992) some of which appear anthropomorphised and a few have female heads. Such anthropomorphised amulets are usually found in women's graves (van Walsem 1978: 236f).

While we are here concerned with the Dynastic *psS-kf*, the common assumption that these are derived from earlier Predynastic fishtailed knives, means that I will briefly discuss these. The fishtail knife is a bifacial, bifurcated tool which, like the Early Dynastic ripple-knife, may be polished on one side only (Massoulard 1936). Hafted examples are

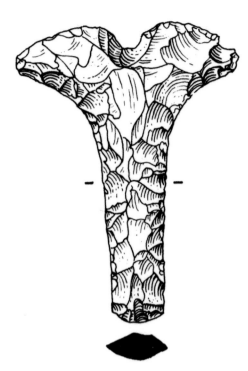

Fig. 2.5. PsS-kf. British Museum EA37279.

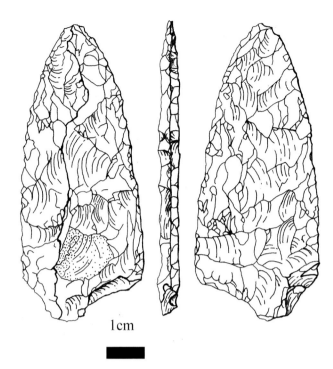

1cm

Fig. 2.6. Large projectile point from Askut. Drawing courtesy of S. Tyson Smith.

known and elsewhere retouch ceases at the point where the stone would have been covered by the handle (Roth 1992: 128). Often, all the exposed edges are evenly serrated while others are serrated only on the interior forked edge. Some examples are clearly not for everyday use, for example the fishtail knife with an ornate gold handle in the Cairo Museum (Currelly 1913: 272, pl. 47). While some examples show wear suggesting heavy use, others were clearly broken for the grave (Hester 1976: 348f).

Function

That the *psS-kf* was used in the 'opening of the mouth' ceremony is shown in the Abusir Papyrus (Posener-Kriéger & Cenival 1968) and in the inclusion of *psS-kf* tools in implement sets clearly matching textual descriptions of tools for that ceremony (Otto 1960; van Walsem 1978). The ceremony was used to reanimate or 'bring to life' mummies and statues. Mummies and statues were transformed by the ritual into vessels for the *ka* (the term *ka* roughly equates to the creative life-force of the individual or god). The ritual was elaborate and involved touching the mummy or statue with various objects to restore its senses.

The reasons why this knife became so important in the ceremony are discussed by Roth (1992) who favours a use partly predicated upon its so-called predecessor, the Predynastic fishtailed knife. However, as Hikade (2003) has

demonstrated, the two are unlikely to be connected and the meaning behind the *psS-kf* must remain a mystery. All that can be said is that the literature states that the purpose of the 'opening of the mouth' ceremony is to 'make firm the jaw' of the deceased.

Large projectile points

In this section, I discuss bifacial points over 9cm long (Figs 2.6 and 2.7). In form, these are the most dagger-like of all Dynastic flint implements; and, as stated above, examples with no evidence of hafting have been mistaken for daggers. It is clear from their form and occurrence on military sites that these points had a military purpose. Attempts have been made to sub-divide the type into spears, javelins and pikes (Vila 1970). While there are differences (thickness and length) which might justify these divisions, I remain unconvinced of their separate purposes, and such subdivisions are not relevant to this paper.

Some have identified Early Dynastic-Old Kingdom large flint projectile points; though, as these are only extant as tips, they could alternatively be knife-tips. The same uncertainty concerns later fragments. However, by the late Middle Kingdom–early New Kingdom there are clear examples, mainly from Egyptian forts in Nubia. Large points were found at the fort of Buhen in conjunction with late Middle Kingdom-Early New Kingdom pottery (Emery *et al.* 1979:

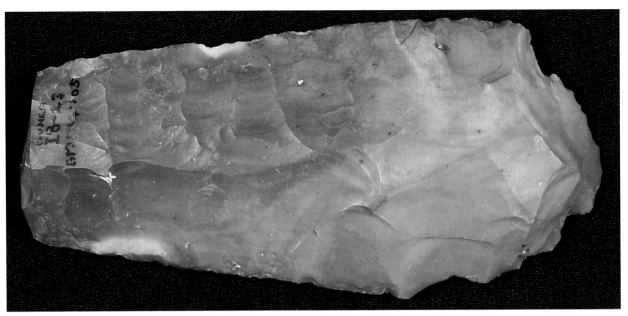

Fig. 2.7. Large projectile point DUROM. 1964.105 (broken). Courtesy of the Oriental Institute, University of Durham.

48). These include: Birmingham Museum 513.1965 (Emery *et al.* 1979: pl. 102.K); Durham Museum DUROM 1964.105 (Emery *et al.* 1979: pl. 102.E.); British Museum EA65771 (Emery *et al.* 1979: 116 no. 271 or 272). Comparable pieces from Semna and Uronarti (Vila 1970: 193; Dunham & Janssen 1967: pl. 45a) resided in Khartoum Museum. The largest collection of large projectile points comes from the early New Kingdom fort of Mirgissa published by Vila (1970). Vila defines 310 'javelots' and 'javelines' and 88 spears. As well as those published by Vila, additional spearheads were found at Mirgissa away from the main armoury (Dunham & Janssen 1967: pl. 92 B & C). At least one large projectile point was found at the fort of Askut dating to the early New Kingdom (Fig. 2.6; Smith 2003: fig. 5.8).

Spearheads are rare on domestic sites, though two early New Kingdom 'probably spear-heads' were found at Memphis (Giddy 1999: 227, 233 no. 951/69 and 227, 234, no. 1066). These are described as crude and bifacial which could imply unfinished or heavily sharpened items (they are not illustrated). Another was found predating the New Kingdom (Giddy 1999: 233 no. 905/57).

One may question why there appear to be so few examples before the Second Intermediate Period. There are, in fact, few weapons of any kind until this date, whether of metal or stone (Tillmann 1992: 208). With the exception of arrowheads, those that are known are metal and funerary, and after the early Old Kingdom, flint ceases to be deposited in graves (it continues in other contexts). Secondly, one might argue that metal weapons are personal weapons and flint weapons military issue; and one would not expect military issue in tombs. Finally, these fort sites may present unusual deposition

characteristics as they were abandoned quickly and would contain quantities of weapons. One might guess that, under normal circumstances, unwanted flint weapons would be appropriated and re-knapped for other purposes. Except in Nubia, there are few purely military buildings built on a large scale, not extensively reused, but extensively excavated.

Despite the amount of flint weapons on fort sites, flint is usually ignored in studies of ancient Egyptian pharaonic warfare (e.g. Yadin 1963; McDermott 2004). Where it is discussed, it is sometimes explained away as a second-best material, only viable against the less advanced Nubians, and, it has been suggested verbally to me, that the material might not even be Egyptian. Part of the problem is the quantity of metal weapons found in tombs by far exceeds that of flint. I turn to these suggestions (Graves-Brown 2015).

While the fort sites are in Nubia, the flint items clearly originate with the occupying Egyptian military. In appearance, the material is similar to Theban flint, and Nubian flint work is entirely different in quality and form. The flint industry is not pre-eminent in Kerma (Nubian) culture, and fine, bifacial Nubian flint working of large pieces unknown (Bonnet 1990: 137). A bifacial, tabular flint knife from the town of Kerma in Nubia, contemporary with Egyptian Middle Kingdom, is considered an Egyptian import as it is unique to Kerma (Bonnet 1990: 137, 153, fig. 119). It is almost identical to a number of Middle Kingdom Egyptian specimens, for example Manchester Museum M239c from Lahun. Nubian types consist of scrapers, sickle blades, microliths, borers, all with little core preparation (Gratien & Olive 1984; Säve-Söderbergh 1989: 122ff, fig. 41; Bonnet 1990:137ff; Bracco & Gratien 2002). The Nubian raw material is largely grey pebbles, quartz, carnelian and agate and rarely flint (Bonnet 1990: 137; Bracco & Gratien 2002), while Egyptian forms, after the Early Dynastic, are almost invariably flint. It appears likely that the material from Mirgissa is Theban, and Tyson Smith (pers. comm.) has stated that the fine bifacial tools found at Askut appear to be from the same source.

It could be argued that the flint use in Nubian forts is only feasible because of Nubia's perceived stone using technology. Metal, one might argue, was in short supply and reserved for Egypt's eastern frontier for use against more 'advanced' metal-using cultures (an idea suggested by Tillmann 1992: 212f, 1998: 265). The idea is questionable.

Firstly, there is little real evidence for a metal shortage, although, following the well-known idiom, absence of evidence is not evidence of absence. Archaeological and textual evidence show that vast quantities of copper and tin were imported into Egypt (Smith 2003:71f), though of course we do not know if this met demand. The price of copper may indicate its rarity value. While slightly later than Mirgissa, in Rameside Egypt a bronze (or copper) spear was worth 1½ to 2 deben (Janssen 1975: 326), by comparison, a bundle of vegetables cost ½ to 1 deben (Janssen 1975: 527). An ordinary workman would get about 11 deben each month (Janssen 1975: 534). So copper was not cheap, but was it rare? Copper was used for mirrors, statuettes and other luxury items; it is certainly not uncommon in New Kingdom tombs, but perhaps such luxuries were considered more important than arms.

Copper may have been more scarce in the outposts of Nubia. However, metal artefacts became increasingly common during the Second Intermediate Period at Askut and dominated the assemblage by the New Kingdom (Smith 2003: 105, fig.5.9). That these tools were not simply weapons, argues against a shortage. It simply does not make sense to use metal for non-military items on a large scale if metal was in short supply and metal weapons were superior.

Yet, it is not perhaps so much copper that was critical but tin for bronze. Sources of tin were available north of Egypt and, hence, may have been difficult for Nubian outposts to acquire. However, the evidence for regular use of bronze in Egypt is not apparent until the Rameside Period (Ogden 2000: 153, 171), the same time as flint weapons decline. Thus, at the time of the Mirgissa hoard, the argument that a shortage of copper or bronze supplies in Nubia forced reliance on flint is debatable.

We may also question the idea that Nubian weapons were primitive. Spalinger (2005: 62) suggests that the Nubians were at a disadvantage compared to the Egyptians because, at the time of Tuthmosis I, the Nubians lacked bronze. However, as stated above, bronze was not in regular use in Egypt until later. Nor did the Nubians lack copper. Nubian daggers and razors were made of copper alloy in the Kerma Classic Period (Second Intermediate Period–early New Kingdom), for example at Kerma (Bonnet 2004: 86). In

fact, the copper alloy dagger is standard in Middle–Classic Kerma burials, and the short copper alloy sword is famous in Classic Kerma burials (O'Connor 1993: 30f). The British Museum, for example, has two Classic Kerma daggers, one of which is of arsenical copper, the other of which is of tin bronze (Davies 1991: 316, pl. 13.2). Of course, we cannot be sure of the quantities available to the Nubians, compared to the Egyptians.

We may also question the claim that Nubians were easier to put down than the enemies of the north-east. Why use Nubian mercenaries, as the Egyptians did, unless they had a reputation for being good fighters, and why build forts there unless there was a problem? However, this does not mean that tactics and weapons differed between Nubia and the north-eastern frontier, though how this relates to use of flint versus metal large projectiles, I am unsure.

Thus, while we cannot prove that copper or tin was not in short supply and rationed for use against the more threatening enemies of the north-east, little evidence supports this view. I know turn to the false impression that metal is more common than flint because of the quantity of metal surviving from burial sites.

With rare exceptions, most substantial metalwork (i.e. not arrowheads) is funerary or unprovenanced (as suggested by a trawl of publications such as Petschel 2011). I know of two important exceptions. The first is the Qantir arms factory, which produced daggers, and javelin heads, probably dating to the reign of Ramesses II (Spalinger 2005: 227 with further references), thus slightly later than the Mirgissa material. Since model soldiers, representing soldiers of everyday life, in the tomb of Meseheti, Middle Kingdom Assiut, are shown with metal spears (Saleh & Sourouzian 1987: pl. 73), it might be thought that soldiers were commonly issued with such items. However, as Vila (1970: 192) points out, it would have been practically impossible to make such tiny items in stone.

Artefacts placed in the grave are always ritual (Whitehouse 1996). They have a purpose relating to this context, which must be other than kinetic, a point made particularly obvious when they are placed with individuals who can have had no utilitarian use for them in life, for example weapons in the graves of children (McDermott 2004:72). We can deduce from the fact that not all materials and artefact forms were placed in tombs, that certain materials and objects were considered particularly suitable in burial contexts. There is evidence that certain types of weapons were employed in funerary rites. For example, McDermott (2004) discusses rituals connected with bowmen and funerals.

It is outside the scope of this paper to discuss in detail the purpose of metal in burials; but, briefly, it may well have display value, arguably linked to its high status compared to flint, because of production costs (Richards 2005). Secondly, it could well have value because of its luminosity (Graves-Brown 2013). I am unsure that metal was indeed expensive; but, certainly, it does have display status for its aesthetic appeal. The public nature of Egyptian funerals would make display apposite. The inherent physical properties of metal may have acted as an aid to the deceased in the afterlife. The revitalising and rebirth properties of luminosity (with which both lightness of colour and shininess are associated) are much discussed by Egyptologists (for faience see Friedman 1998: 15f; Patch 1998: 32ff; for coffins see Serpico & White 2001: 36f; Taylor 2001: 166).

The quality of shininess is associated with the blessed or transfigured dead, the *Axw*, of Egyptian mythology. Their qualities of scintillation have been well studied. For prehistoric Italy, it has been argued that metal daggers were put in graves because of their divine quality of brightness (Keates 2002). One can imagine this too for Egypt. Metal would normally have been brighter than flint. Such an argument would help explain why pale coloured flint was selected for in Predynastic graves (Harris 1961: 139) when metal was rarely available and, secondly, why flint is quickly superseded by metal as a suitable funerary material, despite remaining integral to everyday life.

That metal was specifically selected for the grave is supported by the frequency with which large quantities of lithics are found on settlement sites compared with burial sites, especially after the Old Kingdom. Common use of flint seems to have continued into the New Kingdom, for example at Memphis (Giddy 1999: 226ff), Amarna (Spurrell 1894: 37) and the Valley of the Kings (Carnarvon *et al.* 1912: 10). James Harrell (pers. comm.) has recently discovered a Rameside flint quarry specialising in production of blades at Wadi Umm Nikhaybar in Wadi Araba, in the Eastern Desert. By this date, flint in graves is largely limited to occasional sickle blades and tranchet arrow-heads. The small, visible surface area of such flint tools would restrict its ability to signify shininess or lack thereof.

Consequently, it is plausible that flint weapons were commonly used in the early New Kingdom, and possibly do not appear in graves for ideological reasons. Furthermore, one can suggest that they are used as weapons in life because of their ideological as much as practical importance. There are utilitarian reasons for the use of flint for arms: first, flint is lighter than metal; second, flint cuts better than metal because it is sharper and serrated; and, third, flint is more fragile than metal.

Flint has a specific gravity of 2.65, copper 8.2, and bronze 7.4–7.9. Thus, flint is much lighter than New Kingdom metals. Heavier spears are needed for penetrating armour, but they though are heavy to carry and lighter spears will travel further. According to Forbes (1966 Volume VII:108), as late as the 7th century BC, the Egyptian army preferred stone tipped arrows as they pierced contemporary armour. Certainly arrowheads of this date are known (Graves-Brown 2011: vol. 2, 9.4.5). Flint is superior to metal for penetration (Pope 1962) because it is sharper. The serrated quality of bifacial tools further enhances cutting, and their irregular surface might

additionally encourage haemorrhaging. Modern hunters draw a file across metal arrowheads to produce the same effect (Edmonds & Thomas 1987: 193). For whale hunting, the Koryak used stone projectiles since rifle bullets simply stuck in the blubber without causing injury (Ellis 1997: 51). With respect to fragility; while it is sometimes stated that flint is not fragile, this assumption seems to rest on experimental archaeologists shooting into stationery meat rather than living, moving targets (Ellis 1997: 52). Weapon breakage would be particularly problematic during prolonged combat. However, the fragility of the material might be considered advantageous in certain circumstances. A broken blade within a body will do more damage than a cleanly removed one. Flint's practical efficiency in killing has led to the myth in 'modern' societies, that flint is "naturally poisoned" (Ellis 1997: 47).

However, technological choice is not dependent solely on functional superiority, nor upon effort expenditure. Throughout history, weapon development has been guided by ideology, including such unlikely or seemingly illogical areas as aesthetics (van Creveld 1989: 75f). Therefore, the notion that flint or metal was functionally superior may not even be relevant! The existence of the fragile, bifacial tool, as opposed to an equally efficient but more crudely made weapon, in itself argues an ideological element, as the effort expended in manufacture does not make sense in light of the likely utilitarian return. Organic points are significantly more robust when used in the same way. Historical and ethnographic research clearly shows that weapons are subject to ideological consideration (Larick 1986; van Creveld 1989: 67ff; Bamforth 1993).

The ideological significance of warfare itself, and the subjugation of Nubia, is demonstrated by smiting scenes on Pharaonic religious artefacts. There are indications that weapons in general had ideological import. For the ideological significance of arrows see Brunner-Traut (1956) and McDermott (2004), for spears see Reymond (1963, 1964, 1965) and McDermott (2004). These authors deal largely with metal, but object form as well as raw material would be significant. As we will see below, flint was the weapon of Re, a perfect choice to put down those threatening Egypt and to restore *maat* (roughly translated as 'order'). Within Nubia, flint would have displayed its Egyptian origins and, more specifically its source in Thebes, an important religious site, and the centre of Egyptian government. It embodied the homeland in material form. While basically unprovable, it is surely plausible that the use of emotive materials would have had some effect upon the fighting ability of Egyptian troops.

Religious significance

As is clear from above, flint for the Egyptians had a religious significance. It is only in the Early Dynastic Period that oversize, fragile and possibly curated knives are found in elite graves. Indeed, other flint artefacts appear, from their non-functional characteristics, to have been ideologically important at this period (flint bracelets, bifacial arrowheads, etc.). In this period, certain flint artefacts are associated with the elite and flint is used in ritual cattle slaughter. Use of the flint knife in ritual slaughter continued until the Middle Kingdom, though its exact meaning is unclear.

Ideology is, of course, not static and there are chronological changes in how it is expressed. Generally, there is an increase in the textual evidence for the ideology of flint and increasingly flint is used against the enemies of Re. There is very little archaeological evidence after the New Kingdom, at the time when textual evidence abounds.

The early ideological connection between flint and snakes, shown in text, is largely subtle and non-specific. For example in the *Pyramid Texts* (Old Kingdom, though possibly representing a written version of Early Dynastic oral tradition) we have 'the particoloured knife, which is black and green, has gone forth thereat and it has swallowed for itself that which it has licked'. Here a flint knife is described in ophidian terms (Graves-Brown 2011: vol.1, section 6.2.1.1). From the Middle Kingdom, the connection is more explicit and particular deities are named. The snake on the mountain of Bakhu is said to have a front part made of flint. The direct link between fire and flint is explicit in the Late Period with the Bremner-Rhind Papyrus. A passage reads: a fire 'it shall cut you with its (flint) knife' (Faulkner 1937: 170). However, there are earlier hints in the way flint and fire are described in similar terms. Flint in connection with Re is first attested in the *Pyramid Texts*. For example, 'Re arises, his uraeus upon him, against this snake which came forth from the earth and which is under my fingers. He will cut off your head with this (flint) knife which is in the hand of Mafdet' (Faulkner 1969: 89). The connection between flint and the goddesses who are the Eye of Re, the daughters of the sun-god, is first apparent in the Middle Kingdom, though it continues until the Ptolemaic Period. The fearsome goddess Sekhmet, for example, carries a flint knife (Graves-Brown 2011: vol. 1, section 6.2.2.3).

The storm gods Thoth and Seth have flint connections in the *Pyramid Texts*. Thoth carries a flint knife (Graves-Brown 2011: vol.1, section 6.4.2) which is instrumental in the rebirth of the king. In later periods, Seth had become an enemy of the sun-god and could be defeated using a flint knife. However, while Seth's flint connections continue, Thoth's do not seem to date later than the Middle Kingdom, except perhaps as a 'translation' of Thoth into the *wedjat* Eye, the uraeus which comes forth in flinty form from Seth. Seth's flint connections continue, related to his role as an enemy of Re, but also as the one who gave forth the flinty uraeus.

Two groups of gods can be discerned: the solar deities connected with Re, and those of the northern night sky, such as Seth. A New Kingdom text describes the two mooring posts of flint to which Seth is chained (Graves-Brown 2011: vol.1, section 6.3.2.3).

Conclusions

A study of the three bifacial tool types shows that flint tools were important in the religious and more 'secular' life of the ancient Egyptians. While the *psS-kf* was almost purely ritual, the bifacial knife had both a religious and secular function. The projectile points are usually considered secular, and indeed, their context would support this. There are also practical reasons why flint weapons would have been effective. However, it is also likely that they had an ideological significance. Given the nature of flint as a weapon of the sun-god and as a weapon to be used against the evil Seth, it seems little wonder that flint was used for weapons in ancient Egypt. However, was it that the mythology arose from the use of flint as weapons, or did the mythology cause the continued use of flint? The fact that the mythology continues later than the widespread use of flint does not really tell us which was the cause and which the effect. This knowledge is lost in history.

Notes

1. Detail on knife forms may be found in Graves-Brown 2011:Vol. 2, Appendix 1
2. http://www.eeescience.utoledo.edu/faculty/harrell/Egypt/AGRG_Home.html

References

Bamforth, D. B. 1993. Stone tools, steel tools. In: S. M. Wilson & J. D. Rogers (eds.), *Ethnohistory and Archaeology: Approaches to Postcontact Change in America*. New York: Plenum Press. 49–72.

Bonnet, C. 1990. *Kerma, Royaume de Nubie*. Geneva: Universite de Geneva.

Bonnet, C. 2004. Kerma. In: D. A. Welsby & J. R. Anderson (eds.), *Ancient Treasures: An Exhibition of Recent Discoveries from the Sudan National Museum*. London: British Museum Press. 78–89.

Bracco, J.-P. & Gratien, B. 2002. Les Habitats Ruraux Kerma de Gism el-Arba, Campagne 1997–1998: Analyse Techno-Economique de l'Industrie Lithique Taille de l'Habitat 1. *Archeologie du Nil Moyen* 9: 43–51.

Brunner-Traut, E. 1956. Atum als Bogenschütze. *Mitteilungen des Deutschen Archäologischen Instituts, Abteilung Kairo* 14: 20–28.

Cadogan, G. 1966. An Egyptian Flint Knife from Knossos. *Annals of the British School in Athens* 61: 147–148.

Carnarvon, G. E. S. M. H., Carter, H., Griffith, F. L., Legrain, G., Mèoller, G., Newberry, P. E. & Spiegelberg, W. 1912. *Five Years' Explorations at Thebes: A Record of Work Done 1907–1911*. London: Oxford University Press.

Christensen, M. & Walter, P. 1992. Physico-Chimie en traceologie. Le Cas des Couteaux Égyptiens. In: M. Menu & P. Walter (eds.), *Le Pierre Préhistorique I. Actes du Seminaire du Laboratoire des Recherches des Musées de France 13 et 14 Décembre 1990*. Paris: Laboratoire des Recherches des Musées de France. 149–171.

Currelly, M. T. C. 1913. *Catalogue Général des Antiquités Égyptiennes du Musée du Caire. Nos 63001–64906. Stone Implements*. Cairo: Institut Française d'Archéologie Orientale du Caire.

Davies, N. de G. 1925. The Tomb of Tetaky at Thebes (No. 15). *Journal of Egyptian Archaeology* 11: 10–17.

Davies, W. V. 1991. 'Egypt and Africa' in the British Museum. In: W. V. Davies (ed.), *Egypt and Africa. Nubia from Prehistory to Islam*. London: The British Museum and Egypt Exploration Society. 314–320.

Dunand, M. 1954. *Fouilles de Byblos. 1933–1938*. Paris: Geuthner.

Dunham, D. & Janssen, J. 1967. *Second Cataract Forts Excavated by George Henry Reisner II: Uronarti, Shalfak, Mirgissa*. Boston: Boston Museum of Fine Arts.

Edmonds, M. & Thomas, J. 1987. The Archers: An Everyday Story of Country Folk. In: A. G. Brown & M. Edmonds (eds.), *Lithic Analysis and Later British Prehistory*. Reading studies in archaeology 2. BAR British series 162. Oxford: British Archaeological Report. 187–199.

Eggebrecht, A. 1973. *Schlachtungsbräuche im Alten Ägypten und Ihre Wiedergabe im Flachbild bis zum Ende des Mittleren Reiches*. Munich: University of Munich.

Ellis, C. J. 1997. Factors Influencing the Use of Stone Projectile Tips. An Ethnographic Perspective. In: H. Knecht (ed.), *Projectile Technology*. New York: Plenum Press. 37–74.

Emery, W. B., Smith, H. S., Millard, A. R. & Dixon, D. M. 1979. *The Fortress of Buhen: the Archaeological Report*. London: Egypt Exploration Society.

Faulkner, R. O. 1937. The Bremner-Rhind Papyrus III. *Journal of Egyptian Archaeology* 23: 166–168.

Faulkner, R. O. 1969. *The Ancient Egyptian Pyramid Texts*. Oxford: Clarendon Press.

Forbes, R. J. 1966. *Studies in Ancient Technology*. Leiden: E. J. Brill.

Friedman, F. D. 1998. *Gifts of the Nile: Ancient Egyptian Faience*. London: Thames and Hudson.

Giddy, L. 1999. *Kom Rabi'a: The New Kingdom and Post-New Kingdom Objects*. London: Egypt Exploration Society.

Gilbert, G. P. 2004. *Weapons, Warriors and Warfare in Early Egypt*. BAR international series 1208. Oxford: Archeopress.

Gratien, B. & Olive, M. 1984. Fouilles à Saï 1977–1979: L'Habitat du Kerma Classique: Analyse de l'Industrie Lithique. *Cahiers de Recherches de L'Institut de Papyrologie et d'Egyptologie de Lille* 6: 83–125.

Graves-Brown, C. A. 2009. Flint tools, they were still in use. *Horizon* 5: 7.

Graves-Brown, C. A. 2011. *The Ideological Significance of Flint in Dynastic Egypt*. Unpublished PhD thesis, University College London. Available at: http://discovery.ucl.ac.uk/1306709/

Graves-Brown, C. A. 2013. Luster, Flint and Arsenical Copper in Dynastic Egypt. *Journal of Lithic Technology* 38(3): 150–160.

Graves-Brown, C. A. 2015. Flint and Forts: The Role of Flint in Late Middle Kingdom-New Kingdom Egyptian Weaponry. In

T. P. Harrison & E. B. Banning (eds.), *Walls of the Prince: Egyptian Interactions with Southwest Asia in Antiquity. Essays in Honour of John S. Holladay*. Leiden: Brill. 37–59.

Griffith, F. Ll. 1896. *Beni Hasan* Part III. London: Egypt Exploration Fund.

Harris, J. R. 1961. *Lexicographical Studies in Ancient Egyptian Minerals*. Berlin: Akademie Verlag.

Hester, T. R. 1976. Functional analysis of ancient egyptian chipped stone tools: the potential for future research. *Journal of Field Archaeology* 3: 346–351.

Hikade, T. 1999. An Early Dynastic flint workshop at Helwan, Egypt. *Bulletin of the Australian Centre for Egyptology* 10: 47–57.

Hikade, T. 2003. Getting the ritual right – fishtail knives in Predynastic Egypt. In: S. Meyer (ed.), *Egypt – Temple of the Whole World. Studies in Honor of Jan Assmann*. Leiden and Boston: E. J. Brill. 137–151.

Holmes, D. L. 1987. Problems encountered in high-power microwear study of some Egyptian Predynastic lithic artefacts. In: G. de G. Sieveking & H. M. Newcomer (eds.), *Human Uses of Chert and Flint. Proceedings of The Fourth International Flint Symposium Held at Brighton Polytechnic, 10th–15th April 1983*. Cambridge: Cambridge University Press. 91–96.

Holmes, D. L. 1992. Chipped Stone-Working Craftsmen, Hierakonpolis and the Rise of Civilization in Egypt'. In: R. Friedman & B. Adams (eds.), *The Followers of Horus. Studies Dedicated to Michael Allen Hoffman*. Oxford: Oxbow Books. 37–44.

Houlihan, P. F. 1996. *The Animal World of the Pharaohs*. London: Thames & Hudson.

Jensen, H. J. 1993. *Flint Tools and Plant Working. Hidden Traces of Stone Age Technology*. Aarhus: Aarhus University Press.

Janssen, J. J. 1975. *Commodity Prices from the Ramessid Period: An Economic Study of the Village of Necropolis Workmen at Thebes*. Leiden: E. J. Brill.

Keates, S. 2002. The flashing blade: copper, colour and luminosity in north Italian Copper Age Society. In: A. Jones & G. MacGregor (eds.), *Colouring the Past. The Significance of Colour in Archaeological Research*. New York: Berg. 109–125.

Kelterborn, P. 1984. Towards replicating Egyptian Predynastic flint knives. *Journal of Archaeological Science* 11: 433–453.

Larick, R. 1986. Age grading and ethnicity in the style of Loikop (Samburu) spears. *World Archaeology* 18: 268–282.

Lund, M. 2010. Flintknapping scenes from the Beni-Hasan tombs viewed and interpreted by a contemporary flintknappers. Paper read at Experiment and experience: Ancient Egypt in the Present, 10 May 2012, Swansea, UK. Podcast available at: http://www.egypt.swansea.ac.uk/index.php/events/397-technology-podcasts

Lund, M. 2015. Some observations and experiments regarding depictions of flint knapping in the Old and Middle Kingdoms. In: C. Graves-Brown (ed.), *Experiment and Experience Ancient Egypt in the Present*. Swansea: Classical Press of Wales. 113–137.

Martin, G. T. 1979. *The Tomb of Hetepka and Other Reliefs and Inscriptions from the Sacred Animal Necropolis North Saqqâra 1964–1973*. London: Egypt Exploration Society.

Martin, G. T. 1991. *The Hidden Tombs of Memphis*. London: Thames and Hudson.

Massoulard, M. 1936. Lances Fourches et Peseshkaf. À Propos de Deux Acquisitions Récentes du Musée du Louvre. *Revue d'Égyptologie* 2: 135–163.

McDermott, B. 2004. *Warfare in Ancient Egypt*. Stroud: Sutton Publishing Limited.

Midant-Reynes, B. 1998. *Le Silex de 'Ayn-Asil Oasis de Dakhla-Balat*. Documents de Fouilles de l'IFAO 34. Cairo: Institut Français d'Archéologie Orientale du Caire.

Midant-Reynes, B. & Tixier, J. 1981. Les Gestes de l'Artisan Égyptien. *La Recherche* 120: 380–381.

Miller, R. 1985. Lithic technology in East Karnak. *Journal of the Society for the Study of Egyptian Antiquities* 13: 228–236.

Montet, P. 1910. Les scènes de boucherie dans les tombes de l'Ancien Empire. *Le Bulletin de l'Institut français d'archéologie orientale* 7: 41–65.

O'Connor, D. B. 1993. *Ancient Nubia: Egypt's Rival in Africa*. Philadelphia, PA: University Museum, University of Pennsylvania.

Ogden, J. 2000. Metals. In: P. T. Nicholson & I. Shaw (eds.), *Ancient Egyptian Materials and Technology*. Cambridge: Cambridge University Press. 148–176.

Otto, E. 1960. *Das Ägyptische Mundöffnungsritual*. Wiesbaden: Harrassowitz.

Patch, D.C. 1998. By Necessity or Design: Faience Use in Ancient Egypt. In: F. D. Friedman (ed.), *Gifts of the Nile. Ancient Egyptian Faience*. London: Thames and Hudson. 32–45.

Petrie, W. M. F. 1902. *Abydos. Part 1*. London: Egypt Exploration Fund.

Petschel, S. 2011. *Den Dolch betreffend. Typologie der Stichwaffen in Ägypten von der prädynastischen Zeit bis zur 3. Zwischenzeit*. Wiesbaden: Harrassowitz Verlag.

Pope, S. T. 1962. *Bows and Arrows*. Los Angeles: University of California Press.

Posener-Kriéger, P. & Cenival, J. L. 1968. *Hieratic Papyri in the British Museum: Fifth series: The Abu Sir Papyri*. London: British Museum Press.

Randall-MacIver, D. & Mace, A. C. 1902. *El-Amrah and Abydos, 1899–1901*. London: Egypt Exploration Fund.

Reymond, E. A. E. 1963. The Origin of the Spear I. *Journal of Egyptian Archaeology* 49: 140–146.

Reymond, E. A. E. 1964. The Origin of the Spear II. *Journal of Egyptian Archaeology* 50: 133–138.

Reymond, E. A. E. 1965. The Cult of the Spear in the Temple at Edfu. *Journal of Egyptian Archaeology* 51: 144–148.

Richards, J. E. 2005. *Society and Death in Ancient Egypt: Mortuary Landscapes of the Middle Kingdom*. Cambridge: Cambridge University Press.

Rosen, S. A. 1988. A Preliminary Note on the Egyptian Component of the Chipped Stone Assemblage from Tel 'Erani. *Israel Exploration Journal* 38: 105–116.

Roth, A. M. 1992. The PSŠ-KF and the 'Opening of the Mouth' Ceremony: A Ritual of Birth and Rebirth. *Journal of Egyptian Archaeology* 78: 113–147.

Roubet, C. 1982. Faucille Lithique d'Époque Pharaonique (Aïn Asil, Balat, Oasis De Dakhla). *Bulletin de l'Institut Français d'Archéologie Orientale* 82: 325–331.

Saad, Z. Y. 1951. *Royal Excavations in Helwan, 1945–7. Supplément Aux Annales du Service des Antiquités de l'Égypte* 14. Cairo: L'Institut Français d'Archéologie Orientale du Caire.

Saleh, M. & Sourouzian, H. eds. 1987. *Official Catalogue. The Egyptian Museum Cairo*. Mainz: Verlag Philipp von Zabern.

Säve-Söderbergh, T. 1989. *Middle Nubian Sites*. Scandinavian Joint Expedition to Sudanese Nubia Publications. Partille: Paul Åström.

Scharff, A. 1931. *Die Altertümer der Vor-und Frühzeit Ägyptens*. Mitteilungen aus der ägyptischen Sammlung. Berlin: Karl Curtius.

Schmidt, K. 1992. Tel Ibrahim Awad: Preliminary Report on the Lithic Industries. In: E. C. M. van den Brink (ed.), *The Nile Delta in Transition 4th–3rd Millennium BC. Proceedings of the Seminar Held in Cairo, 21 – 24 October 1990, at the Netherlands Institute of Archaeology and Arabic Studies*. Tel Aviv and Jerusalem: Edwin C.M. Van den Brink. 79–96.

Serpico, M. & White, R. 2001. The Use and Identification of Varnish on New Kingdom Funerary Equipment. In: V. Davies (ed.), *Colour and Painting in Ancient Egypt*. London: British Museum Press. 33–42.

Smith, S. T. 2003. *Wretched Kush. Ethnic Identities and Boundaries in Egypt's Nubian Empire*. London: Routledge.

Spalinger, A. J. 2005. *War in Ancient Egypt*. Maldon: Blackwell.

Spencer, A. J. 1980. *Catalogue of Egyptian Antiquities in the British Museum. V Early Dynastic Objects*. London: British Museum.

Spencer, A. J. 1993. *Excavations at el-Ashmunein III. The Town*. London: British Museum Trust.

Spurrell, F. C. J. 1891. The stone implements. In: W. H. F. Petrie (ed.), *Illahun, Kahun and Gurob*. London: David Nutt. 51.

Spurrell, F. C. J. 1894. Flint Tools from Tell el Amarna. In: W. M. F. Petrie (ed.), *Tell el Amarna*. London: Methuen and Co. 37–38.

Taylor, J.H. 2001. Patterns of colouring on Ancient Egyptian coffins From the New Kingdom to the Twenty-sixth Dynasty: an overview. In: W. V. Davies (ed.), *Colour and Painting in Ancient Egypt*. London: British Museum Press. 164–181.

Tillmann, A. 1992. *Die Steinartefakte des Dynastischen Ägypten, Dargestellt am Beispiel der Inventare aus Tell el-Dab'a und Qantir*. Unpublished PhD thesis, University of Tübingen.

Tillmann, A. 1998. Dynastic stone tools. In: K. A. Bard (ed.), *Encyclopedia of the Archaeology of Ancient Egypt*. London: Routledge. 262–265.

Van Creveld, M. 1989. *Technology and War from 2000BC to the Present*. New York: Free Press.

Vila, A. 1970. L'Armement de la Forteresse de Mirgissa-Iken. *Revue d'Égyptologie* 22: 170–199.

Walsem, R. v. 1978. An Investigation of an Ancient Egyptian Funerary Instrument. *Oudheidkundige Mededelingen uit het RijksMuseum van Oudheden* 59–60: 193–249.

Werschkun, C. 2007. Main Street Lithics. In: M. Lehner & W. Wetterstrom (eds.), *Giza Reports. The Giza Mapping Project. Volume I Project History, Survey, Ceramics, and Main Street and Gallery III.4 Operations*. Boston: Ancient Egypt Research Associate. 153–165.

Whitehouse, R. D. 1996. Ritual objects. Archaeological joke or neglected evidence? In: J. B. Wilkins (ed.), *Approaches to the Study of Ritual*. London: Accordia Research Centre. 9–30.

Yadin, Y. 1963. *The Art of Warfare in Biblical Lands in the Light of Archaeological Discovery*. London: Weidenfeld and Nicolson.

3

ORIGINS AND DEVELOPMENT OF FLINT DAGGERS IN ITALY

Denis Guilbeau

In Italy, flint daggers first appear probably during the first part of the 4th millennium. These daggers were produced mainly in two areas. In the north, the Lessinian Hills flint outcrops were exploited for a production of bifacial daggers distributed throughout the northern part of Italy till the southern part of Germany. In the south, the Gargano flint outcrops were exploited for a production of blade and bifacial daggers distributed throughout the southern part of the Peninsula. In central Italy, the Scaglia Rossa flint was used in a minor way to produce bifacial daggers. Other raw materials were exceptionally used for the manufacture of such artefacts and in the northwestern part of Italy a few blade daggers from Forcalquier (France) were found in Piedmont and Liguria. Sardinia, with only three flint daggers, and Sicily with only one dubious flint dagger seem to have shown little interest in such productions. We show here that the strong differences in the frequency, the technique and the morphology of the daggers between these regions correspond at least partly in local and regional cultural choices and in different traditions in flint knapping techniques.

Introduction

The territory considered in this work covers Italy within its present borders, including Sardinia and Sicily during the 4th and the 3rd millennia BC (Fig. 3.1). This period corresponds to the late Neolithic and the Eneolithic. Defining most of the "cultures" of these regions is not straightforward because of the very incomplete data available (see Steiniger, this volume). Accordingly, they will not be referred to in this paper.

During the two millennia concerned, the available information suggests the presence of agro-pastoral societies throughout this territory, and possibly an increase in reliance on pastoralism in comparison with previous millennia (Guilaine 1998; Robb 2007: 311). It is often suggested that this period corresponds to a rise in violence and to the development of a "warrior" ideology. Weapons are indeed abundant among grave goods of the period and abundant in parietal engravings (e.g. Arca 2009). However, the presence of weapons in these contexts does not necessarily mean an increase of real violence and insecurity. There are fortified sites in several regions, such as villages surrounded by fences or ditches, for example Conelle in the Marche (Cazzella & Moscoloni 1999), Le Cerquette-Fianello (Manfredini 2002) and Selva dei Muli 2 (Cerqua 2011) in Lazio; but fortified sites are not specific to this period, and villages surrounded by fences are present from the early Neolithic, for example in Lugo di Grezzana (Pedrotti *et al.* 2000) or Lugo di Romagna (Degasperi *et al.* 1998). Furthermore, osteological analysis shows that there is more direct evidence of violence between 6000 and 3500 BC than after 3500 BC (Robb 2007: 39).

Across the entirety of the territory considered here, burial practices evolved from the mid–5th millennium BC with the development of necropolises sometimes with abundant grave goods, such as polished axes, flint blades, flint arrowheads, etc. During the 4th and the 3rd millennium BC, the dead are frequently placed in rock-cut tombs, very frequent in most parts of the peninsula, in Sardinia and Sicily.

Fig. 3.1. Italy, with the main sources of the lithic raw materials indicated.

From the beginning of the 4th millennium BC and in following centuries, material products are characterised by the expansion and collapse of the distribution of obsidian pressure-flaked blades, mainly originating from Monte Arci in Sardinia and the island of Lipari in northeastern Sicily (Vaquer 2007; Lugliè 2009). A similar trend is observed in the distribution of greenstone axes from Piedmont and Liguria (Pétrequin *et al.* 2005). In the early 4th millennium BC, small-scale metallurgy began to develop in several regions, for example in Sardinia and central Italy (Lo Schiavo 1989; Pearce 2009). Metal artefacts – most of them in copper – remain rare during this whole period. Metal daggers appear during the first half of the 4th millennium. These are contemporaneous with the appearance of the first flint daggers. Nevertheless, it is necessary to clarify what we mean by "daggers" in the flint assemblage.

Defining flint daggers

In Italy more than elsewhere, what can or cannot be called a dagger is far from obvious.

We must first remember that what we call "daggers" are actually double-edged knives with a tip. We make no assumptions concerning the actual use of these artefacts: they could be used – or not – as a weapon. Most of the time, they were probably used as knives, some may never have had a practical use.

In some areas, such as northern Italy, the typological ambiguity of foliate blades is so great that it is impossible to establish a boundary between the arrowheads, the possible spearheads, the daggers and the possible halberds. It is even conceivable that such boundaries do not exist and, depending on the context, some foliates could have been used for either purpose (see, for example, Fig. 3.4.3 for a large foliate that may correspond to a very long and non-functional arrowhead).

Nevertheless, all the largest foliates, starting from an artificial limit of 14cm long and 4cm wide, of Central and Northern Italy will be described as "daggers". In all other cases, these artefacts will be described as "foliates". In the southern part of the peninsula, we will see that the differences in the morphology and the dimensions of these foliates permit the establishment of clear typological groups.

The origins of the Italian daggers, their morphology and their production technique, as in other countries, is subject to numerous assumptions. We will show here that the diversity of the production of flint daggers in Italy, including their typological and technical diversity, corresponds to regional and local cultural choices as well as local or regional traditions in lithic production.

Description of the Italian flint daggers

In Italy, flint daggers are made from two main raw materials: the flint from the Lessinian Hills on the southeast part of Garda Lake and the flint from the Gargano peninsula near the Adriatic coast of Apulia. The flint from the area of Arcevia in the Marches is also used on a smaller scale for such production; and, elsewhere in Italy, other raw materials are used occasionally for manufacturing daggers.

Northern Italy – Lessinian Hills flint daggers

In Northern Italy, flint foliates appear during the middle of the 5th millennium (Bagolini & Pedrotti 1998). Their dimensions – most of the time they are less than 5cm – and the discovery of a hafted one (Bagolini *et al.* 1973) suggest that foliates were almost exclusively arrowheads. A lot of them are made from Lessinian Hills flint. At the beginning of the 4th millennium BC, we find foliates whose dimensions seem incompatible with such use and which are interpreted as daggers (see Mottes 2001). The oldest ones come from Fiave Carera in the Trento region, dated to 4950±55 BP (3810–3640 cal BC[1]) and Isera-La Torretta in the same region in a horizon dated to 3600–3400 cal. BC. These daggers are documented as late as the end of the 3rd millennium. The most recent archaeological context where we find flint daggers is Lavagnone Phase 2, dated by dendrochronology to not later than 2050–1950 BC (Mottes 2001).

The interpretation of at least some of these artefacts as daggers is confirmed by traceological analyses which show them to have been used as knives, probably with axial hafting (Mottes pers. comm.). Such an hypothesis is confirmed by the dagger found near the Similaun man (Egg 1992: 264) and by a dagger found in Allensbach in southern Germany (Borrello *et al.* 2009:45). These two daggers have retained their wooden hafts.

Until the end of the 5th millennium BC, flint from the Lessinian Hills, a mountainous area over 1000m high, seems to be exploited only from secondary deposits in the valleys below the outcrops (Barfield 1999: 249). According to Barfield, the development of dagger production corresponds to the beginning of the exploitation of the primary deposits. In Colombare di Negrar, in the middle of this area, several daggers and preforms were found. They demonstrate the local production of such artefacts (Cauvin 1963; Peretto & Ronchitelli 1973). This evolution in the exploitation of the flint can be explained by the need for large homogeneous blocks because some of the daggers are over 17cm long, for example the dagger from Soave (Fig. 3.2. 2 on the right). Such big and homogeneous blocks cannot be found in the secondary deposits in the valleys. The outcrops exploited are of Late Cretaceous age and are called the Biancone

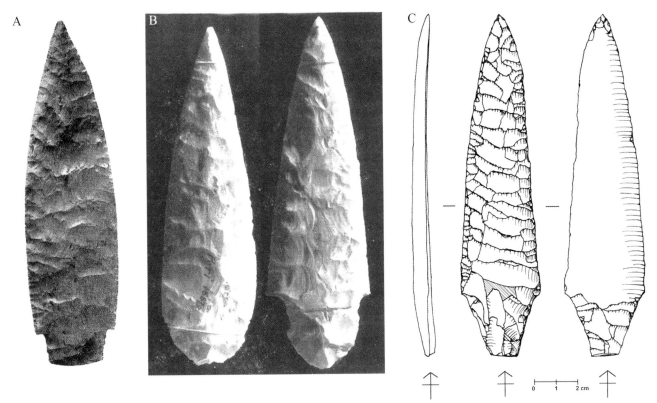

Fig. 3.2. A. Bifacial dagger from Fontanella Mantovana (L: ca. 17cm) (from Acanfora 1956: 333); B. Bifacial daggers from Carotta (L: ca. 16cm) and Soave (L: ca. 17cm; (from Battaglia 1958–1959: 251); C. Blade dagger from Torello (Forcalquier flint, L: 15.5cm – author's drawing).

formation. The Scaglia Rossa formation was also exploited to a lesser extent.

Most of the daggers directly studied by Mottes seem to be manufactured in flint from the Lessinian Hills; so we can assume that most of the over 400 large foliates from more than 300 sites which she described are made from this flint (Mottes 2001).

In almost all cases, the daggers are made through bifacial shaping from large flakes or blocks. The retouch is covering, and at least the final retouch is made by pressure.

The typology of these artefacts is very varied and has been the subject of numerous studies since the earliest research into prehistory (Patroni 1905; Di Lernia & Martini 1988). Nevertheless, Mottes has shown that at least some of the supposed types in earlier studies correspond to the same type of dagger at different states of resharpening (Mottes 2001). She noticed that daggers coming from dwelling sites are shorter and often show traces of edge resharpening; meanwhile, the daggers from graves are usually larger without clear signs of use (Mottes 2001). However, the traceological analysis shows that even the large daggers from graves have probably been used as knives too (Mottes, pers. comm.).

Even considering edge resharpening, there is still an undeniable typological variety, particularly visible in the morphology of the proximal part (Figs 3.2.1 & 3.2.2). Until now, none of the typologies or chronologies proposed for the development of these daggers is satisfying. It is impossible to link a given dagger morphology to a region or a period (Mottes 2001). This problem may reflect bias in our research: for example, we have to consider the fact that a large proportion of the daggers were ancient finds, which were poorly described and, consequently, derive from undated contexts.

These daggers are distributed throughout northern Italy, from the southern parts of the Po Valley up to, perhaps exceptionally, north of Lazio, where we have a dagger from Fosso Conicchio (Fig. 3.3; Mottes 2001; Fugazzola Pelegrini & Delpino 1999). To the North, they reach Switzerland; and some were discovered in southern Germany (Mottes 2001).

They are rarer in northwest Italy, and Honegger shows that there is nearly no overlap between the distribution area of the Lessinian bifacial daggers and the Forcalquier blade daggers from southeastern France (Honegger 2006: 47). The daggers from Forcalquier are manufactured on large blades made by indirect percussion and by lever pressure (Renault 1998, 2006). The retouch may be rather irregular, as in the case of the dagger from Palo in central Liguria, or very fine, made by pressure after surface polishing, as in the case of the Torello dagger in western Liguria (Fig. 3.2.3; Guilbeau

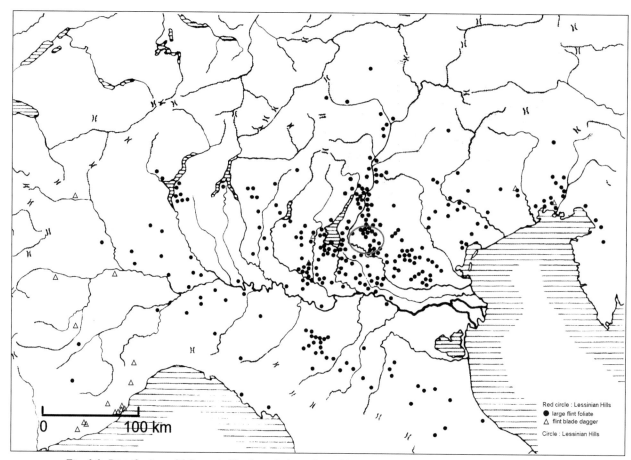

Fig. 3.3. Distribution of foliates in Northern Italy and neighboring areas (redrawn after Mottes 2001: 524).

2010). This production is contemporary with the Lessinian Hills production. It should be noted that only a minority of the large blades produced in Forcalquier are retouched into daggers; the other blades are not retouched or have lateral retouch without a distal tip (see Renault 1998, 2006).

Interestingly, the blade daggers from Grand-Pressigny seem not to have reached Italy even as they are quite numerous in Western Switzerland (Honegger 2006).

In Northern Italy, the flint daggers are only found on a relatively restricted number of sites. For example, in the large necropolis of Remedello Sotto Brescia and Fontanella Mantovana only a few graves have yielded such artefacts (see Colini 1898, 1899; Cornaggia Castiglioni 1971; Acanfora 1956). Nevertheless, they remain far more numerous than the flint daggers found in the central part of the Italian peninsula.

Central Italy – Scaglia Rossa flint daggers

The flint of the Scaglia Rossa outcrops of the Senonian formations in Marche was used for the production of foliates from the middle of the 5th millennium BC. The first daggers are still poorly dated; but they are attested from the late 4th and the beginning of the 3rd millennia BC.

In Pianacci dei Fossi di Genga and Conelle near Arcevia, there is evidence for the knapping of foliates (Cazzella *et al.* 2003; Baglioni 2005–2007). These sites lie in the western part of the Marche, near the flint outcrops. However, we have no direct information concerning the geological context of the outcrops or about the techniques used to extract the flint. In Conelle, excavation of a large ditch has yielded a lot of debris, preforms – both broken and unbroken, and several finished and completed foliates. The traceological analysis has shown that the largest ones (more that 8cm long) were used as daggers, the shorter ones as spearheads and as arrowheads (Lemorini & Massussi 2003).

The final retouch, at least, was carried out by pressure. It is impossible to extend the observations made in Conelle to all the foliates from Central Italy because this site represents only one period – the site is dated to the end of the 4th and the beginning of the 3rd millennia BC – and one particular type of site – a "production site".

Only six foliates from other sites are more than 14cm long and 4cm wide and can be quite convincingly considered to be daggers (Guilbeau 2010: 131). At least two are probably produced in flint from the Scaglia Rossa flint outcrops, one is made from a flint from an unknown provenance, and we have seen that the one from Fosso Conicchio may be Lessinian Hills flint. Smaller foliates are quite numerous.

The quality of the manufacture of these foliates, especially the daggers, is generally very good. They are typologically variable: some pieces have tang, others have a rounded base (Figs 3.4.1 & 3.4.2). Again, it is still impossible to establish specific types for a region or a period.

These daggers come from burials, dwelling sites and isolated finds in the regions south of the Po Valley and north of Molise (Guilbeau 2010). They are relatively rare, and we never find more than one dagger per village or per grave except at production sites, like Conelle. Clearly, the contrast with the southern regions of the peninsula is considerable.

Southern Italy – Gargano flint daggers

The Gargano is a mountainous peninsula *ca.* 30km from north to south and 40km from east to west located on the Adriatic coast just south of the latitude of Rome. Very rich flint outcrops dating from the Senonian-Cenomanian periods and from the middle Eocene are located throughout this area. They were intensely exploited from the early Neolithic through mines and pits (Galiberti 2005). This flint continued to be used in the 4th and 3rd millennia; but, during this period, it is employed at least partly for making daggers.

Even at this late date, the production of flint blades by lever pressure which began during the first half of the 6th millennium BC is still attested (Guilbeau 2010; for the technique, see Pelegrin 1988, 2006). However, the morphology of the blades is quite different from those made in earlier periods. The blades are always around 20–21cm long, but they are now wider and thicker: they measure 4.1cm wide and 1.1cm thick on average, while they were 2.2cm wide and 0.6–0.7mm thick during the Neolithic (Fig. 3.5; Guilbeau 2010). In cross-section, they are also usually triangular instead of trapezoidal during the earlier period. Almost all the large blades documented are retouched into daggers through pressure flaking. The extension of the retouch is variable on the upper face, and covers only the proximal part and the tip on the lower face. Since all the 65 daggers on large blades directly examined are made from Gargano flint, we assume that all daggers of this type are made from this raw material.

Of the 219 blade daggers currently identified, 168 come from graves and only seven from dwelling sites. The context of provenance of 39 of them is unknown because they come from sporadic and ancient finds, five come from caves and from a dubious, non-funerary deposit.

We must put in perspective the overrepresentation of daggers from funeral contexts because 52 of them come from only one site; the necropolis of Spina-Gaudo near

the Tyrrhenian sea on the south of Campania. We also have to consider that the domestic sites are currently very poorly documented, especially in Campania, while recent discoveries tend to clarify the situation in central and southern Lazio (see, for example, Cerqua 2011; Anzidei & Carboni nd.). In the latter region, no dagger is reported in the lithic industry from the villages of Selva dei Muli 2 and Tor Pagnotta (Gangemi 2011); but there are very few lithic tools at all on these sites, so the absence of flint daggers is not conclusive. "Daggers" are reported in the villages of Casetta Mistici, Torino-Mezzocammino 2 and Selva dei Muli 1 in Lazio, and Parco San Nicola near Bari in Apulia; but we still have very few data about their morphology, their size, their raw material, etc. (Bidittu & Segre Naldini 1981; Carboni 2002; Gangemi 2011; Curci & Genchi nd). Even if they are far more numerous here than in central Italy, the flint daggers remain quite rare: for example, there are 11 daggers for 135 individuals (50 adult males) in the Buccino necropolis (Holloway 1973:40).

The typology of the blade daggers is varied. There are some differences in the morphology of the blade, the extension and the regularity of the retouch. For the moment, it is not possible to relate clear types with one period or one area. We must notice that one part of the supposed types actually corresponds to different steps in the resharpening of the blades, an observation confirmed by the traceological analysis still underway (Fig. 3.5.3; Lemorini pers. comm.)

Aside from the blade daggers, we sometimes also find bifacial daggers. Their size and their morphology permit us to distinguish them from the arrowheads. Indeed, most of the time they are longer, and they are always wider. They are between 9.5cm and 33cm long and measure at least 3.5cm wide. Their tang, if they possess one, is always large, unlike the tang of the arrowheads (Fig. 3.6). The latter aspect, along with their increased width, is the most important feature for distinguishing the very long (greater than 10cm long) – and probably non-functional – arrowheads from the smallest daggers.

The bifacial daggers and the arrowheads are made by fine, bifacial pressure flaking. The only preform known to have been subjected to heat treatment was that of the dagger from Telese (Fig. 3.6.1). This technique seems to be far more rarely used than Arcuri (1990) suggested.

In southern Italy, bifacial daggers are rarer than blade daggers as only 62 bifacial daggers are known. Sixteen of the 21 daggers directly examined are made from Gargano flint, the others were produced in diverse flints of unknown provenance.

The typology of the bifacial daggers is very varied and it is still impossible to associate types with regions or periods. Several daggers show clear signs of use and resharpening. This was confirmed by traceological analyses carried out by C. Lemorini (pers. comm.).

Blade and bifacial daggers can be found in the same areas,

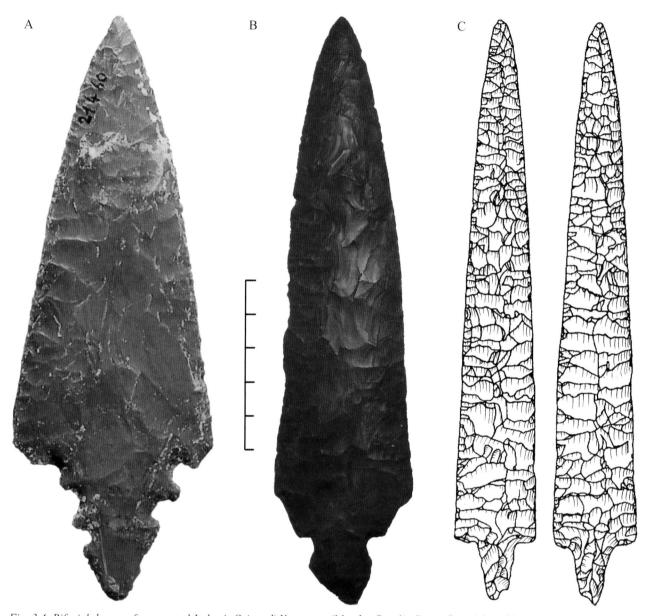

Fig. 3.4. Bifacial daggers from central Italy, A. Osimo di Vescovara (Marche, Scaglia Rossa flint) (altered from Silvestrini 2000: tav. vi no. 5); B. Poggio Aquilone (Umbria, L: 17.8cm, Scaglia Rossa flint); C. Very long foliate from Lattaia (Sticciano, Tuscany, L: 16.5cm, W: 2.3cm) (redrawn after Miari & Negroni Catacchio 1995: 155).

on the same sites and, sometimes, in the same tombs. There may be an overrepresentation of bifacial daggers among stray finds, but this observation has yet to be confirmed.

Their distribution in southern Italy shows concentration of finds in some area for example in central and southern Campania that correspond to areas with the most numerous and the largest necropolis (Fig. 3.7, see Bailo Modesti & Salerno 1998).

Secondary centres and regions almost devoid of daggers

In this brief description of the main flint dagger production centres, we have noted the presence of secondary production centres in several regions. For example, the bifacial dagger from Spilamberto in Emilia Romagna and other daggers found in the same area are in phtanite which probably derives from local outcrops (Bagolini 1996; Mottes 2001). The dagger from Maiolati in the Marche is made in a flint of unknown provenance, clearly different from the Scaglia

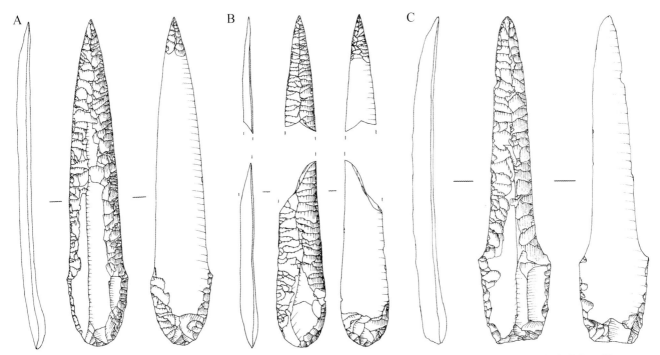

Fig. 3.5. Blade daggers in Gargano flint. A. Altamura (Apulia, L: 18.3cm); B. Monteroduni (Molise, L: ca. 21.2cm); C. Telese (Campania, L: 15.6cm. Probable resharpening of the edges).

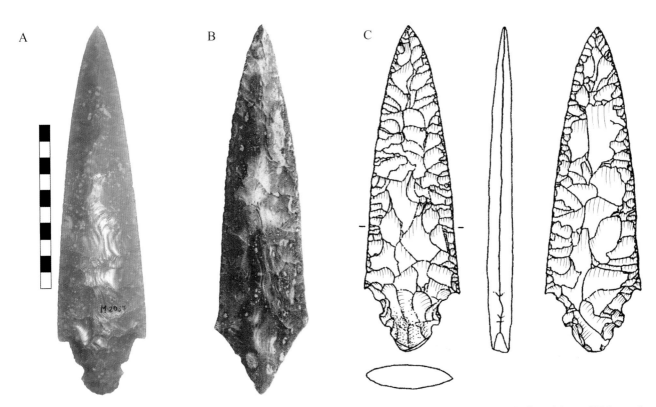

Fig. 3.6. Bifacial daggers. A. Telese (Campania, L: 22.7cm, Gargano flint), B. Riccia (Campania, L: 27cm) (from Maiuri 1926: tav. i); C. Cantalupo-Mandela (Lazio, L: 18.2cm: redrawn after Carboni 2002: 268).

Fig. 3.7. Distribution of blade and bifacial daggers in Southern Italy.

Rossa flint. In southern Italy, at least two bifacial daggers of the 14 studied from Spina-Gaudo necropolis are made from a flint of unknown origin.

Finally, we must note the presence in Sardinia of a dagger manufactured from a lever pressure blade in the Oligocene flint from Perfugas in the northern part of the island. This dagger was found in the megalithic grave of Pranu Mutteddu (Fig. 3.8.1; Atzeni 1985; Atzeni & Cocco 1989). Lever pressure blades were produced from 4200 until about 3500

BC in the Perfugas area; but, except for the one described above, none was retouched into dagger.

This dagger was accompanied by a bifacial dagger made on a very thin, tabular flint blocks from the same source, as evidenced by the extensive cortical surfaces on both sides (Fig. 3.8.2). A fragmentary dagger of the same type, and visibly in the same flint, was found at the site of Monte d'Accoddi in the north of the island. These are the only flint daggers identified for the whole island, unless we consider

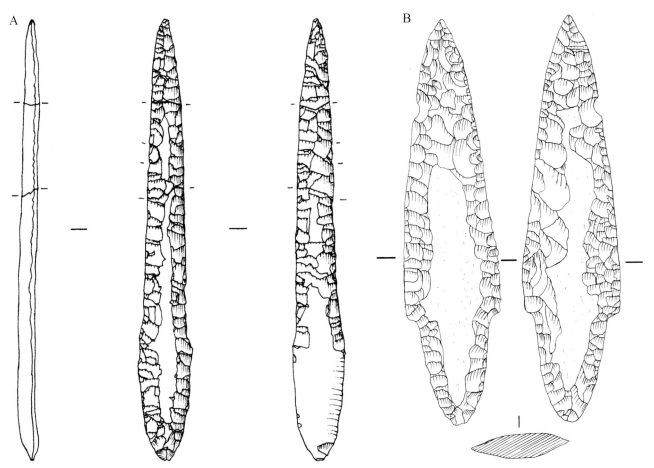

Fig. 3.8. Pranu Mutteddu (Sardinia, Perfugas flint) A. Blade dagger, L: 14.9cm; B. Bifacial dagger, L: 14.1cm (redrawn after Atzeni & Cocco 1989: 216).

foliates from the same contexts. These can sometimes be quite large (a few are over 10cm), are often of poor technical quality, and are made in obsidian from the Monte Arci outcrops and flint from the Perfugas outcrops.

In Sicily, flint daggers are almost absent. There is only one dubious exception: a possible low quality bifacial dagger found in the Syracuse area was reported by Bernabò Brea (Bernabò Brea 1966: 89). On this island, even the small foliates, probable arrowheads, are particularly rare compared to contemporary sites on the peninsula. This scarcity is not the consequence of a lack of data for this period because we know many villages and necropolises, even if most were excavated a long time ago (Tiné & Tiné 1998). In Sicily, the most notable change in the chipped stone industries during the 4th and the 3rd millennia BC is the decline of the distribution networks of obsidian blades at a time when standing pressure and lever pressure blades made from flint from the Hybleans Hills and probably from unknown outcrops in the western part of the island continue to be produced. This production shows no noticeable changes in technique from those used during the 6th millennium

when they first began to be produced. Furthermore, we must remember that the island was not isolated during that period: there are strong similarities in burial practices and in the ceramic assemblage between Sicily and the Peninsula. So, we cannot explain the quasi-absence of flint daggers here by a lack of relationship with continental Italy.

Conclusion

This overview of flint dagger production in Italy shows the huge variety of daggers between periods and regions. The general tendency towards the development of chipped stone foliates from the mid–5th millennium BC and of daggers from the first half of the 4th millennium BC is expressed in very different ways in all the areas concerned. These differences can be related to local and regional cultural trends, in particular to traditions in flint knapping techniques that persist during the Eneolithic.

In Northern Italy, for example, the Lessinian Hills flint distributed from the beginning of the Neolithic, that is from the first half of the 6th millennium BC, is logically used for the manufacture of foliates during the 5th millennium. Flint daggers appear here simply as a larger version of the foliates already being produced. In these conditions, it is impossible to find clear criteria with which to distinguish among the arrowheads, the spearheads, the daggers and the halberds.

In Central Italy, the situation is similar, although to a lesser extent, with flint production being linked to Scaglia Rossa flint from the Marche.

In Southern Italy, the prevalence of blade daggers probably corresponds to an evolution of lever pressure blades which were first produced at the beginning of the Neolithic in the first centuries of the 6th millennium BC in flint from the Gargano peninsula.

Late Neolithic and Eneolithic people in Sicily and, to a lesser extent, in Sardinia showed little interest in the foliates circulating around Italy. With the exception of objects produced in obsidian, the lithic assemblage of the 4th and 3rd millennia BC corresponds, at least in part, to material produced in previous millennia and centuries on these islands.

All these observations lead us to believe that there was a widespread trend toward the creation of "daggers" or "points" from the second half of the 5th millennium BC throughout Italy, but that this trend was expressed in very different ways in each centre of production from the north to the south of the peninsula. Differences appear in their frequency of deposition, their technique or their morphology and probably correspond to regional and local traditions in chipped stone industries as well as to local or regional cultural choices.

It is essential to remember the local roots of Italian flint dagger morphological and technical variety when considering the variable outcomes of typological analyses or attempting to draw out their relationships with contemporary metal daggers (Steiniger, this volume).

Note

1. This date is calibrated at 2 σ with the software Calib 6.0.1 according the calibration curve of Reimer *et al.* 2004.

Acknowledgments

Most of the arguments discussed here were presented first in a PhD ("*Les grandes lames et les lames par pression au levier du Néolithique et de l'Énéolithique en Italie*"), directed by Catherine Perlès and presented in 2010 in the Université Paris Ouest – Nanterre, La Défense (France).

I would like to thank Daniel Steiniger for the very fruitful discussions we had about the Italian late Prehistory and for his help in improving this text and Cate Frieman for the very helpful comments and the (many!) corrections of the first manuscript version.

References

Acanfora, M. O. 1956. Fontanella Mantovana e la cultura di Remedello. *Bullettino di Paletnologia Italiana* 65: 321–385.

Anzidei, A. P., Carboni, G. nd. La Facies del Gaudo nel territorio di Roma nel quadro delle manifestazioni culturali eneolitiche del versante tirrenico. In: *Tra le rocce nascoste agli dei. Incontro di Studi in ricordo di Giancarlo Bailo Modesti*. Università degli studi di Napoli "L'Orientale". Palazzo Du Mesnil, Napoli. 28 ottobre 2011.

Arca, A. 2009. Monte Bego e Valcamonica, confronto fra le più antiche le fasi istoriative. Dal Neolitico al Bronzo Antico, parallelismi e differenze tra marvegie e pitoti dei due poli dell'arte rupestre alpina. *Rivista di Scienze Preistoriche* 50: 265–306.

Arcuri, F. 1990. L'industria litica. In: C. Albore Livadie (ed.), *Archeologia a Piano di Sorrento, Ricerche di preistoria e di protostoria nella penisola sorrentina Soprintendenza archeologica*, Comune di Piano di Sorrento: Musei di Napoli e Caserta, Unité de recherche associée 1220 – École Française de Rome, CNRS. 83–93.

Atzeni, E. 1985. Aspetti e sviluppi culturali del Neolitico e della prima età dei Metalli in Sardegna. In: E. Atzeni, F. Barreca, M.-L. Ferrarese Ceruti, E. Contu, G. Lilliu, F. Lo Schiavo, F. Nicosia, E. Equini (eds.), *Ichnussa, La Sardegna dalle origini all'età classica*. Milano: Garzanti-Scheiwiller. XIX-LI.

Atzeni, E. 2000. *Le collezioni litiche preistoriche dell'università di Cagliari*. Cagliari: Edizioni AV.

Atzeni, E. & Cocco, D. 1989. Nota sulla necropoli megalitica di Pranu Mutteddu – Goni. In: L. Dettori Campus (ed.), *La cultura di Ozieri, problematiche e nuove acquisizioni, Atti del I convegno di studio*. Ozieri: Edizioni il Torchietto. 201–210.

Bailo Modesti, G. & Salerno, A. 1998. *Pontecagnano II, 5. La necropoli eneolitica, L'età del Rame in Campania nei villaggi dei morti*. Napoli: Annali dell'Istituto Orientale di Napoli, sezione di Archeologia e Storia Antica.

Baglioni, L. 2005–2007. Aspetti tecnologici della produzione foliata neo-eneolitica: il caso studio di Pianacci dei Fossi nelle Marche. *Bullettino di Paletnologia Italiana* 96: 109–128.

Bagolini, B. 1996. Il Neolitico e l'Età del Rame, ricerca a Spilamberto-S Cesario 1977–1980. *Preistoria Alpina* 32: 13–305.

Bagolini, B., Barfield, L. H., Broglio, A. 1973. Notizie preliminari delle ricerche sull'insediamento neolitico di Fimon-Molino Casarotto (Vicenza). *Rivista di Scienze Preistoriche* 28: 161–215.

Bagolini, B. & Pedrotti, A. 1998. L'Italie septentrionale. In: J. Guilaine (ed.), *Atlas du Néolithique européen. L'Europe occidentale*. Paris: ERAUL. 233–341.

Barfield, L. H. 1999. Neolithic and Copper Age flint exploitation in Northern Italy. In: Ph. Della Casa (ed.), *Prehistoric alpine environment society and economy, Papers of the International Colloquium*. Universitätsforschungen zur prähistorischen Archäologie 55. Bonn: Rudolf Habelt. 245–252.

Battaglia, R. 1958–1959. Materiali per lo studio del periodo eneolitico del Veneto. *Bullettino di Paletnologia Italiana* 67–68: 249–269.

Bernabò Brea, L. 1966. *Sicily, before the Greeks*. London: Thames and Hudson.

Biddittu, I. & Segre Naldini, E. 1981. Insediamenti eneolitici e dell'anticà età del Bronzo nella valle del Sacco, a Selva dei Muli e Ceccano. In: *Archeologia laziale IV, Quarto incontro di studio del Comitato per l'Archeologia Laziale*. Roma: Consiglio Nazionale delle Ricerche. 35–46.

Borrello, M. A., Mottes, E., Schlichtherle, H. 2009. Traverser les Alpes au Néolithique. *Le Globe* 149: 29–60.

Carboni, G. 2002. Territorio aperto o di frontiera? Nuove prospettive di ricerca per lo studio della distribuzione spaziale delle facies del Gaudo e di Rinaldone nel Lazio centro-meridionale. *Origini* 24: 235–301.

Cauvin, M.-C. 1963. Industrie lithique campignienne de la Colombare di Negrar (Vérone). *L'Anthropologie* 67(3–4): 283–300.

Cazzella, A. & Moscoloni, M. 1999. *Conelle di Arcevia, Un insediamento eneolitico nelle Marche, I- Lo scavo, la ceramica, i manufatti metallici, i resti organici*. Roma: Gangemi Editore.

Cazzella, A., Moscoloni, M. & Recchia, G. 2003. *Conelle di Arcevia, II-I manufatti in pietra scheggiata e levigata, in materia dura di origine animale, in ceramica non vascolari, il contotto*. Roma: Casa Editrice Università La Sapienza, Rubbettino.

Cerqua, M. 2011. Selva dei Muli (Frosinone): un insediamento eneolitico della facies del Gaudo. *Origini* 33: 157–223.

Colini, G. A. 1898. Il sepolcreto di Remedello sotto nel Bresciano e il periodo eneolitico in Italia. *Bullettino di Paletnologia Italiana* 24: 1–47, 88–110, 206–260, 280–295.

Colini, G. A. 1899. Il sepolcreto di Remedello Sotto nel Bresciano e il periodo eneolitico in Italia. *Bullettino di Paletnologia Italiana* 25: 1–32, 218–295.

Cornaggia Castiglioni, O. 1971. La cultura di Remedello, problematica ed ergologia di una facies dell'Eneolitico padano. *Memorie della Società Italiana di Scienze Naturali e del Museo Civico di Storia Naturale di Milano* 20(1): 5–79.

Curci, A. & Genchi, F. Nd. Rituali nel profondo delle grotte. Aspetti culturali eneolitici da Grotta San Biagio (Ostuni-Brindisi). In: *Tra le rocce nascoste agli dei. Incontro di Studi in ricordo di Giancarlo Bailo Modesti, Università degli studi di Napoli « L'Orientale »*. Palazzo Du Mesnil, Napoli, 28 ottobre 2011.

Degasperi, N., Ferrari, A., Steffè, G. 1998. L'insediamento neolitico di Lugo di Romagna. In: A. Pessina & G. Muscio (eds.), *Settemila anni fa il primo pane. Ambiente e culture delle società neolitiche*. Udine: Comune di Udine, Museo Friulano di Storia Naturale. 117–124.

Di Lernia, S. & Martini, F. 1988. Esercizi di tipologia analitica: definizioni morfologiche e nomenclatura dei pezzi foliati peduncolati. *Preistoria Alpina* 24: 183–201.

Egg, M. 1992. Zur Ausrüstung des Toten vom Hauslabjoch, Gem. Schnals (Südtirol). In: F. Höpfel, W. Platzer & K. Spindler (eds.), *Der Mann im Eis. Bericht über das Internationale Symposium 1992*. Innsbruck: Eigenverlag der Universität Innsbruck. 254–272.

Fugazzola Delpino, M. A. & Pellegrini, E. 1999. Il complesso culturale "campaniforme" di fosso conicchio (Viterbo). *Bullettino di Paletnologia Italiana* 90 (nuova serie 8): 61–159.

Galiberti, A. 2005. *Defensola. Una miniera di selce di 7000 anni fa*. Siena: Protagon Editori.

Gangemi, R. 2011. L'industria litica del sito eneolitico di Selva dei Muli (Frosinone). *Origini* 33: 225–232.

Guilaine, J. (ed.) 1998. *Atlas du Néolithique européen. L'Europe occidentale*. Paris: ERAUL.

Guilbeau, D. 2010. *Les grandes lames et les lames par pression au levier du Néolithique et de l'Énéolithique en Italie*. Unpublished PhD thesis, Université Paris Ouest Nanterre-La Défense.

Holloway, R.R. 1973. *Buccino, The Eneolithic necropolis of S. Antonio and other prehistoric discoveries made in 1968 and 1969 by Brown University*. Roma: De Luca Editore.

Honegger, M. 2006. Grandes lames et poignards dans le Néolithique final du nord des Alpes. In: J. Vaquer & F. Briois (eds.), *La fin de l'Age de Pierre en Europe du Sud, Actes de la table ronde de l'E.H.E.S.S.* Toulouse: Éditions des Archives d'Écologie Préhistoriques. 43–56.

Lemorini, C. & Massussi, M. 2003. Lo studio dei foliati in selce di Conelle di Arcevia: approccio tecno-funzionale, sperimentale e delle tracce d'uso. In: A. Cazzella, M. Moscoloni & G. Recchia (eds), *Conelle di Arcevia, II-I manufatti in pietra scheggiata e levigata, in materia dura di origine animale, in ceramica non vascolari, il contotto*. Roma: Casa Editrice Università La Sapienza, Rubbettino: 309–354.

Lo Schiavo, F. 1989. Le origini della metallurgia ed il problema della metallurgia nella cultura di Ozieri. In: L. Dettori Campus (ed.), *La cultura di Ozieri, problematiche e nuove acquisizioni, Atti del I convegno di studio*. Ozieri: Edizioni il Torchietto. 279–294.

Lugliè, C. 2009. L'obsidienne néolithique en Méditerranée occidentale. In: M.-H. Moncel & F. Frohlich (eds.), *L'Homme et le précieux, Matières minérales précieuses*. Oxford: Archaeopress. 213–224.

Maiuri, A. 1926. Pugnale siliceo eneolitico da Riccia, in prov. di Campobasso. *Bullettino di Paletnologia Italiana* 46: 1–4.

Manfredini, A. (ed.) 2002. Le dune, il lago, il mare, Una comunità di villaggio dell'Età del Rame a Maccarese. Firenze: Origines.

Miari, M., Negroni Catacchio, N. 1995. Materiali eneolitici inediti dalla Toscana e dall'Umbria. In: N. Negroni Catacchio, *Preistoria e Protostoria in Etruria, Atti del secondo incontro di studi* 2. Milano: Centro di Studi di Preistoria e Archeologia. 143–155.

Mottes, E. 2001. Bell Beakers and Beyond: Flint daggers of northern Italy between technology and typology. In: F. Nicolis (ed.), *Bell Beakers Today, Pottery, People, Culture, Symbols in Prehistoric Europe, Proceedings of the International Colloquium*. Trento: Provincia autonoma di Trento. 519–545.

Patroni, G. 1905. Tipologia e terminologia dei pugnali in selce italiani. *Bullettino di Paletnologia Italiana* 31: 85–95.

Pearce, M. 2009. How Much Metal was there in Circulation in Copper Age Italy?. In: T.L. Kienlin & B.W. Roberts (eds.), *Metals and Societies: Studies in honour of Barbara S. Ottaway*. Bonn: Rudolf Habelt. 277–284.

Pedrotti, A., Cavulli, F. & Miorelli, A. 2000. Lugo di Grezzana (Verona). Insediamento neolitico della cultura di Fiorano: l'industria ceramica del Settore IX. In: A. Pessina & G. Muscio (eds.), *La Neolitizzazione, Tra Oriente e Occidente*. Udine: Edizioni del Museo Friulano di Storia Naturale. 111–123.

Pelegrin, J. 1988. Débitage expérimental par pression, «du plus petit au plus grand». In: J. Tixier (ed.), *Technologie préhistorique*. Paris: Éditions du CNRS. 37–53.

Pelegrin, J. 2006. Long blade technology in the old world: an experimental approach and some archaeological results. In:

J. Apel & K. Knutsson (eds.), *Skilled Production and Social Reproduction, Aspects of Traditional Stone-Tool Technologies, Proceedings of a Symposium in Uppsala*. Uppsala: Societas Archaeologica Upsaliensis. 37–68.

Peretto, C., Ronchitelli, A.-M. 1973. Il villaggio preistorico delle Colombare di Negrar (Verona). *Rivista di Scienze Preistoriche* 28(2): 431–492.

Pétrequin, P., Pétrequin, A.-M., Errera, M., Cassen, S., Croutsch, S., Klassen, L., Rossy, M., Garibaldi, P., Isetti, E., Rossi, G. & Delcaro, D. 2005. Beigua, Monviso e Valais. All'origine delle grandi asce levigate di origine alpina in Europa occidentale durante il V millennio. *Rivista di Scienze Preistoriche* 55: 265–322.

Reimer, J. P., Baillie, M. G. L, Bard, E., Bayliss, A., Beck, J. W., Bertrand, C., Blackwell, P. G., Buck, C. E., Burr, G., Cutler, K. B., Damon, P. E., Edwards, R. L., Fairbanks, R. G., Friedrich, M., Guilderson, T. P., Hughen, K. A., Kromer, B., MacCormac, F. G., Manning, S., Bronk Ramsey, C., Reimer, R. W., Remmele, S., Southon, J. R., Stuiver, M., Talamo, S., Taylor, F. W., van der Plicht, J. & Weyhenmeyer, C. E. 2004. INTCAL04 Terrestrial Radiocarbon Age Calibration, 0–26 CAL KYR BP. *Radiocarbon* 46: 1029–1058.

Renault, S. 1998. Économie de la matière première. L'exemple de la production, au Néolithique final, des grandes lames en silex zoné oligocène du bassin Forcalquier (Alpes-de-Haute-Provence). In: A. D'Anna & D. Binder (eds.), *Production et identité culturelle*. Juan-les-Pins: APDCA. 145–161.

Renault, S. 2006. La production des grandes lames au Néolithique final en Provence: matériaux exploités, multiplicité des productions, aspects technologiques et chrono-culturels. In: J. Vaquer & F. Brios (eds.), *La fin de l'Age de Pierre en Europe du Sud*, Actes de la table ronde de l'E.H.E.S.S. Toulouse: Éditions des Archives d'Écologie Préhistoriques. 139–164.

Robb, J. 2007. *The Early Mediterranean Village, Agency, Material Culture, and Social Change in Neolithic Italy*. Cambridge Studies in Archaeology. Cambridge: Cambridge University Press.

Silvestrini, M. 2000. L'Eneolitico delle Marche alla luce delle recenti acquisizioni. In: M. Silvestrini (ed.), *Recenti acquisizioni, problemi e prospettive della ricerca sull'Eneolitico dell'Italia centrale*. Ancona: Regione Marche – Centro Beni Culturali. 31–38.

Tiné, S. & Tiné, V. 1998. La Sicile. In: J. Guilaine (ed.), *Atlas du Néolithique européen. L'Europe occidentale*. Paris: ERAUL. 133–163.

Vaquer, J. 2007. Le rôle de la zone nord tyrrhénienne dans la diffusion de l'obsidienne en Méditerranée nord-occidentale au Néolithique. In: A. D'Anna, J. Cesari, L. Ogel & J. Vaquer (eds.), *Corse et Sardaigne préhistoriques: relations et échanges dans le contexte méditerranéen*. Actes des congrès nationaux des sociétés historiques et scientifiques 128e. Paris: Éditions du CTHS. 99–119.

4

ON FLINT AND COPPER DAGGERS
IN CHALCOLITHIC ITALY

Daniel Steiniger

In Chalcolithic Italy, we know about 100 daggers of flint and copper, hundreds of depicted daggers on rock art and a few daggers made of bone. For the flint daggers, we can see the utilisation of different raw material sources in the various regions. Their production technique is rooted in Neolithic traditions of flint knapping and shows continuity into the early metal using period. By the mid–4th millennium cal BC, copper daggers appear in Italy, often in the same context as flint daggers, meaning they are known nearly exclusively from graves. The shape of the cutting edges of daggers of both materials is very similar in each region: in the north, they are mostly triangular and shorter while, in the south, they are very long and slim. While copper could be shaped more freely into any form desired, the possible shape of flint daggers depends strongly on the production technique and size of available flint nodules. We can identify different production and distribution areas with comparable forms of daggers in both materials, interacting in a way we cannot easily explain simply as the imitation of copper daggers in flint. It seems more likely that the shapes of the copper daggers reflect those of flint blades. This observation opens a wide field of possible interpretations concerning the production, function, value and evolution of daggers in Italy, of which we are just beginning to get a glimpse.

Introduction

The Italian Chalcolithic is very rich in flint and copper daggers. The interpretation of their distribution is a serious challenge, when trying to get further than just typological description. Amongst archaeologists the viewpoint is widespread that flint daggers are copies of and inferior to metal ones. In some cases this may be true, but it is an erroneous assumption that this could be a universal law, valid anywhere and at any time. It has to be kept in mind, that the replacement of stone by metal is more complex than just a predetermined progress. It is not possible to cope with the prehistoric way of understanding value and relevance only by following modern, rationalistic ideology, particularly in this case as, obviously, Chalcolithic people did not foresee the complete displacement of stone and flint by metal. Besides the unthinking adoption of modern systems of value to interpret the archaeological material, there is also the basic problem of an incomplete archaeological record

which, in many cases, is not a sound base for modelling. Therefore classifications and typological approaches have to be adapted on the particular situation and question in mind. The following paper tries to give an idea of the situation concerning these topics in the study area.

Thanks to radiocarbon dating, it is possible to place the beginning of the Chalcolithic period in continental Italy around 3500 BC. This dating is based on firm and varied evidence, including the well-known 'Iceman' from the Similaun who dates to the second half of the 4th millennium BC. In addition, new dates for central and southern Italy provide a good base for a chronology of the Italian Chalcolithic from *ca.* 3500 to *ca.* 2200 BC (Dolfini 2010). Especially during the late 4th and the beginning of the 3rd millennia BC, we can identify a developed flint knapping technology as well as an elaborated copper metallurgy, resulting in a wide distribution of flint and copper daggers across the peninsula. The production technique of Italian flint daggers has roots in Neolithic traditions of flint knapping and shows continuity into the early metal using period (Guilbeau, this volume). During the later part of the third millennium BC, the quantity of flint and copper daggers declined in the archaeological record, perhaps due to different burial customs appearing in some regions (for a general synopsis of the Chalcolithic in Italy, see: Cocchi Genick 1996; Steiniger 2005).

In this paper, only a short overview of this complex period is presented. The area under examination is restricted to continental Italy, excluding the islands (for the flint daggers on the islands, see: Guilbeau, this volume; a compilation for the occurrence of flint and copper daggers in Europe and the Near East is given in: Zimmermann 2007 and Zimmermann, this volume). As a matter of course, it is very important to base our study on well-documented material from secure context. Therefore, 108 flint and 51 copper daggers have been chosen as the database for the investigation presented here. All these finds come from burial context (for details and references, see: Steiniger 2005, in press). These graves with daggers have a certain chronological coherence and date to between *ca.* 3500 to 2500 BC, based on the results of sometimes problematic interpretations of the radiocarbon dating. The calibration process in that period is extremely influenced by strong wiggles in the calibration curve (Steiniger 2010). With the analysis of these daggers, we have a representative sample that enables us to identify some main characteristics and to outline the broad structures of Italian Chalcolithic daggers within the funerary sphere. Guilbeau makes use of a partly different and enlarged database of flint daggers, which includes finds from settlements and other context (Guilbeau, this volume). For the present investigation, and our focus on the relationship between flint and copper daggers, grave finds are the primary evidence, especially because copper daggers from Chalcolithic Italy with documented find context come nearly exclusively from burials.

Concerning the general typology of the Italian Chalcolithic material, several traditional typological subdivisions have been proposed in which flint and copper daggers play an important role, because they are one of the main artefact groups (e.g. de Marinis & Pedrotti 1997; Bailo Modesti & Salerno 1998). In some areas, especially in the north (the so-called 'Remedello culture'), pottery is extremely scarce, while stone and metal artefacts are numerous. These typologies are of restricted practical use for the question discussed here. The main problem is that they attempt to portray a classical typo-chronological subdivision of material in the pattern of a framework of clear cut archaeological cultures. This can only be done by using 'clear cut types', that are then ascribed to clear cut 'cultures' and 'single periods' of a chronological sequence. All these general terms: types, cultures and chronological periods (eg. Remedello dagger; Remedello culture, Remedello phase 1, Remedello phase

2; Rinaldone dagger, Rinaldone culture, etc.), are rather monolithic constructs and – in face of the complex patterns visible in the archaeological record – problematic concepts. Concerning the flint and copper daggers, these subdivisions work only and exclusively with the model of a holistic, constructed type (e.g. each dagger belongs to exactly one type). It is obvious that typological subdivisions developed solely on the basis of differences are not an adequate form of data processing for an investigation that intends to focus on the discussion of formal and technological relations and their connections in the material. Even beyond the daggers, the Italian Chalcolithic is a very complex period, and it is not possible to link specific finds to clear-cut entities like archaeological groups or cultures. The situation is much more complex and this not only reflects the fragmentary record, but seems to be a characteristic of Chalcolithic Italy, meaning that from time to time there must be an adjustment of interpretative strategy (Bagolini & Fasani 1982; Barfield 1985, 1986, 1988; 1996; Mottes 2001; Steiniger 2005, 2010). In other words, as regards the north Italian flint daggers, 'there is no evidence that a specific form, is related either to a specific period of time, or a specific cultural group' (Mottes 2001, 532) because neither chronological periods nor cultural groups can yet be defined in a satisfying way. More likely, we must envision a multitude of complex interactions which left fragments of a highly sophisticated distribution pattern that is hard to untangle (e.g. Barfield 1985; Steiniger 2005).

Moreover, the burial customs in Chalcolithic Italy are extremely complex, with inhumation and partial cremation, single graves, collective burials, secondary and tertiary treatment of the bones in different steps with re-excavations and re-burials all present (for an overview, see: Cocchi Genick 2004). On the other hand, there is a comparably smaller archaeological record of settlement structures (a collection of papers on recent discoveries in Southern and Central Italy is published in: Istituto Italiano di Preistoria e Protostoria 2007). This ambivalence in the archaeological record makes it difficult to understand the sequence of individual steps of production and distribution of artefacts and especially the daggers, although we have a great number of finds from the graves.

It is methodologically important that the daggers in this essay were not studied as a single typological entity, like other researchers have done (e.g. Bianco Peroni 1994, where daggers are classified as 'types' or 'varieties of types'). In contrast, the formal expression of the material is understood as a set of variable technical features which can be described as a combination of a wide range of possible choices and technological realisations (Steiniger in press). The material is reviewed from a distinct technological point of view. For example, the shape of the cutting edge, the cross-section, the number and arrangement of rivets (on copper daggers) or the form of the tang or heel[1] can be seen as separate, exchangeable features combined in various ways. The classification of the material develops from considering the daggers as a modular system (German: *Baukastensystem*) of different features combined in diverse ways, creating various types. Although it is obvious that the classification is artificial, in the sense that it was applied to the material by the archaeologist, in this way the finds are not separated into different, pre-existing types – the types were created through the recognition of various features amongst the artefacts. In this sense, the classification evolved based on the archaeological material at hand and not, as in the traditional typological method, on the construction of an idealised concept of type which, in many cases, does not even exist in reality or is borrowed from neighbouring regions because it was never found in the study area (for the problems of unconscious, traditional typology see: Brather 2006; Gauß 2009: 65–76; both with further references). S. Schwenzer also makes use of a broken up concept of type in his work on bronze metal-hilted daggers. In his classification, he uses characteristic features called 'main or core features' and less important, 'secondary features'. He makes use of the traditional terminology of holistic type, mainly because it is quite well-established and widely adopted in prehistoric research; but he points out that some daggers do not fit in this typological classification system and, therefore, their relations with 'core groups and types' have to be described individually (Schwenzer 2004: 33 especially).

For examining the relationship between flint and copper daggers, it is reasonable to choose a feature which is found on daggers of both materials, the shape of the cutting edges, and to use this in the following investigation as a key feature. It is important to note that this feature is neither the only, nor the most important feature amongst the Chalcolithic daggers in Italy. It is just the one the author has chosen because it is all-encompassing. If, for instance, we compared the cross-section of flint daggers (mono- or bifacial) with that of copper daggers (with or without midribs) or the form of the heels/tangs and the arrangement of rivets, we would find that not all daggers could be compared with each other, simply because too many of them lack the one or the other feature. Also these features are of different categories to some extent. However, the shape of the cutting edge is such a fundamental feature of daggers that it can be found on nearly all of them, even if it is fragmentary. The more or less triangular shape of the cutting edge is in other words the constituent criterion to label an artefact 'dagger' (for definitions compare: Schwenzer 2004: 3ff; Zimmermann 2007: 4ff). Although the shape of the edge is crucial for the definition of a dagger, several works refuse to use it for the classification of dagger types because of an anticipated distortion of the database due to unequal patterns of use-wear and re-sharpening. For example, Schwenzer describes the contour of the cutting edge of the bronze metal-hilted daggers as a 'qualitative feature' which lacks the same significance for his classification as the different technical parts of the handle and the rivets (Schwenzer 2004: 26). This point of view is ascribable to the fact that the most complex part of the bronze metal-hilted daggers is the handle and its many components; therefore, a rich field of great variability is available to develop a classification. It has to be kept in mind that, although there is a common reservation against using the cutting edge for typological classification, the direct examination of use-wear is generally a rather common and accepted method. As we will see below, daggers from the funeral sphere across Chalcolithic Italy show a remarkable uniformity in the shape of the cutting edge. Therefore, we can use this feature, even when it is not useful in other areas or chronological periods. Besides this, it has to be mentioned that, although up to now only very limited information for use-wear on Italian daggers has been published (for flint see: Guilbeau this volume; for copper: Dolfini 2011). Severe traces of use have been identified recently on flint daggers from burials in northern Italy (E. Mottes, pers. comm.); but, due to the uniformity of the daggers, we can interpret this pragmatically as a use that caused either very little loss of material or as a regional uniform pattern of use and abrasion due to similar functional application, with a later on similar re-working.

The practical and very pragmatic method of analyzing flint and copper daggers' cutting edges by tracing their silhouette and overlapping the drawings (for details see: Steiniger in press) was inspired by the 'envelope method' that was originally developed by C. R. Orton (1987) for the comparison of pottery profiles.

Flint daggers

In northern Italy, more than 400 flint daggers have been found, but we know nothing about the archaeological context of *ca.* 70% of them (Mottes 1996, 2001). Even when dealing with documented finds, we must pay attention to the find context, because great differences are observable between daggers from burials and daggers from settlements or from other context. Although, to date, there are only a few daggers known from settlements, these are mostly very small and show clear traces of use, fracture and multiple reshaping (as the dagger of the 'Iceman' does); while the daggers from graves are much larger and extremely symmetrical in shape (Mottes 2001). The number of daggers from graves is much greater by far than those from settlements and we will concentrate on these daggers in the following discussion (Steiniger 2005, in press).

When looking at the daggers' overall shape, a difference in the length and width of the daggers immediately becomes apparent which can be correlated with the general production technique. The long and narrow blades have a monofacial cross section while the shorter, wider daggers are bifacial in section (Fig. 4.1). This bipolar structure is not only related

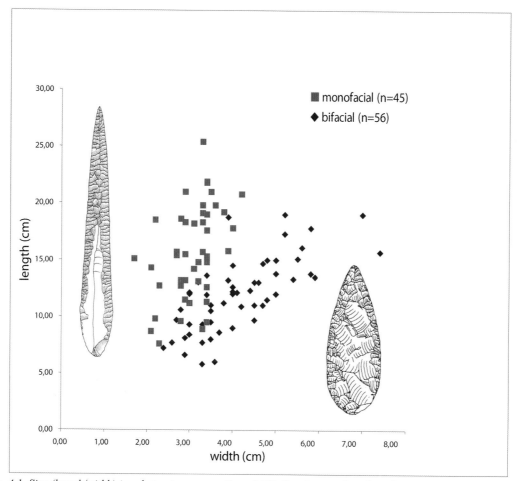

Fig. 4.1. Size (length/width) in relation to cross-section of 101 flint daggers from burial context in continental Italy.

to different production techniques, but also depends on two different distribution patterns that reflect at least two completely different raw material sources (Fig. 4.2).

Most of the daggers in northern Italy are bifacially worked, have a wider and shorter form than the southern ones and are made of Monti Lessini flint from the alpine area (Mottes 2001). Only very few bifacial daggers were found in central and southern Italian graves. Daggers in the south are much longer and (with very few exceptions) monofacially worked, having been produced by indirect percussion on long cores comparable to the blades from Grand-Pressigny (cf. Guilbeau, this volume). This technique requires very big flint nodules, a raw material not found in the north because the flint from the Monti Lessini region occurs only in smaller sized nodules due to tectonic fracture during the alpine orogenesis (Barfield 1990; Goldenberg 2006). Large flint nodules, even some greater than 1m in diameter (Galiberti 2005), are known from the Neolithic and Chalcolithic flint mines on the Gargano peninsula in the southeast of Italy. Pottery and radiocarbon dates from some mines indicate a Chalcolithic exploitation phase (Tarantini 2005). Also, previously unpublished microfacial analysis of flint daggers

Fig. 4.2. Distribution pattern of bifacial (solid line) and monofacial (dashed line) flint daggers from burial context in continental Italy.

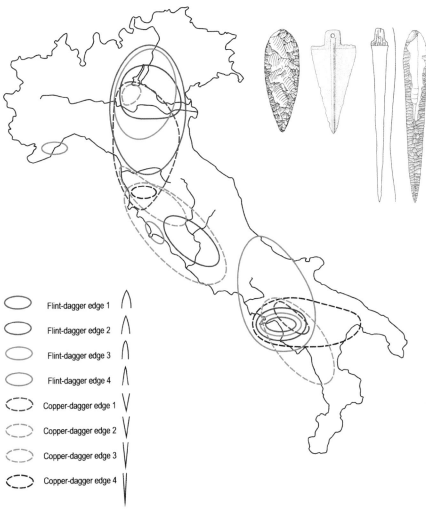

Fig. 4.3. Regional distribution of cutting edge dimensions of 51 copper and 108 flint daggers from burial context in continental Italy (including also the flint dagger from Similaun). Top right: Examples of a flint and copper dagger with edge type 1 from the cemetery of Remedello di Sotto in Northern Italy (left) and two examples of edge type 4 from Pontecagnano in Campania (right). Not to scale (after Bianco Peroni 1994; Longhi 1994; Bailo Modesti & Salerno 1998).

found in the famous Chalcolithic graves in Campania (Bailo Modesti & Salerno 1998) suggest that the provenance of the raw material is the Gargano peninsula (D. Guilbeau, pers. comm.). For a more detailed description of a possible third raw material source, Arcevia in eastern central Italy, and the use of this material that seems to be found only in context near the deposits, compare the contributions of D. Guilbeau (this volume) and Cazzella *et al.* (2003).

When looking at the cutting edge of the flint daggers, the previously mentioned distinction between the southern and the northern blades which corresponds with the production technique and raw material, can give us more than just typological information. If we focus on the shape of the cutting edge, a feature that might still have been visible when the daggers were fitted to their handles, we can neglect for a while the different construction of the tang/heel at the base.

It is important to remember that, although the daggers show a remarkable typological variability, especially at the tang/ heel, the form and measure of the cutting edge changes only gradually, from wide, triangular and short, to slim, triangular and very long as one moves from north to south, while the few central Italian daggers display medium dimensions (Fig. 4.2).

Copper daggers

If we take a closer look at the shape of the copper daggers' cutting edge, we can see different groupings, based on the size and shape of the edge, which are distributed in the same way as the flint daggers in different regions, from wider and shorter to longer and narrower ones as one moves from north to south (see the comparison in Fig. 4.3). The

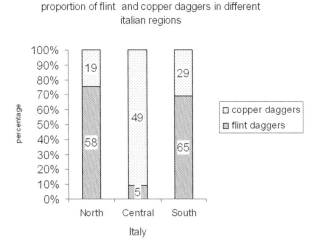

Fig. 4.4. Proportion of flint and copper daggers from burial context in different Italian regions.

striking similarity between the general shape of the cutting edge of the copper daggers and flint blades seems not to be a coincidence because it follows a supra-regional pattern. The only remarkable difference between the general shape of the cutting edges is that the metal blades have a straight and the flint blades a convex edge. The overall impression of the blades' shape is very similar. Another important point is that the copper daggers' cutting edge seems not to have lost very much material due to sharpening/grinding or they were reshaped always in the same way. Most of the blades of one cutting edge type differ just slightly in width from each other, except the corroded ones (Steiniger in press). On the map, we can see that central Italy is the area with the most overlaps and, thus, the most complex copper dagger forms and combinations of different features; while, in the north and the south, less variety is found. This concentration of variability is also the case for many other technical components, such as the shape of the tang/heel, the midrib, the number and position of the rivets etc., which are discussed in detail elsewhere (Steiniger in press).

Another point to be mentioned is that an inverse proportion of flint and copper daggers appears to be present in the various regions. In central Italy, where there are many copper daggers, fewer flint daggers are found; while, in the north and south, the overall number of flint daggers is more than the double to the number of copper daggers (Fig. 4.4). Furthermore, it is possible to identify a certain area where all the copper dagger shapes overlap, but where not one single flint dagger is found. This area is in southern Tuscany and is known as 'Colline Metallifere', meaning 'metal ore hills'. As the name would suggest, this is a region famous for its copper, silver, antimony and iron ores since the time of the Etruscans; unfortunately, no prehistoric copper mining has yet been found in the area (Bodechtel 1972; Giardino

& Steiniger 2011). The trace element patterns indicate that three primary sorts of metal were used in the manufacture of Chalcolithic Italian copper daggers; and they seem to come from three different regions: north, central and south Italy. Within each one of these zones, we can deduce from the interpretation of metal composition, more or less specialised metallurgic techniques and copper production traditions based on the exploitation of local ore sources (Steiniger 2010). This observation points to the fact that there may have been a number of copper mines in central Italy during the Chalcolithic period.

Chalcolithic mining

Unfortunately, no Chalcolithic copper mining in central Italy has been found yet, while there is good evidence for copper mining in Liguria and the Alps (Maggi *et al.* 2011; Pearce 2011) and in the southern part of the peninsula, namely in the Grotta della Monaca/Calabria (Larocca 2005; this mine is – due to the lack of metallurgical traces up to now – supposed to be a source of copper minerals for the production of green pigment). In the course of a research project funded by the Rome department of the German Archaeological Institute and currently underway, several indications for prehistoric mining activity have been identified during extensive field surveys in central Italy. In the Monti della Tolfa (Latium), we have some of the best preserved finds to date (Giardino & Steiniger 2011). They are located within the area of an 18th century AD copper and silver mining complex called Poggio Malinverno.

Various mining related infrastructural elements can be identified, for example some spoil heaps consist nearly exclusively of hammerstones and their fragments. Beside the spoil heaps, subsequently refilled opencast and deeper mining structures are present. A first season of excavation just started investigation at this site in 2012 (Steiniger & Giardino 2013). The hammerstones at Poggio Malinverno are not made of round pebbles like most hammerstones found at prehistoric copper mining sites, but from crude pieces of rock that were quarried and shaped only roughly for use in mining (for western European early copper mining hammerstones see: Groer 2008 with further references; for Liguria: de Pascale 2003; Calabria: Larocca 2005). A comparable situation is known for the Chalcolithic copper mining district of Cabrières in southern France, where hard quartzite rock from outcrops directly beside and inside the galleries was used for making hammerstones (Guendon *et al.* 2011). From preliminary use-wear analyses on the hammerstones from the surface of Poggio Malinverno, we can distinguish different types of tools with different function that seem to have been used in different working phases. Special types were not only made and used in a regular way, they also seem to have been reshaped after

Table 4.1. The three major interpretive models concerning the relationship and direction of influence of flint and copper daggers in prehistoric Europe and their authors.

flint dagger = original metal dagger = copy	metal dagger = original flint dagger = copy	complex, synchronous interaction of flint and metal dagger in function, value and use
Wilde 1862	Müller 1902	Gallay 1981
von Pulszky 1877	Uenze 1938	Mottes 2001
De Rossi 1879	Ströbel 1939	Honegger 2001
Chierici 1884	Strahm 1961/62	
Much 1886	Barfield 1971	
Montelius 1900	Lomborg 1973	
Kraft 1926	Müller-Karpe 1974	
Hillebrand 1929	Barfield *et al.*1992	
Schwab 1970	Matuschik 1997	
Vajsow 1993	Lübke 1997/98	
Ebbesen 1994	Klassen 2000	
	Schlichterle 2004/05	

breakage and recycled into smaller tools (for further information see: Steiniger & Giardino 2013).

Very similar hammerstones are known from another Late Neolithic/Chalcolithic Italian mine – one concerned with the extraction of cinnabar – called Buca di Spaccasasso in Tuscany (Cavanna 2007; for the use of cinnabar in the funerary sphere of Chalcolithic Italy: Cocchi Genick 1996). Radiocarbon dates from secondary burials in what was previously a mining gallery date this mine to prior to *ca.* 2800 BC (Cavanna 2007; Cavanna & Pellegrini 2007). A kind of technological transfer between the extraction of cinnabar (pigment mining) and copper (metal mining) in the same geological environment seems likely as, in both areas, the same type of hard sandstone was used for making the hammers, probably because there is no other hard rock available nearby. Also, the hammers on both sites share many common typological features. The distance between the two mines of Buca di Spaccasasso and Poggio Malinverno is less than 90km as the crow flies, but evidence from further away and yet another type of mining (for flint), shows surprising similarities when looked at from a technological point of view.

This leads us back to the flint mines of the Gargano peninsula, exploited in the Neolithic and Chalcolithic, where an interesting change in the shape and use of hammerstones and picks can be identified between the Neolithic mining phases and the Chalcolithic ones. In this region, we also observe that the Chalcolithic hammerstones are crude and rough and do not display the well-known grooves for hafting the handle; instead, they just have notches along the sides and are very similar to the central Italian tools mentioned above (from Poggio Malinverno and Buca di Spaccasasso). In contrast, the Early Neolithic hammerstones of the Gargano mines were made of ovoid shaped, ground and rounded pieces of rock and flint; and many of them have elaborate grooves that were picked carefully all around the central part of the picks to help fix a handle to them (Tarantini 2005).

In summary, it is possible to see some similarities and maybe connections, not only between flint and copper daggers, but also between flint and copper mining in Chalcolithic Italy. Yet, it is also obvious that much more research must be carried out in this field before we can speak about structural relations, technological transfer and socio-economic developments in detail. Due to the current state of research in mining archaeology and our limited knowledge concerning the settlement structure and organisation of trade routes and exchange systems, it is just possible to start asking questions (for the Alps: Pearce 2011; for Liguria: Maggi *et al.* 2011; for central Italy: Giardino & Steiniger 2011; for Calabria: Larocca 2005; for Gargano: Galiberti 2005).

Facts, problems, perspectives

Finally, some points are worth mentioning as they are key for future research, can serve as a base for discussion and are important to remember in reviewing interpretative models. As mentioned above, it seems very likely that the edges of the copper daggers were intentionally made to have the same general shape as those of the flint daggers rather than the other way around. The slim and long flint and copper daggers are found in the south where suitable raw material for long flint daggers was available. On the other hand, it was impossible to produce such long flint daggers in the north because the raw material was not available; so the copper daggers are shorter there as well. However, it is not currently possible to decide which one of the two materials was the 'primary' or 'prototype' that was 'copied' by the other, if that was the case at all. From a functional point of view, daggers of both materials can be seen as complementary to each other; and it is very likely that there was a tight, reciprocal relationship between the two materials, meaning that neither dagger form would have existed or changed over time without the other.

Surely there have been dynamic technological processes at work for each material alone. It is not only the physical differences between flint and copper which are obvious, but also the diverse distribution of the raw material in the geological environment as well as the means of dressing and beneficiation of the extracted material and its treatment until the final product was obtained. Differences in the technical features that were not visible on the hafted daggers become visible, perhaps even over-emphasised, on the archaeological finds (e.g. the tang/heel can be studied because the handle is not preserved). The differences between the straight and convex shaped cutting edges were mentioned already, but the striking formal similarities in the overall appearance and the similar triangular outline of the blade – on daggers of both materials – may indicate a probable homologous function, although these interpretations are only able to be inferred hypothetically by the archaeologist.

The discussion about the relation of stone and copper tools is as old as the chronological subdivision of prehistory into Stone, Bronze and Iron Age. However, evidence from countries rich in prehistoric copper artefacts, mainly axes and daggers, suggested to our 19th century colleagues that this system ought to be augmented by the creation of a fourth Age: the 'Copper Age' or Chalcolithic (e.g. for Ireland: Wilde 1862; Hungary: von Pulszky 1877; Italy: de Rossi 1879; Chierici 1884). Most of these authors describe, more or less explicitly in a kind of logical exercise, how they try to reconstruct what happened in the past, when someone tried to make a well-known type of tool by using newly discovered material. It seems in their opinion that it was self-evident that the first copper tools were made to the same design as the well-known tools of stone and flint.

The interpretation of this relationship became more complex around the beginning of the 20th century. A short compilation of authors who favour different positions of interpretation is presented in Table 4.1. While this table does not reflect every opinion ever voiced on the subject, it gives an impression of the broad development of the debate. It also must be mentioned that most of the authors listed wrote about different geographical areas and chronological periods in absolute terms. An explanation put forward in one area for a certain archaeological period was sometimes transferred to another area, often without taking specific and individual differences into account, which should have prevented an uncritical adoption of interpretation schemes (for further discussion see: Steiniger in press).

In general, there are two patterns of interpretation. Either the flint daggers were the original form which was copied by the metal blades, or, on the contrary, metal daggers were the archetype for the later copies made of flint. The main arguments for both interpretations mostly concern chronology.

The opinion that copper daggers were the primary object which was later copied in flint evolved mainly because of two circumstances. The first is that there are no obvious flint daggers in the European Neolithic that could serve as prototype for Chalcolithic copper blades, e.g. as it is the case in northern Germany and southern Scandinavia (Klassen 2000). Although it has to be mentioned that in some areas the pre-existence of copper daggers is hard to prove (e.g. Italy or Anatolia; for the situation in the Near East compare Zimmermann 2007, and this volume). The chronological succession of flint and copper daggers is often not clearly definable: both forms appear more or less simultaneously in the Chalcolithic. Secondly, in recognition of their contemporaneity, the assumed high value of copper was held responsible for the interpretation of copper daggers as the archetype. The lack of ore sources in regions without copper metallurgy is envisioned as having stimulated the production of imitations in flint to satisfy the desire for prestige and status objects in Chalcolithic society (Strahm 1961/62). In some areas, this scenario might have occurred, but it is not a universal law. Also, it is difficult to specify without circular reasoning whether copper daggers always had a higher value than those of flint. This cannot be easily determined. Any interpretation offered for Chalcolithic Italy must keep in mind that grave goods necessarily come from highly ritualised prehistoric context and practices. We cannot explain them just by using our present-day rationalistic system of economic values (generally for value in the funerary sphere see: Bernbeck 1997; an example where stone tools can be interpreted as of 'higher value' than comparable metal artefacts is described in: Séfériadès 1991).

A third, moderate position is based on a careful and sophisticated approach that keeps the social and technological complexity of the period in mind. A crucial aspect of this nuanced approach is that it yields the insight that, purely on the basis of the archaeological record and largely due to widespread dating problems – neither of the two previous hypotheses can be proven. In large geographical areas, as in continental Italy, we find most of the copper and flint daggers in practically the same chronological horizon. This third position is not only the more recent, but has also been developed in a geographical area (southern France, Switzerland and northern Italy) with a very dense number of finds in both materials and where the chronological subdivisions are not able to show a clear priority of one of them (Gallay 1981; Honegger 2001; Mottes 2001).

It is obvious that some questions must be solved before our interpretation can move beyond speculation. A recent study of A. Maass was able to demonstrate that an increasing demand for prestige and status objects of different lithological material (hard- and soft-rock, flint/radiolarite, pigment, metal-ore) lead to an extension in mining and a development in mining techniques during the Neolithic and Chalcolithic (Maass 2005; not to forget the 'greenstone axes', cf. Pétrequin *et al.* 2005). Besides extensive use-wear analyses on flint and copper daggers and reliable studies of raw material sources via lead isotopes for copper and microfacies for flint, further investigation of mining and production techniques are needed. Once these data are known, we will not only be able to talk more about the specific technological and socio-economic role of daggers and their relation with other prestigious artefacts (greenstone etc.) but also to decide which one is the imitation or skeuomorph and which is the original (cf. Frieman 2010). It is even possible that the recognition of the 'original vs. copy relationship' shifted from time to time, that it altered or changed in specific situations, such as between everyday use and burial rite. It must also be remembered that we know of daggers made completely of bone from the northern Italian graves of Spilamberto (Bagolini 1981, 1984). These are constantly interpreted as imitations of copper daggers, but is this really the case? In the graves of Spilamberto daggers of copper and flint have also been found, in addition to those made of bone.

Furthermore, as regards function and finished appearance, we have evidence, in the form of their position in the grave, that some flint blades from Spilamberto were used on long handles and were mounted like halberds (Bagolini 1981). Flint halberds are also indicated by Alpine rock art (Cocchi Genick 2004). Moreover, several copper daggers are also interpreted as halberds, mostly because of the asymmetric shape of their cutting edge (partially due to use-wear) and asymmetric hafting arrangement (Bianco Peroni 1994; Horn in press). However, the bone daggers are made in one piece, probably with a handle designed to be held in the hand. Worth noting in this context are the copper daggers of the so called 'type Montebradoni' (cf. Bianco Peroni 1994), which are made of one copper plate (probably produced through forging) that is solid from blade to handle to the mushroom-shaped knob (which greatly resembles the mushroom-shaped knobs preserved on the wooden handles from water logged flint daggers in alpine lakes; examples are found in: Strahm 1961/62). Some authors separate daggers into two groups (hand-held daggers and long-handled halberds) which are strictly divided and, consequently, not studied together. Yet, this distinction is often very problematic because the handle so rarely survives. The widespread similarities between triangular copper and flint daggers seem to point to a close relationship between all kinds of daggers, whether shafted as hand-held dagger or as halberd (an overview of the halberd-phenomenon across Europe, including the Italian flint halberds is prepared by: Horn in press).

Regarding the daggers depicted as halberds on rock art and anthropomorphic statue-menhirs, we can perhaps incorporate them into our discussion by considering them yet another kind of dagger: 'petroglyphic daggers' (F. Nicolis, pers. comm.). Hundreds of daggers are depicted on the rocks of Trentino-Alto Adige, Lombardy and the Maritime Alps (several papers in: Casini 1994; de Lumley 1992). A quite interesting point is that in these areas, not a single real copper dagger or halberd has yet been found; but the depicted 'placeholders' appear in greater numbers than the quantity of real copper daggers found in the whole of Italy. Small crushed, so called 'micro-slags', were found in Chalcolithic layers of the alpine rock art sites of Ossimo-Anvòia (Poggiani-Keller 2009; Fedele 2008) and Cemmo (R. Poggiani-Keller pers. comm.). This may indicate a probable relation of sites with representations of copper daggers to copper metallurgy (for the relationship between copper daggers, their depiction on rock art and metal deposits, see: Rossi & Gattiglia 2005). Especially the two mentioned sites are not far from copper deposits in the Val Camonica (R. Poggiani-Keller and C. Giardino pers. comm.).

Another complex phenomenon concerns some of the south Italian copper daggers which were found mainly in collective burial chambers. Their blade is extremely thin, only 1mm thick. In fact, they are made of a kind of copper sheet and seem not really useable for permanent cutting or thrusting. These 'daggers' can, therefore, be seen as *pars pro toto* or imitations of 'real' copper daggers (an example of a dagger of this type is given in Fig. 4.3, upper right corner, from Pontecagnano Grave 6589, after Bailo Modesti & Salerno 1998; for Buccino, where similar copper daggers have been found see: Holloway 1973). In the cemetery of Pontecagnano two copper daggers of this type were found, besides 15 daggers of flint. Both of the copper daggers appeared not alone in the tombs but together with one, respectively two flint daggers (one of those flint daggers is shown in Fig. 4.3, upper right corner). When taking into account the number of individuals buried in the collective tombs and the grave goods in total, the graves with copper daggers display the same relative number and spectrum of grave goods as all the other tombs. They seem not to be over-equipped in any way and so it is not easy to attest a comparable higher value to the copper daggers, nor do they indicate higher wealth, rank, prestige or status (for details, see Steiniger in press). It is no solution to close the matter with just ascribing an intent supremacy of copper on flint daggers. There are no 'real' copper daggers in this cemetery. So are the flint daggers 'an imitation in flint of an imitation in copper' or a 'flint copy of a metal dagger copy'? But that leaves us asking whether we have only copies in these tombs. Personally, I think not, but here it becomes obvious that further reflective consideration is necessary before we can explain Chalcolithic behaviour, values and meanings properly. The idea of this paper was to present the complex situation in the study area and to stimulate a diversification of discussion by retrieving flint daggers from a secondary position, emphasising cross material relations and bringing into attention similar characteristics across traditional borders of perception.

Acknowledgements

I would like to thank Catherine J. Frieman and Berit Valentin Eriksen for the invitation to the session on 'Flint daggers in prehistoric Europe and beyond' and the possibility to participate the wonderful EAA meeting in Oslo 2011. Thanks also to Frank Weiß of the administration unit at the German Archaeological Institute Rome for supporting my project related travels. For important remarks, discussion and information on different topics, I thank Elisabetta Mottes, Franco Nicolis, Raffaela Poggiani Keller, Christian Horn and Claudio Giardino. Special thanks to Denis Guilbeau for sharing his knowledge on Italian flint daggers on many occasions and Catherine J. Frieman for the detailed revision of the manuscript.

Note

1. "Heel" is the preferred term to describe the part of flint daggers usually referred to as a tang on metal daggers. Only the longer metal daggers appear to have "tangs", while the short, daggers with many rivets placed around a rounded end have "heels", hence the choice of this term for all daggers in this study.

References

Bagolini, B. 1981. *Il neolitico e l'età del rame. Archeologia a Spilamberto – Richerche nel territorio Spilamberto-S. Cesario 1977–1980*. Vignola: Cassa di Risparmio.

Bagolini, B. 1984. *Archeologia a Spilamberto, Riserche nel territorio (Spilamberto-S. Cesario)*. Spilamberto: Gruppe Naturalisti.

Bagolini, B. & Fasani, L. 1982. Problemi sulla fine del Neolitico. In: A. Aspes (ed.), Il passaggio all'età del Bronzo nel versante meridionale della regione alpina centrale. *Atti X Simp. Int. sulla Fine del Neolitico e gli Inizi dell'Età del Bronzo in Europa, Lazise –Verona* 1980. Verona: Museo civico di storia naturale. 343–355.

Barfield, L. H. 1971. *Northern Italy before Rome*. Ancient peoples and places 76. London: Thames and Hudson.

Barfield, L. H. 1985. Burials and boundaries in Chalcolithic Italy. In: C. Malone & S. Stoddart (eds.), *Patterns in Protohistory*. BAR international series 245; Papers in Italian archaeology 4,3. Papers presented at the conference of Italian archaeology 3,3. Oxford: British Archaeological Reports. 152–176.

Barfield, L. H. 1986. Chalcolithic burial in northern Italy – problems of social interpretation. *Dialoghi di Archeologia* Terza Serie 4: 241–248.

Barfield, L. H. 1988. The Chalcolithic of the Po plain. Atti del Congresso Internazionale "L'età del rame in Europa". *Rassegna Archaeologia* 7: 411–418.

Barfield, L.H. 1990. The lithic factor: a study of the relaitionship between stone sources and human settlement in the Monti Lessini and the Southern Alps. In: P. Biagi (ed.), *The Neolithisation of the Alpine Region. Brescia, Monografie di "Natura Bresciana"* 13. 147–157.

Barfield, L. H. 1996. The Chalcolithic in Italy: consideration of metal typology and cultural interaction. In: B. Bagolini & V. Lo Sciavo (eds.), *The Copper Age in the Near East and Europe, XIII International Congress of Prehistoric and Protohistoric Sciences*. Forli: Edizioni: 65–74.

Barfield, L. H., Koller, E., Lippert, A., & von Parleitner, A. eds. 1992. *Der Zeuge aus dem Gletscher*. Wien: Ueberreuter.

Bernbeck, R. 1997. *Theorien in der Archäologie*. Tübingen: Francke.

Bianco Peroni, V. 1994. *I pugnali nell'Italia Continentale*. Prähistorische Bronzefunde VI(10). Stuttgart: F. Steiner.

Bailo Modesti, G. & Salerno, A. 1998. *Pontecagnano II.5 La necropoli eneolitica*. Napoli: Istituto universitario orientale.

Bodechtel, J. 1972. Bemerkungen zur Übersichtskarte der Erzlagerstätten in der Toskana. In: F.-W. von Hase, Zum Fragment eines orientalischen Bronzeflügels aus Vetulonia. *Mitteilungen des Deutschen Archäologischen Instituts, Römische Abteilung* 97: 155–166.

Brather, S. 2006. Typologie. In: H. Beck, D. Geuenich & H. Steuer (eds.), *Reallexikon der Germanischen Altertumskunde* 31. Berlin: Walter de Gruyer. 346–353.

Casini, S. 1994. *Le pietre degli dei. Menhir e stale dell'Età del Rame in Valcamonica e Valtellina*. Bergamo: Centro Culturale Nicolò Rezzara.

Cavanna, C. 2007. Spaccasasso: una cava di cinabro. In: C. Cavanna (ed.), La preistoria nelle grotte del parco naturale della Maremma. *Atti del Museo di Storia Naturale della Maremma*. Supplemento 22. Grosseto: Museo di Storia Naturale della Maremma. 207–220.

Cavanna, C. & Pellegrini, E. 2007. La Buca di Spaccasasso: ricerche 2000–2004. In: C. Cavanna (ed.), La preistoria nelle grotte del parco naturale della Maremma, *Atti del Museo di Storia Naturale della Maremma*. Supplemento 22. Grosseto: Museo di Storia Naturale della Maremma. 117–136.

Cazzella, A., Moscoloni, M. & Recchia, G. 2003. *Conelle di Arcevia: un insediamento eneolithico nelle Marche*. Roma: Gangemi.

Chierici, G. 1884. I sepolcri di remedello nel Bresciano e i Pelasgi in Italia. *Bullettino di Paletnologia Italiana* 10: 133–164.

Cocchi Genick, D. 1996. *Manuale di preistoria III. L'eta del rame*. Firenze: Octavo.

Cocchi Genick, D. 2004. Considerazioni sull'ideologia religiosa nell'Eneolitico italiano. *Bullettino di Paletnologia Italiana* 95: 83–126.

Dolfini, A. 2010. The origins of metallurgy in central Italy: New radiometric evidence. *Antiquity* 84(325): 707–723.

Dolfini, A. 2011. The function of Chalcolithic metalwork in Italy: An assessment based on use-wear analysis. *Journal of Archaeological Science* 38(5): 1037–1049.

Ebbesen, K. 1994. Tragtbægerkulturens dolkstave. *Aarbøger for Nordisk Oldkyndighed og Historie* 1992: 103–136.

Fedele, F. 2008. Statue-menhirs, Human Remains and Mana at the Ossimo "Anvoia" Ceremonial Site, Val Camonica. *Journal of Mediterranean Archaeology* 21(1): 57–79.

Frieman, C. 2010. Imitation, identity and communication: The presence and problems of skeuomorphs in the metal ages. In: B. V. Eriksen (ed.), *Lithic Technology In Metal Using Societies. Proceedings of a UISPP Workshop, Lisbon, September 2006*. Jutland Archaeological Society Publications, 67. Aarhus: Jutland Archaeological Society Press. 33–44.

Galiberti, A. 2005. *Defensola. Una miniera di selce di 7000 anni fra*. Siena: Protagon Editori.

Gallay, G. 1981. *Die kupfer- und altbronzezeitlichen Stabdolche in Frankreich*. Prähistorische Bronzefunde. Abteilung VI, Bd. 5. München: Beck.

Gauß, F. 2009. *Völkerwanderungszeitliche «Blechfibeln»: Typologie, Chronologie, Interpretation*. Ergänzungsbände zum Reallexikon der germanischen Altertumskunde 67. Berlin: Walter de Gruyter.

Giardino, C. & Steiniger, D. 2011. Evidenze di miniere preistoriche nell'Etruria Meridionale. In: C. Giardino (ed.), *Archeometallurgia: dalla conoscenza alla fruizione. Atti del Workshop, 22–25 maggio 2006 (Cavallino (LE), Convento dei Dominicani)*. Beni archeologici – conoscenza e tecnologie 8. Bari: Edipuglia. 289–292.

Goldenberg, G. 2006. Neolithic exploitation and manufacturing of flint in the Monti Lessini, Verona. Italy. In: G. Körlin & G. Weisgerber (eds.), *Stone Age – Mining Age*. Der Anschnitt, Beiheft 19. Bochum: Deutsches Bergbau-Museum. 83–89.

Groer, C. 2008. *Früher Kupferbergbau in Westeuropa*. Universitäts-forschungen zur prähistorischen Archäologie 157. Bonn: Habelt.

Guendon, J.-L., Salazar, D., Figueroa-Larre, V., Salinas, H., Laroche, M., Ambert, P. & Gruneisen, A. 2011. Déblais miniers et marteaux en pierre du Néolithique final. Les mines de cuivre du plateau de Bellarade (district de Cabrières-Péret, Hérault, France). In: I. Sénépart, T. Perrin, È. Thirault, & S. Bonnardin (eds.), *Marges, frontières et transgressions actualité de la recherche: actes de 8e Rencontres Méridionales de Préhistoire Récente, Marseille (13)–7 & 8 novembre 2008*. Toulouse: Archives d'Écologie Préhistorique. 403–412.

Hillebrand, J. 1929. Das frühkupferzeitliche Gräberfeld von Pusztaistvánháza. *Archaeologia Hungarica 4*. Budapest: Franklin-Társulat Nyomdája.

Holloway, R. R. 1973. *Buccino*. Roma: de Luca.

Honegger, M. 2001. *L'industrie lithique taillé du Néolithique moyen et final de Suisse*. Paris: CNRS Ed.

Horn, C. in press. Few and far between – early halberds in Europe. In: M. Kunst & D. Steiniger (eds.), *Strategie insediative e metallurgia – i rapporti tra Italia e la penisola Iberica nel primo calcolitico*. Convegno Internazionale 6–7 ottobre 2011, Museo Nazionale Romano, Palazzo Massimo, Roma. Rom: Deutsches Archäologisches Institut.

Istituto Italiano di Preistoria e Protostoria 2007. *Atti della XL riunione scientifica: strategie di insediamento fra Lazio e Campania in età preistorica e protostorica: Roma, Napoli, Pompei, 30 novembre – 3 dicembre 2005*. Firenze: Istituto italiano di preistoria e protostoria.

Klassen, L. 2000. *Frühes Kupfer im Norden*. Jutland Archaeological Society publications 36. Højbjerg: Jysk arkæologisk selskab.

Kraft, G. 1926. *Die Kultur der Bronzezeit in Süddeutschland*. Augsburg: Filser.

Larocca F. 2005. *La miniera pre-protostorica di Grotta della Monaca (Sant'Agata di Esaro – Cosenza)*. Roseto: Centro Regionale di Speleologia "Enzo dei Medici".

Lomborg, E. 1973. *Die Flintdolche Dänemarks. Studien über Chronologie und Kulturbeziehungen des südskandinavischen Spätneolithikums*. Nordiske Fortidsminder Serie B in quarto I. København: Universitetsforlaget.

Longhi, C. 1994. La necropoli di Remedello Sotto (BS).In: S. Casini (ed.), *Le pietre degli dei. Menhir e stale dell'Età del Ram in Valcamonica e Valtellina*. Bergamo: Centro Culturale Nicolò Rezzara. 203–210.

Lübke, H. 1997/1998. Die dicken Flintspitzen aus Schleswig-Holstein. Ein Beitrag zur Typologie und Chronologie eines Großgerätetyps der Trichterbecherkultur. *Offa* 54/55: 49–95.

de Lumley, H. ed. 1992. *Le Mont Bego: la vallée des Merveilles et la val de Fontanalba*. Paris: Ministère de la culture, Imprimerie Nationale.

Maass, A. 2005. *Silex, Kupfer, Felsgestein: Die Bedeutung des Bergbaus und seine sozio-ökonomischen Strukturen im Neolithikum und Chalkolithikum*. Unpublished Ph.D. thesis, Freiburg University.

Maggi, R., Campana, N. & Pearce, M. 2011. Pirotecnologia e cronologia. Novità da Monte Loreto. In: C. Giardino (ed.), *Archeometallurgia: dalla conoscenza alla fruizione. Atti del Workshop, 22–25 maggio 2006 (Cavallino (LE) Convento dei Dominicani)*. Beni archeologici – conoscenza e tecnologie 8. Bari: Edipuglia. 281–287.

Marinis, R. C. de & Pedrotti, A. L. 1997. L'età del rame nel versante italiano delle Alpi centrooccidentali. In: *Atti XXXI Riunione Scientifica: La valle d'Aosta nel quadro della preistoria e protostoria dell'arco alpino centro-occidentale. Courmayeur, 2–5 giugno 1994*. Firenze: Istituto Italiano di preistoria e protostoria. 247–300.

Matuschik, I. 1997. Der neue Werkstoff – Metall. In: G. Kastl, P. Rau & G. Wesselkamp (eds.), *Goldene Jahrhunderte: Die Bronzezeit in Südwestdeutschland* Stuttgart: Kommissionsverlag K. Theiss. 16–25.

Montelius, O. 1900. *Die Chronologie der ältesten Bronzezeit in Norddeutschland und Skandinavien*. Archiv für Anthropologie 25–26. Braunschweig: F. Vieweg und Sohn.

Mottes, E. 1996. Considerazioni sulle lame di pugnale litiche del territorio veronese nel quadro dell'Eneolitico dell'Italia Settentrionale. In: G. Belluzzo & L. Salzani (eds.), *Dalla terra al museo: Mostra di reperti preistorici e protostorici degli ultimi dieci anni di ricerca dal territorio veronese*. Legnago: Fondazione Fiorini: 35–56.

Mottes, E. 2001. Bell Beakers and beyond: flint daggers of northern Italy between technology and typology. In: F. Nicolis (ed.), *Bell Beakers Today: Pottery, People, Culture, Symbols in Prehistoric Europe. Proceedings of the International Colloquium, Riva del Garda (Trento, Italy) 11–16 May 1998*. Trento, Italy: Provincia Autonoma di Trento Servizio Beni Culturali Ufficio Beni Archeologici: 519–545.

Much, M. 1886. *Die Kupferzeit in Europa und ihr Verhältnis zur Kultur der Indogermanen*. Wien: Zena.

Müller, S. 1902. *Flintdolkene i den nordiske Stenalder*. Nordiske Fortidsminder I, 5. Copenhagen: Gyldendal.

Müller-Karpe, H. 1974. *Handbuch der Vorgeschichte* III. München: Beck.

Orton, C.-R. 1987. The "Envelope": Un nouvel outil pour l'étude morphologique des céramiques. In: J. Chapelot (ed.), *La céramique: (Ve-XIXe s.); fabrication, commercialisation, utilisation; Actes du 1. Congrès d'Archéologie Médiévale (Paris, 4–6 oct. 1985)*. Caen: Société d'archéologie médiévale. 33–41.

Pascale, A. de. 2003. "Hammerstones from early copper mines": sintesi dei ritrovamenti nell'Europa e nel Mediterraneo orientale e prime considerazioni sui mazzuoli di Monte Loreto (IV millennio Be -Liguria). *Rivista di Studi Liguri*, 69: 5–42.

Pearce, M. 2011. Le evidenze archeologiche di estrazione mineraria preistorica in Italia settentrionale. In: Giardino, C. (ed.): *Archeometallurgia: dalla conoscenza alla fruizione. Atti del Workshop, 22–25 maggio 2006 (Cavallino (LE), Convento dei Dominicani)*. Beni archeologici – conoscenza e tecnologie 8. Bari: Edipuglia. 253–266.

Pétrequin, P., Pétrequin, A.-M., Errera, M., Cassen, S., Croutsch, C. 2005. Beigua, Monviso e Valais. All'origine delle grandi asce levigate di origine alpina in Europa occidentale durante il V millennio. *Rivista di Scienze Preistoriche* 55: 265–322.

Poggiani-Keller, R. 2009. Il santuario di Ossimo-Pat. In: R. Poggiani-Keller (ed.), *La valle delle incisioni: 1909–2009 cento anni di scoperte; 1979–2009 trenta anni con l'UNESCO in Valle Camonica*. Brescia: Provincia di Brescia. 223–235.

Pulszky, F. von 1877. L'âge du cuivre en Hongarie. In: *Congrès international préhistorique. Compte rendu de la huitième session à Budapest 1876* 1. Budapest: Franklin–Tárşulat. 220–227, 234–236.

Rossi, M. de 1879. Adunanze dell'Instituto. *Bullettino dell'Instituto di Corrispondenza Archeologica* 5: 65–66.

Rossi, M., & Gattiglia, A. 2005. Les poignards de Remedello hors d'Italie: revision de données. In: P. Ambert & J. Vaquer (eds.), *La première métallurgie en France et dans les pays limitrophes. Actes du colloque international Carcassonne 2002*. Société Préhistorique Française Mémoire 37. Paris: Société Préhistorique Française. 265–271.

Séfériadès, M. 1991. Pierre taillée et métallurgie: Compétition entre deux grandes industries. In: J.-P. Mohen (ed.), *Découverte de métal*. Paris: Picard. 325–330.

Schlichterle, H. 2004/05. Jungsteinzeitliche Dolche aus den Pfahlbauten des Bodenseeraumes. *Plattform* 13/14: 62–86.

Schwab, H. 1970. Prähistorische Kupferfunde aus dem Kanton Freiburg. *Jahrbuch der Schweizerischen Gesellschaft für Ur- und Frühgeschichte* 55: 13–21.

Schwenzer, S. 2004. *Frühbronzezeitliche Vollgriffdolche: typologische, chronologische und technische Studien auf der Grundlage einer Materialaufnahme von Hans-Jürgen Hundt*. Bonn: Habelt.

Steiniger, D. 2005. L'Énéolithique en Italie. In: P. Ambert & J. Vaquer (eds.), *La première métallurgie en France et dans les pays limitrophes. Actes du colloque international, Carcassonne 2002*. Société Préhistorique Française Mémoire 37. Paris: Société Préhistorique Française. 287–301.

Steiniger, D. 2010. The Relation between Copper and Flint Daggers in Chalcolithic Italy. In: P. Anreiter (ed.), *Mining in European History and its Impact on Environment and Human Societies: Proceedings for the 1st Mining in European History-Conference of the SFB-HiMAT, 12.–15. November 2009, Innsbruck*. Innsbruck: Innsbruck University Press. 151–156.

Steiniger, D. In press. Untersuchungen zum Chalkolithikum der Apenninhalbinsel. In: *Palilia*. Rome: Deutsches Archäologisches Institut.

Steiniger, D. & Giardino, C. 2013. Prehistoric mining in centragl Italy: new evidence from the Monti della Tolfa (Latium). In: P. Anreiter, K. Brandstätter, G. Goldenberg, K. Hanke, W. Leitner, K. Nicolussi, K. Oeggl, E. Pernicka, V. Schaffer, T. Stöllner, G. Tomedi, & P. Tropper (eds.), *Mining in European History and its Impact on Environment and Human Societies – Proceedings for the 2nd Mining in European History Conference of the FZ HiMAT, 7.–10. November 2012, Innsbruck*. Innsbruck University Press. 81–87.

Strahm, C. 1961/62. Geschäftete Dolchklingen des Spätneolithikums. *Jahrbuch des Bernischen Hisorischen Museums in Bern* 41–42: 447–477.

Ströbel, R. 1939. *Die Feuersteingeräte der Pfahlbaukultur*. Leipzig: Kabitzsch.

Tarantini, M. 2005. Il fenomeno minerario sul Gargano. In: A. Galiberti (ed.), *Defensola. Una miniera di selce di 7000 anni fra*. Siena: Protagon. 41–58.

Uenze, O. 1938. *Die frühbronzezeitlichen triangulären Vollgriffdolche*. Berlin: W. de Gruyter.

Vajsov, I. 1993. Die frühesten Metalldolche Südost- und Mitteleuropas. *Prähistorische Zeitschrift* 68: 103–145.

Wilde, W. R. 1862. *A Descriptive Catalogue of the Antiquities of Gold in the Museum of the Royal Irish Academy*. Dublin: Hodges, Smith and co.

Zimmermann, T. 2007. *Die ältesten kupferzeitlichen Bestattungen mit Dolchbeigabe: archäologische Untersuchungen in ausgewählten Modellregionen Alteuropas*. Mainz: Verlag des Römisch-Germanischen Zentralmuseums.

5

THE PRESSIGNY PHENOMENON

Ewen Ihuel, Jacques Pelegrin, Nicole Mallet & Christian Verjux
Translated by Marie-Claire Dawson & Brad Gravina

This paper proposes a synthesis of current research about the production of daggers from Grand-Pressigny discovered in France, Belgium, the Netherlands, the western part of Germany and Switzerland and dated between the last century of the 4th millennium and the 3rd millennium BC. It exposes the main results of a collective work, led by N. Mallet over more than 25 years. It describes two main chaînes operatoires *of specialised long blade production well documented in Grand-Pressigny area: "NaCAL" and* livre de beurre; *and shows how long blade production developed from local technological traditions which were improved during the first part of the 3rd millennium in order to achieve longer and longer daggers. Technological studies and experimental approaches help us to draw an organisational model of flint dagger production around the Grand-Pressigny area. This model, proposed by J. Pelegrin, explains how very high know-how could co-exist with the seasonal activities and mobility of the knappers. Long blades were plausibly roughed out, transported and finally retouched in daggers before being hafted, retouched and used in locally significant ways even when broken.*

Introduction

The Pressigny phenomenon encompasses the production of large blades from Upper Turonian flint found south of the Touraine. Produced during nearly six centuries in the 3rd millennium BC, Pressigny 'daggers' were distributed across the whole of France, reaching as far as western Switzerland, Belgium and the Netherlands (Fig. 5.1). Without doubt, these items represent one of the most important European phenomena of production and diffusion of particular lithic products in both quantitative terms and with regard to their overall geographic distribution. In this chapter, we present the various aspects, methods and organisation of this production leading to a brief discussion of the contexts from which these objects have been recovered and how the different modes in which they circulated have been interpreted.

Production

The production of some rather large blades is known as early as the end of the 5th millennium BC at Grand-Pressigny. However, it is not until the end of 4th millennium BC that long blades, transformed into daggers, take on greater importance (Fig. 5.2). The height of these workshops was between 2650 and 2450 BC, after which point their role becomes less certain (Mallet 1992; Honegger 2001; Mallet *et al.* 2008).

Production context

The manufacture of large Pressigny blades took advantage of a particular siliceous resource which was both abundant and relatively easy to access. This flint is available in the form of often quite large slabs (30–100cm) which originally formed in Upper Turonian Limestone (Upper Cretaceous). The slabs had, in fact, been loosened from the matrix in which they formed by decalcification and were extracted

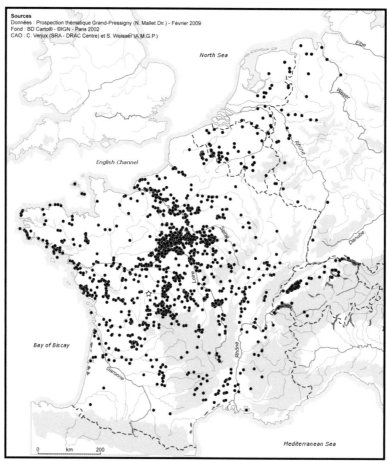

Fig. 5.1. The region around Grand-Pressigny and the diffusion of Grand-Pressigny flint artefacts. Each point represents a site containing objects manufactured in Grand-Pressigny flint. The star marks the region of Grand Pressigny (Indre-et-Loire, France).

from clays or bands of sand following the superficial dissolution of the limestone and Tertiary erosion. Not only was their acquisition therefore easier than in their primary limestone matrix which could be quite tenacious, but it also seems that the overall quality of the flint was subsequently improved following this structural rearrangement (finer grain, more homogeneous).

These flint slabs were available just below the surface and up to several metres deep in a rather extensive region of the southern Touraine, on either side of the Creuse River south of Grand-Pressigny (Fig. 5.3). This hilly region, littered with plateaus and valleys, spreads over 20km from north to south and from east to west, but is mostly documented north of the Creuse, especially around the village of Abilly, as the south is wooded.

This typical and homogeneous flint formed in shallow, open marine environments and is found within a well-delimited geographical area. Macroscopically, the facies is characterised by diverse hues dominated by a waxy yellow-brown variant. This yellowish white speckled stone has a relatively fine texture with a clear translucent granulation

due to the presence of detrital quartz. Traces of fossil organisms can also be observed. Microscopic analyses demonstrate Pressigny flint to result from the silicification of a particularly fine ancient sand principally composed of gravels or limestone pellets ranging from 100 microns to 300 microns and associated with the remains of small or finely fragmented marine organisms. Although not typical of any specific geological horizon, these fossils are consistently distributed in a very specific manner and are dominated by sponge spicules, foraminifera associated with bryozoa, echinoderms and mollusc fragments (Giot *et al.* 1986). This rather unique flint is quite easily distinguishable from other siliceous rocks found in different Upper Turonian deposits.

Products

Large Final Neolithic blades produced in the region of Grand-Pressigny have been recognised in the past (sometimes over zealously when, in actual fact, it was another type of flint altogether) in the form of 'daggers' (pointed blades with regular or lateral retouch and, occasionally, a prepared base).

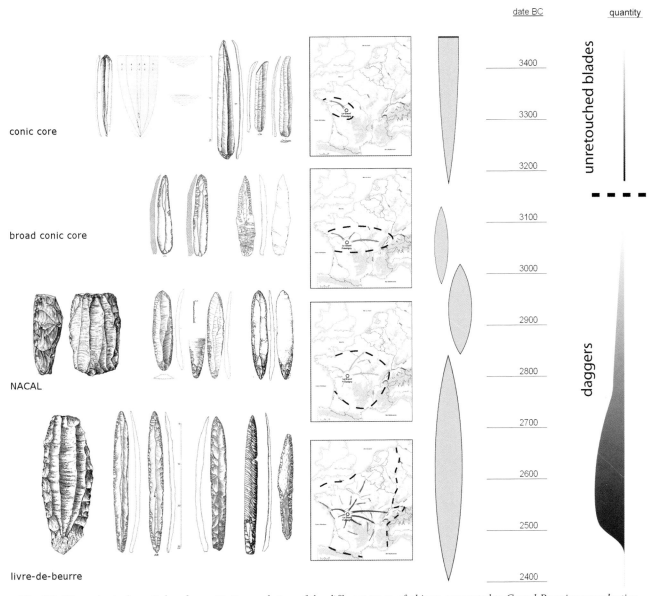

conic core

broad conic core

NACAL

livre-de-beurre

date BC

quantity

unretouched blades

daggers

3400
3300
3200
3100
3000
2900
2800
2700
2600
2500
2400

Fig. 5.2. Chronological, spatial and quantitative evolution of the different types of objects connected to Grand-Pressigny production.

These were recovered from various archaeological contexts in practically the whole of France and in lakeside villages in the Dauphiné region and western Switzerland where they are occasionally found hafted. Several key finds pointed towards their origin.

An initial hoard of over 100 of these large, unmodified blades (Fig. 5.4) was discovered in 1833 at Les Ayez in Barrou, a few kilometres from Grand-Pressigny (Cordier 1961, 1986). A hoard of 15 daggers accompanied by three 'ordinary' end scrapers on blade tips was uncovered in 1890 at Moigny in the Essonne, more than 240km north-east of Grand-Pressigny (Mallet *et al.* 1994).

Most importantly, a new cache of 134 large unretouched blades was discovered in 1970 at 'La Creusette' not far

from the original hoard of Les Ayez and was meticulously excavated (Geslin *et al.* 1975). This material permitted a better understanding of the knapping method already apparent on cores (referred to as *livre de beurre* or 'pound of butter' cores) and a new study has shown that this deposit was actually a portion or representative sample (random, not selected) of an original production of 500–800 blades obtained from 50 to 80 cores, representing 1 to 2 months worth of work by an excellent knapper (Pelegrin 1997).

These numbers are curiously close to those for the *amas* (debitage cluster) of La Creusette, where L.-A. Millet-Richard estimated between 115 and 150 cores to have been shaped out and debited on the site (Pelegrin 1997). The use of two different '*piqueteurs*' (a special tool used to prepare

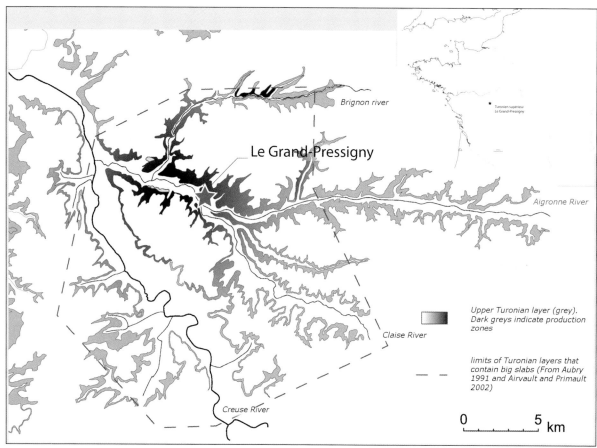

Fig 5.3. The Upper Turonian geological layer in the Touraine (Indre-et-Loire, France). The star represents the town of Grand-Pressigny which is located in the middle of the area where the flint is found.

the striking platform of each blade) suggests that two knappers, or one knapper during two successive seasons, produced the cluster. Therefore, it seems that this activity was seasonal, which is not surprising as the dry summer climate is necessary for the optimal functioning of tools (it decreases the risk of broken the deer antler punches; it's also very difficult to dig argil stone in humid weather).

These large blades were designed to be transformed into Pressigny daggers. During the 'classic' stage, they are at least 22–24cm long (Kelterborn 1981a, b; Pelegrin & Ihuel 2005) with some examples reaching nearly 40cm: 38.5cm for the longest one from La Creusette, 39cm long for a blade scar from a refit of four blades from Ayez (Cordier 1986: fig. 5–3). A certain standardisation is evident in the minimum length of these large blades, as numerous cores were discarded when they could have produced further blades, albeit blades less than 23cm long.

As will become evident from the diffusion of these objects, flakes and other types of blades were also transported from the Grand-Pressigny region.

No dedicated flake production is perceptible: those flakes recovered were simply obtained from shaping out

blade cores. Initially, they may have been waste products; but they were regularly collected from workshops to be used in nearby settlements (Millet-Richard 1997) and even farther away (Mallet 1992). 'Ordinary' blades (less than 20cm long) obtained from standard cores with smooth or rectilinear, faceted striking platforms were also exported, although to a much lesser extent and in fewer numbers. More striking, however, are the short, wide blades produced from characteristic 'flat' cores which can be found on certain *livre de beurre* workshops. This material represents a 'secondary' production of blades at least 5cm wide and 12cm long which were transformed into a particular tool type referred to as a 'notched saw'. Microwear analyses indicate that they served mainly as hand-held sickles designed to harvest cereals (Plisson *et al.* 2002:809; Plisson & Beugnier 2004). This much less numerous production seems to have accompanied that of large blades during the final centuries of the Pressigny phenomenon.

Culmination of the reduction method

The reduction method (the shape and shaping-out of the

core in the form of *livres de beurre*, the preparation and organisation of removals, etc.) is specific to Grand-Pressigny and represents the culmination of a technical tradition whose various steps have now been clearly identified.

As early as the Middle Neolithic, from the end of the 5th millennium or the beginning of the 4th millennium BC, fairly large blades (generally 15–20cm, but sometimes more) were produced at Grand-Pressigny and found, unmodified, in Brittany (Ihuel 2004, 2011). They were obtained from large nodule fragments, debited on their narrow side to take full advantage of a favourable cortical roundedness. Thus, these cores were conical or semi-conical and produced relatively thin blades with convergent edges towards their distal end. Their butts are 'simple', orthogonal and quite thick, corresponding to the most natural form for indirect percussion (the punch technique using an intermediate tool made of deer antler). This production does not appear very significant in quantitative terms and was probably discontinued during the 4th millennium BC.

However, shortly before the end of the 4th millennium BC, 'daggers' appear in earnest, with their large, ogival tips carefully retouched by pressure flaking and their bases which remain quite large and unretouched. They were manufactured on wide and relatively thin blades 18–20cm long such as those from Moigny (Essonne; Mallet *et al.* 1994: fig. 5). To produce a large ogival tip (whose original design remains unknown), a slightly wider core is required, realised on flint slab with a cortical rounded shape.

In what seems to be just a few short decades (according to dendrochronological dates from the sites of Châlain and Clairveaux in the Jura: Pétrequin *et al.* 2001; Viellet 2005), a new core form is perceptible in the dagger blades from that period (3000–2900 cal BC) and equally identifiable from the corresponding cores from Grand-Pressigny. These quadrangular 'NaCAL' type cores have antero-lateral crests and often possess two opposed striking platforms (Fig. 5.4). This method entails the maintenance of the debitage surface through transverse removals combined with the detachment of crested or *débordant* blades during the blade reduction sequence. This technique permits a series of quite wide and regular blades (6–10) to be removed and which are subsequently transformed into daggers with large, ogival tips (Fig. 5.4). Certain NaCAL cores can reach 25cm in length and indicate subsequent developments in the reduction method.

This final step ultimately results in the *livre de beurre* cores typical of the 'classic' period. The simultaneous development of an absolutely specific striking platform preparation method (the 'dihedral pecked butt' procedure: see below) allows longer blades to be detached from cores which, although becoming longer, remain strictly unipolar with lateral crests. Throughout the debitage sequence, a series of shaping and then reshaping flakes are removed from these lateral crests which are no longer detached

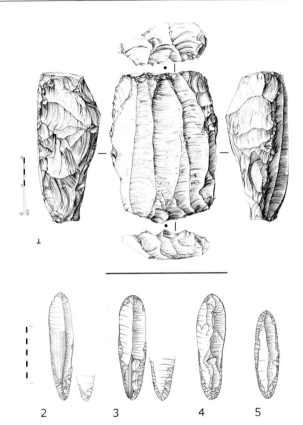

Fig. 5.4. Different types of artefacts issuing from NaCAL productions. 1: long blade core from Abilly, ruins of La Claisière (Indre-et-Loire, France). 2–5: early daggers from Saint-Léger-de-Montbrun, dolmen of Puyraveau II (Deux-Sèvres, France) (no. 1 drawn by A. Villes in Pelegrin & Ihuel 2005, nos 2–5 drawn by Ihuel in Ihuel 2008).

during the actual reduction sequence, but are left in place until the end (Fig. 5.5). This knapping trajectory produces the oblong shape of the *livre de beurre* core as well as its characteristic crenelated or scalloped sides (reminiscent of traditional regional butter moulds).

From this period onwards, and particularly between 2900 and *ca.* 2750 BC, core shapes remain unchanged until large blade production ceases between 2450 and 2400 BC. Daggers from the classic phase are relatively unmodified: a pointed tip is produced at the sharpened extremity and the edges are evened out if necessary, generally without removing the blank's dihedral, pecked butt (Fig. 5.6). This delicate and risky retouch is applied by direct, soft-hammer percussion (deer antler billet), and was probably carried out by the blade knappers themselves just before the new daggers were handed over to its first recipients.

Techniques and preparation for the removal of large blades

Two knapping techniques were utilised for this production.

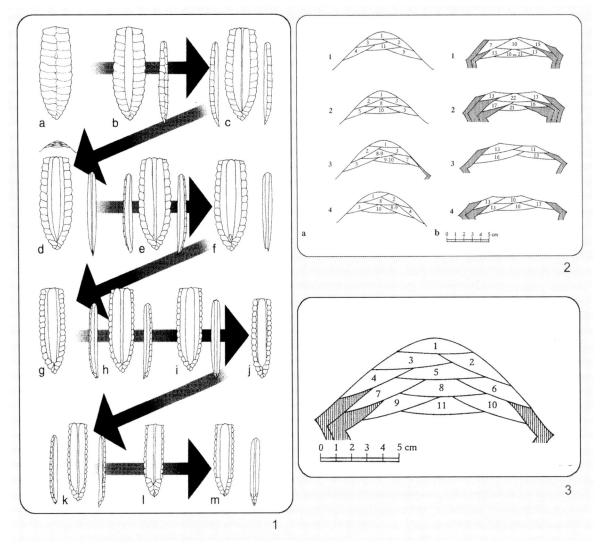

Fig. 5.5. Illustrations of the livre-de-beurre reduction method (from Pelegrin 2002, 1997).

The first is simple, direct hard-hammer percussion for roughing out the slabs. This stage is a rapid (5–10minutes), yet critical, operation, as a missed or imperfect blow can doom the rough-out. No particular hammer-stone has been connected to this procedure; however, portions of blocks weighing several kilos with rounded, cortical extremities bearing numerous incipient cones are present on various workshop sites.

The second technique is indirect percussion (punch technique) used to detach large, thin flakes for shaping the debitage surface, reshaping the striking platform, and removing blades. This technique requires a set of deer antler punches, composed of more or less strong and/or arched tines and whose working extremity was, at times, ground to shape. The butts of flakes are generally plain, more or less concave or dihedral, unprepared, with quite a pronounced bulb.

However, for the extraction of large blades, Grand-Pressigny knappers devised a totally independent preparation process which was remarkably clever. In order to produce a successful initial fracture, several technical innovations had to be developed and combined. First, the size of the butt was reduced; then a relief surface (convex facetted or obtuse dihedral butt) was created; and, finally, an acutely dihedral butt was carefully pecked with a light flint tool in order both to adapt the micromorphology of the small impact zone and to facilitate the initial fracture by creating small incipient cones. This combination of techniques allows for the strength of the blow to be reduced while still detaching blades of the same calibre, an economy of energy which, in turn, diminishes any unintended movement of the core, leading to pronounced percussion waves or hinges on the flaking surface. Careful experimental tests have shown that these knappers also invented an elegant means of

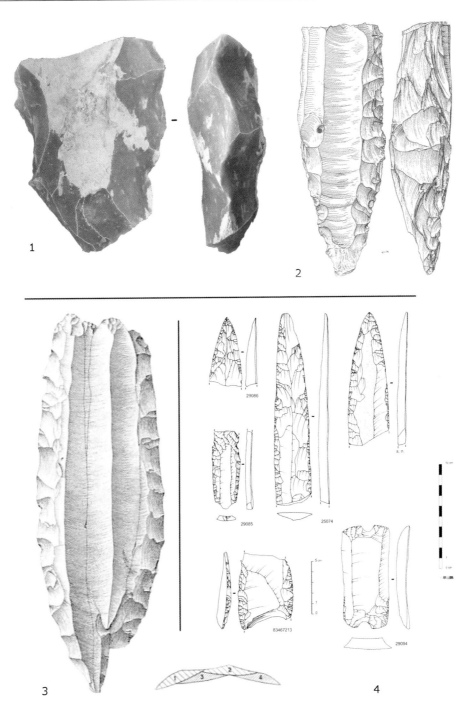

Fig. 5.6. Different types of artefacts connected to the livre-de-beurre reduction method and found in the production area (Indre-et-Loire, France). 1 and 2: core preform and an exhausted livre-de-beurre core from excavations at Abilly, La Claisière. 3: four blades in connection from the hoard of Barrou, Les Ayez. 4: several daggers and notched saws, broken during retouching and found during excavation at Abilly, le Petit-Paulmy (1 and 2 from Villes 2005, 3 from Cordier 1986, 4 from Ihuel 2008).

regulating core recoil by placing cores on an elastic stand (a large wooden bi- or tripod acting like a spring leaf: see Pelegrin 2002).

This particular knapping method involving *livre de*

beurre cores along with a special, pecked, dihedral butt constitute what may be called the 'Pressigny technique'. This technique differs from the knapping trajectories utilised in most other large blade workshops across Europe which relied either on pressure flaking with a lever or on a much more ordinary indirect percussion technique on cores with narrow, flat or orthogonal facetted butts (Pelegrin 2012).

Large blade workshops

During the Final Neolithic, knapping activities become focused on the production of large blades. Numerous dense scatters of characteristic waste have been documented in ploughed fields and represent specialised activity areas sometimes coupled with pits filled with knapping waste, several of which have recently been excavated (Despriée 1983; Aubry 1995; Millet-Richard 2001; Augereau 2002; Villes 2005).

Two different types of workshop reflect two distinct behaviours (Marquet & Millet-Richard 1995). In the first and more common instance, workshops are located directly on the site where flint slabs were extracted. These sites are found on or at the edge of plateaus; and all production stages (core shaping and roughing out flakes, core management flakes, fragments of blades broken during knapping, exhausted cores) are represented on these types of sites, with knapping waste having been deliberately pushed back into the extraction pits, as if to clear the area. The extraction of flint, at least in certain zones, may have been carried out alongside the clearing of fields (uprooting tree stumps) prior to ploughing. Furthermore, this flint quarrying may have been carried out by local farmers and not by the knappers themselves (Pelegrin 2005).

The second type of workshop is situated in valleys at some distance from the flint source. They are composed of knapping clusters or thick layers of waste resulting from the shaping and reduction of cores together with short fragments of blades broken during debitage and core rough-outs imported to the site. One of these, the 'La Creusette cluster', excavated by C. Verjux (1989) and well studied by Millet-Richard (1997), is found in direct proximity to what may be a contemporaneous settlement. The cluster contained several used flint tools, pottery fragments and scattered burnt pieces. Cores, however, had been removed or reused on-site.

The few settlements excavated in the region where flint was both extracted and transformed into large blades have provided little information concerning the Pressigny phenomenon. At Foulon, near Abilly, L.-A., Millet-Richard has shown that the inhabitants received daggers from knappers working nearby, but also retrieved pieces of debitage waste (flakes, blade fragments, cores) found in nearby knapping clusters to use as raw material for the majority of their quotidian tool production (Millet-Richard 1997: 184). At Petit-Paulmy, close to Foulon (excavation J.-C. Marquet, lithic analysis by L.-A. Millet-Richard 1997), several sequences of the shaping out and reduction of *livre de beurre* cores were carried out on site, apparently during brief stopovers by one or more knappers (Millet-Richard 1997: 264; Marquet & Millet-Richard 1995). The lithic industry is also manufactured on recuperated knapping waste. At the site of Ligueil 'Les Sables de Mareuil' (excavation A. Villes and J. Schönstein; cf. Villes 1999), an occupation a few centuries older, lying some 15km north of Grand-Pressigny and 8km from the closest outcrops, it seems that a large blade knapper of the NaCAL period (see below) occasionally visited the site and reduced several blocks left aside by the inhabitants (Pelegrin 2005).

Perennial or occasional satellite workshops

We have gradually come to realise that this very specific Pressigny technology was utilised outside Grand-Pressigny, in other French regions on either a permanent or more sporadic basis.

On the southern end of the Vercors plateau, a 'Pressigny' workshop was identified and excavated by M. Malenfant in 1970 (Malenfant *et al.* 1971). It contained debitage flakes and cores from the reduction of several thousand *livre de beurre* cores to produce blades with pecked dihedral butts. Test pits and surveys suggest that at least 5000 cores were knapped in this manner; but the raw material used was smaller and less easily workable. This production corresponds to the seasonal activity of one or two knappers during one or two generations, producing a minimum of 15,000 blades, of which we have recovered only about 10 from around the Vercors (Riche 1998) and one identified by L.-A. Millet-Richard from the island of Groix, off the Brittany shore of Lorient, more than 900km away. Based on this example, the current recovery rate of such pieces is less than 1 in 1000.

A second 'satellite' Pressigny workshop is located west of Reims in the Champagne region more than 400km from Grand-Pressigny. This site is relatively more important than the one from the southern Vercors, considering that more than 70 daggers are known to have originated from the site (Delcourt-Vlaeminck 1998, 1999). Prior to its discovery, this workshop had long been presumed to exist based on the distribution of Tertiary flint daggers across northern France towards Belgium and the Netherlands. These daggers are known particularly from individual graves with early Bell Beaker vessels, allowing their spread to be dated to the last century of the Pressigny phenomenon, around 2500 BC.

Further evidence of Pressigny technology was found in southwest France, south of Angoulême (Charente; Fouéré 1994) and around Bergerac (Dordogne; Delage 2004), however these sites seem simply to represent clusters of debitage from a single season's production, being composed of several dozen *livre de beurre* cores from occasional knapping episodes (Pelegrin 2002).

As it is effectively impossible for this *savoir-faire* and for detailed knowledge of Pressigny technology to have spread over such distances by word of mouth alone, satellite workshops and 'seasonal clusters' demonstrate that knappers of large blades trained at Grand-Pressigny and then moved around the landscape, creating satellite workshops in the Vercors and in Champagne and occasionally stopping over in the Charente or Dordogne to exploit local, although lesser quality, flint sources.

The circulation of Grand-Pressigny products

Historical background

Various archaeologists began to compile inventories of flint daggers from Grand-Pressigny as early as the end of the 19th century, work which was first presented at the 1910 *Congrès Préhistorique de France in* Tours, by M. Hue (1910) and M. Saint-Venant (1910).

However, identifying different flint varieties at the time remained very intuitive, if not haphazard, especially as we were far from understanding the diversity of siliceous resources across the country. Given these doubts, the scale of the Pressigny phenomenon had been contested up until 1950–1960, especially by G. Cordier (1956).

It was Nicole Mallet, together with the petrographers R. Giot and D. Millet, who first characterised the Upper Turonian flint from the Grand-Pressigny region. Using this initial research as a base, she then began the tedious work of drawing up an inventory and documenting all identifiable pieces made from Grand-Pressigny flint, starting with the richest areas: western Switzerland and the Dauphiné region (Mallet 1992). Other amateur researchers, particularly G. Richard and P. Genty, established a catalogue of Grand-Pressigny flint occurrences in a large region to the north-east of Grand-Pressigny. Marianne Delcourt-Vlaeminck documented and studied identifiable pieces from Belgium, the Netherlands and Northern France (1998, 1999). Ewen Ihuel has recently published an inventory for Brittany (2004) based on his doctoral research which has since been expanded to include west-central France (Ihuel 2008), while Nicole Mallet has expanded her research with the aim of producing an inventory for the rest of France. Containing more than 6750 pieces, this inventory forms the basis of a Geographic Information System managed by C. Verjux and S. Weisser (Verjux 2003).

The banks of the Weser River in northern Germany mark the extent of Grand-Pressigny flint distribution which encompasses Belgium, Luxembourg and the Netherlands. To the east, they are especially well known from western Switzerland, the western shores of Lake Constance in eastern Switzerland and in Germany (Honegger 2001; Schlichterle 1994). The distribution of Pressigny daggers did not extend beyond the Alps, the Pyrenees and the English Channel; so they are absent from Italy, Spain and Great Britain.

Discovery contexts of Pressigny flint objects

Pressigny flints have been found in diverse contexts and in different states of preservation tied to their discovery context: settlements, burials or isolated finds from humid environments and in unidentified contexts (27% for western France).

Settlements

Settlement contexts have produced the greatest number of Pressigny objects (73.3% of identified sites in western France). The notion of a 'settlement' may encompass numerous different realities; but they are nearly always linked to considerable occupation durations. They include genuine housing units, generally made of timber, in the form of small buildings, sometimes within permanent and regularly rebuilt hamlets, for example those from lake shores in the Jura or Switzerland (i.e. lakes Chalain & Clairvaux; Pétrequin 1995; Pétrequin *et al.* 1997, 2001) or on the plains of Bettencourt-Saint-Ouen (Oise; Martin *et al.* 1996). Pressigny material has been found from other settlement types, such as large, isolated buildings located within 30–60m long enclosures, as at Beauclair in Douchapt (Dordogne; Fouéré 1998), Les Marais de Santes at Houplin-Ancoisne, (Nord; Martial *et al.* 2004), as well as within extensive buildings included within fenced enclosure systems like Hersonnais at Pléchatel (Ille-et-Vilaine; Tinevez 2004) or Les Veaux at Moulins-sur-Céphon (Indre; Hamon 1999, 2006).

Pressigny objects have been discovered on living floors (Les Vaux; Hamon 1999), but also in refuse layers, within refuse pits neighbouring settlements, in pits and even in silos. Certain Pressigny tools have occasionally been found in large, poly-lobed pits interpreted as clay quarries close to settlements, such as at Villetoureix (Dordogne; Ihuel in Chancerel & Chancerel 2013) or La Bouchardière in Monts (Fig. 5.7, Indre-et-Loire; Ranger 2002).

These accumulations of refuse are equally common on different types of fortified sites: defensive spurs like Fort-Harrouard at Sorel-et-Moussel (Eure et Loire; Philippe 1936, 1937); banked enclosures, such as the camps of Chassey (Saône-et-Loire; Thévenot 2005) and Challignac (Charente; Burnez 2010); and the numerous ditched enclosures in west-central France, including Diconches in Saintes (Charente-Maritime; Burnez & Fouéré 1999), Chevêtelière at Saint-Mathurin (Vendée; Péridy forthcoming) and also Camp des Prises in Machecoul (Loire-Atlantique; L'Helgouac'h 1981). These sites comprise ditched enclosures covering several hectares and having multiple uses. They include domestic areas associated with farming but also having a defensive dimension that may be symbolic (Burnez & Louboutin 1999). The discovery of the remains of about 400 Pressigny dagger fragments on the site of Fort-Harrouard is both a mystery and a unique occurrence (Philippe 1936, 1937).

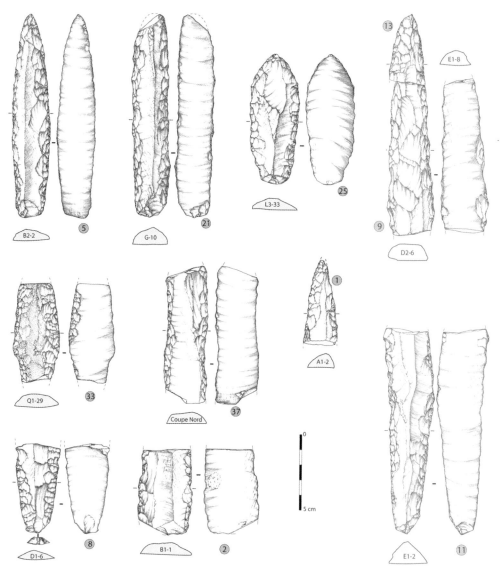

Fig. 5.7. An example of Grand-Pressigny remains in a domestic context from Monts la Bouchardière (Indre-et-Loire, France). Excavations by INRAP. Director O. Ranger. Dagger fragments. n°33 is polished. Illustrations E. Boitard.

Interestingly, aside from the exceptional case of Fort-Harrouard, the multiplicity of domestic contexts does not significantly impact the composition of lithic assemblages. More specifically, pieces in Pressigny flint consistently represent waste discarded at the end of their use-life. These Pressigny tools are overwhelmingly daggers. Although not universally the case, they are very frequently found in these lithic assemblages and generally constitute 3–4% of the domestic tool kit which was otherwise characterised on sites from this period by increasingly simple lithic technologies (Fouéré & Dias-Meirinho 2008). These Pressigny flint daggers were common objects, probably used on a daily basis, and can therefore be considered as technical goods (Féblot-Augustins & Perlès 1992) frequently found as fragments discarded after having been heavily resharpened.

In order to prolong their use, daggers were shortened and reduced in size, having sometimes been used in altogether different ways than originally intended, mainly as end scrapers, notched saws and strike-a-lights with rounded extremity(ies) bearing a characteristic blunting. Sites on which fragments can be refit onto a single dagger are rare as illustrated by the case of a large pit from Bouchardière in Monts (Indre-et-Loire) where a dagger broken during resharpening was retouched to eliminate the break and then continued to be used on a hard mineral material (Linton in Ranger 2002).

Microwear analyses of tools from domestic contexts underscore a variety of motions (cutting, butchery, scraping, rubbing) and processed materials (dry or soft plant materials, animal materials, minerals), corresponding to agrarian activities (especially cereal harvesting), but also to multiple other uses which probably explains their success (Vaughan & Bocquet 1987; Beugnier 1997; Plisson *et al.* 2002; Plisson & Beugnier 2004).

The use of secondary products (short blades and flakes) in Pressigny flint is also evident in settlements. The uniqueness of these objects lies in the fact that they were not systematically retouched and that their use life was rather brief (Les Vaux à Moulins-sur-Céphon; Hamon 2006). Winged and tanged arrowheads are common in the flake component of assemblages with the wide range and quality of retouch indicating them to have been retouched directly by the user.

Daggers and Pressigny tools from domestic contexts, while designed for the agrarian sphere, also allowed a large variety of uses. It is nonetheless remarkable that these exchanged pieces consistently were used over longer periods than tools produced in local flint, a trend which is significantly accentuated in regions devoid of flint such as the Armorican peninsula (Ihuel 2008).

Objects discovered in graves

In the area where Pressigny tools circulated, 3rd millennium BC funerary practices essentially continue traditions known from previous periods, namely inhumations within collective burials, such as those dating to the 5th and 4th millennia BC (Chambon 2003). The majority of Pressigny flints discovered across France come from these graves which follow highly varied regional traditions. Therefore, we find daggers in megalithic monuments, including various types of dolmens (with or without corridors, *Angevin* or *Angoumoisins* types, etc.), gallery graves, semi-megalithic monuments (passage tombs), or even stone-lined pits. Natural caves or artificial ones like hypogea have yielded Pressigny objects in the Paris Basin, however this practice remains rare (L'Helgouac'h 1965; Burnez 1976; Peek 1975). In contrast to these collective inhumations, it should be highlighted that the development of single graves from the 25th century BC coincides with the decline of Pressigny workshops. Besides burials linked to the Beaker period, individual burials are mainly known from the northern part of the Single Grave Culture/Corded Ware zone which was found at the margins of the Pressigny phenomenon.

Burials represent 26.5% of all determined discovery contexts known in the current inventory of Pressigny objects. Once again, we note that Pressigny objects are very frequent in collective burials, although this phenomenon cannot be quantified precisely. Indeed, no information is available for grave goods from a number of burials which were explored during the second half of the 19th century to satisfy the curiosity of a number of wealthy amateurs in the burgeoning field of archaeology.

The number of Pressigny objects contained in these burials is generally low, amounting to just one to three pieces. It is difficult to clearly grasp the representativeness of these objects in each of these contexts and to compare them to other tombs. The extended use of these collective burials is a major factor contributing to the reworking of the bodies and associated grave goods. In the burials, each dagger accompanies a single individual and that they were sometimes placed near the forearm as, for example, at Xanton-Chassenon (Vendée; Joussaume 1977) or near the head (Chambon 2003). Therefore, they represent elements implicated in the gradual process of individualisation of the deceased within collective graves.

As regards the objects themselves, they were for the most part deposited as new or unfinished objects rather than as heavily worked tools. Certain daggers even appear to have been resharpened for the occasion. Contradictory observations concerning the status of these objects show a tension between the desire to individualise objects accompanying the deceased and standardised, non-personal practices inherited from the past (Sohn 2002).

In fact, Pressigny objects accompanying the deceased are not necessarily personal items, but are sometimes interpretable as 'hoarded' elements acquired over an extended period whose social or symbolic value contributed to clearly affirming a social status, as observed, for example, in the Britannic burials (Ihuel 2008).

This latter explanation is clearly the case for a significant component of the unused or freshly resharpened grave goods deposited in the exceptional case of dolmen II at Puyraveau in Saint-Léger-de-Montbrun (Linton in Ard 2011). Located 75km from Grand-Pressigny, this site yielded at least 87 daggers, the majority of which were found whole and in perfect condition. The extreme richness of the grave, equally reflected in other grave goods (vessels, axes, ornaments, etc.), clearly indicates the ease of acquiring daggers as well as the significant social status of these communities. Furthermore, several daggers with unused edges bear traces of a sheath on their arrises, indicating that they were worn for long periods of time without necessarily being used and, therefore, represented *bona fide* social ornaments (Linton in Ard 2011).

The unique deposit of Croix-Blanche in Moigny (Essonne; Mallet *et al.* 1994) exclusively contains unused Pressigny objects (11 daggers on *livre de beurre* blades and three end scrapers on medium long blades) found in a semi-circular cavity cut into clay soil overlying a gritstone deposit which could be interpreted as a rare hoard rather than an actual tomb (Ihuel 2008). This phenomenon of accumulating one particular type of object into 'hoards' is not specific to daggers during the Neolithic, but can involve various objects having a social value, especially axes (Cassen *et al.* 2008). Similar phenomena have also been documented by modern ethnographic studies in Papua New Guinea (Pétrequin & Pétrequin 1997, 2000; Pétrequin *et al.* 1998) where such

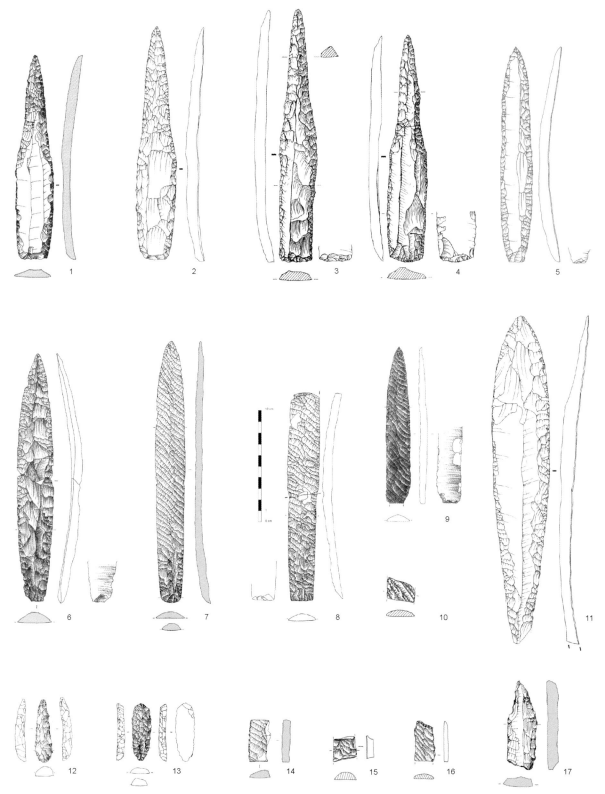

Fig. 5.8. Several examples of classic Grand-Pressigny daggers from Western France found in collective burials (F), without context (WC) or from a domestic context (D). 1 Ploubazlannec (F, Côtes-d'Armor), 2 Beaufort-en Vallée (WC, Maine-et-Loire), 3 and 4 Guidel (F, Morbihan), 5 Moëlan-sur-Mer (F, Finistère), 6 Poullaouen (WC, Finistère), 7 Lanester/Baden (WC, Morbihan), 8 Plougoumelen (F, Morbihan), 9, Saumur (WC, Maine-et-Loire), 10 Saint-Lambert-du-Lattay (D, Maine-et-Loire), 11 Catenoy-Epinard (WC, Maine-et-Loire), 12, 13, 14 Carnac (F, Morbihan), 15 and 16 Coex (D, Vendée), 17 Crac'h (F, Morbihan). All drawings from Ihuel 2008.

practices are particularly tied to the high symbolic and social status of objects and exchange systems and/or a gift economy. The acquisition of prestige goods (shells, feathers, cassowary bones, axes, etc.) is engendered in the various acquisition strategies and search for partners which unfolds in contexts of strong social competition (Malinowski 1922; Pétrequin & Pétrequin 1997; Pétrequin et al. 1998).

Such ethnographic considerations provide new insights into those rare archaeological pieces which reveal clues of over-investment. In terms of Neolithic daggers, this description would apply exclusively to highly polished examples or those presenting a noteworthy and very difficult modification in the form of oblique parallel or en écharpe retouch (Fig. 5.9:1). These ancillary alterations are not linked to functional concerns, but are designed to increase the value of an object which plays an important role in social display.

This sort of over-investment can be seen in a small series of daggers bearing oblique parallel pressure retouch, such as the example from Baden (Morbihan, Fig. 5.8:7) or the one from Neuilly-sur-Eure (Hébert &Verron 1980). The remarkable beauty of these objects lies in the extremely regular retouch. In order to achieve such results, the knapper selects a blade from the most regular blanks, polishes the arrises and proceeds with the long and meticulous retouch work which requires the same area to be reworked two or three times. This retouch is superior in quality to the simple shaping of locally produced arrowheads. The acquisition of such a socially charged object, manufactured at a distance and involving an expertise not shared by any other community member necessarily implies the intervention of foreign agents. Taken together, these factors suggest an elevated social status for the owner of the dagger.

Besides the strong symbolic and social dimension, these finishing touches also have a cultural resonance. While polished daggers are found all over, two particular regions stand out: the Breton peninsula where they are significantly under-represented and Northern Europe (the Netherlands and Germany) which presents a phenomenon of excessive over-polishing. Regarding the latter, such as at Emst-Hanendorp in the Netherlands (Delcourt-Vlaeminck 1998, 1999), polishing may cover the whole of the upper face, the edges and extend over the tip of the dagger. Another parallel can be drawn with jadeite axes, some of which are re-polished and even 'over-polished' in the farthest regions from the production zone, in this case the Carnac area of Brittany and the British Isles, a phenomenon especially prevalent with material deposited in tombs from these regions (Pétrequin et al. 1997).

Grave goods do not always carry such strong social or symbolic implications as the material deposited in these tombs is sometimes much less sensational. In certain graves, such as Kercado at Carnac (Morbihan), simple fragments, sometimes reused as end scrapers, are remnants of what were prestigious pieces. Certain objects even appear to be the mere personal belongings of the deceased. For example, the strike-a-light made from a Pressigny flint blade broken during knapping and deposited in the burial of Bois Pargas at Pageas (Haute-Vienne; Perrin et al. 2007) is evidently a by-product of other knapping activities. Its fairly pronounced use-wear and its presence in the burial signifies a link both with its acquisition and with the rarity of the material itself. In certain burials, particularly in Brittany, the scarcity of high quality material is also evident in the fairly frequent presence of simple flakes, such as in the gallery grave of Mané-Roullarde at Trinité-sur-Mer (Morbihan; Ihuel 2004). Pressigny flint arrowheads are also present alongside the deceased especially in the late stages of the 3rd millennium BC, for example the assemblages within the dolmens of Kercadoret at Locmariaquer and Rogarte in Carnac (Morbihan) can both be attributed to the Beaker culture based on arrowheads types.

To complete this overview of Pressigny elements in funerary contexts, it should be noted that a handful of burials yielded one or two notched saws, despite this agrarian tool being nearly exclusively found around settlements and being frequently produced directly on local raw material sources. The distance from the place of production and, hence, the rarity of the object seems to confer upon them a particular status in burials found at some distance from the Pressigny workshop region, such as the pit of Bois-Pargas at Pageas (Haute-Vienne; Perrin et al. 2007), the dolmen of Quatre Chemins in Marsac (Creuse; Joussaume et al. 2002) or at Argenteuil, Usine Vivez (Val-d'Oise; Mauduit et al. 1977) and layer 37 of Gardon Cave (Ain; Voruz et al. 2004).

Modes of circulation

The fact that these objects, particularly the daggers, circulated for some six centuries necessarily implies complex mechanisms as they represent everyday products which carried a strong social value.

The prolonged use of these tools, whether found in funerary or domestic contexts, has erased much of the information concerning the expertise and shape of these objects, as well as their modes of circulation. However, certain patterns are evident: blades are never found unmodified and only circulate once regularised (Mallet 1992). This pattern is very rarely contradicted (with the exception of the Beaker burial of La Folie near Poitiers (Vienne); Salanova & Tchérémissinoff 2011). This could explain the existence of two hoards of unmodified blades at Creusette and Les Ayez in Barrou (Indre-et-Loire), both in proximity to production areas and interpretable as provisional reserves for future workshop (of their original knapper, according to Pelegrin 1997).

The diffusion of thousands of highly standardised daggers per year requires a long-term structure to be in place as their

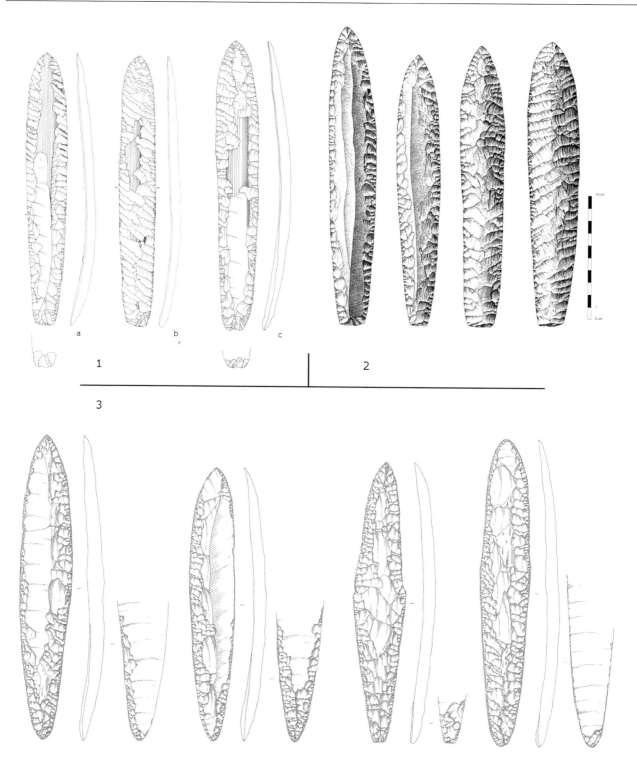

Fig. 5.9. Several examples of classic Grand-Pressigny daggers founds in Northern (1 and 2) and Central France (3). 1: two daggers found in the Seine river at (a) Marolles, Seine-et-Marne and (c) Paris, and (b) from Camps des Sarrazins at Chelles (Oise), 2: four daggers constituting a hoard found in Damps (Eure-et-Loire), 3: four daggers from Saint-Léger-de-Montbrun, dolmen of Puyraveau II (Deux-Sèvres) (Illustrations: 1 Ihuel (Ihuel 2008), 2 Cordier (Cordier 1986) and 3 Blanchet (Ard 2011)).

production present three significant economic constraints: (1) a lengthy learning period to master all the techniques and the larger production scheme (Pelegrin 2002); (2) specialists who exercise their activity over long periods, a few weeks or months minimum per year, during which time they are supported by the community (Pelegrin 1997, 2005); and (3) the regular quantities produced and the considerable distances over which they diffused demand an economic, social and spatial structuring of the production network to ensure continued activity (Renfrew 1977).

Beyond a perimeter of several dozen kilometres around the workshops (Mallet 1992), the circulation of Pressigny objects must not have been subjected (or was barely subjected) to the whims of a passive diffusion according to Renfrew's 'down-the-line' model in which objects spread from person to person (Renfrew 1977). Such might be the case for metadolerite axes produced in the Plussulien region (Côtes-d'Armor; Le Roux 1999) which were designed for a regional diffusion, including circulation of rough outs and completed objects. This model implies a considerable number of exchanges in the immediate area of production, which have left virtually no traces at sites in close proximity to Grand-Pressigny, in particular the burials from Indre-et-Loire (Cordier & Riquet 1957, 1958; Cordier 1968; Cordier et al. 1972).

More sustainable distribution networks dotted with regular stopovers seem more appropriately to explain the first stages of circulation which took advantage of established hamlets rebuilt over several generations as shown by modern excavations (Chalain, Douchapt, Pléchatel, Les Vaures; Pétrequin & Pétrequin 1997; Fouéré 1998, 2011; Tinevez 2004). While it is impossible to assert that this circulation was sustained by knappers alone, as it is improbable beyond a certain distance, the existence of satellite workshops in the south-west and the Vercors implies that they did, however, travel over significant distances and must have actively participated in these areas (Malenfant et al. 1971; Fouéré 1994; Delage 2004). Each knapper could take part in these exchange networks and/or gift economy along these familiar routes according to his or her own wealth and provided it was socially authorised for that person.

The diffusion of Pressigny objects could also be ensured in other ways: hawkers peddling various products, individuals established in fixed locations redistributing bulk products, or both opposing scenarios operating in parallel (Renfrew's 'central point model'; Renfrew 1984). The latter example seems highly likely in the context of fortified camps, such as Fort-Harrouard in the Eure valley which may have served as a control spot along the route towards the Seine, having yielded hundreds of Pressigny daggers (Mallet in prep.). It is unlikely that a single individual could be responsible for the circulation of Pressigny objects beyond a certain distance. Moreover, the idea of a sole individual travelling throughout Europe over numerous weeks to procure a single dagger

(Marquet 2004) also poses logistical problems in regards to transporting the transaction's counterpart. Furthermore, this model finds no support in assemblages from the Grand-Pressigny region where exotic materials are rare.

A limited number of exceptionally finished pieces, such as the dagger from Neuilly-sur-Eure (Orne; Hébert & Verron 1980), when considered in light of the ethnographic record, may correspond to more or less long distance exchange networks such as those described for Kula elites (Malinowski 1922). In this case, the expected benefit is essentially symbolic and social, both of which being augmented by the multiplication of exchanges which thereby heighten the object's symbolic charge (Malinowski 1922; Pétrequin & Pétrequin 1997). Thus, the material benefit is whittled down with each intermediary and does not necessarily return to the specialised producers.

A certain number of secondary products benefit from the flow generated by the demand for daggers. The use of Pressigny flakes is especially of interest in that they are more important in regions devoid of flint (Armorican Peninsula, Massif Central; Ihuel 2004, 2011), without, however, becoming the object of a dedicated circulation in their own right. The study of different distribution patterns (blades, flakes), especially on the Armorican coast, demonstrates that the diffusion of flakes is bound to that of daggers (Ihuel 2011).

Synthesis

The manufacture of flint daggers involved several hubs in Europe, and its emergence seems initially linked to Near-Eastern influences followed by several other zones such as the Balkans where copper metallurgy is on the rise from the 5th millennium. The case of Grand-Pressigny clearly highlights the fact that each of these hubs presents idiosyncrasies and strong identities (choice of laminar products, shaping, blank morphology) which can be tied to their being rooted in older, local technical systems (Ihuel 2008).

The specialised products and production techniques of the Grand-Pressigny region developed over a substantial time period of at least 600 years. The appearance of daggers produced from flint blades begins from the end of the 4th millennium BC, having emerged from local laminar production systems of average quality in a regional context which sees interactions with Central Europe relayed by the western Horgen culture (Honegger 2001; Brunet et al. 2004).

In just a few centuries, perhaps less, production systems see a succession of original technical innovations, some of them extremely highly specialised activities, which reached their pinnacle between the 27th and 25th centuries BC. These specialisations imply long periods of knowledge transmission and apprenticeship, time dedicated exclusively to production and efforts made to secure regular and sufficient outlets. During the height of their production, the various forms of Pressigny daggers are relatively original as they follow a logic of production and innovation specific to Pressigny, rather than representing mere copies of exogenous forms, particularly metallic examples.

A closer examination of Pressigny daggers points to their having had a complex status inherently more developed than that of their metal counterparts which are often viewed simply as weaponry. Is their status as weapons and designation as 'daggers' not misleading for these lithic pieces? Perhaps not, as the presence of a tip embodies notions of piercing, danger and war-craft, potentially affirming a 'contentious' masculine status for these objects in a society replete with strong social competition even while not necessarily representing their day to day purpose as recognised by western societies of the 3rd millennium BC (Guilaine & Zammit 2001).

Flint daggers represent goods likely to have been acquired at quite a high price as they often travelled substantial distances, beyond the local sphere of the village, and were only intermittently available. They are displayed conspicuously as ornaments or as tools worn permanently by their owners.

Several lines of reasoning overlap in terms of symbolic value and the exchange of these objects. Certain prestigious items seem to increase in symbolic value as they are passed between individuals, becoming imbued with greater meaning via transmission and possible personal embellishments. Moreover, evidence exists for hoarded pieces or objects intentionally kept out of circulation and which are eventually found in burial deposits (Fig. 5.9:2). Yet, others are no more than personal technical goods whose status may be compared to that of each family's patriarchal knife during the 19th century. A large portion of daggers seem progressively to lose some of their worth as the inevitable consequence of daily use (diversified uses of the edges for cereal processing) which is sometimes excessively prolonged in the form of waste products (end scrapers or strike-a-lights), especially in areas devoid of flint, such as the Breton peninsula. Based on evidence from settlements in the Jura, some authors have suggested that at the height of this phenomenon, social competition between male members of the group no longer resided in the mere possession of a dagger, but rather was expressed in the capacity of an individual to renew his toolkit (Plisson & Beugnier 2004).

This need for objects whose social value is expressed in different forms (objects worn as jewels, objects daily used, objects kept out far from eyes or on the contrary objects openly exchanged etc.) explains the development of different modes of circulation for items which follow largely pre-existing networks which link communities, the very same networks that have been supporting exchanges of all kinds (essential supplies, technical products, socially valued materials, personal goods, etc.) for millennia.

References

Airvaux, J. & Primault, J. 2002. Considérations sur l'extension géographique du Néolithique final à "livre de beurre" en Touraine et Poitou (France). *L'Anthropologie* 106: 269–294.

Ard, V. ed. 2011. *Le dolmen II de Puyraveau (Saint-Léger-de-Montbrun, Deux-Sèvres). Un monument au mobilier exceptionnel de la fin du Néolithique dans le Centre-Ouest de la France. Collections particulières et collections des musées de Poitiers et des Tumulus de Bougon.* Mémoire 41. Chauvigny: Association des Publications Chauvinoises.

Aubry 1991. *L'exploitation des ressources en matières premières lithiques dans les gisements solutréens et Badegouliens du Bassin versant de la Creuse (France).* Unpublished Ph.D thesis. Bordeaux: Université de Bordeaux I.

Aubry, T. 1995. *Site d'extraction de silex et atelier de débitage de grandes lames selon la méthode des "livres de beurre". La Giraudière (Neuilly-le-Brignon). Document final de synthèse de sondage, mars 1995* (with contribution by Moura, M.-H.). Orléans: Service régional de l'Archéologie du Centre.

Augereau, A., 2002. *Ateliers de taille de silex à Abilly "La Bergeresse". Document final de synthèse d'évaluation, INRAP Centre Ile-de-France* (with contributions by Creusillet, M.-F., Neury, P., Pihuit, P. & Ranger, O.). Orléans: Service régional de l'Archéologie du Centre.

Beugnier, V. 1997. *L'usage du silex dans l'acquisition et le traitement des matières animales dans le Néolithique de Chalain et Clairvaux. La Motte-aux-Magnins et Chalain 3 (Jura, France). 3700–2980 av. J.-C.* Unpublished PhD thesis, l'Université Paris X – Nanterre.

Brunet, P., Cottiaux, R., Hamon, T., Langry-François, F., Magne, P. & Salanova, L. 2004. La céramique de la fin du 4e et du 3e millénaire dans le Centre-Nord de la France. Bilan documentaire. In: M. Vander Linden & L. Salanova (eds.), *Le troisième millénaire dans le nord de la France et en Belgique.* Mémoire de la Société Préhistorique Française 35/Anthropologica et Praehistorica 115. Paris: Société Préhistorique Français. 155–178.

Burnez, C. 1976. *Le Néolithique et le Chalcolithique dans le Centre-Ouest de la France*, Mémoire de la Société Préhistorique Française 12. Paris: Société Préhistorique Français.

Burnez, C. 2010. *Le Camp à Challignac (Charente) au IIIe millénaire av. J.-C. Un établissement complexe de la culture d'Artenac dans le Centre-Ouest de la France.* Oxford: Archeopress.

Burnez, C. & Fouéré, P. 1999. *Les enceintes néolithiques de Diconches à Saintes (Charente-Maritime). Une périodisation de l'Artenac.* Mémoire de la Société Préhistorique Française 25/Mémoire de l'Association des publications Chauvinoises 15. Paris: Société Préhistorique Français.

Burnez, C. & Louboutin, C. 1999. Les enceintes fossoyées néolithiques: architecture et fonction. L'exemple du Bassin inférieur et moyen de la Charente. *Bulletin de la Société Préhistorique Française* 96: 329–353.

Cassen, S., Boujot, C., Errera, M., Marguerie, D., Menier, D., Pailler, Y., Pétrequin, P., Poirier, S., Veyrat, E. & Vigier, E. 2008. Discovery of an underwater deposit of Neolithic polished axe-heads and a submerged stone alignment at Petit Rohu near Saint-Pierre-Quiberon (Morbihan, France). *Antiquity* 82(316). http://www.antiquity.ac.uk/projgall/cassen316/

Chambon, P. 2003. *Les morts dans les sépultures collectives néolithiques en France. Du cadavre aux restes ultimes.* Paris: CNRS éditions.

Chancerel, A. & Chancerel, G. 2013. *Villetoureix, Chez Thuilet. Un habitat du Néolithique final.* Toulouse: Archives d'Ecologie Préhistorique.

Cordier, G. 1956. Le vrai visage du Grand-Pressigny. *Actes du Congrès préhistorique de France de Poitiers-Angoulême.* Paris: Société Préhistorique Français. 416–442.

Cordier, G. 1961. Précisions sur la cachette des lames des Ayez à Barrou (Indre-et-Loire). *Bulletin de la Société Préhistorique Française* 58: 590–591.

Cordier, G. 1968. Le «dolmen» des Marais à Villerable (Loire-et-Cher). *Bulletin de la Société Archéologique, scientifique et littéraire du Vendômois:* 45–69.

Cordier, G. 1986. Les dépôts de lames de silex en France. *Etudes préhistoriques* 17: 33–48.

Cordier, G. & Riquet, R. 1957. L'ossuaire néolithique du Bec-des-Deux-Eaux, commune de Ports (Indre-et-Loire). *L'Anthropologie* 61: 28–44.

Cordier, G. & Riquet, R. 1958. L'ossuaire du Vigneau et le dolmen de la Roche, commune de Manthelan (Indre et Loire). *L'Anthropologie* 62: 1–29.

Cordier, G., Riquet, R., Braban, H. & Poulain, F. 1972. Le site archéologique du dolmen de Villaine à Sublaine (Indre-et-Loire). *Gallia-Préhistoire* 15(1): 31–135.

Delage, J.-P. 2004. *Les ateliers de taille néolithiques en Bergeracois.* Archives d'Ecologie Préhistorique 15. Toulouse: École des Hautes Études en Sciences Sociales.

Delcourt-Vlaeminck, M. 1998. *Le silex du Grand-Pressigny dans le nord-ouest de l'Europe. Le silex tertiaire concurrent possible du Grand-Pressigny?* Unpublished PhD thesis, l'EHESS Toulouse.

Delcourt-Vlaeminck, M. 1999. Le silex du Grand-Pressigny dans le Nord-Ouest de l'Europe. *Bulletin des Amis du Musée du Grand-Pressigny* 50: 57–68.

Despriee, J. 1983. Informations archéologiques, Circonscription du Centre. *Gallia-Préhistoire* 26(2): 262–263.

Féblot-Augustins, J. & Perlès, C. 1992. Perspectives ethnoarchéologiques sur les échanges à longue distance. In: *Ethnoarchéologie: justification, problèmes, limites. XIIe rencontres internationales d'Archéologie et d'Histoire d'Antibes.* Juan-les-Pins: APDCA. 195–209.

Fouéré, P. 1994. *Les industries en silex entre Néolithique moyen et Campaniforme dans le Nord du Bassin aquitain; approches méthodologiques, implications culturelles de l'économie des matières premières et du débitage.* Unpublished PhD thesis, l'Université Bordeaux I.

Fouéré, P. 1998. Deux grands bâtiments du Néolithique final artenacien à Douchapt (Dordogne). In: A. D'Anna & D. Binder (eds.), *Production et identité culturelle. Actualité de la recherche. Actes de la deuxième session, Arles (Bouches-du-Rhône) 8 et 9 novembre 1996.* Antibes: Editions APDCA. 311–328.

Fouéré, P. 2011. Les Vaures à Bergerac: premier témoignage d'un village structuré pour le Néolithique récent du Sud-Ouest de la France. In: I. Sénépart, T. Perrin, E. Thirault & S. Bonnardin (eds.), *Marges, frontières et transgressions. Actualité de la recherche. Actes des 8e rencontres méridionales de Préhistoire récente. Marseille(13) – 7 et 8 novembre 2008.* Toulouse: Archives d'Ecologie Préhistorique. 365–386.

Fouéré, P. & Dias-Meirinho, M.-H. 2008. Les industries lithiques des IVe et IIIe millénaires dans le Centre-Ouest et le Sud-Ouest de la France. In: M.-H. Dias-Meirinho, V. Lea, K. Gernigon, P. Fouéré, F. Briois & M. Bailly (eds.), *Les industries lithiques taillées des IVe et IIIe millénaires en Europe occidentale. Colloque international. Toulouse, 7–9 avril 2005.* BAR international series 1884. Oxford: Archeopress. 231–258.

Geslin, M., Bastien, G. & Mallet, N. 1975. Le dépôt de grandes lames de la Creusette, Barrou (Indre-et-Loire), *Gallia-Préhistoire* 18(2): 401–422.

Giot, D., Mallet, N. & Millet, D. 1986. Les silex de la région du Grand-Pressigny (Indre-et-Loire). Recherche géologique et analyse pétrographique. *Revue archéologie du Centre de la France* 25(1): 26–31.

Guilaine, J. & Zammit, J. 2001. *Le sentier de la guerre. Visages de la violence préhistorique.* Paris: Seuil.

Hamon, T. 1999. *Architectures et culture de l'Artenac en Berry. Le camp des Chateliers à Moulins-sur-Céphons (Indre).* Orléans: Service Régional de l'Archéologie.

Hamon, T. ed. 2006. *Architectures et culture de l'Artenac en Berry. Un bâtiment monumental. Le site des Vaux à Moulins sur Céphon (Indre).* Orléans: SRA Centre.

Hebert, G. & Verron, G. 1980. Quelques poignards en silex de type pressignien recueillis dans le département de l'Eure. In: *Etudes sur le néolithique de la région Centre. Actes du Colloque interrégional sur le néolithique tenu à Saint-Amand-Montrond (Cher), 28–29–30 octobre 1977.* Saint-Amand-Montrond: Association des Amis du Musée de Saint-Vic. 18–31.

Honegger, M. 2001. *L'industrie lithique taillée du Néolithique moyen et final de Suisse.* Monographies du CRA 24. Paris: Editions du CNRS.

Hue, E. 1910. Distribution géographique de l'industrie en silex du Grand-Pressigny. In: *Actes du VIe Congrès Préhistorique de France, Tours 1910.* Paris: Société Préhistorique Français. 386–436.

Ihuel, I. 2004. *La diffusion du silex du Grand-Pressigny dans le Massif armoricain au Néolithique.* Bulletin des Amis du Musée du Grand-Pressigny, Supplément 2. Paris: Comité des Travaux Historiques et Scientifiques.

Ihuel, I. 2008. *De la circulation des lames à la circulation des poignards. Mutation des productions lithiques spécialisées dans l'Ouest de la France du Ve au IIIe millénaires.* Unpublished PhD thesis, l'Université de Paris X – Nanterre.

Ihuel, E. 2011. La circulation des lames dans le Massif armoricain au Néolithique. In: G. Marchand & G. Querré (eds.), *Roches et sociétés de la Préhistoire entre massifs cristallins et bassins sédimentaires.* Rennes: Presses Universitaires de Rennes. 325–340.

Joussaume, R. 1977. Le mégalithe de la Pierre-Virante à Xanton-Chassenon (Vendée). *L'Anthropologie* 81: 5–62.

Joussaume, R., Fouéré, P. & Crédot, R. 2002. Dolmens des Quatres Routes et de Bois Neuf III à Marsac (Creuse). *Bulletin de la Société Préhistorique Française* 99: 49–80.

Kelterborn, P. 1981a. Zur Frage des Livre de Beurre. *Jahrbuch der Schweizerischen Gesellschaft für Ur- und Frühgeschichte* 63: 5–24.

Kelterborn, P. 1981b. The livre de Beurre method. *Flintknappers' Exchange* 4(3): 12–22.

Le Roux, C.-T. 1999. *L'outillage de pierre polie en métadolérite du type A. Les ateliers de Plussulien (Côtes d'Armor): Production et diffusion au Néolithique dans la France de l'Ouest et au delà.* Rennes: Université de Rennes I.

L'Helgouac'h, J. 1965. *Les sépultures mégalithiques en Armorique (dolmens à couloirs et allées couvertes).* Rennes: travaux du laboratoire d'anthropologie de Rennes.

L'Helgouac'h, J. 1981. Machecoul. Informations archéologiques. *Gallia Préhistoire* 24(2): 425–437.

Malenfant, M., Cauvin, M.-C. & Chaffenet, G. 1971. Découverte d'une industrie macrolithique récente de faciès pressignien à Vassieux-en-Vercors (Drôme). *Comptes rendus de l'Academie des Sciences* 272: 1491–1495.

Malinowski, B. 1922. *Les Argonautes du Pacifique occidental.* Paris: Gallimard.

Mallet, N. 1992. *Le Grand-Pressigny: ses relations avec la civilisation Saône-Rhône.* Bulletin des Amis du Musée du Grand-Pressigny, Supplément. Le Grand-Pressigny: Société des Amis du Musée du Grand-Pressigny.

Mallet, N., Ihuel, E. & Verjux, C. 2008. La diffusion des silex du Grand-Pressigny au sein des groupes culturels des IVe et IIIe millénaires avant J.-C. In: M.-H. Dias-Meirinho, V. Léa, K. Germigon, P. Fouéré, F. Briois & M. Bailly (eds.), *Les industries lithiques taillées des IVe et IIIe millénaires en Europe occidentale.* BAR international series 1884. Oxford: Archeopress. 183–205.

Mallet, N., Pelegrin, J. & Reduron-Ballanger, M. 1994. Sur deux dépôts de lames pressigniennes: Moigny et Boutigny (Essonne). *Bulletin des Amis du Musée du Grand-Pressigny* 45: 25–37.

Marquet, J.-C. 2004. *Au pays des tailleurs de grandes lames.* Chambray-le-Tours: Archéa.

Marquet, J.-C. & Millet-Richard, L.-A. 1995. L'habitation-atelier Néolithique final du Petit-Paulmy à Abilly (Indre-et-Loire). Présentation préliminaire. *Revue Archéologique de l'Ouest Supplément* 7: 247–271.

Martial, E., Praud, Y. & Bostyn, F. 2004. Recherches récentes sur le Néolithique final dans le nord de la France. In: M. Vander Linden & L. Salanova (eds.), *Le troisième millénaire dans le nord de la France et en Belgique. Journée d'études SRBAP-SPF (8 mars 2003; Lille).* Mémoire de la Société préhistorique française 35/Anthropologica et Praehistorica 115. Paris: Société préhistorique française. 49–71.

Martin, J.-M., Martinez, R. & Prost, D. 1996. Le site chalcolithique de Bettencourt-Saint-Ouen. *Internéo* 1: 141–168.

Mauduit, J., Tarrête, J., Taborin, Y. & Girard, C. 1977. La Sépulture collective mégalithique de l'usine Vivez à Argenteuil (Val d'Oise). *Gallia Préhistoire* 20: 177–226.

Millet-Richard, L.-A. 1997. *Habitats et ateliers de taille au Néolithique final dans la région du Grand-Pressigny (Indre-et-Loire): technologie lithique.* Unpublished PhD thesis, l'Université de Paris I Panthéon-Sorbonne.

Millet-Richard, L.-A. 2001. Note d'information sur la campagne de fouille 2000 de la Grasse-Coue à Abilly. *Bulletin des Amis du Musée du Grand-Pressigny* 52: 37–39.

Peek, J. 1975. *Inventaire des mégalithes de la France, 4, Région parisienne.* Paris: CNRS.

Pelegrin, J. 1997. Nouvelles observations sur le dépôt de lame de La Creusette (Barrou, Indre-et-Loire). *Bulletin des amis du Musée du Grand-Pressigny* 48: 19–34.

Pelegrin, J. 2002. La production de grandes lames de silex du Grand-Pressigny. In : J. Guilaine (ed.), *Matériaux, productions, circulations du Néolithique à l'Age du Bronze.* Séminaire du Collège de France. Paris: Editions Errance: 131–148.

Pelegrin, J. 2005. L'extraction du silex au Grand-Pressigny pendant le Néolithique final, proposition d'un modèle. *Bulletin des Amis du Musée du Grand-Pressigny* 56: 65–71.

Pelegrin, J. 2012. Grandes lames de l'Europe néolithique et alentour. In: J.-C. Marquet & C. Verjux (eds.), *L'Europe, déjà, à la fin des temps préhistoriques. Des grandes lames en silex dans toute l'Europe. Actes de la table ronde internationale de Tours, sept. 2007.* Supplément à la Revue Archéologique du Centre de la France. Tours: FERACF. 15–42.

Pelegrin, J. & Ihuel, E. 2005. Les 306 nucléus de la ruine de la Claisière. *Bulletin des Amis du Musée du Grand-Pressigny* 56: 45–65.

Perrin, T., Ihuel, E. & Plisson, H. 2007. Les Bois Pargas à Pageas (Limousin). *Bulletin de la Société Préhistorique Française* 104: 543–564.

Péridy P. Forthcoming. *L'enceinte néolithique de la Chevêtelière à Saint-Mathurin (Vendée).*

Pétrequin, A.-M. & Pétrequin, P. 1997. Le poignard en os en Irian Jaya (Nouvelle-Guinée indonésienne). In: M. Schindlbeck (ed.), *Gestern und Heute – Traditionen in der Südsee.* Baessler-Archiv: Beiträge zur Völkerkunde, N.F. Bd. 45. Berlin: Verlag von Dietrich Reimer. 135–150.

Pétrequin, A.-M., Pétrequin, P. & Cassen, S. 1998. Les longues lames polies des élites. Du Néolithique à la Nouvelle-Guinée, un même outil de régulation sociale. *La Recherche* 312: 70–75.

Pétrequin, P. ed. 1995. *Fontenu (Jura) Lac de Chalain. Fouille de Chalain 4. 1993–1995. Rapport de synthèse.* Besançon: SRA Franche-Comté.

Pétrequin, P., Bailly, M. & Viellet, A. 2001. Les villages littoraux néolithiques du Jura français et les chronologies des IVe et IIIe millénaires av. J.-C. Le point de vue de l'archéologue et du dendrochronogue. In: J.-N. Barrandon, P. Guibert & V. Michel (eds.), *Datation, XXIe rencontres Internationales d'Archéologie et d'Histoire d'Antibes.* Antibes: Editions APDCA. 407–431.

Pétrequin, P., Cassen, S., Croutsch, C. & Weller, O. 1997. Haches alpines et haches carnacéennes dans l'Europe du Vème millénaire. *Notae Praehistoricae* 17: 135–150.

Pétrequin, P. & Jeunesse, C. eds. 1995. *La hache de Pierre: carrières vosgiennes et échanges de lames polies pendant le néolithique, 5400–2100 av. J.-C.* Paris: Édition Errance.

Pétrequin, P. & Pétrequin, A.-M. 2000. *Ecologie d'un outil: la hache de pierre taillée en Irian Jaya (Indonésie).* Paris: Editions du CNRS.

Philippe, J. 1936. Le Fort-Harrouard. *L'Anthropologie* 46: 257–301.

Philippe, J. 1937. Le Fort-Harrouard. *L'Anthropologie* 47: 253–308.

Plisson, H. & Beugnier, V. 2004. Les poignards en silex du Grand-Pressigny: fonction de signe et fonctions d'usage. In: P. Bodu & C. Constantin (eds.), *Approches fonctionnelles en Préhistoire. XXVe Congrès Préhistorique de France – Nanterre 24–26 novembre 2000.* Paris: Société Préhistorique Française. 139–154.

Plisson, H., Mallet, N., Bocquet, A. & Ramseyer, D. 2002.

Utilisation et rôle des outils en silex du Grand-Pressigny dans les villages de Charavines et Portalban (Néolithique final). *Bulletin de la Société Préhistorique Française* 99: 793–811.

Ranger, O. 2002. *Monts «La Bouchardière-La pain perdu».* *Rapport de diagnostic archéologique.* Orléans: SRA Centre et Pantin, INRAP.

Renfrew, C. 1977. Alternative models for exchange and spatial distribution. In: T. Earle & J. E. Ericson (eds.), *Exchange systems in Prehistory.* New-York: New-York Academic Press. 71–90.

Renfrew, C. 1984. *Approaches to Social Archaeology.* Cambridge: Harvard University Press.

Riche, C. 1998. *Les ateliers de silex de Vassieux. Exploitation des gîtes et diffusion des produits.* Unpublished PhD thesis, l'Université de Paris X – Nanterre.

Saint-Venant, J. de. 1910. Tailleries de silex du Sud de la Touraine, inventaires des produits exportés aux temps préhistoriques et carte de leur aire de diffusion. *Actes du VIe Congrès Préhistorique de France, Tours 1910.* Paris: Société Préhistorique Français. 256–299.

Salanova, L. & Tchérémissinoff, Y. eds. 2011. *Les sépultures individuelles campaniformes en France.* Gallia-Préhistoire, supplément 41. Paris: CNRS editions.

Schlichtherle, H. 1994. Exotische Feuersteingeräte am Bodensee. *Plattform* 3: 46–53.

Sohn, M. 2002. Place et rôle du mobilier funéraire dans les sépultures collectives du Bassin parisien à la fin du Néolithique. *Bulletin de la Société Préhistorique Française* 99: 501–520.

Thévenot, J.-P. 2005. *Le camp de Chassey (Chassey-le-Camp, Saône-et-Loire): les niveaux néolithiques du rempart de «La Redoute».* Dijon: Revue Archéologique de l'Est.

Tinevez, J.-Y. D. 2004. *Le site de la Hersonnais à Pléchâtel (Ille-et-Vilaine): un ensemble de bâtiments collectifs du Néolithique final.* Société préhistorique française, Travaux 5. Paris: Société préhistorique française.

Vaughan, P. & Bocquet, A. 1987. Première étude fonctionnelle d'outils lithiques néolithiques du village de Charavines, Isère. *L'Anthropologie* 91(2): 399–410.

Verjux, C. 1989. Présentation sommaire des découvertes effectuées à la Creusette sur la commune de La Guerche (Indre-et-Loire). *Bulletin des Amis du Musée du Grand-Pressigny* 40: 37–42.

Verjux, C. 2003. L'informatisation des données de l'inventaire des exportations pressigniennes. *Bulletin des Amis du Musée du Grand-Pressigny* 54: 37–42.

Viellet, A. 2005. Synthèse chronologique des bois d'oeuvre des sites néolithiques de Clairvaux-les-Lacs et de Chalain (Jura, France). Les aléas de la méthode dendrochronologique. *Bulletin de la Société Préhistorique Française* 102: 803–812.

Villes, A. 1999. Quelques observations sur l'architecture domestique au Néolithique final dans la région du Grand-Pressigny et en moitié nord de la France. *Bulletin des Amis du Musée du Grand-Pressigny* 50: 31–56.

Villes, A. 2005. Fouille de sauvetage sur l'atelier de taille pressignien de La Claisière à Abilly. *Bulletin des Amis du Musée du Grand-Pressigny* 56: 13–44.

Voruz, J.-L., Perrin, T. & Sordoillet, D. 2004. La séquence néolithique de la grotte du Gardon (Ain). *Bulletin de la Société Préhistorique Française* 101: 827–866.

6

THE CULTURAL BIOGRAPHY OF THE SCANDINAVIAN DAGGERS IN THE NORTHERN NETHERLANDS

Annelou van Gijn

The Scandinavian daggers which were brought to the northern Netherlands in great numbers during the Late Neolithic and Early Bronze Age display a special biography. First of all they share with other imported flint items from Scandinavia, like the TRB axes and the crescent-shaped sickles, the presence of a piece of cortex on their butt end. They also seem to have had a special use life: they lack 'normal' traces of wear and instead show wear traces from contact with plant material and/or hide all over the surface of the blade. It is suggested that this was due to pulling the dagger in and out of a sheath. Last, the place these daggers were deposited also seems to be 'special': type I and II daggers are usually found as loose finds in peat, probably in the river and brook valleys, the later type III daggers on the other hand were located much further out into the large peat areas.

Introduction

From *ca.* 2350 to 1500 cal BC flint daggers were produced on a mass scale in specialised workshops in the Limfjord area of northern Jutland and on the eastern Danish islands of Sjælland and Møn, where high quality Senonian flint was amply available (Apel 2001, 2008; Barrowclough 2004). It is estimated that more than 13,000 were produced over time, distributed over a large part of north-western Europe (Apel 2001, 2008). Experimental replication of the production process has shown that they involved intricate craftsmanship (Callahan 2006).The technological knowledge was handed down from generation to generation; it is estimated that the technology of how to make daggers was reproduced for more than 24 generations (Apel 2008:94), leading Apel to postulate an institutionalised apprenticeship (Apel 2008:106). They have been subject of a number of detailed typological studies, revealing a morphological variation through time, although their chronology is still debated (Apel 2001). The most common typology is that of Lomborg who distinguished six types (Lomborg 1973).

The daggers also reached the Northern Netherlands but they displayed a different biography from those in southern Scandinavia (Frieman 2012). Only some rare items are found

to the south of the great rivers (Fig. 6.1). The majority was found in the province of Drenthe where peat extraction took place on a massive scale in the 19th and early 20th century revealing numerous archaeological finds. Although these items have not undergone a systematic investigation recently, a cursory inventory of the Archis database in 2008 revealed 127 specimens to be present within the confines of the present-day Netherlands (Van Gijn 2010: 189). It concerned predominantly Lomborg/Apel Type I, II and III (Beuker & Drenth 1999, 2006; Bloemers 1968) (Figs 6.2 & 6.3). It is believed that they first appeared in the Netherlands from the Bell Beaker period onwards but this is difficult to substantiate as hardly any have been found in datable context. It is assumed that Type I is related to the Late Bell Beaker culture, type II to the transition of the Bell Beaker to the Early Barbed Wire culture (Early Bronze Age) and type III to the full Early Bronze Age. Lomborg/Apel types IV-VI have only very rarely been found in the Netherlands (Bloemers 1968). It is without doubt that these items were imported as finished products as so far no production waste has been encountered. It is also quite doubtful that the size of the flint nodules present in the ground moraines of the northern Netherlands – which obviously contain

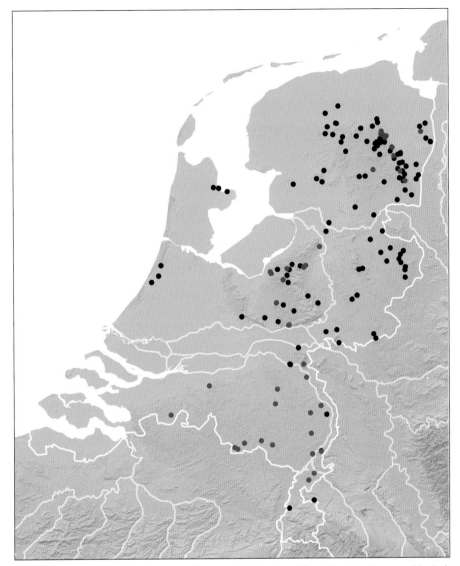

Fig. 6.1. Distribution map of southern Late Single Grave daggers (red dots) and Scandinavian daggers (black dots) in the present-day Netherlands (from Van Gijn 2010: 188).

Scandinavian flint nodules – is insufficient and the quality inferior due to cracks. The Dutch daggers also show that there probably were other production centres apart from the Limfjord and eastern Danish islands workshops. Raw material comparisons led Beuker to conclude that most of the Dutch daggers were made of fine grained flint from Holstein (Beuker & Drenth 2006: 289). The presence of a small number of daggers made of red Helgoland flint in the Netherlands is in support of the former presence of multiple production centres.

Within the context of an on-going project to investigate the meaning of flint for Neolithic communities, 18 daggers were examined microscopically. Use was made of a Wild stereomicroscope with 10–160× magnification and a Nikon Optiphot metallographic microscope with 100–400×

magnification. Two of the daggers were not interpretable due to post-depositional surface modifications. There are two dagger fragments made of red Helgoland flint, but their exact typology could not be further specified as it concerned the tips of the tools. The daggers for the most part came from the province of Drenthe.

The observed use-wear traces and experiments

All of the complete daggers displayed two types of traces, located on the blade and on the hilt respectively. On the blade traces are situated along the edge but also on the crests of the many flake ridges of both retouched surfaces. It concerns a rough, matte polish displaying a distinct directionality

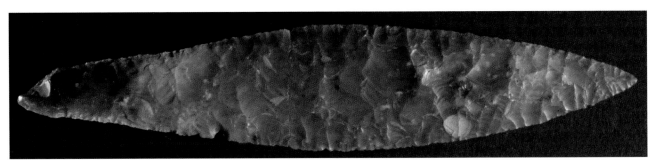

Fig. 6.2. Scandinavian type I dagger: surface find from Westenes, Drenthe (length 28.3cm) (Van Gijn 2010: 36).

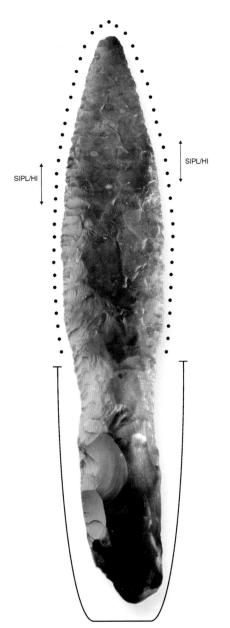

Figure 6.3. Scandinavian type III dagger: find from Exloërveen displaying "sheath" polish and traces of hafting (length 22.3cm) (from Van Gijn 2010: 190).

parallel to the long axis of the object (Fig. 6.4a). The polish resembles the polish from contact with (siliceous) plants and bark, but in places it shares features with experimental hide working polishes. Peculiar is the fact that the traces on the edge are not particularly well-developed nor do they gradually fade out or disappear when going into the centre of the object: the edges are certainly not extensively worn. There is also no evidence for resharpening.

The presence of wear traces is usually interpreted as being related to the former function of the object. In the case of the daggers this was complicated by the peculiar distribution of the traces. Normally, when using a flint tool, the traces are most heavily developed along the working edge to disappear, either gradually fading or ending abruptly, towards the inner surface of the implement. The blades of the daggers do not show this. Instead, the traces are relatively weakly developed along the edges and they are also visible on the crest of the dorsal and ventral flake scar negatives of the blade. This indicates that the entire blade has come into contact with the material responsible for the polish. The fact that the wear traces are not concentrated and more heavily developed along the actual edges suggests that these edges have not been utilised in the 'regular' fashion like for cutting plant materials or hides. Instead it is suggested that this configuration of wear traces is due to contact with a sheath, made of bark or other plant material or possibly of hide.

All daggers display convincing evidence for the former presence of a haft or wrapping on the hilt (Fig. 6.3). Some have a greasy polish with extensive rounding, suggesting that they were enveloped in rawhide. This may indicate that the hilt was covered with hide, wrapped tightly around the flint and fastened with leather bindings. However, raw hide can also form part of a haft of wood or bone, used to fix the tool in the haft as it shrinks upon drying. Several daggers have friction gloss or even small patches of black residue, likely to be associated with the hafting arrangement. Friction gloss indicates a slight movement of the flint implement within a haft made of harder materials like wood or bone. In all cases, however, the most convincing indication for hafting, however, is the distribution of the polish: the polish present on the blade abruptly ends exactly there where the

Fig. 6.4. Use wear traces. A. Type 3 dagger from Wijster (Drents Museum Assen nr. 1979-IX2) (orig. magnify. 200×); B. experimental dagger nr. 1739 (orig. Magnif. 200×); C. Linear traces seen on red Helgoland dagger fragment from Rolde, Drenthe (orig. magnify. 200×); D. Rounding and polish from use as strike-a-light seen on red Helgoland dagger fragment from Rolde, Drenthe (orig. magnif. 100×)

morphology of the dagger facilitates a hafting arrangement, like the narrowing of the blade. This is a sure sign of the former presence of a haft (Rots 2008, 2010). The later dagger types, notably the type III daggers with their rhombic cross section, already have a flaked and ground hilt (Fig. 6.3) which, in combination with the absence of the 'sheath' polish seen on the blades, makes clear that these implements were indeed hafted.

In order to test the interpretation of these daggers three experiments were carried out. Bifacial daggers were made of Scandinavian Senonian flint by Diederik Pomstra, a proficient flintknapper (Fig. 6.5). These daggers were hafted in antler or wooden hafts. The hafting in raw hide has not yet been tested. Three sheaths were made: one of woven *Phragmites*, one of twined lime fibres, and one of cherry bark. The daggers were then pulled in and out of the sheath without having been used before. The traces, especially in terms of distribution, closely resembled those seen on the archaeological specimens (Fig. 6.4b). The traces seem to be due to recurrently pulling the daggers in and out of their sheaths. This activity explains the curious distribution of the polish on the protrusions of the entire surface of the non-hafted part of the tool. Still, a cautionary note is needed. Although the daggers certainly were not used for long term utilitarian tasks like harvesting cereals, butchering animals or performing various craft activities, it cannot be excluded that they were nevertheless incidentally used. One possibility is that they were used to deliver a *coup de grace* when offering for example animals, an explanation already proposed by Skak-Nielsen (2009). Traces are not likely to have developed from such a short term, incidental, activity and if they did, they would be obscured by the overriding

Fig. 6.5. (above) Experimental daggers (Van Gijn 2010: 191).

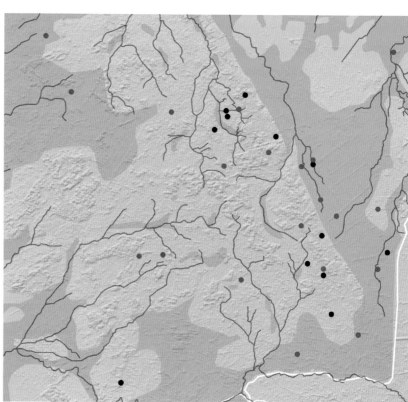

Fig. 6.6. Distribution of the Scandinavian type I/II daggers (black dots) versus type III daggers (red dots) in the province of Drenthe in the north-eastern part of the Netherlands (Van Gijn 2010: 192).

traces from contact with the sheath. It is, however, highly unlikely that the daggers were efficient stabbing weapons, as their name suggests.

Bloemers already noted that some daggers may have functioned as strike-a-lights (Bloemers 1968) and defined these as a specific type. In the sample examined for traces of use, one dagger fragment of red Helgoland flint, found by Jan van Rijn near Rolde, Drenthe, actually displayed such traces (Fig. 6.4c, d). The tips of the daggers are severely rounded and have the distinctive linear distribution of polish and scratches commonly found on such tools (Beugnier & Pétrequin 1997; Van Gijn & Niekus 2001). No traces of pyrite residue were seen. The re-use of these daggers for making fire suggests that not all daggers were taken out of circulation (see below on distribution), but that some were given a second life. It may well be that the special colour of the red Helgoland flint was seen as attractive.

Distribution of the daggers

The Scandinavian daggers in the Netherlands are almost all found in the course of peat collecting activities in the 19th century. As a consequence, their find contexts have rarely been documented in detail. In almost all cases it concerns loose, single finds. Obviously it is very difficult to interpret such finds. However, in many cases the description of the find circumstances (as documented in the sometimes rather detailed find descriptions in the Provincial Museum of Drenthe in Assen) allows a rough reconstruction of the location of the find and the soil type in which they were found. This was the case for 15 of the 18 daggers which were studied in detail. It turns out that they were found in or close to peat, away from settlement areas and also not in areas where we might expect (destroyed) barrows. Instead, these objects seem to be associated with the peat areas or wet context surrounding the settled areas within the north-eastern Netherlands (Fig. 6.6). Due to the lack of association with either settlement or funerary evidence, it is likely that these daggers constituted single deposits from the outset and were not associated with other non-perishable artefacts like stone tools. Obviously, it is impossible to exclude their association with finds that have either not preserved in the peat, like food items, or items that were unmodified and consequently less likely to be distinguished by those who found them like pebbles or unretouched flakes. Nevertheless, it is suggested that one should consider these daggers to be especially deposited in the marginal peat areas surrounding the settled area.

It is noteworthy that the distribution of type I/II daggers differs from that of type III daggers (Fig. 6.6). Whereas the first were deposited in wet zones adjacent to the inhabitable areas, the later type III daggers were found much further into the peat. The interface between inhabitable areas and the peat can be considered a liminal zone where culture and nature meet. The peat itself is beyond the land of the living and although we do find tracks leading into the bogs, these seem to end there (Harsema 1981). One type III dagger was found in association with remnants of a hearth and a configuration of worked pinewood, suggesting the presence of a ritual place (see also the 'temple' of Bargeroosterveld (Van den Broeke 2005)). It is suggested that the daggers formed part of ritual activities in the bog, being deposited not in the land of the living but in the land of the gods or mythical ancestors (Van Gijn 2010).

Discussion and conclusion

The biographical study of the Scandinavian daggers in the present-day Netherlands has shown them to have followed a special itinerary. They were produced in southern Scandinavia in specialised workshops and transported as finished products to the northern parts of the present-day Netherlands. There they did not seem to have been used for utilitarian tasks, as deduced from the lack of 'ordinary' wear traces. Instead they were kept as they were received, considering the lack of rejuvenation on most of the daggers. They may have been used for short term tasks within a more ritual sphere for example to bleed animals or deliver the *coup de grace*. This cannot be assessed anymore as interpretable microwear traces do not develop from such short term use and residue analysis will not be possible because of contamination after extensive handling of the objects by archaeologists and museum employees. However, the daggers do display distinctive, non-utilitarian wear traces concentrating on the surface of the blades of the daggers. It is proposed that these traces resulted from the daggers being pulled in and out of their sheaths many times. At some point in time they ended up in the wet zones and peat away from the settled area. Initially this was still in the vicinity of the inhabitable area, but as times went on the daggers were deposited deeper into the peat zones, in the land of the gods, never to be retrieved again. However, some daggers may have followed a different life path. This was the case with a dagger fragment of red Helgoland flint which displayed distinctive evidence for a second life as strike-a-light. Flint strike-a-lights are 'special' tools (Van Gijn 2010; Van Gijn *et al.* 2006), so it may not be coincidental that this stunning red dagger deserved an itinerary of its own, continuing its life history to make fire, possibly again in ritual context.

References

Apel, J. 2001. *Daggers, Knowledge and Power. The Social Aspects of Flint-dagger Technology in Scandinavia 2350–1500 cal BC.* Uppsala: Uppsala University.

Apel, J. 2008. Knowledge, know-how and raw material – The production of Late Neolithic flint daggers in Scandinavia. *Journal of Archaeological Method and Theory* 15(1): 91–111.

Barrowclough, D.A. 2004. The secrets of the craft production of Scandinavian Late Neolithic flint daggers. *Lithic Technology* 29(1): 74–86.

Beugnier, V. & Pétrequin, P. 1997. Pierres à briquet: utilisation de la marcassite. In: P. Pétrequin (ed.), *Les sites littoraux néolithiques de Clairvaux et Chalain (Jura), III, Chalain, station 3, 3200–2900 av. J.-C.* Paris: Maison des Sciences de l'Homme. 1–8.

Beuker, J. R., & Drenth, E. 1999. 'Scandinavische' dolken in Drenthe. *Nieuwe Drentse Volksalmanak* 116: 3–33.

Beuker, J. R. & Drenth, E. 2006. Scandinavian type flint daggers from the province of Drenthe, the Netherlands. In: G. Körlin & G. Weisgerber (eds.), *Stone Age – Mining Age.* Bochum. Deutsches Bergbau-Museum Bochum. 285–300.

Bloemers, J. H. F. 1968. Flintdolche vom Skandinavischen Typus in den Niederlanden. *Berichten van de Rijksdienst voor het Oudheidkundig Bodemonderzoek* 18: 47–110.

Callahan, E. 2006. Neolithic Danish daggers. An experimental peek. In: J. Apel & K. Knutsson (eds.), *Skilled production and social reproduction. Aspects of traditional stone-tool technologies.* SAU Stone Studies 2. Uppsala: Societas Archaeologica Upsaliensis. 115–129.

Frieman, C. 2012. Innovation and imitation: stone skeuomorphs of metal from 4th–2nd millennia BC Northwest Europe. BAR international series 2365. Oxford: Archeopress.

Harsema, O. H. 1981. Het neolithische vuursteendepot van Nieuw Dordrecht, gem. Emmen en het optreden van lange klingen in de prehistorie. *Nieuwe Drentse Volksalmanak* 98: 117–128.

Lomborg, E. 1973. *Die Flintdolche Dänemarks. Studien über Chronologie und Kulturbeziehungen des südskandinavischen Spätneolithikums.* København: Universitetsforlaget.

Rots, V. 2008. Hafting traces on flint tools. In: L. Longo & N. Skakun (eds.), *'Prehistoric Technology' 40 years later: Functional Studies and the Russian Legacy. Proceedings of the International Congress Verona (Italy), 20–23 April 2005.* BAR international series 1783. Oxford: Arrcheopress. 75–84.

Rots, V. 2010. *Prehension and Hafting Fraces on Flint Tools. A Methodology.* Leuven: Leuven University Press.

Skak-Nielsen, N. V. 2009. Flint and metal daggers in Scandinavia and other parts of Europe. A re-interpretation of their function in the Late Neolithic and Early Copper and Bronze Age. *Antiquity* 83(320): 349–358.

Van den Broeke, P. W. 2005. Gifts to the gods. Rites and cult sites in the Bronze Age and Iron Age. In: L. P. Louwe Kooijmans, P. W. Van den Broeke, H. Fokkens & A. L. Van Gijn (eds.), *The Prehistory of the Netherlands.* Amsterdam: Amsterdam University Press. 659–677.

Van Gijn, A. L. 2010. *Flint in Focus. Lithic Biographies in the Neolithic and Bronze Age.* Leiden: Sidestone Press.

Van Gijn, A. L. & Niekus, M. J. L.T. 2001. Bronze Age settlement flint from the Netherlands. The Cinderella of lithic research. In: W. H. Metz, B. L. Van Beek & H. Steegstra (eds.), *Patina. Essays Presented to Jay Jordan Butler on the Occasion of his 80th birthday.* Groningen: Metz, van Beek & Steegstra. 305–320.

Van Gijn, A. L., Van Betuw, V., Verbaas, A., & Wentink, K. 2006. Flint. Procurement and use. In: L. P. Louwe Kooijmans & P. F. B. Jongste (eds.), *Schipluiden. A Neolithic site on the Dutch north sea coast (3800–3500 BC).* Analaecta Praehistorica Leidensia 37/38. Leiden: University of Leiden. 129–166.

A PARALLEL-FLAKED SCANDINAVIAN TYPE FLINT DAGGER FROM LENT: AN INDICATOR OF CONTACTS BETWEEN THE CENTRAL NETHERLANDS AND NORTHERN JUTLAND DURING BELL BEAKER TIMES

Erik Drenth

A Scandinavian type flint dagger with parallel retouch (Lomborg's type Ic; originally classified as 'I C') was found in 1971 during a period of especially low water of the river Waal near Lent, province of Gelderland, the Netherlands. The object is dated between ca. *2350–1900 BC and can be ascribed to the Late Neolithic Bell Beaker Culture, in particular to the central Dutch Bell Beaker group. The dagger originates in the Limfjord region in northern Jutland, Denmark. Probably it represents a gift, which in view of the overall distribution was brought or taken from the Limfjord region to the Netherlands. The object is, therefore, indicative of the existence of direct contacts between the northern Jutlandic Beaker group and the central Dutch Bell Beaker group, as already hinted at by resemblances in pottery decoration and metalwork. The underlying motif for these supraregional connections may very well have been metallurgy, at least from the northern Jutlandic side. It transpires that, within the Bell Beaker world, metalworking had a centre of gravity in, among other places, the central Netherlands. It is from this district that the dagger in question was recovered. This artefact must have been highly prestigious and valuable in the Late Neolithic, judging from its rarity in Denmark and the technological knowledge as well as skills and time needed to produce a bifacially parallel-flaked flint dagger. Why it ended up in or immediately next to the river Waal is unclear. Possibly the dagger represents a deposition. It has not been reported to have been associated with other artefacts or features.*

Introduction

During low water of the river Waal in 1971, Mr H. Botma discovered a fractured flint dagger of Scandinavian type near Lent in the province of Gelderland, the Netherlands (Figs. 7.1 and 7.2). A short note on this 15.4cm long object has been published by Hulst (1972); and an overview of Scandinavian type flint daggers from the Dutch province of Drenthe also briefly address to the find (Beuker & Drenth 2006: 289f). Nonetheless, it is worthwhile to discuss the Lent dagger again and at more length because, for Dutch standards, it is exceptional.[1] Among the Scandinavian type flint dagger finds, in total well over 130 specimens, from the Netherlands, it stands alone thanks to the parallel retouch covering both the lower and upper face, with the exception of the edges which were secondarily retouched (on this topic, see Beuker & Drenth 1999, 2006; Bloemers 1968). Given the parallel retouch and because the grip and blade have a similar thickness, the Lent dagger is an example of the subtype Ic as defined by Lomborg (1973: 39f, fig. 9). The retouch on daggers of this type ranges from perfectly parallel to semi-parallel (Lomborg 1973: 29). In the former instance, of which the dagger from Lent is an example, the

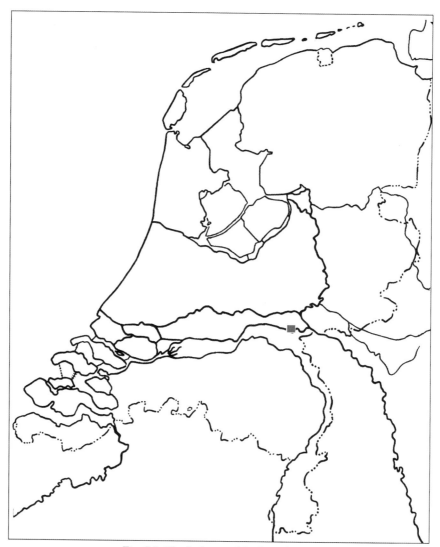

Fig. 7.1. The find spot of the Lent dagger.

parallel negatives run (almost) from one side to the other; while, in the latter case, they reach more or less halfway.

Dating

As no association whatsoever was reported, the Lent dagger should be regarded a single find. Hence, typological and contextual considerations are the only means to date the item. Accordingly, the 'Scandinavian type flint dagger situation' in Late Neolithic northern and northwestern continental Europe should be briefly outlined. Of importance here is the lack of evidence for the production of such artefacts in the Netherlands (Beuker & Drenth 1999: 8ff (100ff), 2006: 288ff). Consequently, specimens found in this country are imports. Their places of origin are northern Germany (Schleswig-Holstein and, among other places, the isle of Heligoland and perhaps also Mecklenburg-Vorpommern) and Denmark (for more information see Beuker & Drenth 1999, 2006). As a consequence, the dagger chronologies established for those regions are also of chronological relevance for the Netherlands.

The earliest Scandinavian type flint daggers occurred in Denmark and northern Germany during Bell Beaker times. It is generally agreed upon that they include specimens of type I (e.g. Kühn 1979: 46ff; Lomborg 1973: Chapter III; Rassmann 1993: 26ff; Vandkilde 1996: 13). Though according to Lomborg (1973: 40, 78f) variety Ic is not among the earliest subtypes, its concurrence with the Bell Beaker Culture is beyond question. Indicative are, for example, type Ic dagger fragments excavated from Late Neolithic I settlements within northern Jutland, to be more precise at Bejsebakken (Sarauw 2006: 234f, fig. 13) and Myrhøj (Jensen 1972:88, fig. 22:10). The Lent dagger may

Fig. 7.2. The Scandinavian type flint dagger with parallel retouch discovered near Lent (photograph F. de Vries). Full size 15.4cm.

thus date to the Bell Beaker Culture. Furthermore, the geographical location from which the artefact was recovered also points in that direction, as will be argued below.

The Bell Beaker Culture in the Netherlands is placed between *ca.* 2400–1900 BC (Lanting & Van der Plicht 1999/2000, 2001/2002: espec. 152f). When exactly the first Scandinavian type flint daggers were imported remains to be seen. If one follows Vandkilde's chronological scheme for Denmark, the earliest specimens, marking the onset of Late Neolithic I, may have appeared around 2350 BC (Vandkilde 1996: espec. 13f and chap. 7). Lanting & Van der Plicht (2001/2002: 124ff, 134) have argued, however, that Late Neolithic I started significantly later: around 2025 BC. Whether Vandkilde's or Lanting and Van der Plicht's ideas are adhered to, Scandinavian type flint daggers are clearly not part of the Bell Beaker Culture's initial phase. As there are no unequivocal associations of such daggers with the earliest Bell Beaker pottery, like maritime bell beakers, such a stance is indeed defendable.

Place of origin

According to Lomborg (1973: 40) the use of parallel retouch in flaking Scandinavian type flint daggers is a local phenomenon, typical of western Denmark. In other words, it is said to have no counterparts elsewhere in Europe.[2] He pointed out the concentration of parallel-flaked (i.e. type Ic) dagger finds around the Limfjord in northern Jutland (Fig. 7.3). The distribution is indeed suggestive of the production in that region of Scandinavian type flint daggers with parallel retouch. Other dagger specialists like Rassmann (1993: 19) sympathise with Lomborg's view and the author also sees no reason to really challenge the latter's hypothesis, especially in light of a recently excavated site where Scandinavian type flint daggers, including subtype Ic, were produced has been excavated at Bejsebakken. The site is located within the Limfjord region (Sarauw 2006). Earlier on, indications of Ic dagger production in the form of flakes displaying parallel flake scars have come to light at Myrhøj (Apel 2001: 165, fig. 6:3).

The obvious inference from the above data is that the Lent dagger was made in northern Jutland. This claim is not contradicted by the raw material used. Judging from its colour, translucence, texture and inclusions it was, in all probability, made from Senonian flint (cf. Högberg & Olausson 2007). The primary and secondary occurrences of this raw material include, amongst other places, northern Jutland.

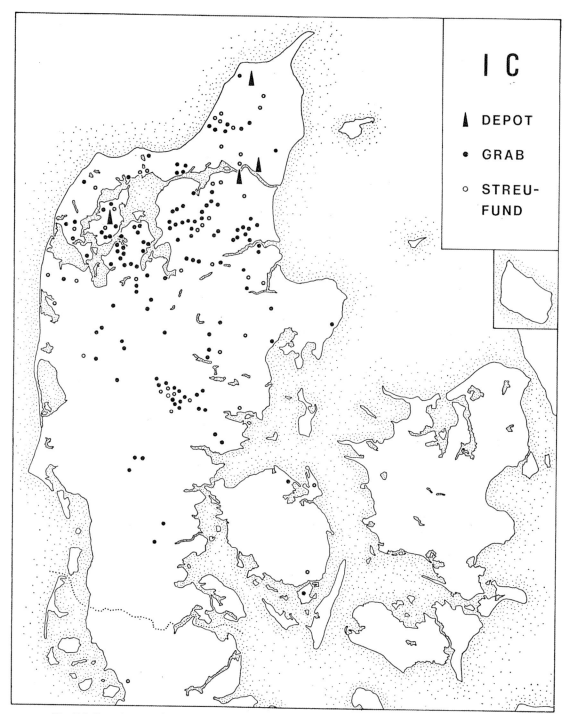

Fig. 7.3. Distribution of type Ic daggers in Denmark and northern Germany (after Lomborg 1973).

How and why did the Lent dagger end up in the Netherlands?

A closer look at the distribution of the type Ic daggers as presented by Lomborg (1973: fig. 14) shows that the Lent dagger is clearly an outlier (cf. Fig. 7.3). As already noted, northern Jutland is the region in which most of these daggers have come to light. A smaller, though dense accumulation is

situated in central Jutland. The area in between the clusters has also yielded specimens. The remainder of the Danish Ic type dagger finds originate from the southern half of the Jutlandic peninsula (seven daggers) and the isles of Fyn and Tåsinge (three and one specimens, respectively). The other Danish islands, including Sealand (Sjælland), are devoid of finds. From the overview by Kühn (1979:

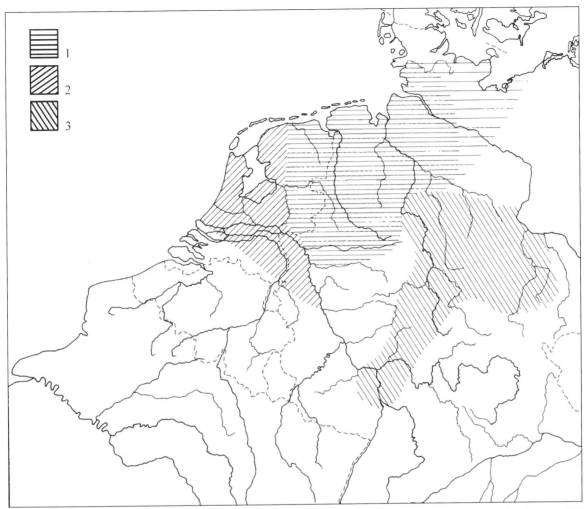

Fig. 7.4. Distribution of different Bell Beaker Culture branches in the Netherlands and the adjacent regions (after Lanting 2007/2008). Area "2" shows the distribution area of the central Dutch Bell Beaker group.

39), it follows that parallel-flaked daggers are very rare in Schleswig-Holstein. Scandinavian type daggers from the same district have also been studied by Siemann, together with those from other districts in northern Germany (northern Brandenburg, the northern part of Lower Saxony, Mecklenburg-Vorpommern and Westphalia). She arrives at the same conclusion (Siemann 2003: 29). From other studies about Germany, in particular concerning Hessen, Lower Saxony, Mecklenburg-Vorpommern, Rhineland and Westphalia a similar picture emerges (Bantelmann 1982; Bargen 1983, vol. A: 128; Rassmann 1993: 19; Siemann 2005: 105; Strahl 1990, vol, 1: 253).

The previously mentioned distribution pattern, in particular the practically empty zone south of Denmark, does not suggest that the dagger from Lent arrived in the Netherlands by exchange down-the-line. Instead, the artefact in question is probably evidence of directional exchange. The dagger most likely reflects a visit that was paid by people from northern Jutland to the central Netherlands

or the other way around. This interpretation accords well with Vandkilde's stance (2005) about the emergence of a Beaker group in northern Jutland, which she relates to the introduction of metallurgy from abroad (cf. Sarauw 2006). As the Danish archaeological record does not hint at large-scale migrations, the local people are thought to have adopted foreign cultural habits, *i.e.* incorporated elements of the bell beaker package, such as pottery. Since contacts over long distances, in particular with the southwest, are claimed to have been an important factor in the transformation, Vandkilde (2005:28) nonetheless surmises that some people did cross cultural borders:

> Foreign people with metallurgical knowledge may well to some limited extent have been involved in the project. Alternatively, agents from northern Jutland may have travelled to foreign lands, learned the craft of metalworking there and returned to Jutland as persons of knowledge and influence.

The author sympathises with this outlook and thinks it may

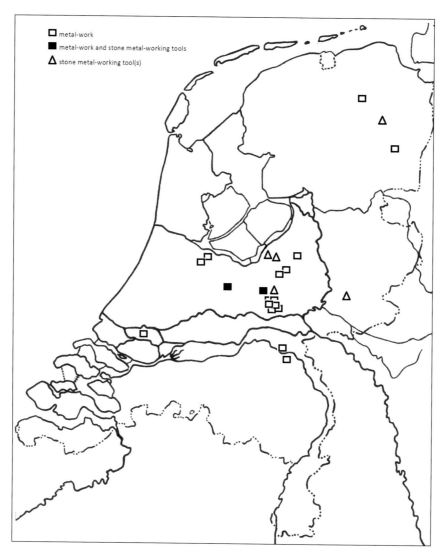

Fig. 7.5. Distribution of metal-work (including a droplet) belonging to the Bell Beaker Culture and stone metal-working tools in the Netherlands. Only undisputable finds have been included (data after Van der Beek 2004; Butler & Van der Waals 1966; Drenth & Freudenberg 2009; Drenth & Schrijer in prep., Drenth & Williams 2011; Lanting 2007/2008; Lanting & van der Plicht 1999/2000; Lanting & van der Waals 1976; Metz 1975; Moree et al. 2011).

serve as an explanatory framework for the Lent dagger. The artefact comes from a location that falls within the distribution area of the central Dutch Bell Beaker group and this can hardly be a coincidence (Fig. 7.4). Following Vandkilde's model, the dagger under consideration can be assigned to this branch of the Bell Beaker Culture. As rightfully signalled by her, similarities in decoration on pottery indicate direct contacts with the Beaker group in northern Jutland. What linked both regions may indeed have been metallurgy. A strong connection between the central Dutch Bell Beaker group and metalworking transpires from the archaeological record (cf. Butler & Van der Waals 1966). The geographical distribution of copper and gold items, as well as their associations, like the characteristic bell beakers

of the Veluwe type, attests to this connection. It appears that, within the Netherlands and the adjacent Belgian and German areas, Bell Beaker metalwork concentrates in the centre of the Netherlands (Fig. 7.5; apart from the references mentioned in the caption to this figure see Bantelmann 1982; Bargen 1983; Warmenbol 2004). This cluster coincides with a concentration of stone metal-working tools. Two of these sites can be attributed with (near) certainty to the central Dutch Bell Beaker group on the basis of associated artefacts.

To substantiate further the claim that metallurgy may have governed the interaction between the northern Jutlandic Beaker group and the central Dutch Bell Beaker group, one can refer to similarities in typology and composition of metal-work (on this topic, see Vandkilde 1996: chap.

8). Illustrative is a gold ornament with oar-shaped ends, presumably a necklace, from a barrow at Bennekom (Butler 1956; Glasbergen 1956). Typologically related objects were discovered in the Limfjord region (Vandkilde 1996: 184ff).

Supposedly, the Lent dagger represents gift exchange meant to establish, maintain or strengthen the network and alliances between the Beaker group in northern Jutland and the central Dutch Bell Beaker group. It must have been a valuable item since, in a detailed study about flint daggers and their production in northern Jutland, Sarauw (2006: 259) writes:

> The first group of daggers, which was intended for daily use and most likely used by men, women and children, encompasses smaller lancet-shaped daggers made on whatever flint was available. The second group comprises larger daggers of good quality exemplified by most of the daggers in the Danish hoards. Such daggers were alienable objects, commodities, intended for exchange. However, when exchanged these daggers became personal belongings of men symbolising maleness and perhaps warriorhood… The last group of daggers belongs to the same general sphere. However, these daggers of superior size and quality, represented by the I C subtype, were the finest and probably most attractive daggers a male could posses[s]. Such daggers ended their life in a burial of a prominent male, hence possibly reflecting the emergence of a ranking system.

Several arguments can be given to endorse the hypothesis that Ic daggers were highly prestigious. Firstly, in Denmark they are relatively rare among the Scandinavian flint daggers of type I (Lomborg 1973; Sarauw 2006: 246). The same holds true for northern and northwestern Germany (see above).

In addition, experimental archaeology shows that the production of a type Ic dagger must have required substantially more time than that of a 'normal' Scandinavian type I dagger. The experiments mentioned below give only an impression of the time investment, as Sarauw (2006: 231, 250) is undoubtedly right in assuming that the production time was originally shorter due to skill and specialisation. He also rightfully points out that the size of daggers determines the production time. Stafford (2003: 1545, table 1) needed on average 10.6–11.1 hours per specimen to make 15 type Ic daggers. Nunn (quoted in Sarauw 2006: 250) estimates that he spent 10 to 29 hours on each replica. In comparison, replicas of Ia and Ib type daggers (typology after Lomborg 1973) were made within a time span (on average) ranging from 2.5 to 3.15 hours (Sarauw 2006: 232; Stafford 2003: 1541). From the previously mentioned experimental replication study by Stafford (2003), it follows that the production of type Ic daggers is relatively time consuming, because the dagger's surface has to be ground and polished for successful parallel flaking. The average time he mentions was 4.9 hours. For the duration of the platform preparation, parallel flaking by pressure and pressure retouch takes an average of 3.7 hours.

A final argument to be mentioned here is the techno-logical skill needed to produce a type Ic dagger. Of all Scandinavian type I daggers, the Ic variety is the most difficult to produce (e.g. Apel 2000: 148, 2001: 40; Sarauw 2006: 247). Only in the Limfjord area did flint smiths have the required knowledge and technological skills.

That the Lent dagger possibly arrived in the central Netherlands as a broken specimen does not mean it had lost its high symbolic value. Sarauw (2006: 256) stresses that shorter daggers apparently also were of high symbolic value, particularly in flint-deprived regions of Scandinavia. Ethnographic analogies, in the form of stone axes, from New Guinea Highland can also support this idea (Højlund 1979 quoted by Sarauw (2006)).

Final remarks

Beuker & Drenth (1999: 24 (116), 31 (123), note 14; 2006: 297f) have noted that, in comparison to Dutch specimens, Scandinavian type flint daggers from Denmark as well Schleswig-Holstein have been found statistically significantly more often in graves. It appears that, within Denmark, type Ic daggers are particularly well-known from graves, more than the other type I varieties (e.g. Lomborg 1973; Sarauw 2006: 247; Vandkilde 1996: 281). The Lent dagger does not follow this pattern. There are no indications of a provenance from a grave. Instead the object might be a deposition in or immediately next to the river Waal, though the meaning as well as underlying motifs and reasons remain unclear. As noted above, there are no clues in the form of associated artefacts or features. Nevertheless, assessed in its wider context, the artefact possibly illustrates a recontextualisation. Thus, import does not imply that artefacts were used in the same way and had identical meanings as they did at their place of origin. In other words, the Lent dagger was perhaps fitted into and treated according to local or regional cultural customs and norms. Though, admittedly, Scandinavian type flint dagger finds from Dutch rivers, streams, etc. are hardly known. As a possible counterpart for the Lent dagger, reference can only be made to two specimens from gullies. One of them, a type I dagger, stems from lot J97 at Emmeloord (Beuker & Drenth 2006: 297, with further references), the other (most probably type II or VI and presumably an item re-used during the Iron Age!) was discovered at Groningen-Kielerbocht (Niekus *et al.* 2011, chap. 5.2).

Lastly, attention should simply be drawn to the clear-cut contextual differences in the Netherlands between, on the one hand, Scandinavian type flint daggers of type I, dated to the Bell Beaker Culture and the Early Bronze Age (*ca.* 1900–1600 BC) and the copper daggers of the Bell Beaker Culture. According to the figures reported by Bloemers (1968) about 11% of the former artefacts found come from graves. A lower percentage was found in more recent investigations by Beuker & Drenth (1999; 2006). By contrast, the 11 Bell Beaker copper daggers listed in the overviews by Butler & Van der Waals (1966) and Lanting & Van der Waals (1976, especially table IV) are without exception grave finds.

This distinction begs an explanation. For this reason alone, research into daggers should be continued.

Notes

1. Kühn (1979: 39) has raised the objection that parallel retouching is already known from 'blade daggers' found, for example, in southern France and Switzerland and which predate the Scandinavian type flint daggers. It should be stressed that these older specimens display semi-parallel retouch and, true as his observation may be, Kühn's criticism with respect to Lomborg's ideas about parallel flaking is therefore of no relevance here. The Lent dagger is an example of full parallel retouch. Kühn (1979) himself acknowledges that this kind of flaking should be regarded as something which developed in northern Jutland.

2. It might, however, be that a second specimen was found in the Netherlands near Oldenzaal, province of Overijssel (Bloemers 1968: 96, fig. 87 and pl. LII: no. 3; Lanting 2007/2008: 295). Unfortunately the author has not yet been able to study the object itself.

Acknowledgments

Thanks are due to Dr C. Frieman who took care that this paper was published in correct and proper English. I am also grateful to drs D. Keijers and drs F. de Vries for helping to gather the information about the Lent dagger and for taking the wonderful photograph shown here as Fig. 7.2, respectively.

References

Apel, J. 2000. Flint daggers and technological knowledge. Production and consumption during LN I. In: D. Olauson & H. Vandkilde (eds.), *Form, Function & Context. Material Culture Studies in Scandinavian Archaeology*. Acta Archaeologica Lundensia, Series in 8° 31. Lund: Almqvist & Wiksell International. 135–154.

Apel, J. 2001. *Daggers, Knowledge & Power. The Social Aspects of Flint-Dagger Technology in Scandinavia 2350–1500 cal BC*. Coast to Coast-book 3. Uppsala: Department of Archaeology and Ancient History, Uppsala University.

Bantelmann, N. 1982. *Endneolithische Funde im rheinisch-westfälischen Raum*. Offa-Bücher 44. Neumünster: Karl Wachholtz.

Bargen, D. 1983. *Die Funde des Spätneolithikums im Weser-Ems-Gebiet*. Unpublished MA thesis, University of Kiel.

Beek, Z. van der 2004. An ancestral way of burial. Late Neolithic graves in the southern Netherlands. In: M. Besse & J. Desideri

(eds), *Graves and Funerary Rituals during the Late Neolithic and the Early Bronze in Europe (2700–2000 BC)*. BAR international series 1284. Oxford: Archaeopress. 157–194.

Beuker, J. R. & Drenth, E. 1999. 'Scandinavische' dolken in Drenthe. *Nieuwe Drentse Volksalmanak* 116: 3–33 (95–125).

Beuker, J. R. & Drenth, E. 2006. Scandinavian type flint daggers from the province of Drenthe, the Netherlands. In: G. Körlin & G. Weisgerber (eds.), *Stone Age–Mining Age*. Der Anschnitt, Beiheft 19. Bochum: Deutsches Bergbau-Museum. 285–300.

Bloemers, J. H. F. 1968. Flintdolche vom skandinavischem Typus in den Niederlanden. *Berichten van de Rijksdienst voor het Oudheidkundig Bodemonderzoek* 18: 47–110.

Butler, J. J. 1956. The Late Neolithic Gold Ornament from Bennekom. II. The Affiliations of the Bennekom Ornament. *Palaeohistoria* 5: 59–71.

Butler, J. J. & Van der Waals, J. D. 1966. Bell Beakers and early metal-working in the Netherlands. *Palaeohistoria* 12: 41–139.

Drenth, E. & Freudenberg, M. 2009. Een bijzondere ontdekking bij Eext: Twee stenen voor metaalbewerking van de klokbekercultuur. *Nieuwe Drentse Volksalmanak* 126: 161–167.

Drenth, E. & Williams, G.L. 2011. Het geheim van de smid? Een opmerkelijk depot van de Klokbekercultuur uit Hengelo (Gld.). In: H. M. van der Velde, N.L. Jaspers, E. Drenth & H.B.G. Scholte Lubberink (eds.), *Van graven in de prehistorie en dingen die voorbijgaan*. Leiden: Sidestone Press: 87–113.

Glasbergen, W. 1956. The Late Neolithic gold ornament from Bennekom. I. The discovery. *Palaeohistoria* 5: 53–58.

Högberg, A. & Olausson, D. 2007. *Scandinavian Flint – an Archaeological Perspective*. Aarhus: Aarhus University Press.

Hulst, R. S. 1972. Elst. *Bulletin van de Koninklijke Nederlandse Oudheidkundige Bond* 71(4): 12.

Højlund, F. 1979. Stenøkser i Ny Guineas Højland. Betydningen af prestigesymboler for reproduktionen af et stammesamfund. *Hikuin* 5: 31–48.

Jensen, J. A. 1972. Bopladsen Myrhøj. 3 hustomter med klokkebægerkeramik. *Kuml*: 61–122.

Kühn, H. J. 1979. *Das Spätneolithikum in Schleswig-Holstein*. Offa-Bücher 40. Neumünster: Karl Wachholtz.

Lanting, J. N. 2007/2008. De NO-Nederlandse/NW-Duitse klokbekergroep: culturele achtergrond, typologie van het aardewerk, datering, verspreiding en grafritueel. *Palaeohistoria* 49/50: 11–326.

Lanting, J. N. & Van der Plicht, J. 1999/2000. De ¹⁴C-chronologie van de Nederlandse pre- en protohistorie, III: Neolithicum. *Palaeohistoria* 41/42: 1–110.

Lanting, J. N. & Van der Plicht, J. 2001/2002. De ¹⁴C-chronologie van de Nederlandse pre- en protohistorie, IV: bronstijd en vroege ijzertijd. *Palaeohistoria* 43/44: 117–262.

Lanting, J. N. & Van der Waals, J. D. 1976. Beaker Culture relations in the Lower Rhine Basin. In: J. N. Lanting & J. D. van der Waals (eds.), *Glockenbechersymposion Oberried 1974*. Bussum, Haarlem: Fibula-Van Dishoeck. 1–80.

Lomborg, E. 1973. *Die Flintdolche Dänemarks. Studien über Chronologie und Kulturbeziehungen des südskandinavischen Spätneolithikums*. Nordiske Fortidsminder Serie B – in quarto I. Copenhagen: Det kgl. nordiske Oldskriftselskab.

Metz, W. H. 1975. Een stenen metaalbewerkingsinstrument uit Ermelo. *Westerheem* 24: 91–100.

Moree, J. M., Bakels, C. C., Bloo, S. B. C., Brinkhuizen, D. C.,

Houkes, R. A., Jongste, P. F. B., Van Trierum, M. C., Verbaas, A. & Zeiler, J. T. 2011. Barendrecht-Carnisselande: bewoning van een oeverwal vanaf het Laat Neolithicum tot in de Midden-Bronstijd. *BOORbalans* 7: 15–154.

Niekus, M. J. L. Th., Stapert, D. & Johansen, L. 2011: Vuursteen. In: A. R. Wieringa (ed.), *Sporen uit de ijzertijd langs de Hunze. Een opgraving aan de Kielerbocht te Groningen*. Groningen: Stadse Fratsen 29. 37–48.

Rassmann, K. 1993. *Spätneolithikum und frühe Bronzezeit im Flachland zwischen Elbe und Oder*. Beiträge zur Ur- und Frühgeschichte Mecklenburg-Vorpommerns 28. Lübstorf: Archäologisches Landesmuseum für Mecklenburg-Vorpommern and Archäologische Gesellschaft für Mecklenburg und Vorpommern.

Sarauw, T. 2006. Early Late Neolithic dagger production in northern Jutland: Marginalised production or source of wealth? *Bericht der Römisch-Germanischen Kommission* 87: 213–272.

Siemann, C. 2003. *Flintdolche Norddeutschlands in ihrem grabrituellen Umfeld*. Universitätsforschungen zur prähistorischen Archäologie 97. Bonn: Dr. Rudolf Habelt.

Siemann, C. 2005. Flintdolche skandinavischen Typs im Rheinland, Westfalen, Hessen und im südlichen Niedersachsen. *Nachrichten aus Niedersachsens Urgeschichte* 74: 85–135.

Stafford, M. 2003. The parallel-flaked flint daggers of Late Neolithic Denmark: an experimental perspective. *Journal of Archaeological Science* 30(12): 1537–1550.

Strahl, E. 1990. *Das Endneolithikum im Elb-Weser-Dreieck*. Veröffentlichungen der urgeschichtlichen Sammlungen des Landesmuseums zu Hannover 36. Hildesheim: August Lax.

Vandkilde, H. 1996. *From Stone to Bronze. The Metalwork of the Late Neolithic and Earliest Bronze Age in Denmark*. Jutland Archaeological Society Publications 32. Aarhus: Jutland Archaeological Society.

Vandkilde, H. 2005. A Review of the Early Late Neolithic Period in Denmark: Practice, Identity and Connectivity. *www.jungsteinSITE.de*.

Warmenbol, E. 2004. Le début des âges des Métaux en Belgique. In: M. Vander Linden & L. Salanova (eds.), *Le troisième millénaire dans le nord de la France et en Belgique*. Mémoire de la Société Préhistorique Française 35, Anthropologica et Præhistorica 115. Brussels, Paris: Koninklijke Belgisch Maatschappij voor Antropologie en Prehistorie/Société royale belge d'Anthropologie et de Préhistoire, Société Préhistorique Française. 27–48.

BLOODY DAGGERS: A DISCUSSION OF THE FUNCTION OF LATE NEOLITHIC FLINT DAGGERS FROM A SOUTH SCANDINAVIAN POINT OF VIEW

Jeanette Varberg

The rise of a trading network in the South Scandinavian Late Neolithic brought a variety of new artefacts and ideas that shaped a new set of personal gear for a major segment of the society. A new kind of male identity appeared in the archaeological material, the dagger being its iconic item – but what was the function of the dagger?

The Late Neolithic in South Scandinavia was part of the trading network established in Early Bronze Age Europe and, more specifically, also underwent the same changes in the institutions of society which can be seen further south. This paper argues that these changes create new social identities in the Late Neolithic centred around warriors, as suggested by Helle Vandkilde and others (Sarauw 2007b; Vandkilde 1996, 2003, 2006). The establishment and control of the trading networks most likely required well-armed men. The concept of silent trade is proposed as a way the trading system could have been introduced in new territory on the outskirts of Europe, such as South Scandinavia, where interpersonal violence, raiding and distrust may have been part of the local perception of and reaction to strangers. The peaceful past is a myth (Vandkilde 2003:126), and the flint dagger must be considered as the weapon it is – at least when it accompanies a warrior.

Function of the flint dagger: unknown

The dagger was evidently of great importance in the 3rd and early 2nd millennia BC throughout Europe; and it does take up much space in both the archaeological record and in the interpretation of the Late Neolithic and Early Bronze Age societies. Yet, we still must ask what its function was. For decades, researchers have been discussing the function of flint daggers, the reason being that the stone tool imitates a metal weapon; but it does not seem to be an efficient combat weapon due to the fragile flint material (Sarauw 2007b: 74), an enigma many scholars have tried to solve. The main conclusion so far is that it is a status object belonging to the male sphere (Earle 2004; Vandkilde 1996). Some suggest that daggers were given to boys becoming men in rites of passage, as a marker of their newfound social identity as men and, perhaps, even as warriors. Others even see the flint dagger as an item used in complicated death rituals (Sarauw 2007b: 77; Stensköld 2004). Jan Apel's studies show that the flint dagger is an excellent hunting tool for slaughtering game. As a consequence, daggers could be considered to be the blades used to deliver the *coup the grâce* in hunting (Apel 2001: 311). A version of this interpretation is put forward by Niels Skak-Nielsen, who convincingly argues that the function of the dagger should be understood as a part of ritualised society where sacrificing livestock played a central role in the cult. In his opinion, the flint daggers were used only to sacrifice animals and, therefore, had no use in battle. He further states that the Late Neolithic was a peaceful period without warfare (Skak-Nielsen 2009: 357). Nevertheless, one can point to the fact that all the interpretations of these daggers require the act of cutting flesh and spilling blood.

Several authors, among them Catherine Frieman, have stated that, as the daggers vary considerably in size and form, they should probably not be interpreted as having had only one, main function, but must be considered to have had more than one purpose (Frieman 2010: 39). Considering the span of almost a thousand years in which the flint dagger was in use; it places the daggers in several spheres in society regarding their function and use, and puts all the interpretations presented above into play.

The web of exchange: dagger production and trade in the Late Neolithic

In the 3rd millennium the Early Bronze Age communities in Central- and Western Europe largely comprised Bell Beaker groups. These culture groups initiated a metallurgical expansion and established an extensive exchange network mainly based on metal (Vandkilde 1996; Kristiansen & Larsson 2005: 112, 116). Thus, the material evidence in the

Fig. 8.1. Type IC bifacial flint daggers. Both daggers measures 40cm. From private collection (right) and a grave excavated in 1873 in Aarhus, Denmark (left) (photo: Bo Lavindsgaard, Moesgaard Museum).

South Scandinavian Late Neolithic I (2350–1950 BC) was influenced by Atlantic Bell Beaker groups. The material evidence in the Late Neolithic I in South Scandinavia is especially characterised by type I flint daggers from North Jutland, Denmark, which were produced by the thousands during the period (Fig. 8.1). The daggers were probably inspired by copper daggers. Both the early lanceolate ones and the later fish-tailed ones were inspired by daggers of flint or metal from the continent: the lanceolate ones indicating contacts with the Bell Beaker culture in south-west Europe and England, the fishtail ones with the Únetice culture south of the Baltic (Lomborg 1973:18ff). The dagger – both metal- and flint daggers – became an iconic item copied and traded through the European landscapes; the very symbol of ideas travelling along new pathways created by a desire for metal in the 3rd millennia BC (Frieman 2012). A web of exchange spread across Europe and showed a high level of interaction not seen before; it created the first building-stones of the Bronze Age societies (Fig. 8.2).

A combination of the desire to be integrated into the European exchange network and the appearance of high quality flint raw material sources probably granted the right conditions for an innovating new Neolithic technology in the northern part of the Danish peninsula. In addition, the South Scandinavian bifacial flint knapping technology in the Late Neolithic is one of the most sophisticated known in the world. The technology was only mastered and produced in the Danish area, mainly because of the high level of skill required of knappers to undertake this bifacial knapping technology and of the need for high quality mined flint, which was only found in the Danish area (Apel 2001; Eriksen 2010; Stafford 1998; Varberg 2007). The intensification of previously known technologies and the introduction of new elements of material culture (i.e. Bell Beakers, archer graves and metal) indicate that there was a new 'know-how' (Apel 2001), a major change that took place in society perhaps over just a few generations (Prieto-Martínez 2008:153).

The centralisation of production enables comparative studies of the South Scandinavian flint daggers, among them the type I daggers which are remarkably widely distributed across Europe. They are found in large quantities as far away as northern Scandinavia, Poland, the Rhine Delta and in graves in the heart of the Únetice culture in Central Europe (Agthe 1989; Apel 2001:296ff). Moreover, as early as the beginning of dagger production in Denmark, the distribution of the flint daggers demonstrates that Rogaland on the Norwegian west coast was involved in, what seems to have been a regular exchange of materials with Jutland (Solberg 1994: 116). The exchange system shows clear evidence of long term interaction between these two regions from the beginning of the Late Neolithic until period III in the Bronze Age; and contacts were probably maintained by seasonal travel by ships which may only have been able to cross the fierce North Sea in the summertime.

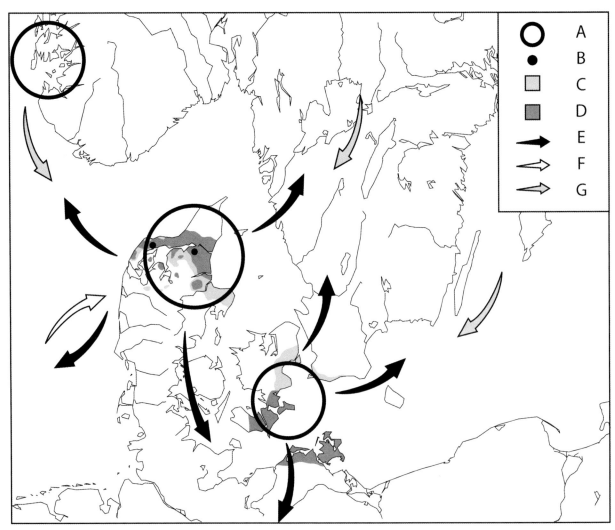

Fig. 8.2. General outline of the contact areas of the exchange networks in the LN I and possible communication routes. A: Primary contact areas based on flint exchange. B: Flint mines. C: Deposits of Danian flint. D: Deposits of Senonian flint. E: Exchange routes of flint products. F: Metal products from the west European Beaker Culture. G: Products from Scandinavia? (based on: Becker 1993; Lomborg 1973; Solberg 1994; Vandkilde 1996; Apel 2001; Varberg 2005a; Graphics Ea Rasmussen, Moesgaard Museum).

Subsequently, in the Late Neolithic, daggers were produced mainly throughout the Danish area, but also in northern Germany and Sweden, and local types evolved; but the distribution of the type I dagger probably originated in the northern part of Jutland in Late Neolithic I. Later, in Late Neolithic II (1950–1700 BC), the area lost influence and the southeast part of Sealand, Denmark, became the prime production and exchange centre for the flint dagger (Fig. 8.3). As early as Late Neolithic I, on the basis of Neolithic technology, it seems very probable that the south Scandinavian area took part in the earliest European Bronze Age exchange network. The old Neolithic tradition of producing fine flint objects was upheld and improved on the verge of the Bronze Age, but it had transitioned into a new form which was influenced by interaction with Western Europe.

It therefore seems possible that the foundations of a stratified society emerged through interaction and exchange with the earliest Bronze Age cultures in the beginning of Late Neolithic I. The production of flint daggers was carried out by highly skilled flint smiths, and it most likely took many years for an apprentice to master the full craftsmanship (Apel 2001). Thus, it can be argued that the production of flint daggers in great numbers required a social organisation or institution that controlled both the production and the exchange. This probably implied an elite's leadership (Earle 2004; Kristiansen 1987; Vandkilde 1996).

Unfortunately, the elites are almost absent in the archaeological material, both in terms of high ranking burials and monumental house structures. In a few cases, monumental burial mounds are built during the first half of the Late Neolithic, which can indicate a certain level

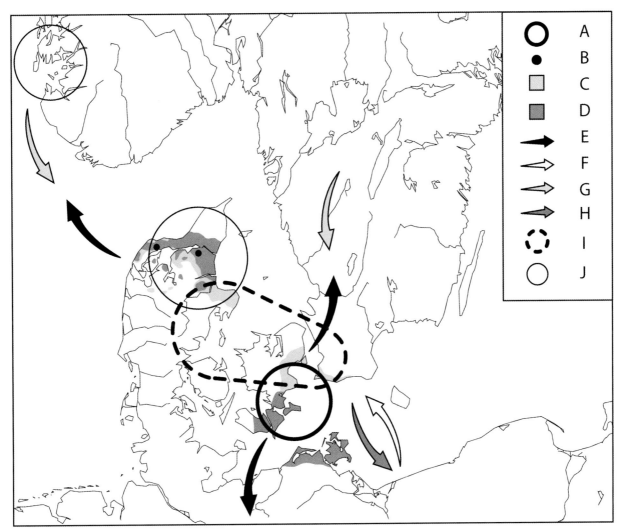

Fig. 8.3. General outline of the contact areas of the exchange networks in the LN II and possible communication routes. A: Primary contact areas based on flint exchange. B: Flint mines. C: Deposits of Danian flint. D: Deposits of Senonian flint. E: Exchange routes of flint products. F: Metal products from the central European Únětice Culture. G: Products from Scandinavia? H: Exchange routes of amber, fur and perhaps salt to continental Europe. I: Primary contact areas based on metal exchange. J: Secondary contact areas based on flint exchange (based on: Lomborg 1973; Becker 1993; Solberg 1994; Vandkilde 1996; Rassmann 2000; Saile 2000; Apel 2001; Varberg 2005a; Graphics Ea Rasmussen, Moesgaard Museum).

of social organisation and interaction (Schiellerup 1991; Varberg 2005a, 2005b). Nevertheless, the graves in the northern part of Jutland are generally sparsely equipped with few personal items. Often, a flint dagger in a stone cist or a megalithic tomb is the only evidence for a Late Neolithic burial (Fig. 8.4). However, exceptions are found in 66 burials known as 'archer's graves' where men were equipped with over-sized daggers (the type IC daggers which could reach 40cm) and arrowheads, showing a clear division between common male graves with smaller daggers and the archer's graves, which indicated warrior-like identities (Sarauw 2007b: 66). This funeral practise was most likely introduced through contacts with the Bell Beaker groups in west and central Europe. Furthermore, the presence of the

archery graves in western Denmark suggests that rank might have been present in Late Neolithic society (Sarauw 2007b: 78). Therefore, this funeral practise can imply that a new order of social structures were forming through contact with differently structured societies in other parts of Europe, most likely indicating a sudden rise in more complex societies in Northern Jutland during the first part of the Late Neolithic. The flint daggers were an outcome of the intensive contact with the Bell Beaker groups and the original flint dagger function may be understood as part of a new set of ideas introduced in a very limited timespan – perhaps only one generation (Prieto-Martínez 2008: 153).

The early trade with metal and other goods – among them Jutlandic flint daggers – which continued to flow along

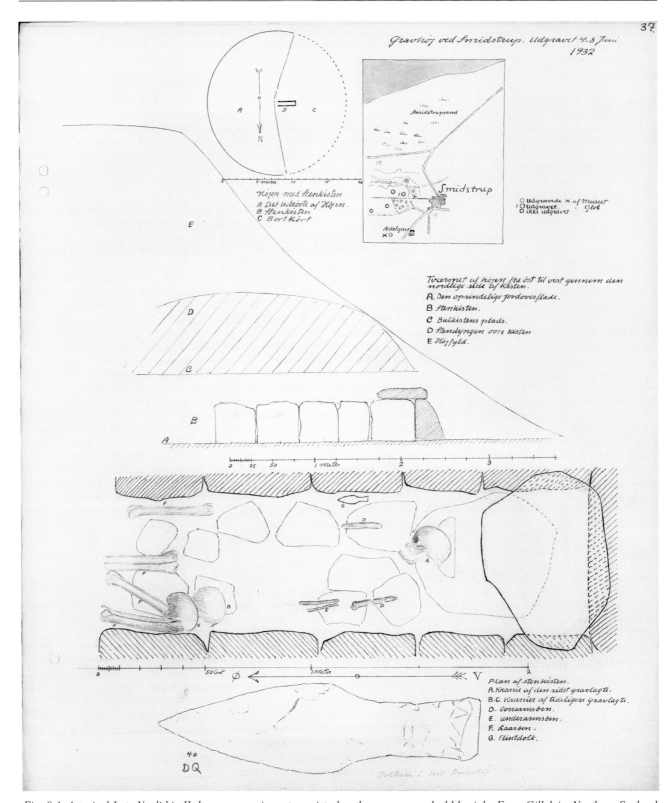

Fig. 8.4. *A typical Late Neolithic II dagger grave in a stone cist placed among several old burials. From Gilleleje, Northern Sealand. Excavated and drawn by Johannes Glob. Illustration dated 1932 (from Glob nd).*

the exchange routes from the north criss-crossing the vast European plain through river valleys and coastlines, could also be seen as resources vulnerable to raids from unfriendly foreigners seeking an opportunity to get hold of metal. There is no question that the travellers must have been armed to defend their goods. Most likely, the travellers were members of a few progressive families, tradesmen, or other groups of people well connected both locally and inter-regionally (Sarauw 2008: 39). Perhaps they strived to travel through the more unpopulated parts of Europe and travel by boat along the rivers – unseen or unreachable from the river bank; but in the end they probably had to be warriors travelling together as a group to protect themselves and their goods. Frieman suggest that the dagger, both metal and flint, was a boundary object bridging social gaps between disparate groups of people, and providing them with a common technological language (Frieman 2012: 456). I agree that the dagger may very well be a sign of a common understanding; but not necessarily a peaceful one.

The web of exchange exposed the travellers to the desire for metal from foreign people and the need for protection became more prominent and urgent than in the past periods (Beyneix 2012: 220). The dagger emerged in a time of increasing conflict; and perhaps it was an item invented to force respect and as defence, the mark of the metal-traders who also travelled in warrior-bands. Later, the dagger became a common object of trade which is found in graves and hoards in all parts of Europe, and it seems very likely that a warrior identity grew strong during the 3rd millennium BC – and that the dagger was part of the weapon-kit.

One could argue, as Skak-Nielsen does, that warfare was absent in the Late Neolithic due to very scarce archaeological evidence of warfare other than the dagger graves (Skak-Nielsen 2009: 357); but research conducted in the last 10–15 years says otherwise. On the contrary, warfare was probably always endemic in the past; and its presence in the Late Neolithic is somewhat clarified by Bell Beaker warrior burials which show uniformity in weapon types from northern Africa to Scandinavia (Osgood & Monks 2010; Vandkilde 2003, 2006, 2011). The dagger was part of the Bell Beaker traveller's weaponry and the flint dagger was perhaps the South Scandinavian version of a new weapon-type that caught on fast. In the following, I will try to widen the perspective concerning exchange and warfare in the 3rd millennium BC.

Distrust and exchange: the concept of silent trade

The Danish Stone Age has a European record in skeletal evidence of violence from the Late Mesolithic and Early Neolithic (Schulting 2006: 227). Nearly ten out of 100 skeletons from the Late Mesolithic show severe blows from an axe to the skull or fractures caused by an arrow

(Schulting 2006; Thorpe 2006). The substantial number of injuries was probably caused by intense raiding among the hunter-gatherers and early farmers. Later, in the Single Grave Culture (i.e. Corded Ware Culture), violence also proved to be a part of society and the battle axe was the prime weapon. Marks from axes or clubs have been found on 12% of 266 skulls from the Danish Neolithic period, clearly demonstrating the use of the weapon in single combat (Bennike 1985; Vandkilde 2011). The later part of the Stone Age in South Scandinavia was not always peaceful, and should probably be considered as characterised by a society not unfamiliar with raiding and interpersonal violence (Vandkilde 2006). Moreover, changes in material culture and some sort of standardisation covering large areas of Europe at approximately the same time is not a new phenomenon in the Late Neolithic. Inventions such as battle axes, daggers and pressure-flaked arrowheads are particularly inventions connected with warfare, prestige or ideology and spread fast over vast areas (Sarauw 2007a: 46), thereby underlining the importance of the warrior in the Late Neolithic.

During the second part of the 3rd millennium BC, herding and livestock played a central part in the South Scandinavian economy. Open areas of land expanded, the houses got bigger and the average height of men and women increased by approximately 10cm (Bennike 1997; Kristiansen 1987). The influences from Bell Beaker societies are apparent not only in the exchange of flint daggers and metal, but also in the funerary sphere. Men were buried with daggers in place of the previously primary weapon the battle axe as can be seen in other parts of Europe where Bell Beaker people settled or influenced the locals (Vandkilde 2006). The dagger burials symbolise a new warrior-elite from an archaeological point of view; but, nevertheless, in battles and during raids the main weapon remained the bow and arrow.

The flint daggers' symbolic and iconic value in Late Neolithic societies must have been very strong since only a small number of metal daggers are found compared with the great number of flint daggers. Instead of metal daggers, people in South Scandinavia used metal axes, but they are seldom found in graves – instead they are found mainly as wetland depositions (Vandkilde 1996: 36, 1998: 255). Consequently, the flint daggers must have had a function and meaning associated with personal prestige, social identity and the human lifecycle. This observation may explain why the strong new wave of metal objects could not replace the symbolic and iconic meanings interlinked with the flint dagger until metal spearheads and swords were introduced in the last part of the Nordic Bronze Age period I, probably indicating a new formation of society and a different perception of the male (warrior) status (Vandkilde 1998: 256). The flint daggers' function in early Metal Age society is a clear example of how new ideas and changes do not always have the same outcome in the archaeological record. Some new forms are accepted as is (e.g. metal axes), but others are reinterpreted within the context of the local ideology and social practices (e.g. flint daggers). Thus, the flint dagger may have had a significant role in constructing the identity of warriors in Northern Europe.

When it comes to describing warfare and the daggers' function, there is a tendency to overlook the fact that the flint dagger was never the main weapon and, therefore, the presence of warriors in the Late Neolithic should not be concluded solely on the utility of flint daggers as weapons. In the 3rd millennium BC, warriors were engaging in battle from a distance. They were archers, and skeletal evidence from Central Europe, mainly France, showed an increase in arrowheads in burials while the part in hunting in the diet was in decline since the beginning of the Middle Neolithic. Simultaneously, in graves, one can note the presence of many arrows near the corpses in what must have been quivers as well as numerous examples of arrow injuries in the vertebral column (Beyneix 2012: 211, 220). Similar examples from Spain and England leave little doubt that the bow was the main weapon in Late Neolithic conflicts (Fitzpatrick 2011; Schulting 2006; Schulting & Fibiger 2012; Vegas *et al.* 2012).

The daggers were also part of the interpersonal violence in the period: a broken copper-dagger blade set in a vertebra found in the burial cave of Pas-de-Joulie at Trèves is a clear example of hand-to-hand violence (Beyneix 2012: 214). The Danish flint daggers are often found in collective graves in open stone cists or megalithic tombs which were, in most cases, opened by amateurs, making it difficult to link the artefact with the remaining bones (Fig. 8.4) if any of these are left. In most cases, we only have the daggers and that leaves very little material for functional interpretation. However, one grave draws attention even though the skeletal remains are gone. In eastern Jutland, just north of Horsens Fjord, a megalithic tomb 'Stenhøj' was excavated in 1978 by archaeologist and former associate professor at Aarhus University Torsten Madsen. In the middle of the chamber, a 1.8m by 0.80m area of the sand was stained with red-brown to dark-brown colours indicating the position of the burial area with decayed organic material. The burial was placed upon a floor laid in the Late Neolithic and covering the previous burial remains in the tomb; and, moreover, it should be stressed that the Late Neolithic burial was the only burial remaining on that particular floor. Here, close to the westerly upright, lay two pressure-flaked flint daggers side by side, a type I A- and type I B dagger datable to Late Neolithic I. In the middle of the dark coloured burial area lay the broken off tip of a type I dagger (Figs 8.5 and 8.6). It is not unlikely that this fragment represents the cause of death (Madsen in prep.). The burial can be interpreted as a male buried with two flint daggers by his side and part of a third inside his upper torso. One could argue that the third piece could be part of the funerary gifts, as fragments of daggers have been found on the chest or waist in other Late Neolithic

burials (Sarauw 2007b: 70); but none of these graves have been excavated in recent times and the find circumstances can be doubted. The Stenhøj grave may very well be the South Scandinavian parallel to the French example from Tréves in that it underlines the function of the type I flint dagger as a weapon used in interpersonal violence.

Arrows, as well as daggers, seldom leave marks on the skeleton when shot by a skilled archer aiming for vital organs, such as the heart or lungs; therefore, it is difficult for us to determine a cause of death (Schulting 2006). If an arrow is embedded in bone, it was probably fired by a less skilled archer or the victim was caught in an ambush and shot at close range. Compared to the previous skeletal evidence for combat in the Single Grave Culture, there is no evidence of that sort in the Late Neolithic in South Scandinavia. Hence, it appears that battles were no longer fought in close combat, face to face as was the case when the battle axe was the main weapon. In that respect, daggers cut and do not leave the same fractures on bone (mainly the cranial bone) as battle axes and would only in rare cases be recognised as a lethal weapon, such as was the case in the burial cave of Pas-de-Joulie at Trèves and perhaps Stenhøj in eastern Jutland.

In conclusion, the Late Neolithic archer had a central function and fighting probably often occurred at a distance. Examples from southern France show a number of healed projectile injuries from various sites, mainly in the limb bones, which might suggest conflict at some distance; first, because the individual was able to withdraw from the scene and survive, and secondly because the limbs would probably not be the target of choice for archers at close range (Schulting 2006; Schulting & Fibiger 2012: 10). In Spain, Sara Monks has argued that Bell Beaker settlements were located on naturally defended locations and that they were geared towards the use of archery with archers being shielded by high protective walls while still able to observe travellers from a distance (Osgood & Monks 2010: 61).

Distrust towards strangers is a part of the human survival strategy in an unstable society where warfare and raiding is a reality. The opening of the vast Bronze Age trading network initiated by the Bell Beaker phenomenon must have been difficult as it required crossing tribal boundaries in search for metal and other goods. Nevertheless, travelling was part of the Bell Beaker lifestyle – if new isotope research from Great Britain should prove not to be an isolated phenomenon. The individuals found within the Bell Beaker burials also known as the Boscombe Bowmen and the Amesbury Archer all travelled great distances within Europe. Two of the Boscombe Bowmen even proved to have taken two large journeys at a young age (Fitzpatrick 2011: 207). Considering the traces of warfare in the Neolithic, one can only begin to speculate how difficult it must have been for the travellers to cross through Europe (Schulting 2006). One way could be to travel in warrior-bands, with skilled men willing to take risks, and trade with the locals from a distance using bows and arrows to keep others away. Several finds of flint daggers are from deposits dug into the ground; and one could speculate that this practice was part of the Bell Beaker trading strategy when approaching new territory on the outskirts of Europe, such as South Scandinavia. Perhaps the warriors were travelling traders using their bows and arrows to defend themselves against the locals, but still be able to trade with them through *silent trade.*

Silent trade or depot trade is a specialised form of barter in which goods are exchanged without any direct contact between the traders. Generally, one group goes to a customary spot, deposits the goods to be traded, and withdraws, sometimes giving a signal such as a call or a gong stroke. Another group then comes to leave a second set of articles and retreats. The first group returns, removing these new goods if satisfied or leaving them until additions are made. The second group then takes the original wares to conclude the transaction. The classic description of silent trade comes from the works of Herodotus (430 BC), who mentioned the exchange of goods between the Carthaginians and peoples of the west coast of Africa. This widespread institution has also been reported from Siberia, Lapland, West Africa, India, Sri Lanka, and New Guinea. Silent trade is often a response to difficulties in communication due to language barriers or to inequality of cultural advancement between neighbouring peoples (Grierson 1903; Price 1967: 67). A historical source, written by Ibn Batuta, described silent trade in *The Land of Darkness* (probably northern Siberia) in the 1300s:

> Each traveller arriving 'at the Darkness' leaves the goods he has brought there and they retire to their camping-ground. Next day they go back to seek for their goods, and find, opposite them, skins of sable, minever and ermine. If the merchant is satisfied with the exchange, he takes them, but if not, he leaves them. The inhabitants then add more skins, but sometimes they take away their goods and leave the merchants. This is their method of commerce. Those who go there do not know whom they are trading with or whether they be jinn or men, for they never see anyone (Ibn Batuta 1929).

All the same, examples of trading without any face to face contact was probably rare; and ethnographic examples from all over the world rather describe silent trade between armed and distrusting men, saying only a few words and keeping their distance with raised weapons such as was the case in the Manus region of Papua New Guinea visited by Margaret Mead in the first half of the 30th century (Price 1967: 68; Mead 1930).

That some of the deposits of flint daggers were leftovers from a silent trade scenario that went wrong could explain the reason why the bow and arrow was the Bell Beaker warriors' favourite weapon: fighting and trading were both undertaken from a distance. Obviously, I do not state that this was the general trading scene in every case of exchange

in the final part of the Neolithic. I only propose to consider silent trade as a possible scenario in establishing the vast exchange network the desire for metal demanded.

The dagger was not the prime weapon and was probably only used when the fighting got close; and it is difficult to imagine that a weapon accompanying a warrior was not intended for use in combat. One of Skak-Nielsen's main arguments against its use in battle are descriptions from Homer's *Iliad* in which the warriors carry a dagger only for the purpose of sacrificing livestock, and daggers are not mentioned in battle scenes (Skak-Nielsen 2009: 357). He overlooks one important detail. The Greek warriors also carried spear and sword; but, in the Late Neolithic, daggers, an earlier form than the sword, were among the only blade weapons. In other words, the function of the dagger is the root from which the combat sword and the sacrificial dagger both emerge. Therefore, flint daggers – in particular, the type I daggers – should be considered a symbol of warriorhood, part of the warrior identity, and be described as a weapon with multiple functions, all interlinked with a warrior's way of life, including fighting, hunting game and sacrificing livestock.

Women and daggers: the flint dagger as part of domestic life?

The dagger was probably introduced into the Northern parts of Europe as a weapon, but during the following centuries it developed into different shapes and sizes and the number of finds suggest it was widely used throughout the Late Neolithic societies. Thus, the function linked with warriorhood and interpersonal violence may have changed for some of the smaller types. The functional discussion has seldom taken into account the concept that the dagger could be anything else but an object belonging to the male gender rather than considering that some of the tens of thousands of daggers could have been used by women. Later in the Danish Bronze Age, rich female burials in some instances included bronze daggers (Randsborg 2006: 34). It is impossible to know whether the dagger was a new item in marking women's identity and status in the Bronze Age or if it was part of an old tradition of dagger carrying women pointing with its roots in the Late Neolithic. Unfortunately, there is no evidence of women with daggers in Late Neolithic or Early Bronze Age burials in South Scandinavia, so that a final link between the flint daggers and the bronze daggers in female burials is lacking. That being said, in the eastern Bell Beaker group in Central Europe, 18% of copper daggers were found in female graves (Müller 2001). These finds suggest that, in some regions, the copper dagger was used to construct social status in ways that didn't imply warriorhood (Fitzpatrick 2011: 212).

In my opinion, it is probable that the smaller flint daggers

Fig. 8.5. Stenhøj. Late Neolithic burial remains seen from East (Photo: Torsten Madsen).

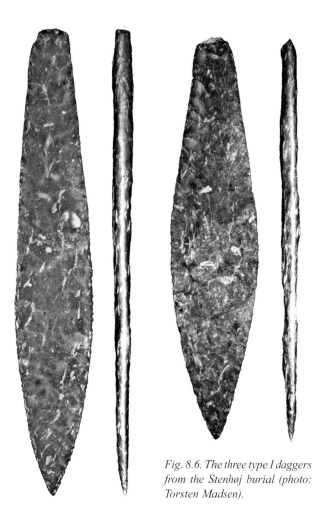

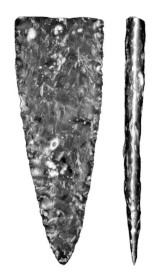

Fig. 8.6. The three type I daggers from the Stenhøj burial (photo: Torsten Madsen).

were used by both sexes. The daggers vary considerably in size and form and most likely also in purpose; especially given the long timespan the dagger was used in South Scandinavia. The smaller daggers could be used in many ways in a busy household; and, in a society where livestock were of great importance, slaughtering animals would have been part of daily life and could very well have been carried out by women.

Final remarks

Flint daggers are excellent tools for cutting flesh and they were probably used for several purposes. The flint daggers of type I were almost certainly both a weapon and a sign of warriorhood; and the dagger idea introduced by the Bell Beaker groups into Northern Jutland was almost certainly associated with a function as a weapon. They could be used in close combat if the fighting happened to be face to face – as was probably the case in the Stenhøj burial, but this does not mean that the same daggers could not be used by warriors in making livestock sacrifices or hunting game. Finally, in the Danish Bronze Age the female dagger burials also opens up a discussion of whether the flint daggers, perhaps just the smaller ones, could also have been used by women in the daily tasks of a farming household.

Acknowledgements

I am very thankful to Torsten Madsen who allowed me to use his unpublished material and photos, without his help this article wouldn't have been the same. I would also like to thank Catherine Frieman and Berit Eriksen for inviting me to participate in this volume, for the support and comments greatly improving the original text.

References

Agthe, M. 1989. Bemerkungen zu Feuersteindolchen im nordwestlichen Verbreitungsgebiet der Aunjetitzer Kultur. *Arbeits- und Forschungsberichte zur sächsischen Bodenkmalpflege* 33: 15–113.

Apel, J. 2001. *Daggers, Knowledge and Power. The Social Aspects of Flint Dagger Technology in Scandinavia 2350–1500 cal. B.C.* Coast to Coast books 3. Uppsala: Uppsala University.

Becker, C. J. 1993. Flintminer og flintdistribution ved Limfjorden. In: J. Lund & J. Ringtved (eds.), *Kort- og råstofstudier omkring Limfjorden. Rapport fra seminarer afholdt 7–8 november 1991 I Bovbjerg samt 23–24 april 1992 I Aalborg*. Limfjordsprojektet rapport 6. Aarhus: Aarhus Universitet. 111–134.

Bennike, P. 1985. *Paleopathology of Danish skeletons: a comparative study of demography, disease and injury*. Copenhagen: Akademisk Forlag.

Bennike, P. 1997. De døde i jægerstenalderen. To gamle mænd fra Korsør Nor. In: L. Pedersen, A. Fisher & B. Aaby (eds.), *Storebælt i 10.000 år. Mennesket, havet og skoven*. Copenhagen: A/S Storebæltsforbindelsen i samarbejde med Kalundborg og Omegns Museum, Miljø- og Energiministeriet, Skov- og Naturstyrelsen samt Nationalmuseet. 99–108.

Beyneix, A. 2012. Neolithic Violence in France: an overview. In: R. Schulting & L. Fibiger (eds.), *Sticks, Stones, and Broken Bones: Neolithic Violence in a European Perspective*. Oxford: Oxford University Press. 207–222.

Earle, T. 2004. Culture Matters in the Neolithic Transition and Emergence of Hierarchy in Thy, Denmark. *American Anthropologist* 106: 111–125.

Eriksen, B. V. 2010. Flintworking in the Danish Bronze Age: the decline and fall of a master craft. In: B. V. Eriksen (ed.), *Lithic technology in metal using societies. Proceedings of a UISPP Workshop, Lisbon, September 2006*. Højbjerg: Jutland Archaeological Society. 81–94.

Fitzpatrick, A. P. 2011. *The Amesbury Archer and the Boscombe Bowmen. Bell Beaker Burials at Boscombe Down, Amesbury, Wiltshire*. Salisbury: Wessex Archaeology.

Frieman, C. J. 2010. Imitation, identity and communication: The presence and problems of skeuomorphs in the Metal Ages. In: Eriksen (ed.) 2010: 33–44.

Frieman, C.J. 2012. Flint daggers, copper daggers, and technological innovation in Late Neolithic Scandinavia. *European Journal of Archaeology* 15(3): 440–464.

Glob, J. ND. Unpublished manuscript, Moesgård Museum's Archives.

Grierson, P. J. H. 1903. *The Silent Trade, a Contribution to the Early History of Human Intercourse*. Edinburgh, Wm. Green & Sons.

Ibn Batuta 1929. *Travels in Asia and Africa, 1325–1354*. Translated by H. A. R. Gibbs. London: Routledge.

Kristiansen, K. 1987. From stone to bronze – the evolution of social complexity in northern Europe 2300 – 1200 B.C. In: E. M. Brumsfield & T. Earle (eds.), *Specialization, Exchange and Complex Societies*. Cambridge: Cambridge University Press. 30–51.

Kristiansen, K. & Larsson, T. B. 2005. *The Rise of Bronze Age Society. Travels, Transmissions and Transformations*. Cambridge: Cambridge University Press.

Mead, M. 1930. Melanesian middlemen. *Natural History* 30: 115–130.

Müller, A. 2001. Gender differentiation in burial rites and grave goods in the eastern or Bohemian-Moravian group of the Bell Beaker Culture. In: F. Nicolis (ed.), *Bell Beakers Today. Pottery, People, Culture, Symbols in Prehistoric Europe*. Trento: Provincia Autonoma di Trento, Servizio Beni Culturali, Ufficio beni Archeologici. 589–599.

Lomborg, E. 1973. *Die Flintdolche Dänemarks. Studien über Chronologie und Kulturbeziehungen des Südskandinavischen Spätneolithikums*. Nordiske Fortidsminder, Serie B in quarto I. Copenhagen: Universitetsforlaget i kommission hos H. H. J. Lynge.

Osgood, R. & Monks, S. 2010. *Bronze Age Warfare*. Stroud: History Press.

Price, J. A. 1967. Conditions in the development of silent trade. *Kroeber Anthropological Society Papers* 36: 67–79.

Prieto-Martínez, M. P. 2008. Bell Beaker communities in Thy: the first Bronze Age society in Denmark. *Norwegian Archaeological Review* 41(2): 115–158.

Randsborg, K. 2006. Opening the oak-coffins. New dates – new perspectives. *Acta Archaeologica* 77: 1–162.

Rassmann, K. 2000. Die Nutzung baltischen Feuerstein an der Schwelle zur Bronzezeit – Krise oder Konjunktur der Feuersteinverarbeitung? *Bericht der Römisch-Germanischen Kommission* 81: 5–36.

Saile, T. 2000. Salz im ur- und frühgeschichtlichen Mitteleuropa

– eine Bestandsaufnahme. *Bericht der Römisch-Germanischen Kommission* 81: 129–234.

Sarauw, T. 2007a. On the outskirts of the European Bell Beaker phenomenon – the Danish case. *www.JungsteinSITE.de*

Sarauw, T. 2007b. Male symbols or warrior identities? The 'Archery Burials' of the Danish Bell Beaker Culture. *Journal of Anthropological Archaeology* 26: 65–87.

Sarauw, T. 2008. Danish bell beaker pottery and flint daggers – the display of social identities*? European Journal of Archaeology* 11(1): 23–47.

Schiellerup, P. S. 1991. St. Valbyvej – et senneolitisk højkompleks ved Himmelev, nord for Roskilde. *Aarbøger for nordisk Oldkyndighed og Historie* (1992): 21–56.

Schulting, R. 2006. Skeletal Evidence and Contexts of Violence in the European Mesolithic and Neolithic. In: R. Gowland & C. Knüsel (eds.), *Social Archaeology of Funerary Remains.* Oxford: Oxbow Books. 224–237.

Schulting, R. & Fibiger, L. 2012. Skeletal evidence for interpersonal violence in Neolithic Europe: an introduction. In: Schulting, R. & L. Fibiger (eds.), *Sticks, Stones, and Broken Bones: Neolithic Violence in a European Perspective.* Oxford: Oxford University Press. 1–16.

Skak-Nielsen, N. V. 2009. Flint and metal daggers in Scandinavia and other parts of Europe. A re-interpretation of their function in the Late Neolithic and Early Copper and Bronze Age. *Antiquity* 83(320): 349–358.

Solberg, B. 1994. Exchange and the Role of Import to Western Norway in the Late Neolithic and Early Bronze Age. *Norwegian Archaeological Review* 27(2): 111–126.

Stafford, M. 1998. In search of Hindsgavl: experiments in the production of Neolithic Danish flint daggers. *Antiquity* 72(276): 338–349.

Stensköld, E. 2004. *Att berätta en senneolitisk historia. Sten och metall i södra Sverige 2350–1700 f.Kr.* Stockholm Studies in Archaeology 34. Stockholm: Stockholm University.

Thorpe, N. 2006. Fighting and Feuding in Neolithic and Bronze Age Britain and Ireland. In: T. Otto, H. Thrane & H. Vandkilde (eds.), *Warfare and Society. Archaeological and Social Anthropological Perspectives*. Aarhus: Aarhus University Press. 141–166.

Vandkilde, H. 1996. *From Stone to Bronze. The Metalwork of the Late Neolithic and Earliest Bronze Age in Denmark.* Jutland Archaeological Society Publications 32. Aarhus: Aarhus University Press.

Vandkilde, H. 1998. Metalwork, depositional structure and social practice in the Danish Late Neolithic and earliest Bronze Age. In: C. Mordant, M. Pernot & V. Rychner (eds.), *L'Atelier du bronzier en Europe du XX au VIII siécle avant notre ére. Actes du colloque international "Bronze'96", Neuchâtel et Dijon, 1996. III: Production, circulation et consummation du bronze.* Paris: CTHS. 243–257.

Vandkilde, H. 2003. Commemorative tales: archaeological responses to modern myth, politics, and war. *World Archaeology* 35(1): 126–144.

Vandkilde, H. 2006. Warriors and warrior institutions in Copper Age Europe. In: T. Otto, H. Thrane & H. Vandkilde (eds.), *Warfare and Society. Archaeological and Social Anthropological Perspectives.* Aarhus: Aarhus University Press. 393–422.

Vandkilde, H. 2011. Bronze Age warfare in temperate Europe. In: S. Hansen & J. Müller (eds.), *Sozialarchäologische Perspektiven: Gesellschaftlicher Wandel 5000–1500 v. Chr. Zwischen Atlantik und Kaukasus. Internationale Tagung 15.–18. Oktober 2007 in Kiel.* Archäologie in Euroasien 24. Mainz: Verlag Philipp von Zabern. 365–380.

Varberg, J. 2005a. Oprindelsen til en ny tidsalder. Mellem stenalder og bronzealder i Sydskandinavien 2350–1700 B.C. *Fornvännen. Journal of Swedish Antiquarian Research* 100(2): 81–95.

Varberg, J. 2005b. Flint og metal – mellem stenalder og bronzealder i Sydskandinavien. In: J. Goldhahn (ed.), *Mellan sten och järn. Rapport från det 9:e nordiska bronsåldersymposiet, Göteborg 2003–10–09/12.* Göteborg: Göteborgs Universitet: 67–80.

Varberg, J. 2007. Dawn of a New Age. The Late Neolithic as third space. In: P. Cornell & F. Fahlander (eds.), *Encounters, Materialities, Confrontations: Archaeologies of Social Space and Interaction.* Newcastle: Cambridge Scholars Press. 58–82.

Vegas, J. I., Armendariz, Á., Etxeberria, F., Fernández, M. S. & Herrasti, L. 2012. Prehistoric violence in northern Spain: San Juan ante Portam Latinam. In: R. Schulting & L. Fibiger (eds.), *Sticks, Stones, and Broken Bones: Neolithic Violence in a European Perspective.* Oxford: Oxford University Press. 265–302.

MAKING A POINT: RE-EVALUATING BRITISH FLINT DAGGERS IN THEIR CULTURAL AND TECHNOLOGICAL CONTEXTS

Catherine J. Frieman

During the last quarter of the 3rd millennium BC, flint daggers were produced and deposited around the British Isles. Yet, unlike in the rest of Europe, they have not been comprehensively studied. Consequently, this paper serves firstly as a brief introduction to these daggers, including their formal variation, production context and patterns of deposition. Secondly, it addresses the relationship of these flint daggers to other third millennium British flintworking and to the other contemporary flint daggers being produced and circulated in continental Europe. Finally, it will examine the role played by flint daggers in later 3rd millennium BC Britain and how it relates both to the development of British regional identities at this time and to the relationship between British communities and their kin and trading partners across the English Channel.

Introduction

There is an unfortunate tendency among British archaeologists to describe developments in British (and Irish) prehistory as if they are somehow distinct or isolated from the social world of contemporary continental Europe – as if Britain were Australia, a continent hundreds of kilometres distant from the nearest large landmass – rather than a large island just 35km offshore. While it is clear that people living in the British and Irish islands in prehistory did, at times, hold themselves apart from developments on the continent, many phenomena, such as the adoption of novel lithic technologies at the end of the third millennium BC, cannot be understood without the continental context. The production and use of flint daggers is a phenomenon which characterised much of western and central Europe during the 4th and 3rd millennia BC (Frieman 2012a); but, until recently, no systematic effort has been made to bring the British evidence in line with the much more closely studied flint dagger assemblages from the continent (Frieman 2014). This paper will introduce the British flint dagger assemblage, describe its links to previous generations of flintworking in the British Isles and examine its place within the British Early Bronze Age as well as its wider European context. As a result of this re-examination of a sadly neglected group of flint tools, a new model of interaction among British societies and the wider European Beaker network will be outlined.

Re-examining British flint daggers

The flint daggers recovered from British and Irish contexts have seen relatively little scholarly interest compared to similar objects found in France, Germany, the Netherlands and Scandinavia. The first and only major summary of the English flint daggers was published in 1932 (Grimes 1932) and has been somewhat supplemented through the publication of a handful of papers covering smaller regions within the distribution area that were poorly served by Grimes' work, such as Wales (Green *et al.* 1982) and northern Britain/Scotland (Saville 2012). Additionally,

Table 9.1. Scandinavian flint daggers found in British and Irish contexts.

Find location	Type	Context	References
Acton Bridge, Cheshire	VI	unknown	Longley 1987; Myers & Noble 2009
Allenby Road, Dunstable, Bedfordshire	VI	?settlement or ?burial	Thomas 1956, 1964
Norfolk?	VI	unknown	Clark 1932b
Fransham, Breckland, Norfolk	VI	single find (dry)	Whitcombe 2010
Ludham, Norfolk	Va	?single find (wet)	
West Row Fen, Mildenhall, Suffolk	VI	unknown	Clark 1932b
Stutton, Babergh, Suffolk	VI	unknown	
Bottisham, Lode, Cambridgeshire	VI	unknown	
Ramsgate [West Cliff], Kent	?IV, ?V (?IVb: lanceolate blade, large fins)	hoard (dry)	Hart 2012; Hicks 1878
Upchurch, Swale, Kent	VI	single find	Anon. 1934
Erith (Thames), London	VI	single find (wet)	
Scariff (Scairbh) [Tulia], Co Clare, Ireland	VI	single find (wet)	Clark 1932b; Corcoran 1964; 1966; Day 1895; Macalister 1921

Needham (2005, forthcoming) has incorporated the small minority of British flint daggers from burial contexts into his discussions of Beaker society and technology. Grimes (1932) developed a rough typochronological outline of flint dagger development and noted their links to Beaker funerary rites. For decades, his catalogue of 146 daggers was the only even somewhat comprehensive list of British flint daggers, their find locations and contexts currently published and available for consultation.

To rectify this situation, a new survey of flint daggers from British and Irish contexts was carried out combining information from antiquarian and archaeological publications, county historic environment records and museum catalogues. All museums which appeared to have three or more flint daggers from British contexts in their collections were visited in order to record the individual artefacts and examine the museum records for further data. In the end, just under 400 objects were recorded which appear to be credible or likely flint daggers (Fig 9.1), greatly increasing on Grimes' count; and full morphological, geological and contextual data was able to be recorded for 170 of them (Frieman 2014).

In order to include previously unrecognised examples and to exclude obviously incorrectly identified pieces, rough morphological criteria were developed and adhered to. Items considered to be credible flint daggers:

- Are fully bifacially knapped;
- Are largely flat in profile, lacking a tendency towards plano-convexity or full convexity;
- Are at least 100mm long when complete and unresharpened - traces of resharpening or breakage have allowed for the inclusion of smaller pieces in the catalogue;
- Have a distinct double-edged cutting part with a reasonably pointed tip and a distinct tang part with several different possible base morphologies;

- May belong to recognised types of flint daggers better known in other parts of Europe, specifically the Nordic area.

While obvious typological variation was observed within the assemblage of daggers (Fig. 9.2), no clear regional or chronological patterns in dagger form appear to exist. In fact, based on data from find contexts, where available, and from the handful of radiocarbon dates on contexts with flint daggers, the British flint daggers all appear to have been deposited within quite a short span of time between 2250 and 2000 BC (Harding & Healy 2007; Levitan & Smart 1989; Needham 2005, 2012, forthcoming; Roberts & Prudhoe 2005). Consequently, developing an elaborate typological schema was deemed to be less than productive, but some formal distinctions are worth noting. Most British flint daggers can be described as having triangular to leaf-shaped blades and tapering tangs which make up 46–52% of their length. In general, the widest point of the dagger is in the blade area (Fig. 9.3). This form is not universal: seven flint daggers have tangs less than 1/3 of their total length (Fig. 9.2a), suggesting that these were designed to be inserted in organic hafts and a further 40 are fully leaf-shaped with no clear distinction between the blade and the tang (Fig. 9.2f). Finally, ten flint daggers from Britain and the only recorded flint dagger in Ireland are clearly Scandinavian flint daggers of Lomborg's (1973) types IV, V and VI, that is flint daggers dating to the centuries after 1950 BC (cf. Apel 2001; Vandkilde 1996; Vandkilde *et al.* 1996). These daggers are clearly more recent than the British dagger forms and do not share the funerary associations of either earlier British flint daggers or contemporary examples in Scandinavia (Table 9.1).

That several distinct British flint dagger forms exist, suggests that there was some shared idea of what the finished objects should look like and, concomitantly, how they should

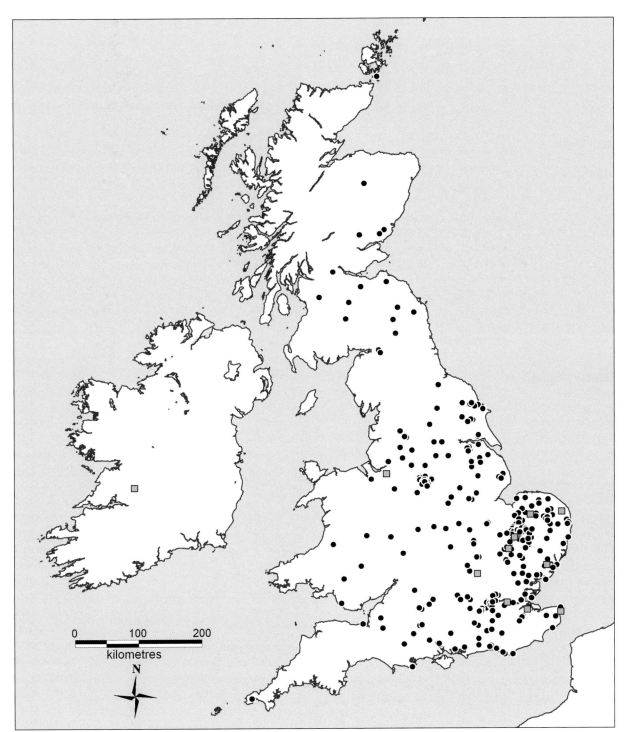

Fig. 9.1: The distribution of flint daggers found in Britain and Ireland. Black circles are British flint daggers, grey squares are handled Scandinavian flint daggers.

be made. In general these flint daggers are flake tools made from relatively large nodules of flint, typically smooth, glossy flints, many apparently from chalk deposits. No clear production site has yet been uncovered, meaning that it is unclear whether flint blanks – for daggers or other tools – were circulating around Britain, whether only roughed out or finished artefacts travelled or whether the distribution pattern reflects a mix of exchanged finished objects and daggers locally produced from flint blanks or local raw materials. However, the two dozen flint dagger finds from

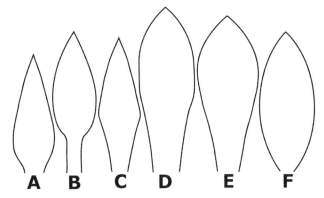

Fig. 9.2: Classification schema developed from the re-examination of the British flint daggers. A) short-tanged daggers or knives; B) Daggers with developed handles which are of Scandinavian origin and date to the second millennium BC; C-E) long-tanged daggers, believed to be of British origin and date to the third millennium BC; F) leaf-shaped daggers which may also overlap with category of foliate knives.

Scotland – consisting of a mix of crudely made daggers made from foreign flints, very fine daggers made from a distinctive cherty flint from Yorkshire and two apparent daggers made from local, non-flint materials – suggest that the latter situation was most likely the case. Nevertheless, their production shows signs of standardisation which were maintained through cycles of use and resharpening, not just in gross morphology but in surface treatment as well. For example, about one in three daggers has an area of cortex preserved on their surface, in almost all cases localised on or around the base of the dagger. This pattern is significant as it can also be found among flint axes and daggers in circulation on the continent where it is generally understood as a conscious choice made by skilled knappers and indicating that the entirety of a flint nodule has been used to make the finished object (Frieman 2012a; Rudebeck 1998).

The function of these daggers remains indeterminate, as little usewear analysis has been carried out; and those studies which have been conducted have produced unambiguous but reasonably unhelpful results: blade faces and edges show traces of having been repeatedly inserted and removed from leather sheaths (Grace 1990; Green *et al.* 1982), at the same time covering or erasing any other use traces that might have existed. Even if their actual function is indeterminate, hints can be drawn from other traces of use. For example, the vast majority of British daggers show signs of resharpening, though not such extensive resharpening as is visible in examples from, for example, Scandinavia (Frieman 2012a; Lindman 1988). Moreover, a number of examples show evidence of quite uniform and tightly bound hafts. Famously, British daggers, unlike most other European flint daggers, sometimes have notches on the edges of their tangs, presumably for securing an organic

haft or wrapping of some sort. About one in three have notched tangs, usually in even numbers with matching pairs on the two tang edges; but about one in four daggers has at least one unpaired notch. It is unclear whether these odd notches were created during the original knapping sequence, or whether they were later additions, perhaps to secure a new or differently designed haft. Other traces of hafting on British flint daggers take the form of microscopic traces of adhesive residue observed on the tangs of four daggers (e.g. Green *et al.* 1982) and dark brownish criss-crossed streaks or stains on the faces at the junction of blade and tang – often between edge notches (Fig. 9.3).

What clear evidence we do have for the function of British flint daggers comes from the choices made in depositing them. Following Grimes, British flint daggers, much like their continental counterparts, have been widely discussed as primarily linked to the funerary sphere (cf. Needham 2005, forthcoming). However, while flint daggers are definitely found in funerary contexts in Britain, their find locations are certainly more heterogeneous than that. Contextual information is lacking for over half of the flint daggers from British sites, but the 160 daggers with some information about their find context and associations give an interesting insight into flint dagger use and deposition. For example, a number of daggers come from apparent occupation or settlement contexts, including a large lithic scatter recovered from Chichester College Brinsbury Campus, Pulborough, (West Sussex, England) from which 70 barbed-and-tanged arrowheads were also recovered. Others were recovered in proximity to ritual sites, such as Arbor Low henge and stone circle (Derbyshire, England) (Burl 2000: 289ff), or with material suggesting a votive deposit, for example the Scandinavian flint dagger and axes recovered together at Ramsgate (Kent, England) (Hicks 1878).[1]

Certainly, funerary contexts, particularly Beaker single inhumations, are the best known find spots for flint daggers in the British Isles, and many of these contexts with flint daggers are strikingly rich. The vast majority of the 43 interments with flint daggers are single burials of adult males, all tightly crouched on their left side (Needham forthcoming); and just under half are associated with whole or fragmented Beaker pottery. Within these graves, the most common associations for flint daggers are flint flakes and tools, including knives and arrowheads as well as other lithic implements, such as axes (battle axes and other ground-stone axes), cushion stones and sponge fingers. A notable association are bone or antler spatulae, eight (of less than two dozen known examples: Duncan 2005) of which were found with flint dagger burials, and which have previously been suggested to be specialist pressure flaking tools (Olsen in P. Harding 2011b; P. Harding & Olsen 1989: 104). Six daggers were also found associated with lumps of iron pyrite or hematite, often placed in proximity with or touching the

Fig. 9.3: The flint dagger recovered from a Beaker burial at Shorncote, Somerford Keynes, Gloucestershire – arrows indicate binding traces (© Trustees of the British Museum).

dagger, suggesting daggers may have been linked to fire starting kits (cf. Stapert & Johansen 1999) or to the larger sphere of pyrotechnology, including metalworking. Metal is almost unknown in burial contexts with flint daggers; but the cushion stones, sponge fingers and boars' tusks found in some burials are all associated with metalworking (Fitzpatrick 2009, 2011: 221f). This pattern of associations suggests that flint daggers and elaborate flint knapping may have been highlighted in these funerary contexts as belonging to the same technological sphere as metal and metallurgy.

Less widely discussed, but greater in number than the flint daggers from funerary contexts, are the 53 daggers recovered from wet locations, in particular riverine contexts. Notably, 33 of the 43 flint daggers found in rivers were found in the Thames, mostly in Greater London, but one was found as far up the river as Henley (Oxfordshire, England) (Frieman 2013). Later prehistory saw a long tradition of depositional activity focussed on the Thames and its tributaries (Bradley 1979, 1990; York 2002); and, while the best known river finds date to the middle of the 2nd millennium BC and later, these depositional rites clearly originate in the Neolithic and may be linked to the funerary sphere (Edmonds 1995: 150; Lamdin-Whymark 2008). As most of these river finds come from southeast England, the centre of flint dagger deposition, while most obvious funerary contexts are slightly more peripheral (Fig. 9.4), we might be looking at regional variations in the funerary rite or contrasting ideas of the value, function or use of flint daggers themselves.

British flint daggers in their local and international contexts

Following Edmonds (1995: 103f), the end of the 3rd millennium BC witnessed a distinct division between everyday flint knapping techniques and procedures which become increasingly less uniform and specialised and the concomitant appearance of a number of highly specialised, and widely shared, *chaînes opératoires* used to produce a variety of elaborate flint tools, including daggers. Among the tool types which appear at this time, barbed-and-tanged arrowheads (Green 1980) are among the most numerous and closely studied alongside thumbnail scrapers and a variety of types of flint knives (Butler 2005: 166ff).

A deep and long-standing archaeological interest in the early and widespread adoption of metallurgy in the British Isles has meant that, unlike on the continent, relatively little comprehensive work has been carried out on the flint industries of the later third and early 2nd millennia BC. Grimes Graves has yielded immense information about the technology of 3rd millennium BC flint mining and production in southeast England (Longworth *et al.* 1991), but this site is largely without parallel for the study of contemporary flint knapping technologies; and, moreover, it is closely associated with Grooved Ware rather than Beaker material culture. Few syntheses or accepted typologies of British later prehistoric flint tools exist, and those that do are often decades old (e.g. Clark 1929, 1932a; Green 1980) or so general as to be more field guides to flint tools than analytical resources (Butler 2005). While individual flint

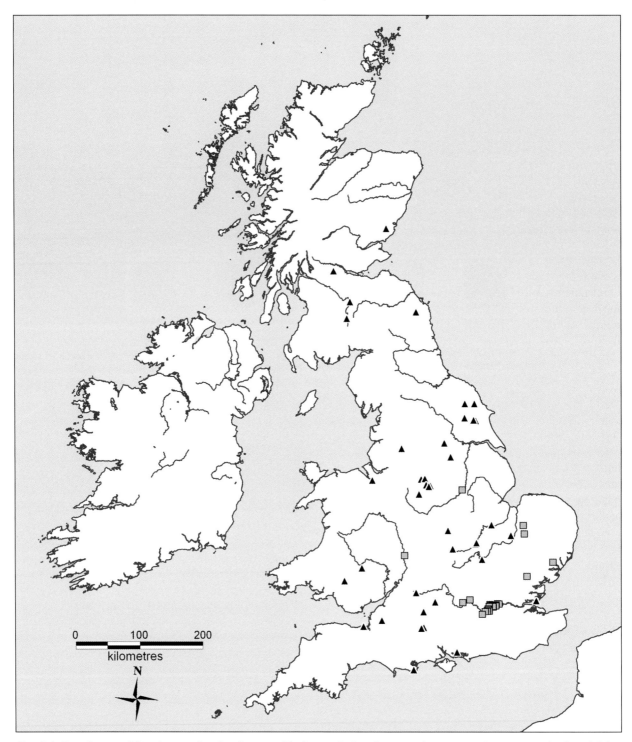

Fig. 9.4: Distribution of flint daggers found in funerary (black triangles) and riverine (grey squares) contexts in the British Isles.

researchers have a wide and deep body of knowledge about flint technologies and tool varieties, in Britain, these have rarely been published except as discussions in excavation reports (e.g. Ballin 2011a).

Consequently, while we can compare British flint daggers to continental varieties (see below), it is considerably more difficult to relate them to the flint objects being produced in Britain contemporary with and in the generations preceding their adoption. Certainly, a variety of types of flint knives were being produced in the British Isles during the late 3rd and early 2nd millennia BC; and many have been recovered from apparent ritual and funerary contexts. Plano-convex knives, typically associated with Food Vessel ceramics and dated to the 3rd and well into the 2nd millennium BC (Clark 1932a), are characterised as being knapped from long flakes or blades which retain a distinct plano-convex curvature and having unifacial pressure flaking, sometimes very fine, on the dorsal surface, with the ventral surface typically remaining untouched. Other than plano-convex knives, various ovoid knife forms are also known. Laurel leaves, bifacially worked implements 'not elongated enough to be spearheads, or sharp enough to be knives' (Radley 1970: 132) are an Early Neolithic tool type found around Britain; but some appear to have Grooved Ware, that is mid–3rd millennium BC, associations. Several particularly fine, possible laurel leaf points were found with Seamer axes and tens of other flint objects dated to the mid to late 3rd millennium BC near Holgate in York (Radley 1970), although this find is somewhat dubious (A. Saville, pers. comm.). Ovate knives have also been found in hoards as well as in production contexts around Grimes Graves, Norfolk (Robins 2002). Adding to the typological confusion, a number of quite refined doubled-edged blades have been recovered from funerary contexts around Britain. Among the best known are those from the burial of the 'Amesbury Archer' in southwest England (Harding 2011a: 94); these might well have been hafted as daggers, and are often described as such by the excavator (A. Fitzpatrick, pers. comm.). Indeed, the small flint blade hafted as a dagger with a wooden handle found with the remains of a Copper Age man in the Alps provides an example for this sort of hafting (Spindler 1994). It is possible that these double edged blades and the short-tanged daggers described briefly above might fit into the same social or functional category; but, at the moment, too little is known about their distribution, usewear or technology for more than speculation.

Of particular relevance to the British flint daggers are a particularly fine class of ovoid knives which Ballin (2011b: 450) has termed foliate knives. These knives arguably draw on similar technological and functional traditions as the British flint daggers, but they are more recent and tend to be slightly smaller. They are fully leaf-shaped with no distinction between the two pointed ends and, where usewear is present and observable, show wear – including gloss – on diagonally opposing edges. This pattern of wear suggests that they were not hafted like daggers, but that the tool was rotated in the hand during use. Like the flint daggers which they resemble, they are also recovered from ritual and funerary contexts, for example, a 90mm long foliate knife was found with a multiple cremation burial in a Collard Urn from Barrow 5 in West Cotton, Raunds area (Northamptonshire, England) (Harding & Healy 2007: 141, 2011: fig. SS3.1). Foliate knives are often misidentified as flint daggers; and it is entirely possible that some leaf-shaped

flint daggers, recorded based on photographs and drawings rather than direct observations, should better be thought of as foliate knives.

Although flint knives, some of very high quality, proliferate in the British Isles in the 3rd and 2nd millennia BC, there is no obvious local precursor for the British flint daggers. Moreover, their appearance is quite sudden, and they appear to be as suddenly abandoned as they are adopted, so it becomes difficult to conceptualise them as a local development. Consequently, making sense of the British flint dagger assemblage cannot be done without reference to the wider context of flint dagger production, use and distribution in Europe. Flint daggers were in circulation in various parts of Europe, from Italy to Norway, from the 4th to the 2nd millennia BC (Delcourt-Vlaeminck 2004; Delcourt-Vlaeminck *et al.* 1991; Honegger 2002; Honegger & de Montmollin 2010; Kühn 1979; Lomborg 1973; Mallet & Ramseyer 1991; Mottes 2001; Siemann 2003; Solberg 1994; Steiniger 2010; Strahm 1961–1962; Struve 1955; Zimmermann 2007).

Among the best known, are the long, plano-convex blades, hafted as daggers and made primarily from flint from Grand-Pressigny in the Massif Central (France), which were largely produced and circulated in the first half the 3rd millennium BC (Ihuel *et al.*, this volume; Ihuel 2004; Mallet *et al.* 2004). These Grand-Pressigny daggers circulated as blanks and finished daggers via riverine networks to Brittany and Switzerland and up the North Sea coasts to Denmark, Germany and the Netherlands (cf. Delcourt-Vlaeminck 2004; Delcourt-Vlaeminck *et al.* 1991; Honegger & de Montmollin 2010; Lomborg 1973; Siemann 2003; van der Waals 1991; Vander Linden 2012). They, and smaller imitations in local and northern French flints typically referred to as 'pseudo-Grand-Pressigny' blades (Siemann 2003; Zimmermann 2007), were deposited in a variety of contexts, most notably alongside late Dutch Single Grave Culture burials (Van Gijn 2010a: 142, 2010b).

The youngest major flint dagger industry to develop in Europe and to circulate widely, appeared towards the end of the 3rd millennium BC in Scandinavia and was characterised by the production of large, flat and bifacially worked flint blades made preferentially (although not universally) from very high quality mined flint (Apel 2001; Forssander 1936; Lomborg 1973; Müller 1902). The earliest of these Scandinavian daggers were largely lanceolate and included a group of extremely long and very finely made examples which appear to have been produced for the funerary sphere, particularly to accompany male burials along with archery equipment and Danish Beakers (Varberg, this volume; Sarauw 2007, 2008). Later examples of Scandinavian flint daggers are known for their elaborate handle morphologies and complex knapping sequences, suggesting the development of a thriving community of specialist flint knappers and a value system in which specialised products, including lithic tools, were highly desirable (Apel 2000, 2004; Frieman 2012a). Both the lanceolate and the fishtail daggers were widely valued and appear in contexts in northern Scandinavia, central Europe and the North Sea borders, where they are typically deposited in wet locales (Drenth, this volume; Van Gijn 2010a, 2010b)

Despite the prevalence of flint daggers in circulation networks abutting the North Sea, there is little evidence that people living in Britain during the majority of the 3rd millennium BC had any interest in adopting, using or displaying them. There are no Grand-Pressigny (or pseudo-Grand-Pressigny) blades anywhere in the British Isles or Ireland and only a handful of obviously Scandinavian daggers – all of which are of the elaborately handled varieties which date to after 2000 BC and, thus, are subsequent to the period of local dagger production and deposition in Britain. However, there do appear to be links between the British flint daggers and the lanceolate Scandinavian varieties which were circulating around northern Europe. Lomborg (1973:91f) erroneously believed that the appearance of British flint daggers pre-dated the Scandinavian dagger industry and likely served as prototypes for Scandinavian daggers. Certainly, a handful of flint daggers with particularly wide blades or notches on their tang edges are known both in Scandinavia (Lomborg 1973: fig. 61) and elsewhere in northern Europe (Kühn 1979). However, radiocarbon dating tells us that the Scandinavian daggers were in circulation several generations prior to the adoption of flint daggers in Britain; and, moreover, the Scandinavian examples draw on a long tradition of extremely fine flint knapping in the Nordic region, including the production of pseudo-Grand-Pressigny blades in the 3rd millennium BC (Lomborg 1973: 88f). Consequently, it might be better to understand lanceolate flint daggers of Scandinavian origin as the inspiration or prototype for the flint daggers produced in Britain, some of which (or the people who knew how to produce them) may have travelled back up the North Sea coast to northern Germany and Denmark.

Based on the heavy density of flint daggers in southeastern England and the lack of concrete evidence for direct connections between southern Scandinavia and the British Isles at this time, the Netherlands seems like the most likely source for this knapping tradition in Britain. Certainly, links between southern England and the Netherlands were particularly strong in the second half of the 3rd millennium BC. The adoption of Beaker ceramics in Britain has traditionally been linked to cross-Channel connections between the two regions (Clarke 1970; Sheridan 2008); and the 'Dutch model' of Beaker ceramic typology dominated British Beaker studies until very recently (Fokkens 2012a, 2012b; van der Beek & Fokkens 2001 with references). This connection has also been suggested as the origin of early British Beaker funerary rites (Vander Linden 2012:

77), with several Scottish sites recently having been (somewhat controversially) identified as having been designed by and for Dutch migrants (Fokkens 2012b; Sheridan 2008). In the Netherlands, Grand-Pressigny and pseudo-Grand-Pressigny daggers are associated with All Over Ornamented (AOO) ceramics, a suggested parent form of Beaker pottery, in funerary contexts (Vander Linden 2012: 76f with references). Lanceolate flint daggers from Scandinavia appear in Dutch contexts in the last third of the 3rd millennium BC (Beuker & Drenth 2006; Bloemers 1968), generally found deposited in wet locales away from settlement contexts (Van Gijn 2010a, 2010b). One or two are known from funerary contexts, notably a dagger found with a stone battle axe in a grave near Emmen (Bloemers 1968; Kühn 1979: 51). As few systematic studies of lithic raw materials in Britain have been conducted, it is not yet known whether any of the finer lanceolate daggers from the British Isles has a Scandinavian origin, but it is certainly possible.

British flint daggers and British societies in the wider Beaker network

While flint daggers are regularly described as a key status symbol used in Beaker funerary rites, in fact, they are a later, and reasonably small-scale, addition to Beaker assemblages in Britain. Yet, their adoption and their use in highly visible funerary and ritual activities cannot be ignored, particularly in light of the long-standing significance of flint daggers on the continent. In Britain, they are particularly associated with the material culture and practices linked to what Needham (2005) refers to as the 'fission horizon'. This horizon – dating to the centuries following *ca.* 2250 BC – is characterised by the rise of competing, localised identities within the British Beaker sphere. Beaker material culture and practices remain in use, but they are manipulated to allow for the emergence of localised and distinctly British identities within the broader Beaker horizon. For example, Long Necked Beakers, the ceramic type most closely associated with flint daggers, appear to be decorated with motifs originated in Grooved Ware ornamentation (Needham 2005). A similar interest in connecting with local British ancestors can be seen in burial sites and contexts where curated heirlooms and human remains begin to appear with greater frequency and burial alignments become increasingly visible (Garwood 2012).

This focus on regionalisation and ancestral identities after 2250 BC has been linked to an increasingly competitive and socially fragmented social context in which individuals and communities were seeking out alternate strategies for signalling status and identity (Needham forthcoming). However, the apparent emphasis on *Britishness* visible in the ceramic material and aspects of the funerary rite are undercut by the sudden adoption of widespread continental lithic technologies, including ground-stone battle axes and flint daggers. Instead, the adoption of flint daggers primarily in southern and eastern England, likely via the Netherlands, and their deposition in wet locales, echoing Dutch deposition patterns, might better be understood as effort to highlight or call back to the early Beaker period Dutch connection. In other words, deploying flint daggers within British Beaker contexts suggests an attempt to affiliate oneself or one's community with a specifically continental ancestral Beaker identity, rather than the more British identities which were emerging at the same time. In this light, the regional distinction between river finds and burial finds might indicate a time lag in the adoption of flint daggers, with the former retaining their Dutch associations while the latter, deposited further away, began accruing more locally significant meanings.

Clearly, flint daggers in British contexts are part of the wider European flint dagger phenomenon, even if their period of use was considerably briefer. Within their continental context, flint daggers have been described as developing out of and, in their wide circulation and regular use, contributing to a widely understood 'dagger idea' (*sensu* Vandkilde 2001: 337; Vandkilde 2005: 17; cf. Heyd 2007) linked to new ideas about individual prestige and status, specific gendered identities and access to new ways of carrying out and thinking about technology. In this model, possessing (and presumably wielding or displaying) a dagger of some variety – and of any raw material, including flint, metal, bone or antler – would indicate participation in networks of trade and communication which relied on the adoption of standardised and specialised production processes (Frieman 2012a). Flint daggers, in combining a very traditional technology and raw material with a new form and novel, frequently specialised, production processes were able to act as 'boundary objects', tangible expressions of people's engagement in shared value-systems (Frieman 2012a, 2012b).

While this model was formulated without reference to the British flint dagger assemblage, adding them to it both strengthens the model and clarifies the significance of the adoption of these objects in the British Isles. While they may have been deployed within social situations, such as burials and ritual activities, to signify status and regional British identities, they also clearly underline the continued engagement of British individuals and communities with wider European networks. In other words, even as the British Beaker package became more insular in composition than international, the adoption of flint daggers (and battle axes), could have served as a mitigating factor, signalling to continental friends, kin or trading partners that there remained a desire to participate in wider networks of contact and exchange.

The reasons for emphasising these cross-Channel connections remain unclear; but they seem likely to be linked to a specific ancestral identity or lineage which was newly valuable after 2250 BC. In particular, the value of cross-Channel affiliation may have increased in response to the contemporary shift in trade from Ireland. In the last quarter of the 3rd millennium BC, the spread of Irish practices and material culture – and particularly Irish copper and gold – became closely concentrated around lines of communication linking Ireland to Scotland, shifting Ireland away from the broader Atlantic Facade exchange network (Carlin & Brück 2012: 203; Needham 2004). A consequence of this shift is that increasing quantities of copper and gold objects were flowing into northern and northwestern Britain, perhaps causing tensions to develop as these new centres of wealth threatened established contact and exchange networks, particularly in southern and eastern England which seem to have been both geographically and socially most distant from these new nodes. Adopting flint daggers can be understood as part of a shift to emphasising continental connections in order to remain engaged in the continent-spanning exchange networks which were of evident social and economic importance at this time. In this light, the reasonably swift abandonment of flint dagger production in England after about 2000 BC makes perfect sense, as this is the period when bronze metallurgy became widely adopted on the continent and southern England once more became central to Atlantic trade networks with tin from Cornwall becoming one of the most valuable materials in circulation (cf. Needham 2000).

Conclusions

Compared to the better known assemblages of flint daggers from elsewhere in Europe, the flint daggers deposited in British contexts are less technologically impressive, less typologically diverse, less widespread and considerably less numerous. They have also suffered from less archaeological interest due to the presence of considerable amounts of metal in contemporary contexts. Yet, as this paper has shown, they have the capacity to yield a wealth of information about social practices, ritual activities, technological innovations and networks of communication. The British flint daggers were developed in a region with a rich local tradition of flintworking and were part of a floruit of the technology which included the production of elaborate barbed-and-tanged arrowheads alongside a variety of scrapers, knives and other fine flint tools. Many of these were deposited in special contexts, most notably burials. Flint daggers clearly served a variety of roles in society, though their function or functions outside the ritual sphere are not yet well understood. Nevertheless, it is clear that, within the ritual sphere, they were valued objects for deposition in ritual locales, including riverine and funerary contexts.

Dating to the last quarter of the 3rd millennium BC, these flint daggers are part of the so-called fission horizon, a period characterised by increasing regionalisation within Britain which occurred, at least in part, in response to the introduction of copper alloying and contemporary (though not necessarily connected) shifts in the networks of trade and communication around the British Isles. As northern Britain gained prestige and wealth from increasingly close communication with Ireland, people living in southern and eastern Britain likely struggled to maintain access to these networks which brought not just valued materials, but also new ideas and practices to the British Isles. In adopting flint daggers, with their long history of use and deposition across the Channel, they were able to highlight ancestral links to the wider Beaker network in the North Sea region, and particularly to the Netherlands, a putative point of origin for British Beaker materials and practices. Moreover, by the end of the 3rd millennium BC, flint daggers had accrued a considerable significance from their close association with long-distance exchange, communication of new ideas and the value of specialist and specialised technologies. Consequently, their adoption signalled first, to cross-Channel friends and trading partners, a continued willingness to engage with them and a desire to be part of the networks of trade and communication flourishing on the continent and, second, to groups elsewhere in Britain, that people in the south and east were not reliant on their connections to Ireland. The speed with which flint daggers fell out of favour, and the very small number of Scandinavian daggers which were deposited in Britain and Ireland after 2000 BC only serve to highlight that their adoption was a temporary strategy, abandoned as soon as a more compelling reason for copious cross-Channel exchange was found in the form of Cornish tin.

Note

1. This example, however, must be treated as an outlier as the Ramsgate flint dagger is, based on photographic evidence, a very fine fishtail dagger – probably Lomborg's type IV or V – a Scandinavian type dated to after 1950 BC. Consequently, it is several generations more recent than the main period of flint dagger production and deposition in Britain and may be part of a separate set of exchange relationships and functional/symbolic contexts.

Acknowledgements

Thanks in particular to my very patient co-editor Berit V. Eriksen. Thanks are also due to Hugo Anderson-Whymark, Stuart Needham, Alan Saville and Frances Healy for comments on the text, references, corrections and general hand-holding as this research project developed. Museum curators and assistants around Britain were enormously helpful in pulling this research together, but particular thanks are due to Ben Roberts for providing regular and comprehensive access to the British Museum collections. This research was funded by the Fell Fund at the University of Oxford, a Prehistoric Society research grant and the Research School of Arts and Humanities at the Australian National University. As always, any factual errors or leaps of logic are, of course, my own responsibility.

References

Anon. 1934. Flint dagger from Upchurch. *Antiquaries Journal* 14: 298–299.

Apel, J. 2000. Flint daggers and technological knowledge. Production and consumption during LN1. In: D. S. Olausson & H. Vandkilde (eds.), *Form, function & context: material culture studies in Scandinavian archaeology*. Stockholm: Almqvist and Wiksell International. 135–154.

Apel, J. 2001. *Daggers, Knowledge and Power: The social aspects of flint-dagger technology in Scandinavia 2350–1500 cal BC*. Coast to Coast Books 3. Uppsala: Uppsala University Press.

Apel, J. 2004. From marginalisation to specialisation: Scandinavian flint-dagger production during the second wave of neolithisation. In: H. Knutsson (ed.), *Coast to Coast - Arrival. Results and Reflections. Proceedings of the final coast to coast conference 1–5 October in Falköping, Sweden*. Coast to Coast Books 10, Uppsala: Uppsala University Press. 295–308.

Ballin, T. B. 2011a. Overview of the lithic evidence. In: Harding & Healy (eds.) 2011. 506–526.

Ballin, T. B. 2011b. Struck flint from West Cotton, Irthlingborough and Stanwick. In: Harding & Healy (eds.) 2011. 433–505.

Beuker, J. R. & Drenth, E. 2006. Scandinavian type flint daggers from the provinces of Drenthe, the Netherlands. In: G. Körlin & G. Weisgerber (eds.), *Stone Age - Mining Age*. Bochum: Deutsches Bergbau-Museum. 285–300.

Bloemers, J. H. F. 1968. Flintdolche vom Skandinavischen Typus in den Niederlanden. *Berichten van de Rijksdienst voor het Oudheidkundig Bodemonderzoek* 18: 47–110.

Bradley, R. 1979. The interpretation of later Bronze Age metalwork from British rivers. *International Journal of Nautical Archaeology* 8(1): 3–6.

Bradley, R. 1990. *The Passage of Arms. An Archaeological Analysis of Prehistoric Hoards and Votive Deposits*. Cambridge: Cambridge University Press.

Burl, A. 2000. *The Stone Circles of Britain, Ireland, and Brittany*. New Haven, CT: Yale University Press.

Butler, C. 2005. *Prehistoric Flintwork*. Stroud: Tempus.

Carlin, N. & Brück, J. 2012. Searching for the Chalcolithic: continuity and change in the Irish final Neolithic/Early Bronze Age. In: M. J. Allen, J. Gardiner & A. Sheridan (eds.), *Is there a British Chalcolithic? People, Place and Polity in the Later 3rd Millennium*. Prehistoric Society research paper 4. Oxford: Oxbow books. 193–210.

Clark, J. D. G. 1929. Discoidal polished flint knives - their typology and distribution. *Proceedings of the Prehistoric society of East Anglia* 6: 41–54.

Clark, J. D. G. 1932a. The date of the plano-convex flint-knife in England and Wales. *Antiquaries Journal* 12: 158–162.

Clark, J. D. G. 1932b. Note on some flint daggers of Scandinavian type from the British Isles. *Man* 32: 186–190.

Clarke, D. L. 1970. *Beaker Pottery of Great Britain and Ireland*. Cambridge: Cambridge University Press.

Corcoran, J. X. W. P. 1964. A Scandinavian flint dagger from Scarriff, Co. Clare. *North Munster Antiquarian Journal* 9(3): 83–88.

Corcoran, J. X. W. P. 1966. An adze and an axehead from Co. Wexford. *Journal of the Royal Society of Antiquaries of Ireland* 96(1): 93-95.

Day, R. 1895. Danish spear-head. *Journal of the Royal Society of Antiquaries of Ireland* 5th Ser. 5(2): 176.

Delcourt-Vlaeminck, M. 2004. Les exportations du silex du Grand-Pressigny et du matériau tertiaire dans le nord-ouest de l'Europe au néolithique final/Chalcolithique. In: M. Vander Linden & L. Salanova (eds.), *Le troisième millénaire dans le nord de la France et en Belgique: Actes de la journée d'études SRBAP-SPF, 8 mars 2003, Lille*. Paris: Société Préhistorique Française. 139–154.

Delcourt-Vlaeminck, M., Simon, C., & Vlaeminck, J. 1991. Le silex du Grand-Pressigny sur le complexe SOM/chalcolithique du Brunehaut (Tourain-Belgique). In: J. Despriée, C. Verjux, J. Piédoue, G. Richard, R. Albert, P. Pilareck, L. Tudal, F. Varache & A. Manchet (eds.), *La région Centre, carrefour d'influences? Actes du 14e Colloque Interrégional sur le Néolithique, Blois, 16–18 octobre 1987*. Argenton-sur-Creuse: Société Archéologique, Scientifique et Littéraire du Vendômois. 201–205.

Duncan, H. 2005. Bone artefacts. In: I. Roberts & J. Prudhoe (eds.), *Ferrybridge Henge: the Ritual Landscape. Archaeological Investigations at the Site of the Holmfield Interchange of the A1 Motorway*. Leeds: Archaeological Services WYAS. 163–165.

Edmonds, M. R. 1995. *Stone Tools and Society: Working Stone in Neolithic and Bronze Age Britain*. London: Batsford.

Fitzpatrick, A. P. 2009. In his hands and in his head: the Amesbury Archer as a metalworker. In: P. Clark (ed.), *Bronze Age Connections. Cultural Contact in Prehistoric Europe*. Oxford: Oxbow Books: 176–188.

Fitzpatrick, A. P. 2011. *The Amesbury Archer and the Boscombe Bowmen: Bell Beaker Burials on Boscombe Down, Amesbury, Wiltshire*. Salisbury: Wessex Archaeology.

Fokkens, H. 2012a. Background to Dutch Beakers. A critical review of the Dutch model. In: H. Fokkens & F. Nicolis (eds.), *Background to Beakers. Inquiries in Regional Cultural Backgrounds of the Bell Beaker Complex*. Leiden: Sidestone Press: 9–36.

Fokkens, H. 2012b. Dutchmen on the move? A discussion of the adoption of the Beaker package. In: M. J. Allen, J. Gardiner & A. Sheridan (eds.), *Is there a British Chalcolithic: People, Place and Polity in the Later 3rd Millennium*. Prehistoric Society research paper 4. Oxford: Oxbow Books. 115–125.

Forssander, J. E. 1936. *Der ostskandinavische Norden während der ältesten Metallzeit Europas*. Lund: C. W. K. Gleerup.

Frieman, C. J. 2012a. Flint daggers, copper daggers and technological innovation in Late Neolithic Scandinavia. *European Journal of Archaeology* 15(3): 440–464.

Frieman, C. J. 2012b. *Innovation and Imitation: Stone Skeuomorphs*

of Metal from 4th–2nd Millennia BC Northwest Europe. Oxford: Archaeopress.

Frieman, C. J. 2013. Lost and found: A flint dagger from the River Thames at Henley. *Oxoniensia* 78: 225–226.

Frieman, C. J. 2014. Double edged blades: Re-visiting the British (and Irish) flint daggers. *Proceedings of the Prehistoric Society* 79: 33–65.

Garwood, P. 2012. The present dead: The making of past and future landscapes in the British Chalcolithic. In: M. J. Allen, J. Gardiner & A. Sheridan (eds.), *Is There a British Chalcolithic? People, Place and Polity in the Later 3rd Millennium*. Prehistoric Society research paper 4. Oxford: Oxbow books. 298–316.

Grace, R. 1990. The limitations and applications of usewear data. *Aun* 14: 9–14.

Green, H. S. 1980. *The Flint Arrowheads of the British Isles*. BAR British series 75. Oxford: British Archaeological Reports.

Green, H. S., Houlder, C. H. & Keeley, L. H. 1982. A flint dagger from Ffair Rhos, Ceredigion, Dyfed, Wales. *Proceedings of the Prehistoric Society* 48: 492–495.

Grimes, W. F. 1932. The Early Bronze Age flint dagger in England and Wales. *Proceedings of the Prehistoric Society of East Anglia* 6(4): 340–355.

Harding, J. & Healy, F. eds. 2007. *A Neolithic and Bronze Age Landscape in Northhamptonshire*. Swindon: English Heritage.

Harding, J. & Healy, F. eds. 2011. *The Raunds Area Project: A Neolithic and Bronze Age landscape in Northamptonshire*. Vol. 2: Supplementary Studies. Swindon: English Heritage.

Harding, P. 2011a. Flint. In: Fitzpatrick (ed.) 2011: 88–103.

Harding, P. 2011b. Spatula. In: Fitzpatrick (ed.) 2011: 158–159.

Harding, P. & Olsen, S. 1989. Flint and the burial group in 1017 with a note on the antler spatulae. In: P. J. Fasham, D. E. Farwell & R. J. B. Whinney (eds.), *The Archaeological Site at Easton Lane, Winchester*. Winchester: Hampshire Field Club & Wessex Archaeology. 99–107.

Hart, P. 2012. *Special artefacts*. The Museum of Thanet's Archaeology, [cited 30 October 2013]. Available from http://www.thanetarch.co.uk/Virtual%20Museum/3_Displays/GBeaker%20Displays/GBeaker_Display3_Link1artefacts.htm.

Heyd, V. 2007. Families, prestige goods, warriors and complex societies: Beaker groups in the 3rd millennium cal BC. *Proceedings of the Prehistoric Society* 73: 327–380.

Hicks, R. 1878. Roman remains found at Ramsgate. *Archaeologia Cantiana* 12: 13–18.

Honegger, M. 2002. Les influences méridionales dans les industries lithiques du néolithique Suisse. In: M. Bailly, R. Furestier & T. Perrin (eds.), *Les Industries lithiques taillées holocènes du bassin rhodanien: problèmes et actualités: actes de la table ronde tenue à Lyon les 8 et 9 décembre 2000*. Montagnac: Mergoil. 135–147.

Honegger, M. & de Montmollin, P. 2010. Flint daggers of the Late Neolithic in the Northern Alpine area. In: B. V. Eriksen (ed.), *Lithic Technology in Metal Using Societies*. Aarhus: Jutland Archaeological Society. 129–142.

Ihuel, E. 2004. *La diffusion du silex du Grand-Pressigny dans le massif armoricain au Néolithique*. Paris: Comité des Travaux Historiques et Scientifiques.

Kühn, H. J. 1979. *Das Spätneolithikum in Schleswig-Holstein*. Neumünster: K. Wachholtz.

Lamdin-Whymark, H. 2008. *The Residue of Ritualised Action: Neolithic Deposition Practices in the Middle Thames Valley.* Oxford: Archaeopress.

Levitan, B. W. & Smart, P. L. 1989. Charterhouse Warren Farm swallet, Mendip, Somerset. Radiocarbon dating evidence. *Proceedings of the University of Bristol Speleological Society* 18(3): 390–394.

Lindman, G. 1988. Power and influence in the late Stone Age: A discussion of the interpretation of the flint dagger material. *Oxford Journal of Archaeology* 7(2): 121–138.

Lomborg, E. 1973. *Die Flintdolche Dänemarks: Studien über Chronologie und Kulturbeziehungen des südskandinavischen Spätneolithikums.* København: Universitetsforlaget I kommission hos H. H. J. Lynge.

Longley, D. M. T. 1987. Prehistory. In: B. E. Harris & A. T. Thacker (eds.), *A History of the County of Chester.* Oxford: Oxford University Press.

Longworth, I. H., Herne, A., Varndell, G., & Needham, S. 1991. *Excavations at Grimes Graves, Norfolk, 1972–6 Fascicule 3: Shaft X: Bronze Age Flint, Chalk and Metalworking.* London: British Museum Press.

Macalister, R. A. S. 1921. *Ireland in Pre-Celtic times.* Dublin: Maunsel and Roberts.

Mallet, N. & Ramseyer, D. 1991. Un exemple d'importations de silex du Grand-Pressigny dans un village de la civilisation Saône-Rhône: Partalban (Canton de Fribourg, Suisse). In: J. Despriée, C. Verjux, J. Piédoue, G. Richard, R. Albert, P. Pilareck, L. Tudal, F. Varache & A. Manchet (eds.), *La région Centre, carrefour d'influences? Actes du 14e Colloque Interrégional sur le Néolithique, Blois, 16–18 octobre 1987.* Argenton-sur-Creuse: Société Archéologique, Scientifique et Littéraire du Vendômois. 167–192.

Mallet, N., Richard, G., Genty, P., & Verjux, C. 2004. La diffusion des silex du Grand-Pressigny dans le Basin parisien. In: M. Vander Linden & L. Salanova (eds.), *Le troisième millénaire dans le nord de la France et en Belgique: Actes de la journée d'études SRBAP-SPF, 8 mars 2003, Lille.* Paris: Société Préhistorique Française. 123–138.

Mottes, E. 2001. Bell Beakers and beyond: flint daggers of northern Italy between technology and typology. In: F. Nicolis (ed.), *Bell Beakers Today: Pottery, People, Culture, Symbols in Prehistoric Europe. Proceedings of the International Colloquium, Riva del Garda (Trento, Italy) 11–16 May 1998.* Trento, Italy: Provincia Autonoma di Trento Servizio Beni Culturali Ufficio Beni Archeologici: 519–545.

Müller, S. 1902. *Flintdolkene i den nordiske Stenalder.* Nordiske Fortidsminder I, 5. Copenhagen: Gyldendal.

Myers, A. & Noble, P. 2009. On the discovery and regional context of an Early Bronze Age flint dagger at Mellor, Stockport. *Derbyshire Archaeological Journal* 129: 173–182.

Needham, S. 2000. Power pulses across a cultural divide: cosmologically driven acquisition between Armorica and Wessex. *Proceedings of the Prehistoric Society* 66: 151–207.

Needham, S. 2004. Migdale-Marnock: sunburst of Scottish metallurgy. In: I. A. G. Shepherd & G. Barclay, J. (eds.), *The Neolithic and Early Bronze Age of Scotland in their European Context.* Edinburgh: Royal Society of Antiquaries of Scotland. 217–245.

Needham, S. 2005. Transforming Beaker culture in north-west Europe: processes of fusion and fission. *Proceedings of the prehistoric society* 71: 171–217.

Needham, S. 2012. Case and place for the British Chalcolithic. In: M. J. Allen, J. Gardiner & A. Sheridan (eds.), *Is There a British Chalcolithic? People, Place and Polity in the Later 3rd Millennium.* Prehistoric Society research paper 4. Oxford: Oxbow Books. 1–26.

Needham, S. forthcoming. *Material and Spiritual Engagements: Britain and Ireland in the First Age of Metal. The Rhind Lectures 2011,* Edinburgh: Society of Antiquaries of Scotland.

Radley, J. 1970. The York hoard of flint tools, 1868 [1]. *Yorkshire Archaeological Journal* 42: 131–132.

Roberts, I. & Prudhoe, J. eds. 2005. *Ferrybridge Henge: the Ritual Landscape. Archaeological Investigations at the Site of the Holmfield Interchange of the A1 Motorway.* Leeds: Archaeological Services WYAS.

Robins, P. 2002. A late Neolithic flint hoard at Two Mile Bottom, Near Thetford, Norfolk. *Lithics* 23: 29–32.

Rudebeck, E. 1998. Flint extraction, axe offering, and the value of cortex. In: M. R. Edmonds & C. Richards (eds.), *Understanding the Neolithic of North-western Europe.* Glasgow: Cruithne Press. 312–327.

Sarauw, T. 2007. Male symbols or warrior identities? The 'archery burials' of the Danish Bell Beaker Culture. *Journal of Anthropological Archaeology* 26 (1): 65–87.

Sarauw, T. 2008. Danish Bell Beaker pottery and flint daggers - the display of social identities. *European Journal of Archaeology* 11(1): 23–47.

Saville, A. 2012. Three Early Bronze Age flint daggers from north Northumberland and their typological context. *Archaeologia Aeliana* 5th Series 41: 1–17.

Sheridan, A. 2008. Upper Largie and Dutch-Scottish connections during the Beaker period. *Analecta Praehistorica Leidensia* 40: 247–260.

Siemann, C. 2003. *Flintdolche Norddeutschlands in ihrem grabrituellen Umfeld.* Bonn: Habelt.

Solberg, B. 1994. Exchange and the role of import to western Norway in the Late Neolithic and Early Bronze Age. *Norwegian Archaeology Review* 27(2): 111–126.

Spindler, K. 1994. *The Man in the Ice: the Preserved Body of a Neolithic Man Reveals the Secrets of the Stone Age.* London: Weidenfeld and Nicolson.

Stapert, D. & Johansen, L. 1999. Flint and pyrite: making fire in the Stone Age. *Antiquity* 73: 765–777.

Steiniger, D. 2010. The relation between copper and flint daggers in Chalcolithic Italy. In: P. Anreiter, G. Goldenberg, K. Hanke, R. Krause, W. Leitner, F. Mathis, K. Nicolussi, K. Oeggl, E. Pernicka, M. Prast, J. Schibler, I. Schneider, H. Stadler, T. Stöllner, G. Tomedi & P. Tropper (eds.), *Mining in European History and its Impact on Environment and Human Societies – Proceedings for the 1st Mining in European History-Conference of the SFB-HIMAT, 12.–15. November 2009, Innsbruck.* Innsbruck: Innsbruck University Press. 151–156.

Strahm, C. 1961–1962. Geschäftete Dolchklingen des Spätneolithikums. *Jahrbuch des Bernischen historischen Museums in Bern* 41/42: 447–478.

Struve, K.W. 1955. *Die Einzelgrabkultur in Schleswig-Holstein.* Neumünster: Karl Wachholtz Verlag.

Thomas, N. 1956. Material for the study of the prehistory of

Bedfordshire I: the Neolithic and Bronze Age. *Bedfordshire Archaeologist* 1: 67-92.

Thomas, N. 1964. A gazetteer of Neolithic and Bronze Age sites and antiquities in Bedfordshire. *Bedfordshire Archaeological Journal* 2: 16–33.

van der Beek, Z. & Fokkens, H. 2001. 24 years after Oberried: the 'Dutch Model' reconsidered. In: F. Nicolis (ed.), *Bell Beakers Today: Pottery, People, Culture, Symbols in Prehistoric Europe. Proceedings of the International Colloquium, Riva del Garda (Trento, Italy) 11–16 May 1998*. Trento, Italy: Provincia Autonoma di Trento Servizio Beni Culturali Ufficio Beni Archeologici. 301–308.

van der Waals, J. D. 1991. Silex du Grand-Pressigny aux Pays-Bas. In: J. Despriée, C. Verjux, J. Piédoue, G. Richard, R. Albert, P. Pilareck, L. Tudal, F. Varache & A. Manchet (eds.), *La région Centre, carrefour d'influences? Actes du 14e Colloque Interrégional sur le Néolithique, Blois, 16–18 octobre 1987*. Argenton-sur-Creuse: Société Archéologique, Scientifique et Littéraire du Vendômois. 193–200.

Van Gijn, A. 2010a. *Flint in Focus: Lithic Biographies in the Neolithic and Bronze Age*. Leiden: Sidestone Press.

Van Gijn, A. 2010b. Not at all obsolete! The use of flint in the Bronze Age Netherlands. In: B. V. Eriksen (ed.), *Lithic Technology in Metal Using Societies*. Aarhus: Jutland Archaeological Society: 45–60.

Vander Linden, M. 2012. The importance of being insular: Britain and Ireland in their north-western European context during the 3rd millennium BC. In: M. J. Allen, J. Gardiner & A. Sheridan (eds.), *Is there a British Chalcolithic? People, Place and Polity in the Later 3rd Millennium*. Prehistoric Society research paper 4. Oxford: Oxbow Books. 71–84.

Vandkilde, H. 1996. *From Stone to Bronze: the Metalwork of the Late Neolithic and Earliest Bronze Age in Denmark*. Aarhus: Aarhus University Press.

Vandkilde, H. 2001. Beaker representation in the Danish Late Neolithic. In: F. Nicolis (ed.), *Bell Beakers Today: Pottery, People, Culture, Symbols in Prehistoric Europe. Proceedings of the International Colloquium, Riva del Garda (Trento, Italy) 11–16 May 1998*. Trento, Italy: Provincia Autonoma di Trento Servizio Beni Culturali Ufficio Beni Archeologici. 333–360.

Vandkilde, H. 2005. A review of the early Late Neolithic period in Denmark: practice, identity and connectivity. *www. jungsteinSITE.de*.

Vandkilde, H., Rahbek, U., & Rasmussen, K.L. 1996. Radiocarbon dating and the chronology of Bronze Age southern Scandinavia. *Acta Archaeologica* 67: 183–198.

Whitcombe, E. 2010. *A Bronze Age dagger*. [cited 5 April 2011]. Available from http://finds.org.uk/database/artefacts/record/id/397283.

York, J. 2002. The life cycle of Bronze Age metalwork from the Thames. *Oxford Journal of Archaeology* 21(1): 77-92.

Zimmermann, T. 2007. *Die ältesten kupferzeitlichen Bestattungen mit Dolchbeigabe: archäologische Untersuchungen in ausgewählten Modellregionen Alteuropas*. Mainz: Verlag des Römisch-Germanischen Zentralmuseums.

BIFACIAL FLINT DAGGERS FROM THE EARLY BRONZE AGE IN VOLHYNIA – LESSER POLAND

Witold Grużdź, Witold Migal & Katarzyna Pyżewicz

The production of bifacial flint daggers started in the Late Neolithic and the Early Bronze Age in particular parts of Europe. Few production centres during that time were located in Poland and Ukraine (in the area between the regions of Volhynia and Lesser Poland). In this paper, we present the brief history of research, production technology, typology and function of flint daggers from these areas. To that end, we analyzed bifacial forms from the collections of three Polish museums. The study focuses on describing the research history of flint daggers in these regions. We also present the classification of bifacial forms from Western Ukraine and Poland. However, due to the focus of this research we excluded the forms originating from the Scandinavian and Northern Pontic dagger traditions. The technology studies section shows the methods of platform preparation and the techniques used during the flake removal process. We then studied selected finished daggers to assess how they were repaired and reshaped. Finally, we present microscopic analyses that were used to interpret the function of selected artefacts, which allow us to demonstrate how daggers were possibly hafted and used.

Introduction

The bifacial daggers from the Volhynia and Lesser Poland areas have been studied since the second half of the nineteenth century. The history of this research is presented in the literature (Kopacz & Valde-Nowak 1987a, 1987b; Libera 2001). We can differentiate two trends in these studies. The first one is focused on various classification systems which determine the cultural attribution, genesis, diffusion and chronology of various tools and their possible functions by macroscopic observation (e.g. Przyborowski 1873; Ossowski 1886; Kozłowski 1923, 1924; Bryk 1928; Kostrzewski 1924–1925, 1939–1948; Sulimirski 1957–1959; Swiesznikow 1967; Machnik 1960, 1967, 1978; Głosik 1962; Libera 2001). The second one is associated with the emergence of the *New Archaeology*. The researchers following this trend attempt to analyse bifacial forms with new methods and interpret processes affecting the material culture. The effect of these studies are publications about methods that determine raw material economy (e.g.

Budziszewski 1991, 1998), the influence of environment on the types of lithic toolkits (Kopacz & Valde-Nowak 1987a, 1987b) and the technology of bifacial reduction (Migal & Urbanowski 2009). Despite this long research history, there is still a lack of knowledge concerning production sites and the distribution of flint daggers around the Volhynia – Lesser Poland area.

The main aim of this paper is to characterise the features of bifacially worked flint daggers that appeared at the turn of the third and second millennia BC in the so-called Volhynia – Lesser Poland zone. To do so, we synthesised previous research and analyzed selected materials from this territory.

We compared the technologies used for producing daggers and tried to estimate the knowledge and know-how of flintknappers based on the selected bifaces. We also performed analyses to determine if daggers from Volhynian flint and chocolate flint were made using the same methods and if their forms were similar or whether the *local* forms were merely the imitations of *imported*

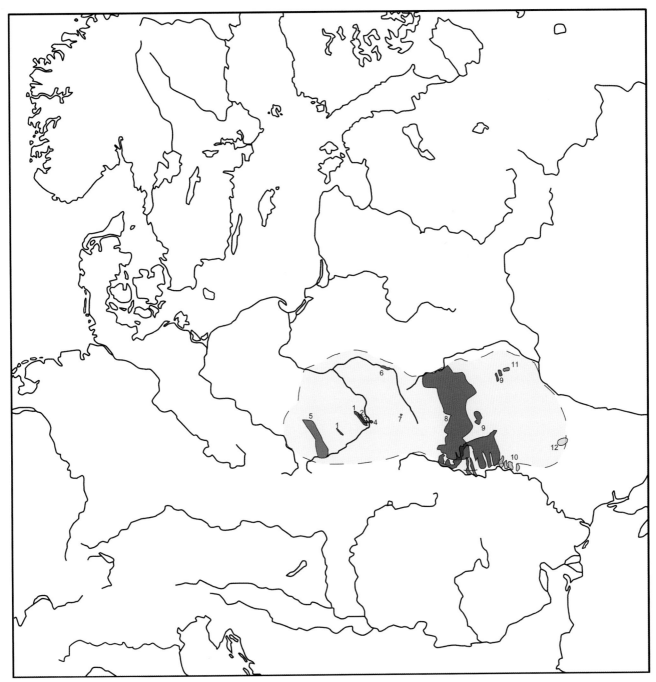

Fig. 10.1. Lithic raw materials within the Volhynia – Lesser Poland zone (some of the erratic flint outcrops were not marked on the map): 1 – chocolate flint; 2 – banded flint of Krzemionki type; 3 – Ożarów flint; 4 – Świeciechów flint; 5 – Jurassic flint from the Cracow region; 6 – Cretaceous flints from Poland (Mielnik) and Belarus; 7 – Cretaceous flint from Rejowiec; 8 – Cretaceous flints from the Volhyno-Podolian Upland; 9 – Middle Dniester and Prut chert; 10 – Middle Dniester flint; 11 – Desna type flint; 12 – Dnieper flint (after Ryzhov et al. 2005; Król & Migaszewski 2009) (drawing: W. Grużdź).

artefacts? Additionally, we tried to answer the questions of how selected daggers were utilised, what their function was and how they were repaired and reshaped. In order to answer these questions, we applied use-wear analyses to present *the biographies* of selected pieces.

Localisation and raw material background

The Volhynia – Lesser Poland zone (Fig. 10.1) consists of Lesser Poland, Mazovia, Podolia, Polesia and Volhynia regions (Libera 2001: 104). The centre of this area is located on the outcrops of Cretaceous flint from the Volhyno-

Podolian Upland (Zakościelna 1996; Konoplia 1998; Ryzhov *et al.* 2005). This raw material usually occurs in big concretions and has different colour shades, ranging from black and brown through grey to white, frequently with bands. Some researchers classify this flint (West Volhynian and Podolian flint with their varieties) into varieties based on the location where they outcrop (Balcer 1983; Zakościelna 1996; Konoplia 1998; Ryzhov *et al.* 2005). In this paper, we do not follow this classification, because certain defined features of raw materials are difficult to identify on finished bifaces (e.g. shape of the cortex, inconsiderable or slight differences between the varieties). On the western range of the Volhynia – Lesser Poland zone we find outcrops of various kinds of flint: chocolate, Krzemionki, Świeciechów, Ożarów, Rejowiec and so-called Jurassic flint from the Cracow region (Rejniewicz 1985; Król & Migaszewski 2009). These raw materials were also used for the production of bifacial forms (such as daggers, sickles or axes) which, in some contexts, are found with daggers and sickles made from Volhynian flint (Budziszewski 1998; Libera 2001).

Volhynia – Lesser Poland daggers classification

Flint daggers from the Volhynia – Lesser Poland area have been sorted into a wide range of classification systems and types (Przyborowski 1873; Ossowski 1886; Kozłowski 1923, 1924; Kostrzewski 1924–1925, 1939–1948; Sulimirski 1957–1959; Machnik 1960, 1978; Głosik 1962; Libera 2001). Their descriptions sometimes differ significantly. In this chapter, we present a simplified version of Jerzy Libera's classification (2001) without a broad range of subtypes and with some modifications of our own. However, this kind of typology should be considered *artificial* – we used elaborated forms with evident morphological features to define selected types. Additionally, there is not enough data to apply this typology within precise chronological frames. We also try to avoid directly associating various dagger types with specific Early Bronze Age cultures (although the daggers were used in Mierzanowice, Strzyżów and Trzciniec cultures) which are distinguished on the basis of ceramics and metal artefacts (Kadrow & Machnik 1997; Kadrow 2001; Klochko 2001; Makarowicz 2010). Additionally, it is worth mentioning that some more specific forms originating from Volhynia and Lesser Poland traditions, such as the Czerniczyn-Torczyn type, are rarely found outside the described area (Czebreszuk & Kozłowska-Skoczka 2008; Razumov 2011: 143f; Kaczmarek 2012: 126ff, 388).

Type 1

Daggers attributed to this type usually do not have tangs (rarely, there are slightly pronounced tangs) and are lanceolate (Fig. 10.2: 1). If their base is marked, it can be convex, pointed or straight. The blades of these daggers are long and narrow, sometimes broadest in the middle of the section. Generally there are no differences in thickness along the entire length of a form.

In Libera's classification, these daggers were divided into variety AA (II-III) and AB (II-III), and they were distinguished by the shapes of bases and sub-varieties derived from the morphology of the blades. In the literature related to relative chronologies, these types are known to be used in the Strzyżów culture and also could have existed in the Trzciniec and Lusatian cultures (Libera 2001: 123ff; Bargieł & Libera 2005; Makarowicz 2010: 184ff).

Type 2

This category includes daggers with lanceolate or rhomboid blades and slightly pronounced tangs that are lenticular in cross-section (Fig. 10.2: 2). The bases are convex or straight. Usually, the daggers are widest in the lower section of the blades. The thickness of the tangs is usually identical to or slightly greater than the thickness of the blades.

Daggers of this type correspond to the Libera variety AB (I) and BA (I-II) which are differentiated based on the shapes of the blades. These forms are linked to the early phase of the Mierzanowice culture and Strzyżów culture – in this case only rhomboid bladed forms with straight base (Machnik 1967: 72; Libera 2001: 123ff; Bargieł & Libera 2005).

Type 3

These types of daggers are distinguished by well-marked tangs and leaf-shaped blades (Fig. 10.2: 3). As in the case of the previous type, their base can be convex or straight. The part between the sides and the base of the blade is rounded or has an obtuse angle. The ratio of width to length is usually the greatest of all the dagger types. The thickness of the tangs is differentiated – they can be equal, thinner or thicker than their blades. In some cases, small notches can be seen at the bottom part of the blade.

Analogies to this category can be observed in the examples of the BA (II) type according to Libera's classification. These daggers appeared in the early phase of the Mierzanowice culture (Machnik 1967: 72; Libera 2001: 123ff; Bargieł & Libera 2005).

Type 4

This dagger type is identified by very pronounced tangs and leaf-shaped or triangular blades (Fig. 10.2: 4). The bases are convex or straight. The part between the sides and the base of the blade is nearly straight or even sharply angular. The tangs are usually thinner or have the same thickness as the rest of the forms. Occasionally, small notches are present at the bottom part of the blades.

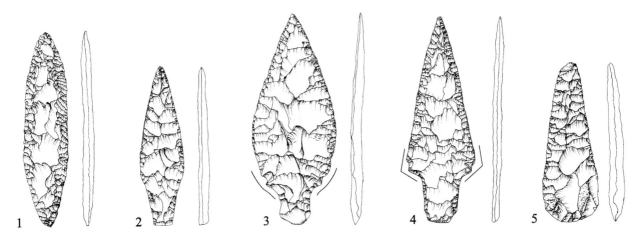

Fig. 10.2. Classification of daggers from Volhynia – Lesser Poland (drawings: K. Pyżewicz).

Libera classified these artefacts as the variety BB (I-II). According to relative chronology, these kinds of daggers are linked to the early phase of Mierzanowice culture (Libera 2001: 123ff; Bargieł & Libera 2005).

It is worth noting that, in the literature, the term Czerniczyn-Torczyn is used to describe a wide range of different morphological forms found in graves on the Czerniczyn (Kokowski & Koman 1985) and Torczyn (Fitzke 1975) sites. Volhynian flint daggers (types 2–4) were identified in the recorded assemblages. On the Czerniczyn site, graves could be dated to around the 20th century BC. These daggers were associated with materials linked to the early phase of the Mierzanowice culture (Głosik 1968; Kopacz 1971; Kempisty & Włodarczak 1996; Libera 2001:78f; Bargieł & Libera 2005).

Type 5

This type of dagger is characterised by having its greatest width at the base and by the lack of a tang (Fig. 10.2: 5). Generally, the shape of the blade is close to triangular. The base of these daggers is straight or slightly convex. These kinds of artefacts are very difficult to classify due to similarities between the morphology of daggers, sickles and preforms of bifacial axes found in the Volhynia – Lesser Poland zone.

This category is related to type AB (IV) in Libera's classification, where they were associated with Kołpiec-Kawsko assemblages and possibly with the late phase of the Mierzanowice culture (Libera 2001:123ff; Bargieł & Libera 2005).

As we have shown, the daggers from the Volhynia – Lesser Poland area share some general features. Their most prominent feature is a high width-to-thickness ratio

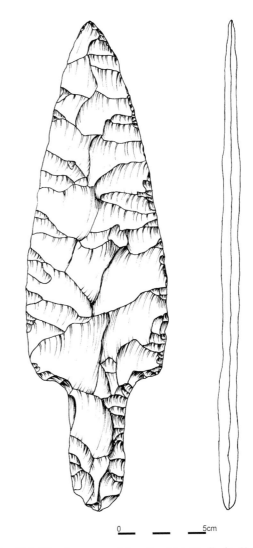

Fig. 10.3. Flint dagger type 4 from Grodzisk (Podlaskie Voivodeship) (drawings: K. Pyżewicz).

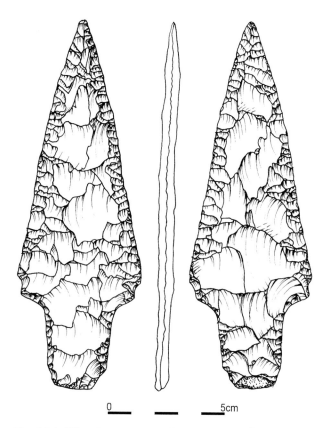

0 _____ _____ 5cm

Fig. 10.4. Flint dagger type 4 from Baranów (Świętokrzyskie Voivodeship) (drawings: K. Pyżewicz).

on finished, elaborated blades (e.g. Figs. 10.3 and 10.4). The cross-section of these forms is slightly lenticular. The faces of these bifaces are frequently parallel to each other, becoming curved only towards the edges where they were finished off with precise, pressure flaking retouch. The second distinctive attribute lies in the morphology of their tangs which are different from the handles noted in the Scandinavian tradition. These tangs are very thin and shaped in the same manner as the rest of the artefact. In some cases, notches were made along the edges of these daggers; and these notches should also be considered as a specific feature of the Volhynia – Lesser Poland flint daggers.

During the Early Bronze Age in the area between Volhynia and Lesser Poland, another type of dagger appeared: asymmetric daggers that are often referred to as *transitional* forms. In the literature, they are linked to the classical phase of the Mierzanowice culture (Libera 2001: 123ff; Bargieł & Libera 2005). Budziszewski (1998) noticed that some of these daggers were made from *local* lithic raw materials (e.g. chocolate and Świeciechów flint). Therefore, he suggested that these bifaces were a result of influence from the small workshops within the distribution area of the Volhynia – Lesser Poland dagger tradition. These forms belong to a category that is morphologically differentiated and limited

in number of artefacts, so the present state of research does not allow for their inclusion in the typological classification.

Technology and function of flint daggers – a case study

We analyzed the production and function of daggers in Early Bronze Age societies by undertaking detailed studies of selected flint bifaces.

The first step was to conduct technological research and use-wear analysis (cf. Keeley 1980:28; Vaughan 1985: 41f; Ibáñez *et al.* 1990; Byrne *et al.* 2006; Méry *et al.* 2007; Rots *et al.* 2011; Vergès & Andreu 2011). The microscopic analyses, used to investigate function, hafting and technological aspects, were carried out with a metallographic microscope (Nikon LV150) which allows magnification from 50× to 500×. Before analysis, the lithic bifaces were cleaned of contaminants on their surfaces with warm water and detergent as well as pure acetone. To verify our hypotheses, we conducted additional, experimental tests.

The analysed artefacts came from the collection of the State Archaeological Museum in Warsaw, the Museum of Archaeology in Krakow and the District Museum in Sandomierz. The daggers were mostly stray finds or were obtained during excavation. They were usually made of Cretaceous flint from the Volhyno-Podolian Upland and, in some cases, from other (local) raw materials. While carrying out our research, we found some limitations which affected the quality of our work. Firstly, within the Volhynia – Lesser Poland area, there was no previously analyzed workshop which could be associated with the production of daggers. Therefore, in order to interpret the technology, we based our research on the results of analyses of finished forms and individual preforms. Additionally, we used the data obtained from the analysis of flint mines in Ożarów, known to be linked to bifacial sickles production workshops and dated to the same period as production centers of Volhynian daggers. The second important limitation of our study was the poor state of preservation of the analyzed daggers (patination, burnt pieces etc.). These constraints often made it difficult to identify raw materials and to interpret microscopic observations on lithic surfaces.

Bifacial reduction

Methods of bifacial reduction have often been the subject of case studies in the Scandinavian dagger tradition. Researchers generally divide the production process into several stages demonstrating gradual transformation of the raw material and enabling a good visualisation of the entire shaping sequence. However, this kind of observation is always influenced by the researcher making the division between certain stages of lithic processing and should not

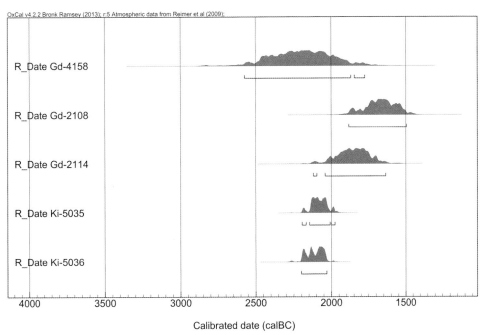

Fig. 10.5. Calibrated radiocarbon dates from the Ożarów mine shafts I/5 (Gd–4158, 3760±140 BP) and I/3 (Gd–2108, 3370±80 BP; Gd–2114, 3520±80 BP) and the Czerniczyn graves III (Ki–5035, 3690±30 BP) and XI (Ki–5036, 3720±30 BP).

be regarded as describing the perception of prehistoric producers. The current state of research on the bifacial technology from the Volhynia – Lesser Poland territory does not allow us to present the manufacturing process accurately, as has been done in the Scandinavian tradition (Arnold 1990; Apel 2001, 2006; Callahan 2006; Nunn 2006). For this reason, our discussion of bifacial reduction was based on comparing the bifacial stages proposed by Callahan (1996) with later modifications made by other researchers (Andrefsky 2005; Whittaker 1999) to the lithic materials from the Ożarów (Lesser Poland) mine where local Turonian flint was obtained. Two of the analysed shafts from Ożarów are linked to bifacial production (sickles) and are dated (Shaft I/5: Gd–4158 3760±140 BP, 2573–1775 cal BC; Shaft I/3: Gd–2108 3370±80 BP, 1884–1496 cal BC; Gd–2114 3520±80BP, 2120–1636 cal BC) roughly to the same period as the flint daggers (Czerniczyn graves III: Ki–5035 3690±30 BP, 2196–1977 cal BC and XI: Ki–5036 3720±30 BP, 2202–2031 cal BC, both with Type 4 daggers) made from Volhynian flint (Fig. 10.5) (Budziszewski 1980, 1997; Libera 2001; Bargieł & Libera 2005). The results of this research have already been discussed in a separate paper (Grużdź 2012). Here, we briefly present a few distinctive features from this case study that differentiates the Volhynia – Lesser Poland tradition from the reduction sequences presented by Callahan.

These observations lead to two trends in the analyzed assemblage. The first trend is the detachment of large flakes from the natural sides of the blank through the use of

direct, hard-hammer percussion (Fig. 10.6: 3). This method proves that the second stage of bifacial reduction (*Initial Edging, Edged Biface, Rough Out*) could look somewhat different from the one proposed in the Scandinavian schema (Callahan 1996; Whittaker 1999; Apel 2001; Andrefsky 2005). The analysis of the flaking pattern showed that, before the detachment of full-face flakes, a large platform (usually continuous) was prepared (Fig. 10.6: 1–2). The platform was located away from the center line of the biface. This method is quite similar to those described by Bradley (Aubry *et al.* 2008; Bradley *et al.* 2010). The only difference is that it was probably rarely used during the advanced stage of production. This procedure was quite risky and was noted only on the specimen from the area of the mine. The majority of forms with evidence of this technique were made from tabular flint, indicating that it was intentionally used to remove natural square edges from a preform (Bradley *et al.* 2010). Although there is an example of using extensive full face flaking with use of direct soft percussion on more advanced stages of dagger production noted on preform made from Volhynian flint, which comes usually in nodules (Fig. 10.7).

The microscopic traces that could be a result of contact with material used for flake detachment were difficult to interpret as technological traces cannot always be distinguished from wear caused by usage or by keeping the daggers in sheaths. Therefore, the interpretation of microscopic traces and the determination of flaking technique was limited to selected artefacts. This study

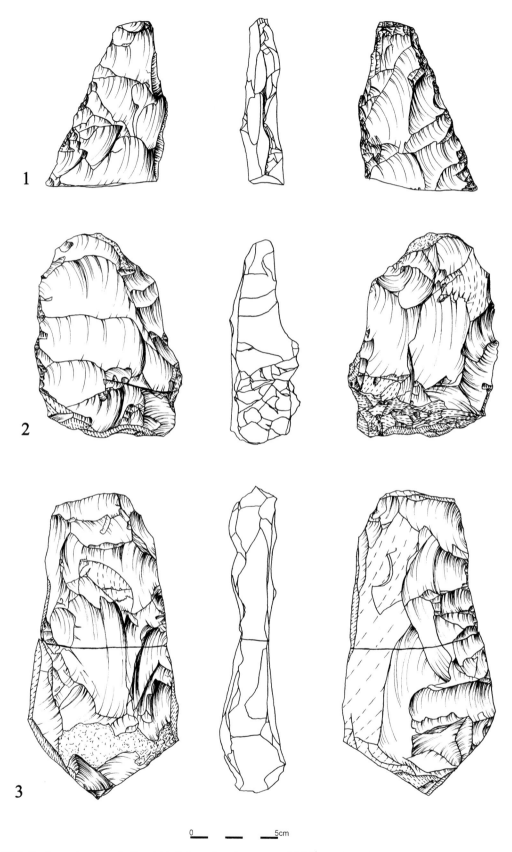

Fig. 10.6. Preforms (most probably sickles) from Ożarów mining field (Świętokrzyskie Voivodeship) (after Grużdź 2012).

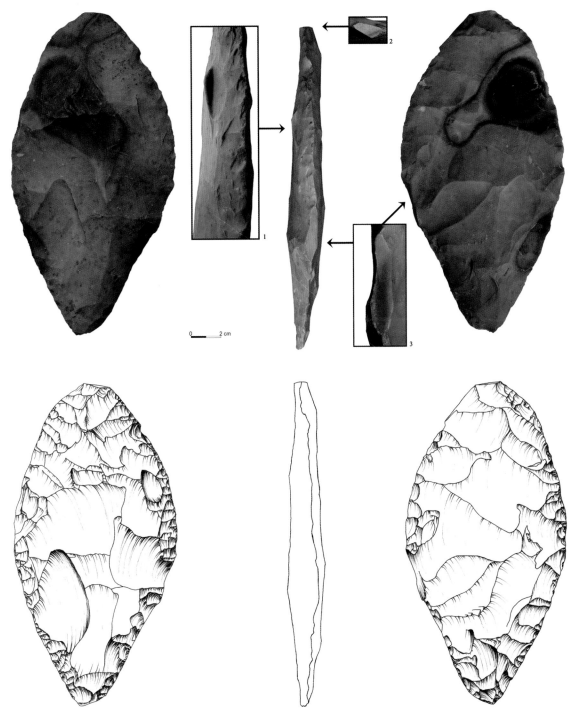

0 _____ 2 cm

Fig. 10.7. Bifacial preform from Mirohoszcza (Volyn Oblast): 1– "continuous" platform prepared on one of the sides, 2 – "natural" tip, 3 – negative after plunging flake (drawings & photo: W. Grużdź & K. Pyżewicz).

enabled us to distinguish materials that were used as tools in bifacial shaping.

The microscopic analyses confirmed the results of the technological observations concerning the early stage of production of the materials from the Ożarów flint mines. Bifaces from this shaping phase showed traces of hammerstones on their striking platforms. On bifaces from the later stages of reduction there are characteristic traces on the surface where hammer and flint came into contact which confirms that billets of organic material were also used.

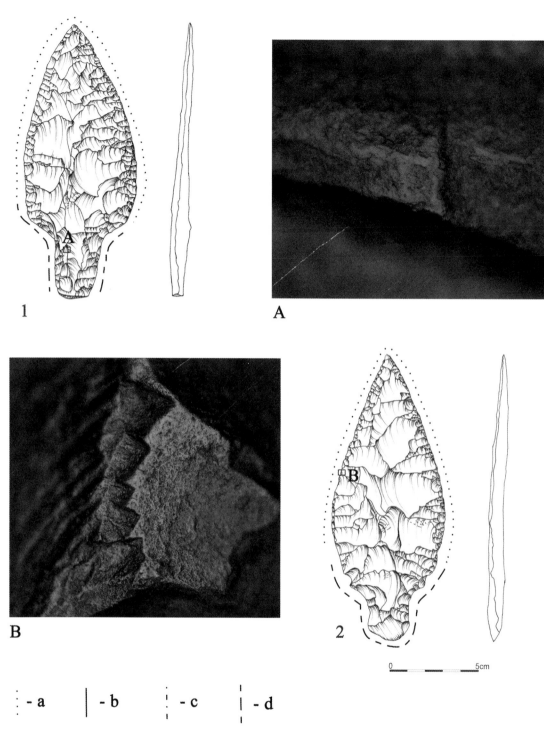

Fig. 10.8. Type 3 flint daggers: 1. Wilanów (Masovian Voivodeship); 2. Moszczanica (Rivne Oblast); A. orig. magn. 200×; B. orig. magn. 100×. Symbols used in the figures: a – sheath; b – siliceous plants; c – sheath/hafting; d – hafting (drawings & photo: K. Pyżewicz).

These micro-traces correspond to the marks of deformation observed on experimental forms made with antler tools. Most of these traces were noted on unfinished bifaces from Dermań (Fig. 10.10: 1A) and Ożarów that were discarded during the final phases of reduction. Traces that probably resulted from the application of organic billets were noted on forms that retained evidence of manufacture (morphology of negatives with diffused bulbs of percussion, remnant of the lip and acute flaking angle) interpreted as resulting from soft direct percussion. In conclusion, microscopic studies

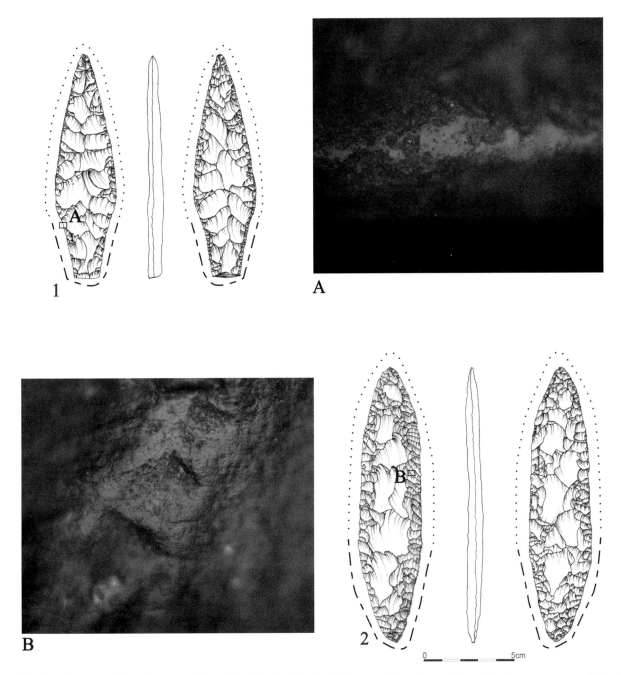

Fig. 10.9. Flint daggers: 1. Type 2 – Zawadyńce (Khmelnitsky Oblast); 2. Type 1 – Marianówka (Volyn Oblast); A. orig. magn. 200x; B. orig. magn. 200× (drawings & photo: K. Pyżewicz).

provide support for our general knowledge about hammers used in bifacial reduction (e.g. Apel 2001; Andrefsky 2005; Callahan 1996; Whittaker 1999).

Function of daggers

The results of use-wear analysis show clear differences between the daggers and the sickles in the Early Bronze Age in the Volhynia – Lesser Poland area. These differences are found both in the utilisation and in the hafting of these items.

On the daggers that were not altered as a result of post-depositional factors, we observed traces which usually did not indicate their *function*. The structure and location of traces is analogous to those of the wear which is interpreted as resulting from hafting, protecting bifaces in sheaths or keeping flint bifaces in containers made from organic

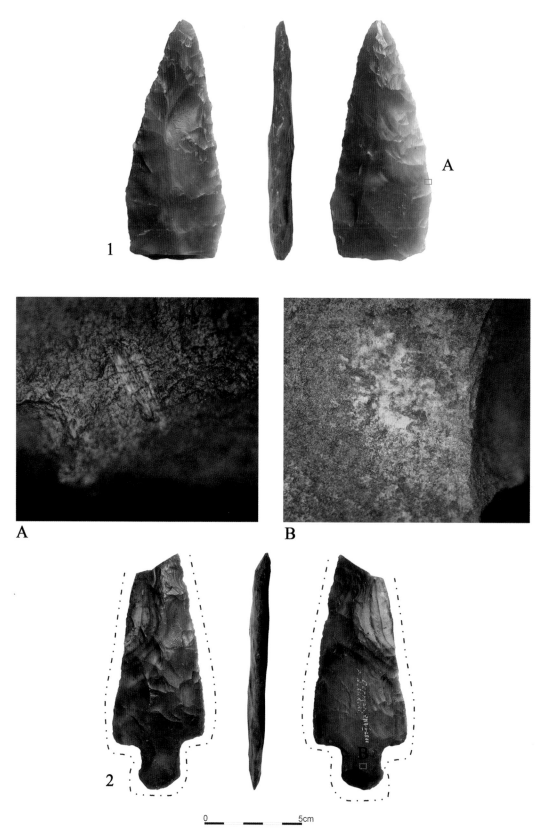

*Fig. 10.10. 1. Bifacial preform from Dermań (Rivne Oblast); 2. Type 4 flint dagger from Dermań (Rivne Oblast); A. orig. magn. 200×;
B. orig. magn. 100× (drawings & photo: K. Pyżewicz).*

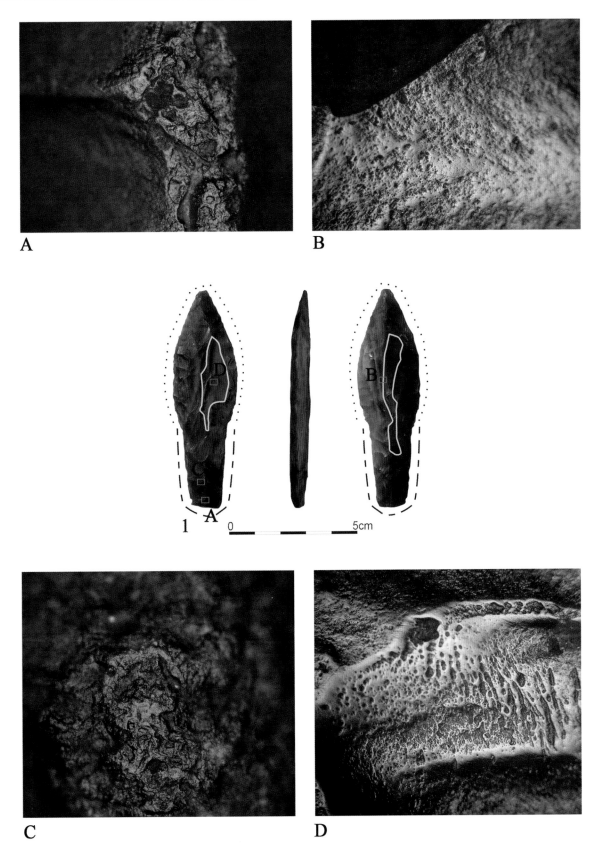

Fig. 10.11. Type 2 flint dagger from Dermań (Rivne Oblast): A. orig. magn. 100×; B. orig. magn. 50×; C. orig. magn. 100×; D. orig. magn. 50× (drawings & photo: K. Pyżewicz).

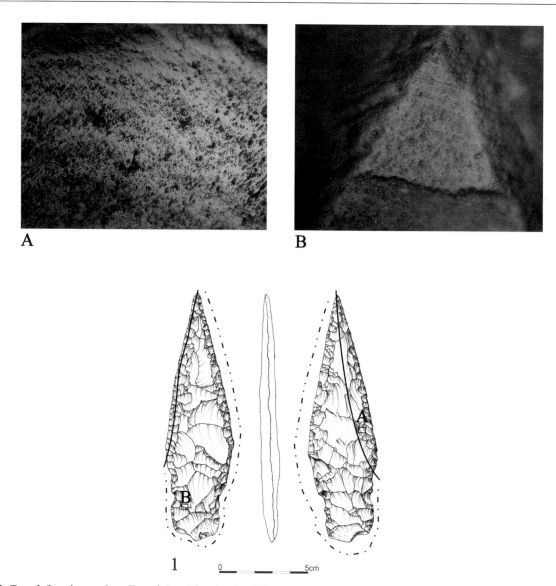

Fig. 10.12. Type 2 flint dagger from Zawadyńce (Khmelnitsky Oblast): A. orig. magn. 100×; B. orig. magn. 200× (drawings & photo: K. Pyżewicz).

material (cf. Libera 2001: 38ff; Plisson *et al.* 2002; Rots 2010; Van Gijn 2010a, 2010b). In addition, we noticed that, in some cases (when the marks are more distinctive), the wear located on the tangs diverges from that noticed on other parts of the daggers. The blades are covered with wear occurring on the edges and protruding parts (along the whole item), resulting from contact with a soft organic material – skin and/or plant fibre (Figs 10.8: 2B and 10.9: 2B). We can presume that these types of materials were used to make sheaths in which flint daggers were kept. On the protruding parts of the tangs we noticed traces which could result from contact with a haft made from a slightly harder material, such as antler, bone or wood (Figs 10.8: 1A, 10.9: 1A, 10.10: 2B and 10.12: 1B).

Other very interesting features were noticed on some smaller daggers which differ from more typical ones not only in size but also in morphology. On the surfaces of these pieces we noted the traces of siliceous plants and the evidence of reshaping.

One of them – a small dagger – is characterised by various traces formed at different stages of its use-life which reveals its biography. Marks which we recorded only on the fragments of the *old* negative flake scars, located at the central parts of both sides of the tool should be interpreted as resulting from intense contact with siliceous plants (Fig. 10.11: 1B, 1D). In contrast, on the negatives of smaller flakes and chips resulting from final retouch, we recorded only traces associated with some kind of sheath or haft, as well as unidentified wear (Fig.10. 11: 1A, 1C). This artefact exhibits a transformation of form and change of use (perhaps it was originally a sickle, because most of the analysed items of this type were covered by evident traces of siliceous plants in contrast to daggers). The second dagger is characterised by traces of use extending along one side of the blade and consistent with cutting siliceous plants (Fig. 10.12: 1A). We can assume that the form was utilised in a similar way to the sickles analysed (cf. below), perhaps the final retouch (differing from the common one in the analysed set of daggers) was designed to modify the working edge for functional purposes.

It should be noted that the analyzed daggers probably functioned for a long time in the prehistoric societies, as indicated by the intensity of the microscopic traces. The present research confirms that flint daggers were probably more prestige items than conventional tools used in daily life, as suggested by the lack of visible signs of usage and intensive traces of long-term storage in organic containers or sheaths.

The forms classified as sickles which, in this paper, we treated as a background to our discussion about the daggers' function, are characterised by completely different traces of utilisation and hafting (cf. Balcer & Schild 1978a, 1978b, 1980; Bąbel & Budziszewski 1978; Libera 2001: 67ff). These specimens have homogeneous, intense use-wear traces, different to those which we observed on most of the daggers. On all such tools, we noted traces associated with the intensive processing of siliceous plants, especially cereals. Evidence of cutting plants can be seen in the form of a distinctive polish and striations indicating the direction of work. The clearly delineated border of the gloss enables us to interpret the position of the sickles in their hafts. Among the varieties of sickles we recorded various methods of hafting including traces which covered only the tops of the tools and those which extended into its central part.

Conclusions

Flint daggers that appeared in the Volhynia and Lesser Poland regions were distributed from production centres that played an important role in Early Bronze Age societies. One of the key elements of such a situation could be linked to difficulties among local groups in obtaining bronze. At the beginning of the 2nd millennium BC this metal was used in Lesser Poland mostly for small items and flint was still the main raw material for tool production (Kadrow & Machnik 1997; Kadrow 2001). This continued quotidian use of flint could be one of the factors that led to the distribution of bifacial tools; but, according to this interpretation, the bifaces would only serve as conventional tools. Use-wear

analyses already presented in the literature and in our studies would suggest that daggers could be used as prestigious objects kept for a very long time in which case they were not always used in everyday activities. We may also assume that bifacial tools could have both symbolic and functional roles at the same time.

We can assume that Early Bronze Age societies preferred daggers made from imported Volhynian flint as opposed to the sickles which were often made from local raw materials. A similar situation can be seen even in flint rich regions, such as Lesser Poland. In this area, Świeciechów, Ożarów and chocolate flints were used for the production of sickles in contrast to daggers which were rarely made from this kind of raw material. However, we can observe many similarities in bifacial technology in both of these object types. These similarities are prominent especially in reduction strategies which involved critical thinning of the blade with the detachment of a few large flakes at the early stage of shaping. This observation could indicate that some craftsmen from societies that were located far from each other nevertheless shared knowledge about flint technology. On the other hand, we noticed that some of the daggers were repaired by unskilled knappers who were probably the users of these items. One of the interesting aspects lies in the production of *transitional* daggers. We could interpret their irregular morphology as a result of a lack of *know-how* in tool production (in repairing or in attempting to imitate the imported pieces). We noticed one more tendency associated with the final retouch along the edges. In the case of the daggers, which were not quotidian tools, we recorded a regular, thinning retouch, whereas artefacts characterised by intensive use-wear traces (as shown by the examples of analyzed sickles and daggers) have more dull and robust types of retouch, sometimes with denticulation.

Further investigations should be focused on analyzing bifacial workshops from Volhynia and Lesser Poland. There is also a need to obtain more accurate absolute dating which would indicate more precise chronological frames for the daggers in this region. There should also be an extended discussion about whether the typological forms correspond with prehistoric mental templates.

Acknowledgements

We are grateful to Dr Berit V. Eriksen and Dr Catherine J. Frieman for inviting us to contribute a chapter in this book. Additional thanks go to Monika Bajka, Dr Wojciech Brzeziński, Dr Janusz Budziszewski, Agnieszka Dziedzic, Dr Jacek Górski, Barbara Sałacińska, Sławomir Sałaciński, and Elżbieta Trela-Kieferling for helping us during this project.

References

Andrefsky, W. 2005. *Lithics. Macroscopic Approaches to Analysis.* Cambridge: Cambridge University Press.

Apel, J. 2001. *Daggers, Knowledge and Power: The Social Aspects of Flint-dagger Technology in Scandinavia, 2350–1500 cal. BC.* Uppsala: Uppsala University Department of Archaeology & Ancient History.

Apel, J. 2006. Skill and experimental archaeology. In: J. Apel & K. Knutsson (eds.), *Skilled Production and Social Reproduction. Aspects of Traditional Stone-Tool Technologies. Proceedings from an International Symposium held in Uppsala August 20–24, 2003.* SAU Stone Studies 2. Uppsala: Societas Archaeologica Upsaliensis. 207–218.

Arnold, V. 1990. Refitting of waste material from dagger production of site Tegelbarg (Quern-Neukirchen, Schleswig-Holstein). In: E. Cziesla, S. Eickhoff, N. Arts, & D. Winter (eds.), *The big puzzle: International Symposium on Refitting Stone Artefacts.* Bonn: Holos. 211–216.

Aubry, T., Bradley, B., Almeida, M., Walter, B., Neves, M.-J., Pelegrin, J., Lenoir, M. & Tiffagom, M. 2008. Solutrean laurel leaf production at Maîtreaux: an experimental approach guided by techno-economic analysis. *World Archaeology* 40(1): 48–66.

Balcer, B. 1983. *Wytwórczość narzędzi krzemiennych w neolicie ziem Polski.* Wrocław - Warszawa - Kraków - Gdańsk - Łódź: Zakład Narodowy im. Ossolińskich, Wydawnictwo Polskiej Akademii Nauk.

Balcer, B. & Schild, R. 1978a. A jednak sierpy! *Z Otchłani Wieków* 44(1): 44–48.

Balcer, B. & Schild, R.1978b. Sierpem i głowę można uciąć... *Z Otchłani Wieków* 44(2): 145–147.

Balcer, B. & Schild, R. 1980. Traces of Wear and Stone Tool Function: Do They Really Mean What They Show? In: R. Schild (ed.), *Unconventional Archaeology. New Approaches and Goals in Polish Archaeology.* Wrocław – Warszawa – Kraków – Gdańsk: Zakład Narodowy im. Ossolińskich.109–116.

Bargieł, B. & Libera, J. 2005. Zespoły grobowe z krzemiennymi płoszczami w Małopolsce i na Wołyniu. *Wiadomości Archeologiczne* 57: 3–27.

Bąbel, J. T. & Budziszewski, J. 1978. Noże wielofunkcyjne! *Z Otchłani Wieków* 44(2): 139–145.

Bradley, B., Collins, M. B. & Hemmings, A. 2010. *Clovis Technology.* Michigan: International Monographs in Prehistory.

Bryk, J. 1928. *Kultury epoki kamienia na wydmach zachodniej części południowego Wołynia.* Lwów: Towarzystwo Naukowe we Lwowie.

Budziszewski, J. 1980. Der Ożarówer Feuerstein und die Probleme seiner Nutzung und Verteilung. In: G. Weisgerber, R. Slotta & J. Weiner (eds.), *5000 Jahre Feuersteinbergbau. Die Suche nach dem Stahl der Steinzeit.* Veröffentlichungen aus dem Deutschen Bergbau – Museum Bochum 22. Bochum: Deutsches Bergbau-Museum Bochum: 318–320.

Budziszewski, J. 1991. Krzemieniarstwo ludności Wyżyny Środkowomałopolskiej we wczesnej epoce brązu. *Lubelskie Materiały Archeologiczne* 6: 181–208.

Budziszewski, J. 1997. C–14 dating of shallow flint mine sites. Case study from th 'Za Garncarzami' mining field in Ożarów (Central Poland). In: R. Schild & Z. Sulgostowska (eds.), *Man and Flint. Proceedings of the VIIth International Flint Symposium, Warszawa – Ostrowiec Świętokrzyski, September 1995.* Warszawa: Institute of Archaeology and Ethnology, Polish Academy of Sciences. 87–109.

Budziszewski, J. 1998. Świętokrzyski Okręg Pradziejowej Eksploatacji Krzemieni w dobie kultury trzcinieckiej. In: A. Kośko & J. Czebreszuk (eds.), *Trzciniec System kulturowy czy interkulturowy proces?* Poznań: Wydawnictwo Poznańskie. 285–299.

Byrne, L., Olle, A. & Vergès, J. M. 2006. Under the Hammer: Residues Resulting from Production and Microwear on Experimental Stone Tools. *Archaeometry* 48(4): 549–564.

Callahan, E. 1996. *The Basics of Biface Knapping in the Eastern Fluted Point Tradition: A Manual for Flintknappers and Lithic Analysts,* 3rd ed.. Archeology of Eastern North America 7. Connecticut: Eastern States Archaeological Federation.

Callahan, E. 2006. Neolithic Danish daggers: an experimental peek. In: J. Apel & K. Knutsson (eds.), *Skilled Production and Social Reproduction. Aspects of Traditional Stone-Tool Technologies. Proceedings from an International Symposium held in Uppsala August 20–24, 2003.* SAU Stone Studies 2. Uppsala: Societas Archaeologica Upsaliensis. 115–137.

Czebreszuk, J. & Kozłowska-Skoczka, D. 2008. *Sztylety krzemienne na Pomorzu Zachodnim, Muzeum Narodowe w Szczecinie.* Szczecin: Uniwersytet im. Adama Mickiewicza, Poznańskie Towarzystwo Prehistoryczne.

Fitzke, J. 1975. Cmentarzysko kultury strzyżowskiej w Torczynie pod Łuckiem na Wołyniu. *Wiadomości Archeologiczne* 40: 53–62.

Głosik, J. 1962. Wołyńsko-podolskie materiały z epoki kamiennej i wczesnej epoki brązu w Państwowym Muzeum Archeologicznym w Warszawie. *Materiały Starożytne* 8: 125–216.

Głosik, J. 1968. Kultura strzyżowska. *Materiały Starożytne* 11: 7–114.

Grużdź, W. 2012. *Wybrane aspekty form dwuściennych we wczesnej epoce brązu na przykładzie materiałów z pola górniczego w Ożarowie. Wiadomości Archeologiczne* 63: 3–31.

Ibáñez, J. J., Gonzáles, J. E., Lagüera, M. A. & Gutièrrez, C. 1990. Knapping traces: their characteristics according to the hammerstone and the technique used. In: R. Séronie-Vivien & M. Lenoir (eds.), *Le silex de sa genèse à l'outil, Actes du Ve Colloque international sur le Silex, Bordeaux, 17 sept. – 2 oct. 1987. Cahiers du Quaternaire* 17. Paris: Éditions du Centre national de la recherche scientifique. 547–553.

Kaczmarek, M. 2012. *Epoka brązu na Nizinie Wielkopolsko-Kujawskiej w świetle interregionalnych kontaktów wymiennych,* Poznań: Wydawnictwo Poznańskiego Towarzystwa Przyjaciół Nauk.

Kadrow, S. 2001. *U progu nowej epoki. Gospodarka i społeczeństwo wczesnego okresu epoki brązu w Europie Środkowej.* Kraków: Instytut Archeologii i Etnologii Polskiej Akademii Nauk.

Kadrow, S. & Machnik, J. 1997. *Kultura mierzanowicka, chronologia, taksonomia i rozwój przestrzenny.* Kraków: Wydawnictwo Oddziału Polskiej Akademii Nauk.

Keeley, L. H. 1980. *Experimental Determination of Stone Tool Uses. A Microwear Analysis.* Chicago: University of Chicago Press.

Kempisty, A. & Włodarczak, P. 1996. Chronologia absoluta

cmentarzyska w Żernikach Górnych, woj. kieleckie. In: W. Nowakowski (ed.), *Concordia: studia ofiarowane Jerzemu Okuliczowi-Kozarynowi w sześćdziesiątą piątą rocznicę urodzin*. Warszawa: Instytut Archeologii Uniwersytetu Warszawskiego. 127–140.

Klochko V.I. 2001. *Weaponry of Societies of the Northern Pontic Culture Circle: 5000–700 BC*. Baltic-Pontic Studies 10. Poznań: Adam Mickiewicz University.

Kokowski, A. & Koman, W. 1985. *Néolithique et la période romaine aux environs de Hrubieszów, Pologne de l'Est*. Inventaria Archaeologica: Corpus des ensembles archéologiques, Pologne 54. Warszawa-Łódź: Państwowe Wydawnictwo Naukowe.

Konoplia V.M. 1998. Klasyfikatsiia kremianoi syrovyny zakhodu Ukrainy. *Naukowi zapysky* 7: 139–157.

Kopacz, J. 1971. Nieznane zabytki kultury strzyżowskiej z cmentarzyska w Torczynie. *Wiadomości Archeologiczne* 36: 354–355.

Kopacz, J. & Valde-Nowak, P. 1987a. Episznurowy przykarpacki krąg kulturowy w świetle materiałów kamiennych. *Archeologia Polski* 32: 55-92.

Kopacz, J. & Valde-Nowak, P. 1987b. From studies of flint industries of the Circum-Carpathian Epi-Corded Ware cultural circle (C.E.C.C.). In: J. K. Kozłowski & S. K. Kozłowski (eds.), *New in Stone Age Archeology*, Archaeologia Interregionalis. Warszawa: Wydawnictwo Uniwersytetu Warszawskiego. 183–210.

Kostrzewski, J. 1924–1925. Młodsza epoka kamienna w Polsce. (Z powodu pracy prof. L. Kozłowskiego). *Wiadomości Archeologiczne* 9(3–4): 262–296.

Kostrzewski, J. 1939–1948. Od mezolitu do okresu wędrówek ludów. In: S. Krukowski, J. Kostrzewski & R. Jakimowicz (eds.), *Prehistoria ziem polskich. Encyklopedia Polska* 4(1/5). Kraków: Polska Akademia Umiejętności. 118–360.

Kozłowski, L. 1923. *Epoka kamienia na wydmach wschodniej części Wyżyny Małopolskiej*. Lwów: Książnica polska.

Kozłowski, L. 1924. *Młodsza epoka kamienia w Polsce /Neolit/*. Lwów: Towarzystwo Naukowe.

Król, P. & Migaszewski, Z. M. 2009. Rodzaje, występowanie i geneza krzemieni. Zarys problematyki. In: P. Król (ed.), *Historia krzemienia*. Kielce: Muzeum Narodowe w Kielcach. 12–45.

Libera, J. 2001. *Krzemienne formy bifacjalne na terenach Polski i Zachodniej Ukrainy (od środkowego neolitu do wczesnej epoki żelaza)*. Lublin: Wydawnictwo Uniwersytetu Marii Curie-Skłodowskiej.

Machnik, J. 1960. Ze studiów nad kulturą ceramiki sznurowej w Karpatach polskich. *Acta Archaeologica Carpathica* 2: 55–86.

Machnik, J. 1967. *Stosunki kulturowe na przełomie neolitu i wczesnej epoki brązu w Małopolsce (na tle przemian w Europie Środkowej)*. In: W. Hensel (ed.), *Materiały do prahistorii ziem polskich*. Warszawa: Instytut Historii Kultury Materialnej Polskiej Akademii Nauk. 1–235.

Machnik, J. 1978. *Wczesny okres epoki brązu*. In: A. Gardawski & J. Kowalczyk (eds.), *Prahistoria ziem polskich III, Wczesna epoka brązu*, Wrocław – Warszawa – Kraków – Gdańsk: Ossolineum. 9–136.

Makarowicz, P. 2010. *Trzciniecki krąg kulturowy - wspólnota pogranicza Wschodu i Zachodu Europy*. Poznań: Wydawnictwo Poznańskie.

Méry, S., Anderson, P., Inizan, M. L., Lechevallier, M. & Pelegrin J. 2007. A pottery workshop with flint tools on blades knapped with copper at Nausharo (Indus civilisation, *ca.* 2500 BC). *Journal of Archaeological Science* 34: 1098–1116.

Migal, W. & Urbanowski, M. 2009. *Narzędzia bifacjalne jako wskaźniki chronologiczne?* Technologie środkowego paleolitu i wczesnej epoki brązu na przykładzie materiałów ze stanowiska Polany II. In: W. Borkowski, J. Libera, B. Sałacińska & S. Sałaciński (eds.), *Krzemień czekoladowy w pradziejach. Materiały z konferencji w Orońsku, 08–10.10.2003*. Studia nad gospodarką surowcami krzemiennymi w pradziejach 6, Warszawa – Lublin: Państwowe Muzeum Archeologiczne w Warszawie, Stowarzyszenie Naukowe Archeologów Polskich Oddział w Warszawie, Instytut Archeologii Uniwersytetu Marii Curie-Skłodowskiej w Lublinie. 215–243.

Nunn, G.R. 2006. Using the Jutland Type IC Neolithic Danish Dagger as a model to replicate parallel, edge-to-edge pressure flaking. In: J. Apel & K. Knutsson (eds.), *Skilled Production and Social Reproduction. Aspects of Traditional Stone-Tool Technologies. Proceedings from an International Symposium held in Uppsala August 20–24, 2003*. SAU Stone Studies 2. Uppsala: Societas Archaeologica Upsaliensis. 81–114.

Ossowski, G. 1886. Przyczynek do wiadomości o grotach krzemiennych znajdowanych na ziemiach dawnej Polski. *Zbiór Wiadomości do Antropologii Kulturowej* 10: 24–37.

Plisson, H., Mallet, N., Bocquet, A. & Ramseyer D. 2002. Utilisation et rôle des outils en silex du Grand-Pressigny dans les villages de Charavines et de Portalban (Néolithique final). *Bulletin de la Société préhistorique française* 99(4): 793–811.

Przyborowski, J. 1873. Z epoki kamiennej w Sandomierskiem. *Wiadomości Archeologiczne* 1: 9–16.

Razumov, S.M. 2011 *Flint artefacts of Northern Pontic populations of the early and middle Bronze Age:3200–1600 BC*. Poznań: Adam Mickiewicz University in Poznań.

Rejniewicz, Ł. 1985.Wytwórczość krzemieniarska oparta o surowiec rejowiecki w Dorohuczy, woj. Lubelskie. *Lubelskie Materiały Archeologiczne* 1: 9–19.

Rots, V. 2010. *Prehension and Hafting Traces on a Flint Tools. A Methodology*. Leuven: Leuven University Press.

Rots, V., Van Peer, P. & Vermeersch, P. M. 2011. Aspects of tool production, use, and hafting in Palaeolithic assemblages from Northeast Africa. *Journal of Human Evolution* 60: 637–664.

Ryzhov, S., Stepanchuk, V. & Sapozhnikov., I. 2005. Raw material provenance in the Palaeolithic of Ukraine: state of problem, Current approaches and first results. *Archeometria Műhely* 2005(4): 17–25.

Sulimirski, T. 1957–1959. *Polska przedhistoryczna II*. Londyn: Gryf Printers.

Swiesznikow, I. 1967. Krzemieniarstwo kultury ceramiki sznurowej na Wołyniu. *Z Otchłani Wieków* 33 (4): 222–226.

Van Gijn A.L. 2010a. *Flint in focus. Lithic Biographies in the Neolithic and Bronze Age*. Leiden: Sidestone Press.

Van Gijn A. L. 2010b. Not at all obsolete! The use of flint in the Bronze Age Netherlands. In: B. V. Eriksen (ed.), *Lithic Technology in Metal Using Societies. Proceedings of a UISPP Workshop, Lisbon, September 2006*. Aarhus: Jutland Archaeological Society. 45–60.

Vaughan, P. C. 1985. *Use-Wear Analysis of Flaked Stone Tools*. Tucson: University of Arizona Press.

Vergès, J. M. & Andreu, O. 2011. Technical microwear and residues in identifying bipolar knapping on an anvil: experimental data. *Journal of Archaeological Science* 38: 1016–1025.

Whittaker, J. C. 1999. *Flintknapping: Making and Understanding Stone Tools*, Austin: University of Texas Press.

Zakościelna, A. 1996. *Krzemieniarstwo kultury wołyńsko-lubelskiej ceramiki malowanej*. Lublin: Wydawnictwo Uniwersytetu Marii Curie-Skłodowskiej.

SILICITE DAGGERS FROM THE TERRITORIES OF THE CZECH REPUBLIC AND SLOVAKIA (A PRELIMINARY STUDY)

Antonín Přichystal & Lubomír Šebela

At the end of the Eneolithic (2200 BC) and in the Early Bronze Age (2200–1700 BC) silicite (flint) daggers appeared in the territory of former Czechoslovakia. They are believed to be prevalently imported because there is no evidence of their local production. We have recorded 88 daggers in the Czech Republic (42 pieces in Bohemia, 45 pieces in Moravia and one piece in Czech Silesia); while, in Slovakia, we found only five such artefacts (from a total of 94 pieces). In relation to raw material utilised, we could analyse only 58 finds from the Czech Republic. Northern flint (i.e. flint raw material of the Danian and Maastrichtian age, generally imported from the north based on the archaeological finds) is the most common in the studied collection. Only two daggers made of local raw material (Moravian Jurassic chert) have been recorded in Moravia. In the collection from Bohemia we also found, besides the previously mentioned northern flint, chocolate silicite from central Poland, chert breccia of red-yellowish colour and Cretaceous spongolite (the latter two of unclear provenance). The presence of Bavarian cherts, confirmed for three daggers from central Bohemia, has been ascertained for the first time. In one of these cases, the raw material is comparable with the Bavarian tabular chert (Plattensilex) of the Baiersdorf type; and one dagger was shaped from a Bavarian chert, probably of the Flintsbach type. Dominant flint daggers from the Czech territory and probably also from Slovakia most likely represent evidence of contacts with Poland, Germany or northern Europe where production centres of these artefacts were located. We suggest these raw materials were collected from glacial sediments in northern Central Europe; but, in some cases, we cannot exclude the primary sources on the northern coast of Germany or perhaps in Scandinavia.

Introduction

At the end of the Stone Age and at the beginning of the Bronze Age new stone artefacts appeared in the territory of the former Czechoslovakia: silicite daggers shaped on both sides by flat retouching. In the literature, they are interpreted as imports from the north (Zápotocký 1961; Šebela 1997/98; Marková 2004), as the stone sources most often used for their production are not present in the Czech Republic and Slovakia.

The Czech Republic and Slovakia are located in the eastern part of Central Europe. The Czech Republic comprises three historical countries: Bohemia, where the capital city of Prague is situated, is in the west. In the eastern part of the Republic there is Moravia with its administrative centre in Brno. Czech Silesia (main city Opava) lies to the north of Moravia. These three countries saw partly different developments in prehistoric times because of their diverse geomorphological conditions and the accessibility to of raw material sources. Slovak historic territories are encompassed today by the Republic of Slovakia.

The silicite or flint daggers in former Czechoslovakia are connected with cultures of the Young and Late Eneolithic (around 2900/2800–2300/2000 BC) and the Early Bronze Age (2200–1600 BC). The Young Eneolithic period comprises in the mentioned area two important cultures – the Corded Ware (2900/2800–2500 BC) and Bell Beaker (roughly 2500–2300 BC) cultures (Neustupný 2008). The Late Eneolithic represents the Protoúnětice culture (the first of the Únětice Culture; the end of 3rd millennium BC). The Early Bronze Age is represented by the Únětice culture (from the 2nd up to 5th Phase in Moravia and up to the 6th Phase in Bohemia) and Věteřov group. The long period of the existence of the Únětice culture has been divided into five consecutive phases. The Věteřov group is a Moravian component of a vast complex, often referred to as the Věteřov-Maďarovce culture. It is believed the Věteřov group developed from the Únětice culture (Jiráň 2008; Podborský 1993).

As is raw material terminology, we prefer the correct comprehensive petrographic term silicite instead of the very often used flint in archaeological papers. The silicite (for more details see Přichystal 2010) comprises all varieties of chert (Proterozoic to Quaternary, nodular, layered) including flint as a special variety of silicite coming from the Cretaceous (Maastrichtian) chalk and Early Tertiary (Danian) limestones. Besides silicites, there were used especially for segments and rarely for daggers also sedimentary clastic rocks such is orthoquartzite or chert breccia. Chert breccia represents a fossil weathering crust in which chips of chert up to a few centimetres big prevail and are cemented by silica groundmass together with very small particles of chert or quartz.

Evidence

The present work is based on silicite daggers found in both the republics in question, discovered during archaeological excavations and located in various museum collections or just referred in the literature, up to 2012.

Presently, from Bohemia there are known 42 daggers, eight of them in fragments. Forty-one artefacts come from 38 cadastral areas, while the exact find location of one piece is unknown (it is referred under the designation "Litoměřice and the vicinity"). The finds are concentrated along the most important Bohemian rivers, the Labe (Elbe), Sázava, Vltava, Ohře, and the Bílina (Fig. 11.1).

Moravia has yielded 45 daggers (15 of which are in fragments) from 37 cadastral areas. They appear mainly between the rivers of Morava and Svitava and between the Svratka and Dyje (Fig. 11.2). From Czech Silesia there only one dagger is known so-far; it comes from Holasovice near Opava (Fig. 11.2).

The archaeological literature records finds of six silicite daggers from Slovakia. Five of them were found in the five various cadastral areas (Fig. 11.3). The sixth artefact comes from an unknown locality and is referred to as "from Slovakia". Such a small number of finds prevents us from identifying any specific concentrations of them (Fig. 11.3).

The circumstances of dagger discoveries are interesting to observe. Most of the analysed artefacts are surface finds without cultural context (57 from the Czech Republic and five from Slovakia), while fourteen of them (all from the Czech Republic) come from funerary contexts. Nine daggers (eight from the Czech Republic and one from Slovakia) were found in settlement layers. The remaining nine daggers (from the Czech Republic), although found on the surface, probably also represent settlement finds but are without specific cultural assignation (they were accompanied by atypical artefacts of unclear chronology).

Raw material analysis

For the petrographic determination of artefacts produced from siliceous rocks which are hardly distinctive in macroscopic observations, a method introduced almost 30 years ago by A. Přichystal (1984) has been utilised. It appeared very useful in studying Neolithic chipped assemblages from the famous Neolithic sites at Bylany, Těšetice-Kyjovice, and Mšeno near Mělník, but also in recent years in studies of materials from the Late Eneolithic and the Early Bronze Age from the Czech Republic (A. Přichystal in Kopacz & Šebela 2006; Kopacz et al. 2009).

The main principle of the method lies in the comparison of raw material structure, contents of inclusions and microfossils of examined artefacts with samples obtained from source areas. Observations of samples are carried out under microscope in the water immersion. It utilised the fact that the index of light refraction in water (1.33) is close to that of the light refraction in silicites (about 1.53). In contrast, the refraction index of light in air is 1.00. After applying a thin film of water on an artefact (or its immersion in water), its siliceous mass becomes more transparent. This transparency facilitates observation of its details and – if needed – allows for photographic documentation.

Our petrographic analysis has been applied to 59 siliceous daggers from the Czech Republic (the remaining 29 artefacts were not available for the research). The results obtained are presented in Table 11.1. They indicate that most of daggers from Bohemia and Moravia have been made of the northern flint (44 artefacts, i.e. 75%).

A new element in the analysed series is the evident occurrence of raw materials of German provenience used for daggers found in Bohemia – Bavarian tabular chert (Plattensilex) of the Baiersdorf type (three pieces: Evaň, Dražkovice, Vraný), probably spotted Bavarian chert of Flintsbach type (one piece: Loučeň), and a quartzite of unclear provenience (one piece: Kopisty). Moreover, for the first time in the Bohemian/Moravian milieu, a dagger of

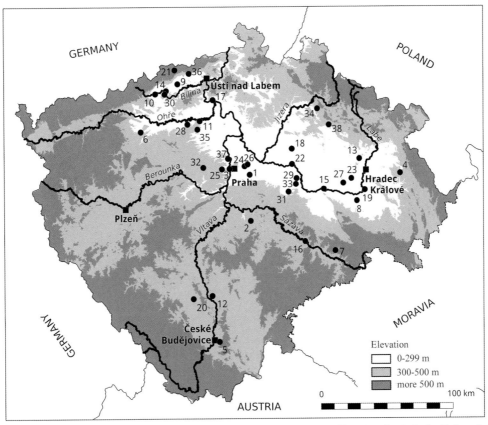

Fig. 11.1. Silicite daggers from Bohemia. 1 - Běchovice (Prague capital); 2 - Benešov (Benešov district); 3 - Bubeneč (Prague capital); 4 - Byzhradec (Rychnov nad Kněžnou district); 5 - Dobrá Voda u Českých Budějovic (České Budějovice district); 6 - Dolánky (Louny district); 7 - Dolní Krupá (Havlíčkův Brod district); 8 - Dražkovice (Pardubice district); 9 - Duchcov (Teplice district); 10 - Ervěnice (Most district); 11 - Evaň (Litoměřice district); 12 - Hosty (České Budějovice district); 13 - Chlum (Hradec Králové district); 14 - Kopisty (Most district); 15 - Labské Chrčice (Pardubice district); 16 - Ledeč nad Sázavou (Havlíčkův Brod district); 17 - Litoměřice (Litoměřice district);18 - Loučeň (Nymburk district); 19 - Lukovna (Pardubice district);20 - Myšenec (Písek district); 21- Nové Město (Teplice district); 22 - Nymburk (Nymburk district); 23 - Osice (Hradec Králové district); 24. Praha, cadastral part Kbely (Prague capital); 25 - Praha, cadastral part Liboc (Prague capital); 26 - Praha, cadastral part Vinoř (Prague capital); 27 - Rohovládová Bělá (Pardubice district); 28 - Slavětín (Louny district); 29 - Sokoleč (Nymburk district); 30 - Souš (Most district); 31 - Svojšice (Kolín district); 32 - Unhošť (Kladno district); 33 - Velim (Kolín district); 34 - Volavec (Semily district); 35 - Vraný (Kladno district); 36 - Vrchoslav (Teplice district); 37 - Žalov (Praha-west district); 38 - Železnice (Jičín district) (map assembled by P. Jansa).

chocolate silicite from central Poland has been recognised (Bohemia, Osice – Locality I). The sole occurrence of spongolite dagger is also probably not linked Czech territories. In the collection of Moravian daggers, apart from the northern flint, two artefacts of Moravian Jurassic chert have been recognised (two pieces from Křepice; Kopacz & Šebela 2006:123f, Tab. XLII: 1, 2).

In Slovakia, the authors had the possibility to examine a dagger from Nitriansky Hrádok, which was made of the northern flint. The dagger from Prešov was recognised by Ľubomíra Kaminská as made of the Volhynian flint from Ukraine (Kaminská 1998).

Characteristics of recognised rocks

Northern flint

Most daggers were made of northern flint (Fig. 11.4). This term refers to silicites (flints) that were transported to territories in Poland, Germany and to the northern outskirts of the Czech Republic by the continental ice sheet, that is, erratic silicites from glacial sediments. Natural fragments of that rock, as well as artefacts made of it, occasionally show external traces caused by rock chunks having been moved over a hard surface – clearly proof of their erratic (glacial) origin. Daggers, due to their fashioning by surface retouch, usually lack such traces. Moreover, as prestigious artefacts,

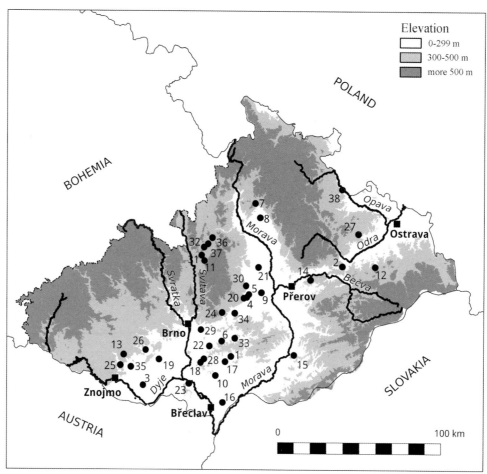

Fig. 11.2. Silicite daggers from Moravia (1–35), including those now within administrative borders of the Pardubice region (36–37) and Czech Silesia (38). 1 - Archlebov (Hodonín district); 2 - Blahutovice (Nový Jičín district); 3 - Božice (Znojmo district); 4 - Brodek u Prostějova (Prostějov district); 5 - Dobrochov (Prostějov district); 6 - Heršpice (Vyškov district); 7 - Horní Libina (Šumperk district); 8 - Horní Sukolom (Šumperk district); 9 - Klenovice na Hané (Prostějov district); 10 - Knínice u Boskovic (Blansko district); 11 – Kobylí (Břeclav district); 12 - Kopřivnice (Nový Jičín district); 13 - Křepice (Znojmo district);14 - Lhota (okr. Přerov district); 15 - Mistřice (Hodonín district); 16 - Moravská Nová Ves-Hrušky (Břeclav district); 17 - Násedlovice (Hodonín district); 18 - Nikolčice (Břeclav district); 19 - Olbramovice (Znojmo district); 20 - Ondratice (Prostějov district); 21 - Olšany (Prostějov district); 22 - Otnice (Vyškov district); 23 - Pavlov (Břeclav district); 24 - Pístovice (Vyškov district); 25 - Plaveč (Znojmo district); 26 - Rybníky (Znojmo district); 27 - Stará Ves (Nový Jičín district); 28 - Šitbořice (Břeclav district); 29 - Šlapanice (Brno-country district); 30 - Určice (Prostějov district); 31 - Vanovice (Blansko district); 32 - Velké Opatovice (Blansko district); 33 - Vícemilice (Vyškov district); 34 - Vyškov (Vyškov district); 35 - Žerotice (Znojmo district); 36 - Chornice (Svitavy district); 37 - Jevíčko (Svitavy district); 38 - Holasovice (Opava district) (map assembled by P. Jansa).

they might have been imported over long distances from workshops near primary flint outcrops in north Germany or Scandinavia.

For producing daggers, Danian silicite (flint) with microfossils (mainly bryozoans) was most often used. Tabular blocks of this raw material with flat surfaces were convenient for shaping bigger artefacts. However, even if the northern provenience of the raw material of daggers from Bohemia and Moravia is accurate, we still do not know whether this raw material was transported dozens or hundreds of kilometres from relatively close glacial

sediments or whether it was extracted from natural flint deposits in the western Baltic or even Scandinavia.

Western raw materials – Bavarian tabular Jurassic chert (Plattensilex), Flinstbach silicite, and may be quartzite

Platy Jurassic chert from Frankish Alba (Bavaria), utilised in the Bohemian Neolithic, is also known to have been used in the production of Neolithic chipped tools from Moravia. However, so far no daggers of this material have been

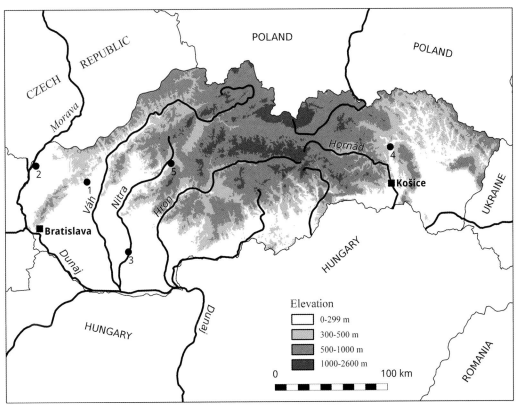

Fig. 11.3. Silicite daggers from Slovakia. 1 - Dolný Lopašov (Piešťany district); 2 - Kúty (Senica district); 3 - Nitriansky Hrádok (Nové Zámky district); 4 - Prešov (Prešov district); 5 - Prievidza (Prievidza district) (map assembled by P. Jansa).

Table 11.1. Raw materials used for the production of silicite daggers found in the Czech Republic and Slovakia.

Raw material	Bohemia	Moravia	Czech Silesia	Czech Republic	Slovakia
Northern Flint	21	23	–	44	1
Bavarian spotted chert of the Flintsbach type	1	–	–	1	–
Bavarian tabular chert (*Plattensilex*), Baiersdorf type	3	–	–	3	–
Chocolate silicite	1	–	–	1	–
Chert breccia	1	–	–	1	–
Cretaceous spongolite	1	–	–	1	–
Orthoquartzite	1	–	–	1	–
Moravian Jurassic chert	–	2	–	2	–
Volhynian flint	–	–	–	–	1
Patinated silicite	–	1	–	1	–
Burnt silicite	2	–	–	2	–
Undetermined siliceous rocks	–	1	1	2	–
Non vidi (rock not verified by the authors)	11	18	–	29	4
Total	42	44	1	88	6

recorded in the Czech Republic. Recently, we have found them only in Bohemia. Its source areas were presented in detail most recently by A. Binsteiner (2005). The same author also published a dagger made of platy chert of the

Arnhofen type from Mitterbreitsach (district of Inn) in Upper Austria (Binsteiner 2011: 22), classifying the find as Late Neolithic, probably belonging to the Cham culture. Analogous daggers are certainly known from Bavaria, for

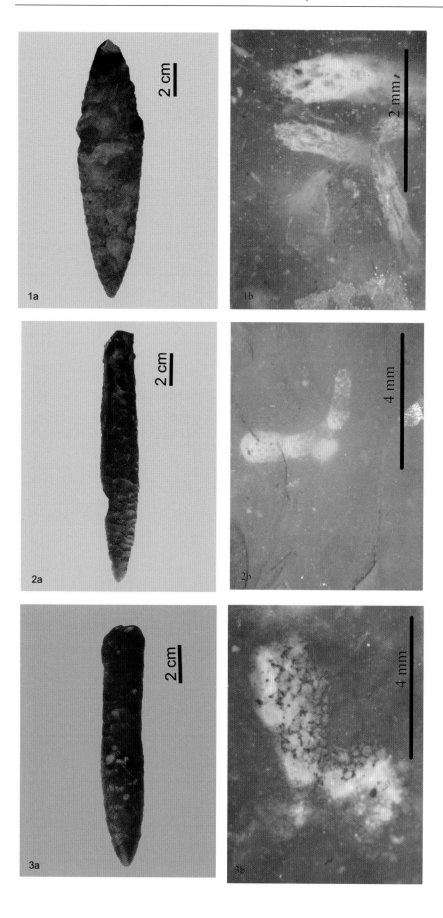

Fig. 11.4. 1a,b - Praha-Běchovice (central Bohemia), grave 1. The Protoúnětice culture. Northern flint of the Danian age with numerous relics of bryozoa. Length of the picture is 4mm; 2a,b - Dolní Krupá (eastern Bohemia). The Early Bronze Age. Northern flint of the Danian age. Length of the picture is 8mm; 3a,b - Hosty (southern Bohemia). The Early Bronze Age. Northern flint of the Danian age. Length of the picture is 8mm. All microphotos are made in the water immersion under stereomicroscope (photos: L. Plchová and A. Přichystal).

Fig. 11.5. 1a,b - Vraný (central Bohemia), Late Eneolithic, Bavarian tabular chert (Plattensilex) of the Baiersdorf type; 2 - Byzhradec (eastern Bohemia), Late Eneolithic or Early Bronze Age, chert breccia; 3 - Osice, Locality 1 (eastern Bohemia), Late Eneolithic, chocolate silicite from central Poland (photos: L. Plchová and A. Přichystal).

example from Straubing-Alburg, Straubing-Bogen, where they are also found in graves of the Corded Ware and Bell Beaker cultures (Binsteiner 2011: Tab. 58).

In the collection of Bohemian daggers we have one piece (Loučeň) probably made of spotted Bavarian chert of the Flintsbach type, also of the Jurassic age. Its source area, again located in Bavaria, is nonetheless closer to Bohemia. There is also an example of a dagger prepared of orthoquartzite (Kopisty), a raw material coming either from Bohemia or from Germany.

Chocolate silicite from central Poland

Use of chocolate silicite from central Poland for producing daggers has been confirmed in the Czech Republic for the first time (Bohemia, Osice-Locality I; Fig. 11.5:3). This raw material, one of the best in Europe, has been extracted through mining from at least the Mesolithic. Radiocarbon dates indicate that it was also extracted at the end of the Neolithic and during the Early Bronze Age (e.g. Lech & Lech 1995).

Other rocks

Single examples of other raw materials have been recorded: chert breccia (Byzhradec in Bohemia), Cretaceous spongolite (Ervěnice in Bohemia), and Moravian Jurassic chert (Křepice in Moravia). As regards the first two rock types, we are not sure about provenience. The chert breccia that occurred in the collection does not display characteristics typical for chert breccia from the Krumlovský les Upland, Moravia (a famous raw material source exploited in prehistory); and the spongolite appears to be different from spongolites from the Bohemian Cretaceous Basin. The raw material of the analysed artefact from Czech Silesia has been tentatively classified as erratic silicite from glacial sediments. However, it does not correspond exactly with any of the recognised classical types of these erratic siliceous rocks.

Classification and typology of silicite (flint) daggers

The first scheme of development of northern flint daggers was published at the beginning of the 20th century by S. Müller (1902). His concept was adopted by R. Beltz (1910) and A. Tode (1935). Eventually, it was J. E. Forssander's 1936 division of flint daggers into six main types, with subdivision into local variants, which has been commonly accepted in the literature (*cf.* Lomborg 1973; Kühn 1979; Agthe 1989a, 1989b; Apel 2001). For silicite daggers from Poland and Ukraine, there is a typological scheme elaborated by J. Libera (2001). In our study, we utilise the typology elaborated for Denmark, presented by E. Lomborg 1973; *cf.* Apel 2001: figs 8:1; 8:2).

Czech Republic

The collection of daggers which have been typologically identified comprises 88 artefacts. They fall into two major groups. The first (47 artefacts) includes daggers with no handle, with a blade with a willow leaf form, with a pentagonal cross-section and with an obtuse-angled outline in the middle part (Fig. 11.4:1a; Fig. 11.7:8). The artefacts' surfaces are fashioned by fine retouching. Due to their lenticular outline, the daggers described here correspond with those of the northern European Type I, recognised there as the earliest. The piece from Archlebov (Moravia), 245mm long, with the broadest part in one-third of the length (Šebela 1997/98: Tab. 3:8) is the biggest in this group. Slightly smaller is the dagger from Sokolče (Bohemia) – 234mm long and widest 122mm from the tip (Fig. 11.6:9). The shortest daggers in the group are daggers from Chlum (Bohemia) and Vacenovice (Moravia). The length of the former is 62mm (Stocký 1924: Tab. XXXVII:1) and of the latter is 60mm (Šebela 1997/98:206, Tab. 3:2).

Seven artefacts have their widest points at their mid-point. For that reason, it is impossible to say which part of the dagger served for blade and which for handle. In Moravia, there are artefacts from Rybníky – grave 2, Šlapanice – grave 6, Olšany, Stará Ves, and – inferring from the preserved photographic documentation – from Brodek u Prostějova (Šebela 1997/98: Tab. 2:2; 3:6 & 7; 4:2 & 5:3). In Bohemia, daggers of that form are known from Chlum (Stocký 1924: Tab. XXXVII:1) and Louček (Stocký 1924: Tab. XXXVII:2). Analogies to them can be found in Germany where, in the late 1980s, four similar forms were recorded. All the described daggers can be classified as Type Ie, according to the division of M. Agthe which is based on German finds from territories to the south of Mecklenburg (Agthe 1989a: 28, Abb. 45:2).

Two other similarly shaped daggers are from Moravia – from Heršpice and Božice (Šebela 1997/98: Tab. 1:7 and 3:5). However, in contrast to the German type Ie, they have handles which are sometimes terminated but not pointed (the end might have been purposely truncated).

The handle of the dagger from Heršpice has two retouched notches placed opposite each other, possibly to facilitate fixing to it an organic grip. Another notch, located on the left edge of the blade close to the point, served another unknown purpose. Two opposing notches are also present on the artefact from Osice–Locality I (Bohemia; Fig. 11.5:3) which has a rounded handle termination. The dagger from Ondratice (Moravia: Kopacz & Šebela 2006: Tab. LXVII:1) was broken at the handle part. The dagger from Duchcov (Bohemia) is distinctive by the presence of two pairs of retouched notches opposite each other on the handle (Fig. 11.7:1). Similar forms from Germany are included by M. Agthe and H. J. Kühn within their variant Id. In the Danish typological system of E. Lomborg, daggers with opposing retouched notches are classified as type Ie. If they have one pair of such notches, they fall into variant 2 of that type (Lomborg 1973: fig. 17:c), while forms with minimum two pairs – into variant 1 (Lomborg 1973: fig. 17:a, b).

Of particular note is the dagger from Božice (Moravia) which lacks any retouched notches (Fig. 11.7:3). We can think of almost no parallels to it. By its overall outline, the artefact resembles daggers from Schleswig-Holstein with their maximal width close to the point; these were linked by H. J. Kühn with the milieu of the Bell Beaker culture (Kühn 1979: 58).

Finally, we should mention lenticular daggers of pentagonal outline which were transformed to various degrees. For that reason, their typological classification is uncertain. We can presume that, in the most part, they represent imperfect forms intended to be Type I. In Moravia, such daggers are known from Moravská Nová Ves-Hrušky, Vyškov (grave 1), Pavlov (grave 11 and 353), Rybníky (grave 3), Ondratice, and Určice (Šebela 1997/98: Tab. 1:1,5–6; 2:7; 3:1); while, in Bohemia, they are known from

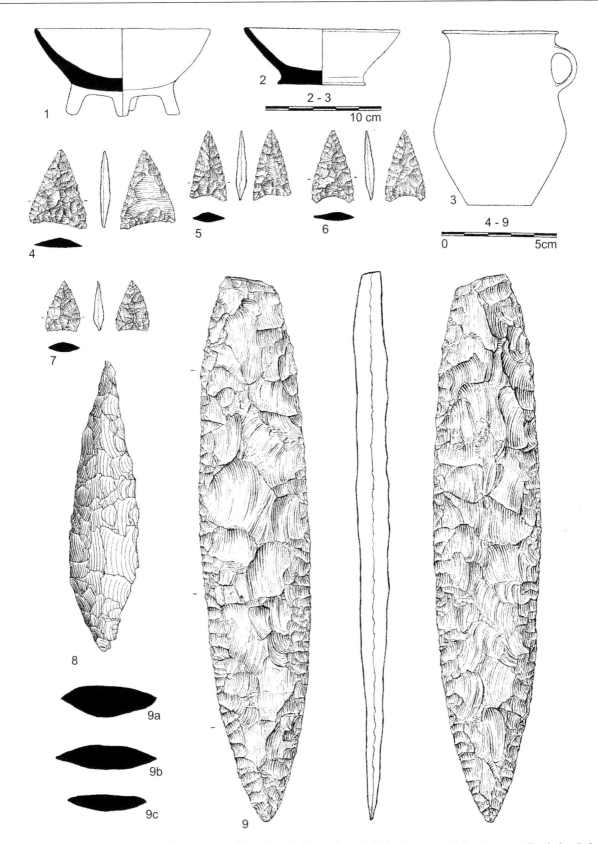

Fig. 11.6. Silicite daggers of the type I from graves of the Protoúnětice culture in Bohemia: 1, 9 – Sokoleč, grave (?); 2–8 – Bubeneč, grave 3. Drawing by J. Brenner and B. Ludikovská.

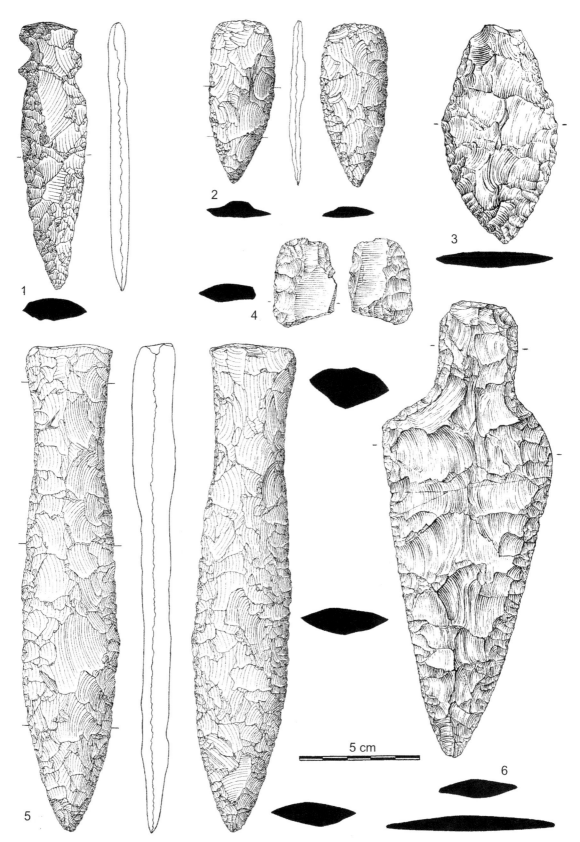

Fig. 11.7. Silicite daggers with handle from Bohemia (1, 5, 6), Moravia (3,4) and Czech Silesia (2). 1 – Duchcov; 2 – Holasovice; 3 – Božice, grave; 4 – Velké Opatovice (dagger/segment); 5 – Nové Město; 6 – Svojšice (drawing: J. Brenner & B. Ludikovská).

Dražkovice (Stocký 1928: Tab. LV:16), Praha-cadastral part Kbely (unpublished; National Museum, Prague), and Železnice (Kalferst & Prostředník 1993: Tab. XII:9). It is possible that the artefacts found in sepulchral contexts (in Moravia) were intentionally damaged during funerary rituals.

The dagger from Násedlovice (Moravia) should also be classified as of probable pentagonal form. In contrast to the daggers previously described, its handle has a rounded termination (Šebela 1997/98: Tab. 3:3). Parallels to it can be found in the German literature (Agthe 1989a: fig. 43:1). In Moravia, the artefact in question is interpreted in various ways. According to J. Svoboda, it is a point of the Font Robert type, a typical form of the Western and Central European *Périgordien* (Svoboda *et al.* 1994: 149). Karel Valoch (mentioned in Šebela 1997/98: 212) interprets it as a fragment of silicite dagger. L. Šebela and P. Škrdla are of the same opinion, and suggest parallel forms in the milieu of the Leibacher Moor culture (*cf.* Korošec & Korošec 1969: Tab. 73:3, 5; 74:7; Šebela 1997/98: 201, Tab. 3:3; Šebela & Škrdla 1997).

The second, less numerous, group of silicite daggers encompasses forms with a distinctive handle. Eight such daggers are known from Moravia (Blahutovice, Horní Libina, Horní Sukolom, Kobylí-grave, Kopřivnice, Křepice, Pístovice, and Žerotice); and twice as many (*i.e.* 16) from Bohemia (Benešov, Dobrá Voda u Českých Budějovic, Dolní Krupá, Hosty, Labské Chrčice, Ledeč nad Sázavou, Litoměřice, Myšenec, Nové Město, Nymburk, Osice – Locality I, Svojšice, Velim, Vrchoslav, Žalov, and Litoměřice and vicinity). They correspond with northern daggers of types III to VI.

Similar to daggers of the willow leaf shape are forms with a blade that gradually merges with a handle which is evenly wide, including termination. The handle has four edges and is rhomboidal in cross-section. In Bohemia, such daggers are known from Dolánky (Zápotocký 1961: fig. 2: 1), Dolní Krupá (Fig. 11.4:2a), Labské Chrčice (Rous 1981: Tab. 16:8), Osice – Locality I (unpublished; Museum in Pardubice), and Velim (unpublished; National Museum, Prague); and, in Moravia, they are only known from Žerotice (Šebela 1997/98: Tab. 4:7). Similar forms from Germany are classified as Type III D (Agthe 1989a: 31, fig. 37:9; 44:5). In E. Lomborg's Danish scheme, they also fall into Type III (Lomborg 1973: fig. 24).

Daggers which have their maximum width at the termination have similar blade outlines. Handle cross-sections can be rhomboidal, oval, triangular, or even rectangular. The artefact from Horní Sukolom (Moravia; Šebela 1997/98: Tab. 4:6) falls into this category. It has a wide blade and a distinctive handle with triangular cross-section (with rounded edges) and a fan-like termination. On the upper side of the handle a lateral edge (in German: *Mittelgrat*) which is centrally located is visible. This feature is also visible on the partially preserved dagger from Dobrá Voda near České Budějovice (Bohemia; Zavřel 1986: fig. on p. 291) and on a fragment from Myšenec (Bohemia; Museum in České Budějovice). Daggers from Vrchoslav (Bohemia; unpublished) and Nymburk (Bohemia; Zápotocký 1961: fig. 1:1) are similar in outline to the dagger from Horní Sukolom, but the cross-section of their handles is rhomboidal. In the northern milieu, daggers with this sort of profile are classified as Type IV (Agthe 1989a: 32; Kühn 1979: 44f) which is subdivided into several variants based on handle cross-section. Thus, rhomboidal cross-sections are found in variants IVa – IVc (Lomborg 1973: fig. 29: A-C) while triangular cross-sections appear among variants IVd and IVe (Lomborg 1973: fig. 29:D-E).

The silicite dagger from Nové Město in Bohemia also has an expanding handle termination which, in contrast to forms presented above, has an angular-oval cross-section (Fig. 11.7:5). It corresponds with northern daggers of Type V, variant A, according to Lomborg's typological scheme (Lomborg 1973: 58, fig. 35A).

Daggers with the widest part of the blade located closest to the handle come from Kopřivnice (Šebela 1997/98: Tab. 4:3), Kobylí (grave 1; Kopacz & Šebela 2006: Tab. XLI:1) and Pístovice (Šebela 1997/98: Tab. 4:5) in Moravia and from Svojšice (Fig. 11.7:6) in Bohemia. The handles of the first two are pointed and those of the others rounded. The transversal blade and handle cross-sections of all four artefacts are lenticular. In the case of the piece from Kopřivnice, the blade and handle are almost identical in cross-section. In other cases, the differences between these two measure up to 2mm (*e.g.* the handle of the dagger from Pístovice is thicker by 2mm than the blade). Northern forms with such a profile are classified as Type VIb (Agthe 1989a: fig. 43:4, 8; 47:5; Lomborg 1973: 93, fig. 40: Type VIb; Kühn 1979: 46, Tab. 17:7-9). The pieces from Pístovice and Svojšice have parallels in Poland – in Piotrowice Wielkie and Piasky (Libera 2001: Tab. XI:b, d).

The silicite dagger from a hillfort at Hosty, Bohemia also has a rounded handle (Fig. 11.4:3a). In this case, however, the transformation from blade to handle is gradual and the handle itself becomes slightly wider at the end. Referring to Lomborg's scheme we can link the dagger from Hosty to type VIb (Lomborg 1973: fig. 40:B).

Three daggers have not been identified during our research because they were available only as simplified drawings or photographs. They are: the dagger from Blahutovice, Moravia (Šebela 1997/98: Tab. 5:1) and the dagger handles from Křepice, Moravia (Kopacz & Šebela 2006: Tab. LXVIII:15) and Žalov, Bohemia (Rýzner 1883: 216, 247, Tab. XII:43, 46). As the cross-sections of these artefacts are unknown, they cannot be more precisely classified in the scope of typology.

Fragments of dagger blades reworked into rectangular forms fall into another, very specific group. In the

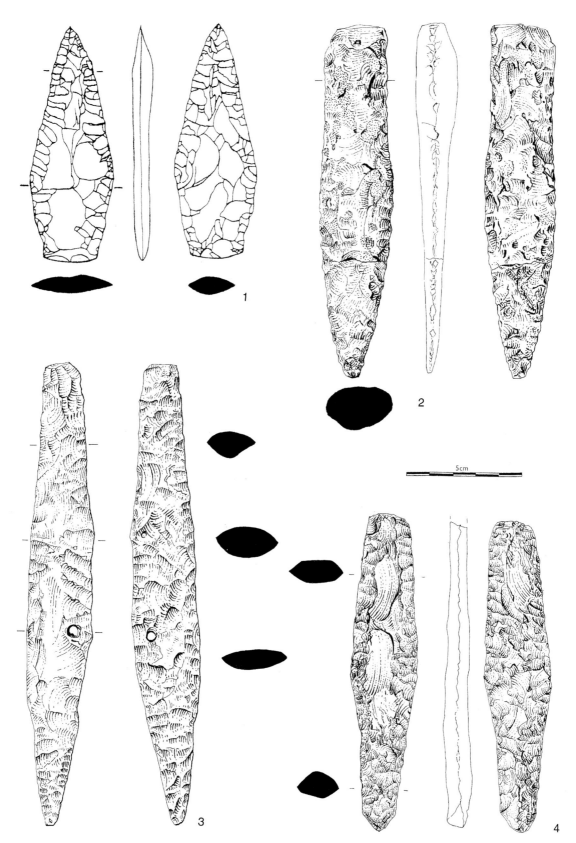

Fig. 11.8. Silicite daggers from Slovakia: 1 – Prešov; 2 – Prievidza; 3 – Kúty; 4 – Nitransky Hrádok (1 – after Kaminská 1998; 2–4 – after Marková 2004).

Table 11.2. Types of silicite daggers and their raw materials in the Czech Republic (B - Bohemia; M - Moravia and Czech Silesia).

Raw material	Type I B/M	Type II B/M	Type III B/M	Type IV B/M	Type V B/M	Type VI B/M	Dagger/ Segment B/M	Unclassified	Total
Northern flint	6/15	–	4/1	2/1	1/0	4/4	1/1	3/1	44
Bavarian spotted chert, Flintsbach type	1/0	–	–	–	–	–	–	–	1
Bavarian tabular chert (*Plattensilex*), Baiersdorf type	3/0	–	–	–	–	–	–	–	3
Chocolate silicite	1/0	–	–	–	–	–	–	–	1
Chert breccia	–	–	–	–	–	–	1/0	–	1
Cretaceous spongolite	–	–	–	–	–	–	–	1/0	1
Qrthoquartzite	1/0	–	–	–	–	–	–	–	1
Moravian Jurassic chert	–	–	–	–	–	–	–	0/2	2
Patinated silicite	0/1	–	–	–	–	–	–	–	1
Burnt silicite	–	–	–	1/0	–	–	–	1/0	2
Undetermined siliceous rocks	0/1	–	–	–	–	–	–	0/1	2
Non vidi (rock not verified by authors)	5/13	–	2/0	1/0	1/0	1/1	–	1/5	29
Total	7/30	–	6/1	3/1	2/0	5/4	2/1	6/9	88

Bohemian/Moravian collection there are two such forms: one from Byzhradec, Bohemia (Fig. 11.5:2) and the other from Velké Opatovice, Moravia (Fig. 11.7:4). In the northern literature, they are described as silicite (flint) axes (Lomborg 1973: fig. 5:b). However, in our opinion, we should speak instead about silicite dagger blades converted into bifacially retouched rectangular forms, referred to by Moravian authors as segments. In the eastern part of Central Europe, artefacts of this type were developed by bearers of the Bell Beaker culture (Kopacz *et al.* 2009: 98ff). Subsequently, the concept was adopted by people of the Únětice culture and the Věteřov group (Kopacz & Šebela 2006: 63ff). More problematic is the classification of the find from Lukovna, Bohemia (unpublished, Museum in Pardubice). It is either a diminutive dagger (length: 36mm) or a segment. The authors of this paper are rather inclined to the second option.

Slovakia

In the Slovak collection, there are three handle-less silicite daggers. Artefacts from Prešov (Fig. 11.8:1) and Nitriansky Hrádok (Fig. 11.8:4) have pentagonal outlines and lenticular transverse cross-sections while the one from Kúty (Fig. 11.8:3) is of the willow-leaf form. All of them belong to the northern Type I. The former two display traces of intensive wear. Parallels can be found among the silicite daggers of the Moravian collection (Šebela 1997/98: Tab. 1:6), but also in Poland and west Ukraine (Libera 2001: Tabs III:e & IV:f). Forms similar to the artefact from Nitriansky Hrádok are known from Germany (Wormstedt, Polda district; Agthe 1989a: 94, fig. 45:1).

The dagger from Prievidza is different from forms described above. It has a "fish tail" handle termination and

a willow-leaf blade (Fig. 11.8:2). These features are typical for Type Vb (Lomborg 1973: fig. 55:A). However, the piece identified only as coming from Slovakia has been recognised by us only from photographic documentation (Novotný 1958: Tab. LIV:1) and its transverse and longitudinal cross-sections are unknown. For that reason, it cannot be more precisely classified.

Relations between raw material and types of silicite daggers

This issue can be studied on the basis of the Bohemian/ Moravian collection, comprising 88 artefacts (Tab. 1). Two-thirds of them were petrographically determined and linked to northern typological schemes. Our analysis encompassed not only daggers *sensu stricto*, but also forms classified into the group "dagger/segment". Results of the research are presented in Table 11.2.

In the analyzed series, northern flint was predominant. It was the exclusive raw material for handled daggers (Types III-VI). As far as Type I (handle-less daggers) is concerned, the northern flint was dominant only in Moravia. In Bohemia, the situation is different for Type I. In that region, we only recorded one artefact of central Polish chocolate silicite (Osice-Locality I) along with daggers of Bavarian tabular chert of the Baiersdorf type (Dražkovice, Evaň, and Vraný) and spotted Bavarian chert of the Flintsbach type (Loučeň).

Artefacts from the dagger/segment group are made mainly of northern flint, but not exclusively. The form from Byzhradec is manufactured from chert breccia, the lithic type utilised in Moravia in the Early Bronze Age for producing segments (Kopacz & Šebela 2006: 40f). Despite the fact that similar tools are described in the northern literature as "flint axes" (Lomborg 1973: 24), all presently known silicite axes from Moravia, Czech Silesia, and Bohemia are considerably different to the artefact from Byzhradec and chert breccia was never used for their production.

Chronological and cultural analyses of silicite daggers

Czech Republic

Chronology and cultural analysis of silicite daggers from those territories considered here is based on artefacts found in specific "closed assemblages", that is either from graves or settlement structures. There are 14 artefacts which comply with these criteria (ten from Moravia and four from Bohemia). With two exceptions, they are daggers of Type I (handle-less). In Moravia, they are known from graves with pottery dating them to the Proto-Únětice culture from the very end of the Eneolithic. However, this "accompanying pottery" does not appear throughout the whole duration of that culture, but only in its early stage (*cf.* Ondráček 1967: 430f; Šebela 1997/98: 213).

Also, observations from Bohemia confirm the association of daggers of Type I with the Proto-Únětice culture (e.g. Bubeneč, grave 3; Fig. 11.6:2–8). However, the handle-less dagger from Sokoleč was accompanied in a grave by a legged-bowl (Fig. 11.6:1, 9). It is a form typical for the second stage of the Únětice culture – the Old Únětice Phase (e.g. Velké Žernoseky, grave 54; Moucha 1963: Tab. X:3–4), both in Bohemia (Moucha 1963: fig. 6) and Moravia (Ondráček 1967: 416). On that basis, we assume that, in Moravia, daggers with handles were utilised only for a short period of time (the Old Proto-Únětice culture); while, in Bohemia, they continued to be used through the beginning of the Bronze Age. Therefore, in the latter territory they might have also been made from various silicites from Central Europe (of central Polish or Bavarian provenience).

The chronological position of Moravian handled daggers can be determined only on the basis of the funerary assemblage of grave 1 from Kobylí, Moravia. Pottery from that site, preserved in a very fragmentary state, is related to the Únětice culture, but not to any specific phase.

In Denmark, handled daggers (of Type III) appear in assemblages from phase B of the local Late Neolithic, corresponding with phases 3 and 4 of the Únětice culture in Central Europe. Slightly less ancient are daggers of types IV and V. They are dated to phase C of the Late Neolithic in Denmark, that is to the classic period of the Únětice culture. The most recent daggers, Type VI, come from the Danish Early Bronze Age, contemporary with the latest stage of the Únětice culture in Bohemia, corresponding with its

sixth phase according to V. Moucha (1963: fig. 6) and, in Moravia, with the Post-Classic phase and the Věteřov group (Ondráček 1967: 440, note 334).

A comparison of numerous finds of handled daggers in individual historical regions within today's Czech Republic is very interesting. In Czech Silesia, they are unknown. In Moravia, eight such artefacts have so far been recorded and they are twice less frequent as in Bohemia (16 artefacts). Such a distribution of finds can be related to the fact that, in Bohemia, silicite daggers occur over a long period of time over the course of the development of the Únětice culture; while, in Moravia, their appearance was only a short episode in the scope of the Proto-Únětice culture. Moreover, the Bohemian milieu maintained more intensive contacts with Germany and Denmark, especially along the Labe River.

Slovakia

Considering the small number of silicite daggers recorded so far in Slovakia (six artefacts), we can suppose that people living in these areas at the turn of the Stone and Bronze Ages did not maintain very intensive contacts with Northern Europe. This lack of contact might have been caused by bad trade passages through the Carpathian bow-shaped range. For the period concerned here, territories on both sides of the Carpathian range and those of western Ukraine were encompassed by the Epi-Corded Circum-Carpathian complex which had little contact with the north. The handle-less dagger from Kúty on the left bank of the Morava River, near the state border with the Czech Republic (Fig. 11.3) is evidently linked with the Moravian milieu (Šebela 1997/98: fig. 1a). The artefact of a similar profile as the piece from Prešov, made of Volhynian flint from Ukraine, is unique in eastern Slovakia. It testifies to contacts between the Košťany culture and the Strzyżów culture (Kaminská & Tomášová 1998: 147).

Summary

Comparing collections of silicite daggers from Bohemia and Moravia, we find a very significant diversity of raw materials utilised in Bohemia. Among them there are Bavarian tabular chert, well suited for making bifacial tools and excellent chocolate silicite from central Poland, as well as rocks of lesser knappability, such as Cretaceous chert and orthoquartzite. As regards the artefact of chert breccia we cannot exclude that, rather than being a dagger, it was an unusually big segment (Kopacz *et al.* 2009). Artefacts of that type made of Moravian chert breccia were used in Moravia in the Early Bronze Age (the Únětice culture and the Věteřov group). It is possible that the use of more various lithic types for Type I daggers in Bohemia might have been related to the longer life of these artefacts there (as they were in use during the Proto-Únětice and Old Únětice Phases of the Únětice culture).

Determining the provenience of raw materials usually referred to as erratic silicites (flints) from glacial sediments poses a serious problem. Pieces of these rocks were brought to Poland, Germany and the northernmost margin of Moravia and Bohemia by the continental ice sheets; but those obtained from their original deposits on the shores of the Baltic and in Scandinavia do not differ in the structure of siliceous mass and microfossil contents. Moreover, bifacially shaped artefacts (such as daggers) are practically always lacking any relicts of the original surface which might have retained traces of glacial transportation (such traces have been identified on some chipped artefacts from the Upper Paleolithic and Neolithic in the Czech Republic). An argument against the glacial origin of the raw material used to make Bohemian and Moravian daggers is the relatively small size of erratic chunks. According to observations by Z. Gába (1972: 16), a sample of 1282 pieces collected from glacial sediments by pupils of the elementary school at Vidnava (Czech Silesia) contains chunks with a diameter 1–14cm (in comparison, the usual length of silicite daggers is about 15cm). It is also significant that only two silicite daggers (Holasovice near Opava and Stará Ves near Nový Jičín) are known from the areas with silicites (flints) in their glacial sediments. That is why, for some Bohemian/Moravian daggers prepared from raw materials related to flint types distinguished by Scandinavian archaeologists (Högberg & Olausson 2007), we cannot exclude a northern provenience.

The important and interesting problem of the origin of East-Central European daggers may be resolved (or at least made more clear) by cooperation between local and Scandinavian specialists. Of especial importance would be studies on the relationship between varieties of northern flints and specific types of daggers. If such relationships are confirmed, we would be more positive in the opinion that the analysed artefacts were really imported from the areas of the primary flint deposits in northern Germany or Scandinavia.

Acknowledgement

The authors of this work received financial support from research projects: MSM0021622427 (A. Přichystal) and IAA800010705 (L. Šebela).

References

Agthe, M. 1989a. Bemerkungen zu Feuersteindolchen im nordwestlichen Verbreitungsgebiet der Aunjetitzer Kultur. *Arbeits- und Forschungsberichte zur Sächsischen Bodendenkmalpflege* 33: 15–133.

Agthe, M. 1989b. Bemerkungen zu Feuersteindolchen im nordwestlichen Verbreitungsgebiet der Aunjetitzer Kultur. In:

E. Pleslová-Štiková & M. Buchvaldek (eds.), *Das Äneolithikum und die früheste Bronzezeit (C¹⁴ 3000–2000 b. C.) in Mitteleuropa: kulturelle und chronologische Beziehungen. Acta des XIV. Internationalen Symposiums Prag-Liblice 210.–24. 10. 1986.* Praehistorica, 15. Praha: Univerzita Karlova. 305–309.

Apel, J. 2001. *Daggers Knowledge and Power.* Uppsala: Department of Archaeology and Ancient History, University of Uppsala.

Beltz, R. 1910. *Die vorgeschichtlichen Altertümer des Großherzogtums Mecklenburg-Schwerin.* Berlin: Dietrich Reimer.

Binsteiner, A. 2005. Die Lagerstätten und der Abbau bayerischer Jurahornsteine sowie deren Distribution im Neolithikum Mittel- und Osteuropas. *Jahrbuch des Römisch-Germanischen Zentralmuseums* 52: 43–155.

Binsteiner, A. 2011. *Rätsel der Steinzeit zwischen Donau und Alpen.* Linzer archäologische Forschungen, 41. Linz: Guttenberg-Werbering GmbH.

Gába, Z. 1972. Příspěvek k poznání ledovcem transportovaných pazourků. Beitrag zur Erkenntnis der durch das Islandeis transportierten Feuersteine. *Zprávy Vlastivědného ústavu v Olomouci č.* 157: 16–17.

Högberg, A. & Olausson, D. 2007. *Scandinavian Flint – an Archaeological Perspective.* Aarhus: Aarhus University Press.

Jiráň, L. ed. 2008. *Archeologie pravěkých Čech/5. Doba bronzová.* Praha: Archeologický ústav AV ČR, Praha.

Kalferst, J. & Prostředník, J. 1993. Nálezy kultury se šňůrovou keramikou ve východních Čechách. *Pojizerský sborník* 1: 16–47.

Kaminská, Ľ. 1998. Listovitý hrot z včasnej doby bronzovej z Prešova. *Archeologické nálezy a výzkumy na Slovensku* (1996): 93.

Kaminská, Ľ. & Tomášová, B. 1998. Ojedinelý nález listovitého hrotu z Prešova. *Východoslovenský pravek* 5: 145–148.

Kopacz, J., Přichystal, A. & Šebela, L. 2009. *Lithic Chipped Industry of the Bell Beaker culture in Moravia and its east-central European Context.* Kraków – Brno: Polska Akademia Umiejętnośći – Archeologický ústav Akademie věd České republiky, Brno.

Kopacz, J. & Šebela, L. 2006. *Kultura unietycka i grupa wieterzowska na Morawach na podstawie materiałów krzemieniarskich.* Kraków: Polska Akademia Umiejętnośći.

Korošec, P. & Korošec, J. 1969. *Najdbe s koliščarkih naselbin pri Igu na Ljubljanskem barju. Fundgut der Pfahlbausiedlungen bei Ig am Laibacher Moor.* Catalogi Archaeologici Sloveniae, III. Ljubljana: Narodni muzej.

Kühn, H. J. 1979. *Das Spätneolithikum in Schleswig-Holstein.* Offa-Bücher 40. Neumünster: Karl Wachholtz Verlag.

Lech, H. & Lech, J. 1995. Wierzbica „Zele", Radom Province. In: J. Lech (ed.), Appendix to the Bochum catalogue of prehistoric flint mines in Europe. *Archaeologia Polona* 33: 465–480.

Libera, J. 2001. *Krzemienne formy bifacjalne na terenach Polski i zachodnie Ukrainy (od środkowego neolitu do wczesnej epoki żelaza).* Lublin: Wydawnictwo Universytetu Marii Curie-Skłodowskiej.

Lomborg, E. 1973. *Die Flintdolche Dänemarks. Studien über die Chronologie und Kulturbeziehungen des südskandinavischen Spätneolithikums.* Nordiske Fortidsminder, Ser. B - in quarto 1. Copenhagen: H. J. Lynge.

Marková, K. 2004. Zu Silizitdolchen in der Slowakei. In: J. Bátora,

V. Furmánek & L. Veliačik (eds.), *Einflüsse und Kontakte Alteuropäischer Kulturen. Festschrift für Jozef Vladár zum 70. Geburtstag*. Nitra: Archeologický ústav SAV. 205–215.

Moucha, V. 1963. Die Periodisierung der Úněticer Kultur in Böhmen. *Sborník Československé společnosti archeologické* 5: 9–60.

Müller, S. 1902. *Flintdolkene i den nordiske Stenalder*. Nordiske Fortidsminder 1. Copenhagen: Gyldendal.

Neustupný, E. ed. 2008. *Archeologie pravěkých Čech/4. Eneolit*. Praha: Archeologický ústav AV ČR, Praha.

Novotný, B. 1958. *Slovensko v mladšej dobe kamennej*. Bratislava: Vydavateľstvo Slovenskej akademie vied.

Ondráček, J. 1967. Moravská protoúnětická kultura. *Slovenská archeológia* 15(2): 389–446.

Podborský, V. ed. 1993. *Pravěké dějiny Moravy*. Vlastivěda Moravská. Země a lid. Nová řada svazek 3. Brno: Muzejní a vlastivědná sapolečnost.

Přichystal, A. 1984. Petrografické studium štípané industrie Petrographic investigation of chipped industry. In: E. Kazdová, *Těšetice-Kyjovice 1. Starší stupeň kultury s moravskou malovanou keramikou*. Brno: Univerzita Jana Evangelisty Purkyně v Brně. 205–211.

Přichystal, A. 2006. Surowce kamienne morawskich inwentarzy krzemieniarskich z wczesnego okresu epoki brązu. In: J. Kopacz & L. Šebela, *Kultura unietycka i grupa wieterzowska na Morawach na podstawie materiałów krzemieniarskich*. Kraków: Polska Akademia Umiejętnośći. 37–45.

Přichystal, A. 2010. Classification of lithic raw materials used for prehistoric chipped artefacts in general and siliceous sediments (silicites) in particular: the Czech proposal. *Archeometriai Mühely* 7(3): 177–181.

Rous, P. 1981. *Katalog pravěkých nálezů (okres Havlíčkův Brod)*. Hradec Králové: Krajské muzeum východních Čech.

Rýzner, Č. 1883. Řivnáč. Hradiště u Levého Hradce. *Památky archeologické* 12: 216, 240–247, 299–315.

Stocký, A. 1924. *Čechy v době kamenné*. Praha: Jan Štenc.

Stocký, A. 1928. *Čechy v době bronzové*. Praha: Jan Štenc.

Svoboda, J., Havlíček, P., Ložek, V., Macoun, J., Musil, R., Přichystal, A., Svobodová, H. & Vlček, E. 1994. *Paleolit Moravy a Slezska*. Dolnověstonické studie I. Brno: Archeologický ústav AV ČR v Brně.

Šebela, L. 1997/98. Spätäneolithische und altbronzezeitliche Silexdolche in Mähren. *Saarbrücker Studien und Materialien zur Altertumskunde* 6/7: 199–226.

Šebela, L. & Škrdla, P. 1999. *A flint tool from Násedlovice: the Problem of its Dating. Archeologické rozhledy 51: 876–879*.

Tode, A. 1935. Zur Entstehung der Germanen. *Mannus* 27: 19–67.

Zápotocký, M. 1961. Severské zbraně a nástroje starší doby bronzové v Čechách. *Památky archeologické* 52: 166–176.

Zavřel, P. 1986. Rukojeť severské pazourkové dýky z Českých Budějovic 9 – Dobré vody. *Archeologické rozhledy* 38: 290–292.

METAL ADOPTION AND THE EMERGENCE OF STONE DAGGERS IN NORTHEAST ASIA

Shinya Shoda

This paper discusses the characteristics of production of elaborately polished stone weapons from Northeast Asia (NE-A), including northeast China, the Russian Maritime Province, the Korean peninsula, and the Japanese islands, during the time of metal adoption, from the 2nd to the 1st millennia BC. First, it reviews studies of lithic weapons in NE-A carried out in various countries and by various schools of research. A chronology for the entire area is set out which divides the lithic daggers into five stages which reflect their regionally and chronologically varying forms. There is a clear pattern of these stone weapons appearing in the stage just before the emergence of bronze in each region, a period which saw the contemporary adoption of bronze in neighbouring areas. Additionally, taking recently excavated Korean materials as examples, I discuss the production and use of stone daggers in the Korean Peninsula where the densest distribution of stone daggers is found. First, particular types of the daggers are highly regular in their production. Second, petroglyphs of daggers excavated at cemetery sites show the strong connection between funeral rites and bronze or ground-stone daggers which are among the major offerings within tombs. Third, daggers seemed to be connected with males and are affixed to the right side of the lower body in a regular way, a pattern which is also found in northeast China where the daggers originate. Thus, the idea or usage of daggers seems to be transferred with the form.

Introduction

This paper discusses the lithic weapons distributed in northeast Asia at the eastern periphery to the Eurasian continent, a region which includes northeast China, the Maritime Province of Russia, the Korean peninsula and the Japanese islands (Fig. 12.1). During the period of metal adoption, from the 2nd to 1st millennia BC, people in this region developed highly exquisite lithic daggers and spearheads. In this article, I will further explore the characteristics of these materials to investigate the nature of metal adoption in NE-A and to propose an example of a case study which will be compared with the European material described in other papers in this volume.

Over recent decades, a considerable number of studies have been conducted on these lithic weapons in NE-A.

Most studies have been focused on the phasing, chronology and craft specialisation in this period; and only a few were written in English. Thus, we must begin with a brief review of the research history on this topic. Following this literature review, I discuss the period to which these lithic weapons belong and their distribution, especially as these topics concern the relationship between lithic daggers and the process of metal adoption. In the final section, I focus on the production and use of lithic daggers, taking recent studies and excavation data as examples. In bringing together the data from various areas and ordering them within the different regional and radiocarbon chronologies, I am able to show the variety of lithic weapons in each with local situation, as well as the way that the idea of daggers became widely spread.

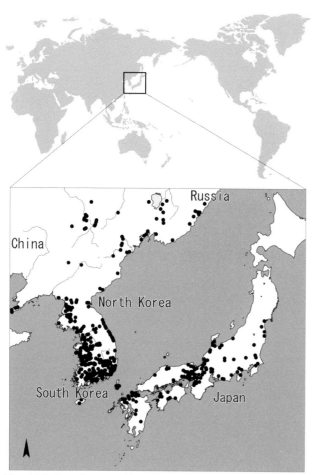

Fig. 12.1. Distribution of lithic weapons in NE-A. Figure by S. Shoda, J. Son, N. Teramae & O. Yanshina.

Archaeological studies of lithic weapons in NE-A

Stone weapons in NE-A have been studied in various national and intellectual contexts, sometimes independent from each other, and written about in various languages including Chinese, Russian, Korean, English and Japanese, leading to serious differences in opinion between different archaeologists and schools of research (see discussion in Shoda *et al.* 2009).

After the early antiquarian studies of Japanese and Korean lithic weapons (Takahashi 1923; Umehara 1924), starting in the 1950s, Russian (Okladnikov 1956) and Japanese (Arimitsu 1959) archaeologists began to study the elaborately polished stone daggers in the Maritime Province of Russia and the Korean peninsula to investigate the social changes in local societies under the influence of the more developed cultures of China, Central Asia and Siberia. They commonly considered these daggers to be imitations of bronze weapons used by these developed cultures. Since the lithic material were regarded as indicating the existence of bronzes nearby, they also

denoted the beginning of new eras, such as the "Bronze Age", and were useful in explaining the chronology of peripheral areas in NE-A.

In Russia, followers of Okladnikov (Andreeva *et al.* 1986; Dyakov 1989; Konkova 1989) further developed his scheme with the following criteria in mind: 1) lithic weapons in the Maritime Province were linked to bronze in Siberia; 2) The series of stages in lithic weapon production corresponded to subsequent bronze-using cultures in Siberia, such as the Seima-Turbino, Karasuk and Tagar; and 3) Russian, Korean and Japanese lithic weapons were all related. Although this interpretative framework has also found some sympathy in Korea (Kang 2007), other studies (Hirai 1961; Usuki 1989) have criticised the first and second criteria based on a comparison with the materials in China and Korea. Recently, this criticism was made more specific through the use of a new corpus of material and new chronological data, including radiocarbon dates from archaeological sites (Shoda *et al.* 2009; Yanshina 2012).

In Japan, followers of Arimitsu developed the chronology of lithic weapons in the Korean peninsula (Komoto 1973) and the Maritime Province (Usuki 1989) based on Arimitsu's assumption that the narrow-shaped bronze daggers were the prototype of stone weapons. However, the excavation of the Baju Oksok-ri dolmen site in the Korean peninsula has revealed that the narrow-shaped bronze dagger appeared later than the stone daggers. This reversed chronology was supported by the stratigraphy of this site and radiocarbon dating (Kim & Yun 1967). Accordingly, this type of bronze dagger cannot be the prototype of stone daggers. Although this report was published in the 1960s, Arimitsu's scheme remained in use for several decades because it appeared typologically logical. Moreover, "the short chronology" corroborated by the "inclined chronology" of the 1st millennium BC of NE-A which was broadly accepted in Japanese archaeology at this time (Onuki 2005) supported this scheme firmly.

From the 1970s in Japan and the 1990s in South Korea, both countries witnessed the explosive increase in rescue excavation (Tsuboi 1986; Shoda 2008); a situation which led many archaeologists to focus on typological and chronological studies of narrower regions and single materials (e.g. stone, metal, bone, or wood) (Teramae 2010). Variations and functions of the lithic weapons were studied in detail (Hashiguchi 1986; Negita 1986; Tanesada 1990; Lee 1997); while a few studies had broader aims, such as identifying interactions among regions in NE-A (Shimojo 1977) or determining the social meanings behind metal adoption (Kim 1971), as well as using cross-craft approaches to reconstruct production systems or craft specialisation (Nakamura 1987).

In the 2000s, as research integrating material from larger areas began to appear, many assemblages were brought together and compared in regional typo-chronologies: Korean

Table 12.1. Chronology of metal adoption and of the spread of lithic weapons across NE-A.

Phase	Date	Liaoxi	Liaodong/Jilin/ North Korea	Maritime region	Middle Korea	South Korea/Kyushu	West Honshu
I	Early-Mid 2nd millennium BC	SY	SP				
II	Late 2nd millennium BC		SP	SP?	PD	PD?	
III	Early 1st millennium BC		SP, PD	SP, PD	PD	PD	
IV	Mid 1st millennium BC		SP, PD	SP, PD	PD	PD, HA	PD, KD
V	Late 1st millennium BC			PD?		PD, HA	PD, KD

▮ bronze	SY:	"Yue"axe	PD: Polished Daggers
▮ iron	SP:	Spearheads	KD: Knapped Daggers
	HA:	Halberds	

materials by Son (2006), Japanese materials by Teramae (2010), Russian materials by Yanshina (2012), and knives from Korea and the Maritime Province were compared by Bae (2007). It is especially noteworthy that Kondo (2000) suggests a relationship between Liaoning Bronze daggers in the Upper Xiajiadian culture and stone daggers in South Korea. This opinion is widely accepted in spite of the geographical distance – finds of these two types of object are separated by up to 1000km – because the specimens belong in the same period within the new long chronology described below. According to Kondo, Korean stone daggers might have appeared as early as the end of the 9th century BC. We also compared the materials from Russia, China and Korea as mentioned above (Shoda *et al.* 2009).

In addition, in the past decade there has been a drastic change in the chronology from the 2nd to the 1st millennia BC in NE-A, that is, from a short chronology to a long chronology. This change is the result of new AMS radiocarbon dating and the re-examination of metal objects in NE-A (Shoda 2010). Consequently, the dates of bronze adoptions in areas of NE-A are being re-evaluated. Within this new chronology, the stone daggers are coeval with lute-shaped bronze daggers which are, in turn antecedent to the narrow-shaped bronze daggers traditionally regarded as the putative prototypes of stone daggers in the Korean peninsula. Interestingly, the new long chronology dovetails with the chronology of stone daggers in Korea (Park 1993; Shoda 2005) and the Maritime Province (Yanshina 2004, 2012) as discussed below.

Chronology and distribution

In this section, the chronology and distribution of lithic weapons in NE-A is discussed within the context of the studies reviewed above. As shown in Figure 12.1, lithic weapons are broadly distributed across NE-A aside from the western part of Liaoning province China where a dense distribution of bronzes is observed and from more peripheral

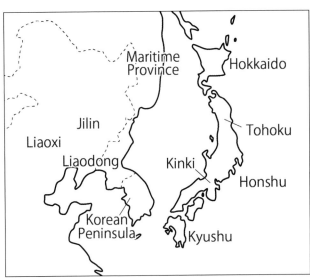

Fig. 12.2. Map of NE-A with the locations of regions discussed in the text.

area such as Tohoku and Hokkaido. We can see a remarkable concentration in the southern part of the Korean peninsula as well as some smaller concentrations in northern Kyushu and the Kinki area in Japan. Of course, we still lack adequate information from North Korea.

According to the new long chronology, bronze and iron adoption in NE-A has been reassessed (Table 12.1 & Fig. 12.2). To put it briefly, there is a clear pattern of these stone weapons appearing in the stage just before the emergence of bronze in each region – the stage in which one also observes bronze being adopted in neighbouring areas. There are also patterns in the disappearance of lithic weapons. This disappearance nearly always corresponds to the beginning of active local production of bronze, followed by the rapid, large-scale spread of iron in the late 1st millennium BC (Shoda & Frieman forthcoming).

The shapes of these lithic weapons vary with location. The stone "Yue" axe which shows influences from the

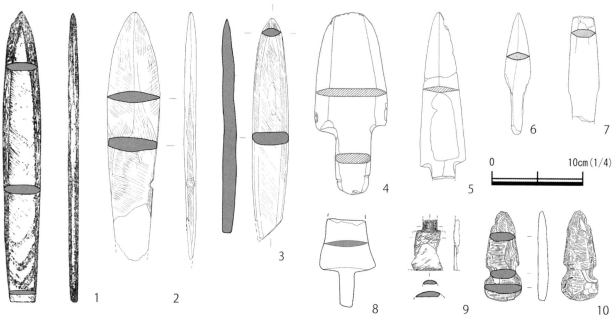

Fig. 12.3. Lithic weapons in phases I-II. 1: Gaotaishan (Shengyang Cultural Relics Administrative Committee 1986); 2, 3: Xiaoyingzi (Kang et al. 2009); 4: Kuryounggang (Seok & Kim 2003); 5: Oesampo-ri (Gangwon Research Institute of Cultural Properties 2008); 6: Jucheon-ri (Yemaek Institute of Cultural Properties 2010) (modified by S. Shoda).

Chinese central plain is found in the Liaoxi area, while the stone halberds which are often drawn on Yayoi pottery in Japan (Fukasawa 1998) are found in Honshu, showing that there existed local traditions concerning the appearance of weapons. Also, in some areas almost exact copies of the bronze prototypes were produced while in others the shapes were absolutely different. We shall examine these varieties in more detail below (Figs. 12.3–12.6), dividing them into the five phases showed in Table 12.1.

In phase I (Fig. 12.3: 1–3), lithic weapons such as "Yue" axes and spearheads are found, although they are small and distributed only in the Liaoxi and Liaodong area. A stone "Yue" was found on a site of the Lower Xiajiadian culture and was considered to be an imitation of bronze (Guo & Zhang 2004: 299). Also, there is the example of a spearhead from the Gaotaishan site made in polished stone (Shengyang Cultural Relics Administrative Committee 1986: 24) which was regarded as a non-functional, symbolic material (Guo & Zhang 2004: 340).

In phase II (Fig. 12.3: 4–10), although the existence of lithic weapons in the Maritime Province and the southern part of Korean peninsula remains controversial, we know that they clearly began to appear in Liaodong, Jilin, and the north and middle of Korea, based on the materials from the Shuangtuozi site (Institute of Archaeology, Chinese Academy of Social Science 1996), the Dazuizi site (Dalian Institute of Cultural Relics and Archaeology 2000), the Xiaoyingzi site (Fujita 1941; Kang *et al.* 2009), the Kuryounggang site (Seok & Kim 2003, the Oesampo-

ri site (Gangwon Research Institute of Cultural Properties 2008) and the Jucheon-ri site (Yemaek Institute of Cultural Properties 2010). However, they seem to result only from small-scale production activities.

Much more material is found in phase III (Fig. 12.4) across the majority of NE-A. Stone daggers with elaborate hilts are found at Pyeongseong-ri (Shim 1984) and other sites in the southeastern part of the Korean peninsula where bronze is not found in this stage. Daggers in this phase are represented by the stepped-hilted daggers, such as those from Gahyeong-dong (Gangwon Research Institute of Cultural Properties 2011), Jogyo-ri (Lee & Son 2004) and other sites. Stone spearheads are also found in Pyodae (Kim 2003) and Namgyeong (Kim & Seok 1984), both sites in the northern part of the Korean peninsula. As mentioned by Onuki (1998: 165), daggers are densely distributed to the south of NE-A, while spearheads tend to be found in north; a pattern which seemingly relates to the differing subsistence patterns in these areas because spearheads are not clearly divided from the hunting tools. This tendency which continued until phase V, supports the co-existence model of daggers and spearheads in the Maritime Province (Yanshina 2004).

During the subsequent phase IV (Fig. 12.5), we find a characteristic similarity between the straight-hilted daggers from Kyushu Island, Japan to those from the Russian Maritime Province. Close similarities can be observed between the daggers from the Zasshonokuma site (Fukuoka City Board of Education 2005) in Japan and the Majeon-ri

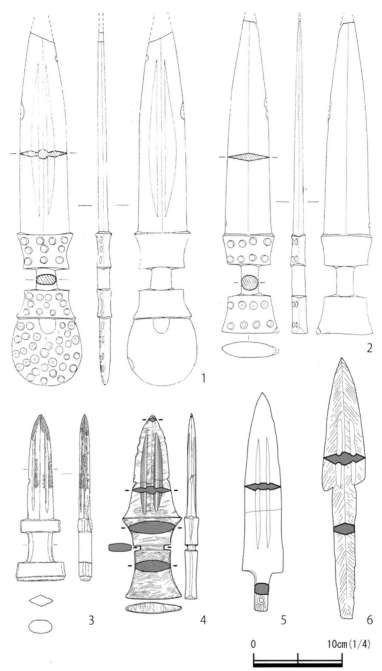

Fig. 12.4. Lithic weapons in phase III. 1, 2: Pyeongseong-ri (Shim 1984); 3: Gahyeon-dong (Gangwon Research Institute of Cultural Properties 2011); 4: Jugyo-ri (Lee & Son 2004); 5: Namgyeong (Kim & Seok 1984); 6: Pyodae (Kim 2003) (4 drawn by S. Shoda, others modified by S. Shoda).

site (Lee *et al*. 2004) in Korea as well as between spearheads from the Xinguang site (Jilin Wangyan Archeological Unit 1992) in China and Slavyanka 1 (Andreeva *et al*. 1986: 64) in Russia. Moreover, the exaggeratedly large, elaborated daggers are found at Jinra-ri (Yongnam Institute of Cultural Properties 2005), Pyeongchon-ri (Gyeongsang-bukdo Institute of Cultural Properties 2010) and other sites in Korea.

In the final phase V (Fig. 12.6), greater numbers of daggers, many of which are much closer in form to metal prototypes are found in the Japanese islands than in the preceding stages, for example those found on the Otoba (Kaminaka Town Board of Education 1975) and Uriudo sites (Osaka Center for Cultural Heritage 1980). Also, clear regionality of forms can be observed in the various

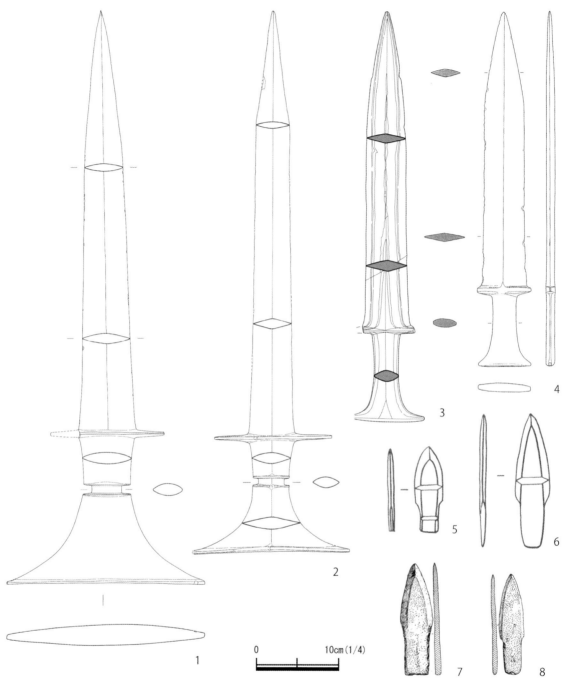

Fig. 12.5. Lithic weapons in phase IV. 1: Jinra-ri (Yongnam Institute of Cultural Properties 2005); 2: Pyeongchon-ri (Gyeongsang-bukdo Institute of Cultural Properties 2010); 3: Majeon-ri (Lee et al. 2004); 4: Zasshonokuma (Fukuoka City Board of Education 2005); 5, 6: Slavyanka 1 (Andreeva et al. 1986:64); 7, 8: Xinguang (Jilin Wangyan Archeological Unit 1992) (3 redrawn, others modified by S. Shoda).

Japanese regions. In Kyushu, people produced stone halberds, such as those found at the Kanamaru site (Onga Town Board of Education 2007), which were not produced in any other region in NE-A even though bronze halberds are found across much of this area. Additionally, people did not only produce polished stone daggers like those

from Kyushu or the Korean peninsula, but also knapped andesite into daggers, such as those found on the Karako-kagi (Tawaramoto Town Board of Education 1983) and Tamatsu-tanaka sites (Hyogo Prefecture Board of Education 1996) in the Kinki area on Honshu.

Additionally, there are also some examples of daggers

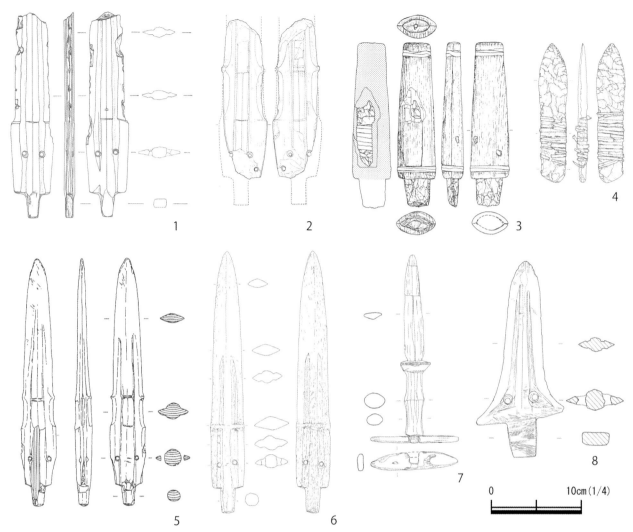

Fig. 12.6. Lithic (1–4, 8), wood (5, 7) & bone (6) weapons in phase V. 1: Otoba (Kaminaka town Board of Education 1975); 2: Uriudo (Osaka Center for Cultural Heritage 1980); 3: Karako-kagi (Tawaramoto Town Board of Education 1983); 4: Tamatsu-tanaka (Hyogo Prefecture Board of Education 1996); 5: Minamikata (Okayama Prefecture Board of Education 2005); 6: Aoya-kamijichi (Tottori Prefectural Archaeological Centre 2000); 7: Shinchang-dong (Kwangju National Museum 1997); 8: Kanamaru (Onga Town Board of Education 2007) (modified by S. Shoda).

made of materials other than stone, such as wood and bone, from Korea and Japan. These include the wooden daggers from the Shinchang-dong site (Kwangju National Museum 1997), the wooden daggers from the Minamikata site (Okayama Prefecture Board of Education 2005) and the bone dagger from the Aoya-kamijichi site (Tottori Prefectural Archaeological Centre 2000). In this phase, the production of stone daggers ceased in large parts of NE-A, most likely because active bronze casting spread across most of this area, soon followed by the rapid adoption of iron. However, in the peripheral areas – mainly in central and eastern Japan – people kept on producing lithic weapons, such as knapped or ground-stone daggers. The situation in the Maritime Province at this time remains controversial.

Production and use of stone daggers in the Korean Peninsula

Having clarified the chronology and distribution of lithic weapons in NE-A, I will now discuss the characteristics of their production and use, especially focusing on recently excavated materials from South Korea where the densest distribution of stone daggers is found. Although Neolithic ground-stone axes and arrowheads are known from northeast China and the Maritime Province as well as the Korean peninsula, the dagger shape was first introduced in the beginning of the Bronze Age, that is from the later 2nd millennium BC. Thus, investigations into the production and use of these daggers are essential in order to understand the nature of metal adoption in each region.

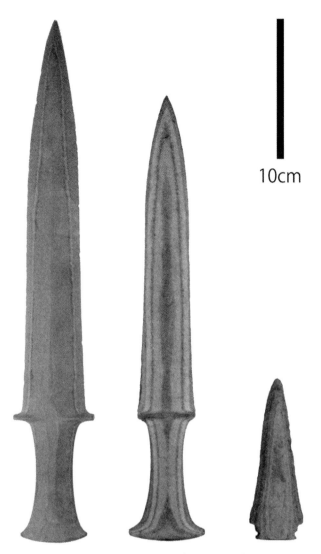

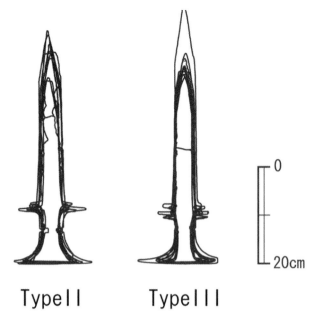

Fig. 12.8. Regularity of dagger morphology and dimensions as shown by superimposing outline drawings of numerous lithic daggers (Jang & Hiragori 2009: fig. 9).

Fig. 12.7. Stone daggers with striped patterns (after Lee & Son 2004).

The sources and physical properties of lithic raw materials used to make daggers in Korea have not been studied in particular, aside from a pioneering study by Hwang (2011) focusing on the hornfels daggers. However, some knappers in the southern Korean peninsula were obviously exploiting sedimentary rocks with distinctive striped patterns and using their natural banding to emphasise the dagger shape (Fig. 12.7). Tuff, slate and mudstone have also been suggested as raw materials which were utilised based on macroscopic observation (Daegu National Museum 2005: 261).

Contrasting with the diversity of stone raw materials exploited, there is clear regularity in the production technique used to manufacture the particular type of stone daggers found in the southeastern part of the Korean peninsula, indicating that knowledge of how to manufacture daggers was distributed along with the daggers themselves (Jang &

Hiragori 2009; Fig. 12.8). This communication network also seems to be connected to the way production regularities and funeral rites are shared within single river basins, a pattern revealed by the analysis of stone tubular beads in this period (Shoda 2006).

Regarding the use of the stone daggers, only 16 of the 352 Late Bronze Age tombs (5%) in the Nam river basin, located near the southern end of the peninsula, have stone daggers as their burial goods (Ko & Bale 2008: 97). Considering that most of tombs of the Korean Bronze Age lack burial accessories, the possession of stone dagger seemed to be highly restricted in these societies. On the other hand, stone daggers are among the most frequent burial goods (such as there are) in this period along with stone ornaments and arrowheads as well as pottery.

Additionally, daggers are found in rock art (Fig. 12.9), suggesting that they played important roles in ritual behavior in local societies. Petroglyphs of daggers were excavated at cemetery sites, such as Salnae (Center of History & Culture, Gyeongnam Development Institute 2005), Sinan (Center of History & Culture, Gyeongnam Development Institute 2007), Boncheon-ri (Jo *et al*. 2011) and Inbidong (Lee *et al*. 1985), distributed in the southeastern part of the Korean peninsula. Their context shows the strong connection between funeral rites and bronze or ground-stone daggers, among the major offerings within tombs of this period. In particular, the petroglyph on the dolmen in Olimdong (Lee & Jeong 1992) is much more similar in shape to stone daggers than it is to bronze daggers.

Fig. 12.9. Petroglyphs of daggers on the rock art in Korea. 1, 2: Inbidong (Lee et al. 1985); 3: Sinan, 4: Olimdong, 5: Salnae, 6: Massang (Ulsan Petroglyph Museum 2011) (modified by S. Shoda).

Fig. 12.10. A stone dagger with human skeletal remains under excavation at the Pyeongchon-ri site (Gyeongsang-bukdo Institute of Cultural Properties 2010: pl. 74).

Due to the chemical character of soil, skeletal remains are rarely found in the Korean peninsula. However, the Pyeongchon-ri site (Gyeongsang-bukdo Institute of Cultural Properties 2010) yielded skeletal remains in an extraordinarily good condition for this area, allowing me to investigate the relationship between the presence/absence of stone daggers and sex as well as the manner in which the stone daggers were affixed to their body. First, when it was possible to assign a sex, all of the stone daggers are found with males; so, at Pyeongchon-ri we find seven cases of stone daggers being associated with male skeletal remains, while the sex of three sets of skeletal remains associated with stone daggers remains unclear. There is also one example from Hwangsoek-ri dolmen no. 13 (Kim & Yun 1967) where skeletal remains determined to be male and stone daggers were found together inside a coffin. On the other hand, we have no known finds of female remains associated with stone daggers. Apparently, the idea of daggers or weapons, possibly of warfare itself, was embedded in the stone daggers, and connected to male identity, at least at these sites.

More interestingly, daggers in the coffins at Pyeongchon-ri were all positioned in the same manner: they were placed under or next to the right knee of the deceased, with the blade pointed towards his feet (Fig. 12.10). This pattern of associations is also observed in tombs with bronze daggers at the Shiertaiyingzi site (Zhu 1960) in China: in one tomb, male and female remains were excavated and the former was associated with two bronze daggers while the latter was accompanied by accessories other than weapons. It seems that the idea or usage of daggers was transferred with the material from the Liaoxi region to the southern part of the Korean Peninsula.

Summary and conclusion

In this paper, I reviewed studies of lithic weapons in NE-A and set out their chronology. I divided lithic daggers into five stages, dating from the 2nd to the 1st millennia BC to explain the geographic and chronological variety in their forms. Furthermore, taking Korean materials as an example, I discussed the character of the production and use of stone daggers in the Korean Peninsula. In particular, daggers seemed to be connected with males and fixed at the right side of the lower body, in common with the dagger's origin in northeast China.

In conclusion, most studies of lithic daggers and spearheads have focused on their shapes or chronology within small regions. Very few attempts have been made to grasp the broader distribution of the weapons, not to mention the idea of weapons writ large, which is seemingly characteristic of bronze adoption in the northern part of Eurasia (Shoda & Frieman forthcoming). Therefore, in this paper, I began by bringing together a wealth of data from various areas and ordering them within the various regional and radiocarbon chronologies.

The characteristics of lithic weapon production and use are regionally variable. There are different materials used and shapes preferred according to time and place. They also differ in find context: I showed the examples from tombs in the Korean peninsula, but few daggers were found from tombs in the Maritime Province. In this paper, only the examples from Korea were discussed in depth. In the future, comparative studies not only between areas within NE-A, but also on a global scale should be carried out to help understand one of the most discussed topics in human history: the nature of metal adoption and the attendant social changes.

Acknowledgements

I thank Catherine J. Frieman, Igor Ya. Shewkomud, Oksana V. Yanshina, Lena Sushko, Yegor Bagrin, Yubin

Song, Huili Liang, Jing Yu, Jingtang Cheng, Joon-ho Son, Sang-mok Lee, Byeongseop Kim, Sieun Yang, Inuk Kang, Yongjoon Jang, Jongmo Choi, Emiko Kusunoki, Daisuke Nakamura, Tatsuya Hiragori, Yoshiki Fukasawa, Keiji Umezaki, Tadashi Takimoto, Mikio Tsunematsu, Katsuhiro Nakanishi, Toshiyuki Kimijima, Akiko Nakamura and Naoto Teramae who helped me undertake this research. This study is supported by a Grant-in-Aid for Young Scientists (A), Japan Society for the Promotion of Science (no. 23682012).

References

Andreeva, J.V., Zchuchihovskaya, I. S. & Kononenko, N. A. 1986. *Yankovsky Culture*. Moscow: Nauka. [In Russian]

Arimitsu, K. 1959. *Study of Polished Stone Daggers in Korea*. Kyoto: Kyoto University. [In Japanese]

Bae, J.S. 2007. An essay on the Dongbuk-type stone knife. *Yeongnam Archaeological Review* 40: 5–25. [In Korean]

Center of History & Culture, Gyeongnam Development Institute 2005. *The Report of Excavation at Miryang Salnae Site*. Changwon: Center of History & Culture, Gyeongnam Development Institute. [In Korean]

Center of History & Culture, Gyeongnam Development Institute 2007. *The Report of Excavation Sinan Prehistory Site at Miryang*. Changwon: Center of History & Culture, Gyeongnam Development Institute. [In Korean]

Daegu National Museum 2005. *The Adapted People, The Adapted Stones*. Seoul: Tongcheon. [In Korean]

Dalian Institute of Cultural Relics and Archaeology 2000. *Dazuizi: A Report on Bronze Age Site Excavatoin in 1987*. Dalian: Dalian Press. [In Chinese]

Dyakov, V.I. 1989. *The Bronze Age in the Prymorye Region*. Vladivostok: Izd-vo Dal'nevostochnogo. [In Russian]

Fukasawa, Y. 1988. Men holding halberds. *Mizuho* 24: 47–58. [In Japanese]

Fukuoka City Board of Education 2005. *The 14th and 15th Excavation Report of Zasshonokuma Site*. Fukuoka: Fukuoka City Board of Education. [In Japanese]

Fujita, R. 1941. *Excavation Report on the Xiaoyingzi Site, Yanji*. Shinjian: Manju Press. [In Japanese]

Gangwon Research Institute of Cultural Properties 2008. *The Excavation Report on The Oesampo-ri Site in Hongcheon*. Chuncheon: Gangwon Research Institute of Cultural Properties. [In Korean]

Gangwon Research Institute of Cultural Properties 2011. *The Excavation Report on The Gahyeon-dong site in Wonju*. Chuncheon: Gangwon Research Institute of Cultural Properties. [In Korean]

Guo, D. S. & Zhang, X. D. 2004. *Dongbei Culture and Youyan Civilization*. Nanjing: Jiangsu Education Publishing House. [In Chinese]

Gyeongsang-bukdo Institute of Cultural Properties 2010. *The Pyeongchon-ri and Aeahyun-ri Site, Dalseonggun*. Yeongcheon: Gyeongsang-bukdo Institute of Cultural Properties. [In Korean]

Hashiguchi, T. 1986. Sacrifice. In: H. Kanazaeki & M. Sahara

(eds.), *Archaeology of the Yayoi Period* 9. Tokyo: Yuzankaku: 120–129. [In Japanese]

Hirai, N. 1961. On the stone daggers found in the Sikhota Alin coast – to compare with Korean material. *Journal of the Academic Association of Koreanology in Japan* 18: 32–45. [In Japanese]

Hwang, C. H. 2011. The current view, study on a place of presumed production of hornfels-polished stone daggers in the Bronze Age. *Archaeological Square* 9: 25–49. [In Korean]

Hyogo Prefecture Board of Education 1996. *Tamatsu-Tanaka Site 5*. Kobe: Hyogo Prefecture Board of Education. [In Japanese]

Institute of Archaeology, Chinese Academy of Social Science 1996. *Shuangtouzi and Gangshang*. Beijing: Science Press. [In Chinese]

Jang, Y. J. & Hiragori, T. 2009. The Management of Ceremonial Activities in the Mumun Pottery Period. *Journal of the Korean Archaeological Society* 72: 36–71. [In Korean]

Jilin Wangyang Archeological Unit 1992. Excavation Report on Xinguang site in Yanjishi, Jilin. *Kaogu* 1992(7): 615–623. [In Chinese]

Jo, Y. J., Song, Y. & Jeong, J.S. 2011. *Boncheonri Site in Sacheon*. Jinju: Gyeongsang University Museum. [In Korean]

Kaminaka Town Board of Education 1975. *Cultural Properties in Kaminaka*. Kaminaka: Kaminaka Town Board of Education.

Kang, I. U. 2007. Cultural Interaction between the Maritime Province and Korea in the Bronze Age. In: *The Formation of Prehistoric Societies and Their Cultural Interaction around the East Sea*. Seoul: Korean Ancient Historical Society: 89–123. [In Korean]

Kang, I. U., Lee, J. J., Yang, S. E., Jo, G. Y., Kim, J. Y., Kim, E. N. & Lee, J. U. 2009. *The Seoul National University Museum Collection of Prehistoric Duman River Area*. Seoul: Seoul National University Museum. [In Korean]

Kim, W. R. 1971. A study on the origin of stone daggers of Korea. *The Paek-San Hakpo*: 1–31. [In Korean]

Kim, J. H. 2003. The excavation report on the Locality 1 in Pyodae Site. The excavation reports on Masan-ri, Bangun-ri and Pyodae Sites. Seoul: Paeksan: 215–388. [In Korean]

Kim, J. W. & Yun, M. B. 1967. *Study of Korean Dolmens*. Seoul: National Museum of Korea. [In Korean]

Kim, Y. G. & Seok, K. J. 1984. *Study on the Namgyeong site*. Pyeongyang: Science and Encyclopedia Publisher. [In Korean]

Ko, M. J. & Bale, M. T. 2008. Craft production and social differentiation in the Bronze Age. *Journal of Korean Bronze Culture* 2: 82–115. [In Korean]

Komoto, M. 1973. Polished stone daggers in Northeast Asia. *Cultura Antiqua* 25(4): 140–149. [In Japanese]

Kondo, T. 2000. Bronze culture in East Asia and the dagger from Mukatsuku. *History of Yamaguchi prefecture: Archaeology* 1: 709–794. Yamaguchi: Editing Room of History of Yamaguchi Prefecture. [In Japanese]

Konkova, L. V. 1989. *The Bronze industry in the south of the USSR's far east. The boundary of the second-first millennia BC*. Leningrad: Nauka. [In Russian]

Kwangju National Museum 1997. *Shinchang-dong Wetlamd Site I*. Kwangju: Kwangju National Museum. [In Korean]

Lee, H. J. & Son, J. H. 2004. *The Jugyo-ri Site*. Jochiwon: Research Institute for Archaeological Resource, Korea University. [In Korean]

Lee, H. J., Park, S. H. & Lee H. J. 2004. *The Majon-ri Site – Locality C*. Jochiwon: Research Institute for Archaeological Resource, Korea University. [In Korean]

Lee, K. M., Choi J. K., Park, P. R. & Kim S. M. 1985. Field survey in Wolsong-gun and Yongil-gun. *Report of the Research of Antiquities of the National Museum of Korea XVII*. Seoul: National Museum of Korea. 104–157. [In Korean]

Lee, Y. M. 1997. Study on the ground-stone daggers from Jeonnam region. *Journal of Korean Ancient Historical Society* 24: 61–65. [In Korean]

Lee, Y. M. & Jeong, K. J. 1992. *Yeosu Olimdon Dolmens*. Kwangju: Jeonnam University Museum. [In Korean]

Nakamura, T. 1987. Weapon-shaped ritual tools. In: H. Kanazaeki & M. Sahara (eds.), *Archaeology of the Yayoi Period* 8. Tokyo: Yuzankaku: 23–31. [In Japanese]

Negita, Y. 1986. Knapped daggers, spearheads and halberds. In: H. Kanazeki & M. Sahara (eds.), *Archaeology of the Yayoi Period* 9. Tokyo: Yuzankaku. 77–82. [In Japanese]

Okayama Prefecture Board of Education 2005. *Minamikata Saiseikai Site – Wooden tools*. Okayama: Okayama Prefecture Board of Education. [In Japanese]

Okladnikov, A. P. 1956. Primorye during the 1st millennium BC. *Soviet Archaeology* 26: 54-96. [In Russian]

Onga Town Board of Education 2007. *Ozaki-Temjin site V, Kanamaru site II*. Onga: Onga Town Board of Education. [In Japanese]

Onuki, S. 1998. *Archaeology of Northeast Asia*. Tokyo: Doseisha. [In Japanese]

Onuki, S. 2005. A review of the recent debate about the date of the Yayoi period. *Anthropological Science (Japanese Series)* 113: 95–107. [In Japanese]

Osaka Center for Cultural Heritage 1980. *Uriudo*. Osaka: Osaka Center for Cultural Heritage. [In Japanese]

Park, S. B. 1993. Bronze and Iron cultures in the Han River Basin. In: *The History of Han River Basin*. Seoul: Mineunsa. 115–223. [In Korean]

Seok, K. J. & Kim, J. Y. 2003. Excavation Report on Kuryounggang Site. In: *Excavation Reports on Kangan-ri, Koyeon-ri and Kuryounggang Sites*. Seoul: Paeksan Press: 160–263. [In Korean]

Shengyang Cultural Relics Administrative Committee 1986. Report of the second excavation in Gaotaishan site, east of Shinmin prefecture. *Laiohai Cultural Relics* 86(1): 16–29. [In Chinese]

Shim, B. G. 1984. Relics from Namjeon-ri in Milyang and Pyeongseong-ri in Wuichang sites. In: *Dedicated Papers for the 60th Anniversary of Dr. Yoon Moo Byeong's Birth*. Seoul: Tongcheon. 53–66. [In Korean]

Shimojo, N. 1977. Birth and development of Korean type polished stone artefacts of Yayoi period in Kyushu. *Journal of History* 114: 179–215. [In Japanese]

Shoda, S. 2005. Yayoi dating – using the lute-shaped bronze daggers in Hoseo Region. *Journal of the Hoseo Archaeological Society* 12: 35–62. [In Korean]

Shoda, S. 2006. An analysis of production technique and standardization of tubular beads in the Korean Bronze Age. *Journal of the Hoseo Archaeological Society* 14: 55–83. [In Korean]

Shoda, S. 2008. A Brief Introduction to Rescue Archaeology in South Korea. *Early Korea* 1: 201–212.

Shoda, S. 2010. Radiocarbon and Archaeology in Japan and Korea: What has changed because of the Yayoi dating controversy? *Radiocarbon* 52(2–3): 421–427.

Shoda, S. & Frieman, C. J. forthcoming. Just a coincidence? The similar but contrasting history of bronze adoption in Northeast Asia and Northwest Europe. In: T. Rehren, X. Tianjin, C. Jianli, L. Nickel & P. Rui (eds.), *Making Metals and Moulding Society: a Global Perspective on the Emergence of Bronze Age Social Complexity*. Oxford: Oxbow Books.

Shoda, S., Yanshina, O., Son, J. H. & Teramae, N. 2009. New Interpretation of the Stone Replicas in the Maritime Province, Russia. *Review of Korean Studies* 12(2): 187–210.

Son, J. H. 2006. *An Archaeological Study on the Polished Stone Tools in the Korean Bronze Age*. Seoul: Seokyong. [In Korean]

Takahashi, K. 1923. Studies on the bronze daggers and spearheads XI. *Journal of the Archaeological Society of Nippon* 13(6): 372–391. [In Japanese]

Tanesada, J. 1990. Ground-stone daggers in Hokuriku region. *Bulletin of the Fukui Prefecture Archaeological Association* 8: 7–26. [In Japanese]

Tawaramoto Town Board of Education 1983. *Brief Review of Archaeological Research in Tawaramoto* 1. Tawaramoto: Tawaramoto Town Board of Education. [In Japanese]

Teramae, N. 2010. *Weapons and Societies in the Yayoi Period*. Osaka: Osaka University Press. [In Japanese]

Tottori Prefectural Archaeological Centre 2000. *Aoya-Kamijiti Site 4*. Tottori: Tottori Prefectural Archaeological Centre. [In Japanese]

Tsuboi, K. 1986. Problems concerning the preservation of archaeological sites in Japan. In: R. J. Pearson, G. Barnes & K. Hutterer (eds.), *Windows on the Japanese Past: Studies in Archaeology and Prehistory*. Ann Arbor: Center for Japanese Studies, University of Michigan. 481–490.

Ulsan Petroglyph Museum 2011. *Petroglyphs in Korea I*. Ulsan: Ulsan Petroglyph Museum. [In Korean]

Umehara, S. 1924. On the bronze daggers and spearheads. *Shilin* 9(2): 205–216. [In Japanese]

Usuki, I. 1989. A reconsideration of the Bronze Age Sites in the Maritime Region. *Prehistoric and Archeological Studies in Tsukuba University* 1: 97–119. [In Japanese]

Yanshina O. V. 2004. *The Problem of the Bronze Age in the Primorye Region*. Saint Petersburg: Peter The Great Museum of Anthropology and Ethnography, RAS. [In Russian]

Yanshina, O. V. 2012. Weapon-shaped stone tools from the Russian Far East. *Cultura Antiqua* 64(2): 69–81. [In Japanese]

Yemaek Institute of Cultural Properties 2010. *Report on the Excavation of Jucheon-ri Site, Yeongwol*. Chuncheon: Yemaek Institute of Cultural Properties. [In Korean]

Yongnam Institute of Cultural Properties 2005. *The Ancient Site at Jinra-ri, Cheongdo*. Daegu: Yongnam Institute of Cultural Properties.

Zhu, K. 1960. Bronze dagger tombs at Shih Er Ying Tai Tzu, Ch'aoyang county, Liaoning. *Chinese Journal of Archaeology* 1960(1): 63–72. [In Chinese]

'ART THOU BUT A DAGGER OF THE MIND?' UNDERSTANDING LITHIC DAGGERS IN EUROPE AND BEYOND

Catherine J. Frieman

...or art thou but
A dagger of the mind, a false creation,
Proceeding from the heat-oppressed brain?
I see thee yet, in form as palpable
As this which now I draw.
Macbeth Act II Scene I

If archaeologists can be said to be experts in anything it is holes. We burrow into hills and fields, finding bits and pieces of the past at the bottom of deep trenches and shallow pits; but we also constantly skirt holes in our knowledge, making neat narratives from bone fragments and flint flakes. We reconstruct the past just as we would reconstruct a pot, using plaster and plausibility to fill in the gaps until it stands up by itself and is ready for display. In some cases, these reconstructions stand the test of time, gaining support from subsequent finds and new data, while, in others, they are dismantled and reconstructed over and over as new techniques allow for more accurate and precise examination of the ancient past. In the end, what makes archaeology such a challenging and exciting discipline is that because our knowledge is, in fact, a scaffold built around a series of impossibly deep lacunae in the data available for investigation, a single find or a new methodology can overturn years if not decades of received wisdom about the past.

Flint dagger research has certainly not seen the level of change that has shaken archaeometallurgy, scientific dating or even early domestication studies over the last several decades. Nevertheless, new interpretive approaches, new analytical techniques and a new interest in flint daggers as a product of complex and interwoven technological systems have had a profound effect on our understanding of lithic daggers. Not only are we now able to reconstruct their technological processes, including in some cases the

sorts of choices prehistoric people were making about raw materials and the transmission of knapping knowledge and know-how, but we are gaining a new appreciation for their significance, not (just) as copies of metal daggers, but as valued implements in their own right. Moreover, flint daggers are emerging as possibly one of the more significant archaeological materials for studying the birth of the networks of exchange and contact which gave rise to the European Bronze Age. Yet, this research has generally been conducted within the confines of pre-existing national boundaries and through the lens of many different, sometimes only tangentially connected, national traditions of lithic analysis. As the papers in this volume have demonstrated, we know a considerable amount about individual corpora of lithic daggers, but how these groups of daggers, their production technology and functions relate to each other and to other contemporary materials and technologies remains a major question.

It is no longer adequate to suggest that flint daggers appear because metal daggers were valued, and we must work to align the highly variable regional dagger groups with significant long-term social and technological trends, such as the beginnings of metal technology and the emergence of new social structures. Moreover, the eye-catching form of lithic daggers and their perceived imitation of metallic forms have often separated flint dagger studies from the general thrust of lithic analysis. Yet, the research presented in the previous chapters demonstrates that flint daggers must be understood as part of a widespread, knowledgeable and highly technically proficient lithics industry built on long-standing ways of perceiving and working with lithic raw materials. In the end, if we are going to build on our understanding of flint daggers, we are going to need to broaden our approach, taking into account the technological sphere in which they were produced, the preceding lithics industry from which they developed, the social and material worlds in which they were exchanged, used and resharpened and the wider networks over which they were valued.

Making the daggers speak to each other

A key challenge to our developing understanding of the flint dagger assemblages in Europe and beyond is the partitioned knowledge base from which we can draw. Not only are there different national traditions of lithics research, but there are also different levels of interest in flint daggers (or even lithic technology) in different countries which leads to very different depths of knowledge about these implements. While there are many possible directions for future research into individual assemblages of flint daggers, I would propose four avenues of research which should improve our knowledge not just of specific groups of flint daggers but also of the entire flint dagger phenomenon in Europe and beyond.

1. Re-evaluating established typologies

One of the most basic tools for the study of archaeological materials is the typology. While these systems are not without problems and have been thoroughly criticised and discussed over the last several decades (Adams & Adams 1991; Read 2007; Whittaker *et al.* 1998), they remain useful to archaeologists seeking to understand regional and chronological variation, the development and spread of technological knowledge and the movement of people, objects and ideas. It has become clear that the flint dagger typologies developed in the early part of the twentieth century are incomplete and would benefit from further attention by contemporary archaeologists (see concerns raised by Guilbeau, this volume). For example, Mottes' (2001) work on Italian flint daggers demonstrates that long-standing typological schema are flawed in not taking resharpening and re-use into account, thus heavily worn down pieces have been classed as different archaeological types, rather than implements which saw greater wear or perhaps remained in circulation for longer periods. Scientific dating has undermined some typologies as well, for example, as Frieman (this volume) notes, while twentieth-century researchers accepted Grimes' (1932) protracted sequence of development for British flint daggers, claiming them as prototypes for the Scandinavian varieties, radiocarbon dating suggests just the opposite, that is that there is little chronological variability within the British dagger assemblage and that these daggers were more than likely inspired by Scandinavian types rather the opposite scenario. Similarly, national boundaries have often divided research areas, resulting in separate typological schema for

identical flint daggers. Thus, we have Lomborg's (1973) typochronology for the Danish (and, by proxy, wider Scandinavian) flint daggers, but Kühn's (1979) is also used when discussing the same objects when they are found further south in Jutland and northern Germany and Bloemers (1968) describes the very same pieces when recovered in the Netherlands. Clearly, some variation in the dagger assemblage over space is to be expected, not just because different regional traditions in manufacture, preference for specific raw materials and varying methods of resharpening can all lead to different final forms, but also because the uses to which they were put clearly varied regionally and also affected the size, shape and final morphology of flint daggers. That said, future work, particularly in northern and central Europe where the Scandinavian daggers were known and were, apparently, highly valued and influential, might do well to include a transnational re-evaluation of flint dagger typology. In doing so, scholars might take the outstanding work on the Grand-Pressigny flint dagger assemblage, discussed in this volume by Ihuel *et al.*, as a key source of inspiration for incorporating technological, functional and morphological data and applying it to better understand the similarities and differences within a widespread and quite variable assemblage of daggers and other lithic implements.

2. Comparing like to like

Building on this first suggestion, a further key goal of future flint dagger studies should include an attempt to standardise, or at least popularise, the various analytical approaches archaeologists can take to study these implements. By allowing national traditions of lithic research to dominate our study of flint daggers (and, frankly, of the wider lithic industries of which they form part), we have reduced our ability to compare results of research on different assemblages and, consequently, to draw together larger narratives about the spread, function and meaning of flint daggers. In particular, while in some countries (e.g., Britain and Ireland) we have a very patchy understanding of the raw materials from which flint daggers were made, in others numerous qualitative and scientific approaches have been developed to identify specific raw materials, pinpoint their sources and analyse their physical properties (Přichystal & Sebela, this volume; Högberg & Olausson 2007; Hughes *et al.* 2012). Raw material studies are key to developing a concrete idea of which flint daggers were exchanged long distances, in what direction and over what time-scale.

A further absolutely crucial avenue for future research lies in use-wear analysis. At the moment, the most extensive (and only intensive) use-wear studies on flint daggers have been carried out in the Netherlands by Annelou Van Gijn (this volume, 2010a, 2010b) who has examined both unifacially retouched Grand-Pressigny blades and flat, bifacially retouched Scandinavian blades. Her research suggests that these pieces saw little physical use in the Netherlands, but were largely curated in organic sheathes from which they were regularly removed, perhaps to be brandished publically in demonstrations of wealth or status. These results are comparable with use-wear analyses on two British flint daggers which also show signs of sheathing (Grace 1990; Green *et al.* 1982), but not with analyses of Grand-Pressigny blades found elsewhere (Beugnier & Plisson 2004; Vaughan & Bocquet 1987) or with the Volhynian pieces described by Gruźdź *et al.* (this volume), some of which bear sickle gloss. The large number of resharpened flint daggers attests to their having had some sort of physical function, but without considerable, systematic use-wear analysis the nature of those functions and their variability in time and over space cannot even begin to be discussed.

3. Positioning flint daggers within the broader sphere of lithic technology...

In addition, a better understanding of the technology and manufacture of flint daggers would allow us to trace the development of their unique *chaînes opératoires* in order to better understand the origins of the dagger form and the development and transmission of specialist know-how and knowledge from one generation to the next. This approach sidesteps (but complements) traditional typological or contextual analyses, allowing us to look beyond the museum cases and pristine flint daggers to the beaten up, broken and generally poorly made examples housed ignominiously in dark basements and dusty cardboard boxes. These pieces often lack the visual impact or contextual data of the daggers we generally illustrate and display, but they also provide insight into the variety of knapping techniques and differing levels of skill within specific dagger assemblages (cf. Olausson 2008).

Moreover, the sequence of development of the techniques involved in flint dagger manufacture would also merit future research. For example, the origins and spread of different pressure flaking and parallel retouch techniques used in the manufacture of daggers from Anatolia to Denmark deserve considerable attention, particularly in light of the anomalous daggers and dagger fragments from Çatalhöyük (Zimmermann, this volume; cf. Apel 2012). Similarly, the wider lithic industry in which various types of flint daggers were developed and then produced in great numbers, should be considered as a rich source of data for understanding these specific implements. Certainly, research on the origins and early development of the Grand-Pressigny daggers has demonstrated that technological studies within the production regions can yield valuable information for flint dagger researchers even when flint daggers are not the primary implement being studied (Ihuel *et al.*, this volume). Studies of flint technology, particularly in areas which lack a rich tradition of later

prehistoric lithic research, have potential to yield significant information not just for archaeologists seeking to develop a better understanding of flint daggers, but also for more general archaeological narratives concerning technological innovation, specialisation and the movement of people and ideas.

For example, as our understanding of Bronze Age and Iron Age stone tools continues to improve (Eriksen 2010), it is no longer tenable to position the beginning of the Metal Ages (when many of these flint daggers were in circulation) as the time of the last flowering of specialist lithic technology. While much of the later prehistoric lithic assemblage is demonstrably *ad hoc*, recent re-evaluations suggest that some flint tools were produced with great skill and through the application of specialist knapping sequences (Högberg 2010). Similarly, Van Gijn (2010a) has demonstrated that fine, bifacially knapped "sickles" remained not only in circulation, but also in use for sod cutting in Dutch later prehistory. A better grasp of the development and eventual attenuation of specialist flint dagger production, and the intersection of this specialist knapping technology with more mundane flint knapping activities, might serve to illuminate how lithic technology continued to be practiced and transmitted even as bronze, and subsequently iron, replaced stone tools in most quotidian tool kits.

Finally, by focusing on the lithic-ness of lithic daggers we foreground some of the bigger questions in flint dagger studies, particularly connections between the different dagger assemblages and how those might reflect patterns of contact and exchange. Raw material studies, for example, give us enormous insight into the movement of specific implements. More standardised protocols for recording and identifying the raw materials from which lithic implements were produced will allow for the examination of myriad object types and where and when they travelled. *Projet JADE*, an internationally helmed project studying the spread of Neolithic polished stone axes made from north Italian jade, was developed along exactly these lines and has demonstrated the power of raw material-focussed lithic research to contribute to debates around the spread of new ideas, new technologies and social practices (Pétrequin *et al.* 2012). Based on their findings, specifically that Italian stone axes were deposited from Ireland to Denmark to Bulgaria during the Neolithic, raw material studies – as well as more minute studies of specific technological developments – might be usefully applied to the question of what, if any, connection exists between the elaborate Anatolian and Egyptian flint implements discussed by Zimmermann and Graves-Brown and those which circulated in Europe. On a smaller scale, recent work in Scandinavia has demonstrated that flint daggers and flint axes were consciously and regularly produced from different flints with different physical properties (Högberg & Olausson

2007), making clear the role that knowledgeable specialist practitioners played in the entire sequence of flint dagger and axe production. Instead of singling out flint daggers as a totally unique variety of lithic implement, we should instead remember that they were produced alongside other flint and stone tools, that they circulated in worlds where stone tools were in daily use and that at least some of their significance probably derived from the tension between their elaborate form and mundane raw material (Frieman 2012).

4. … but viewing them from a cross-craft perspective

One final suggestion for future research into flint daggers lies less in the use of specific methodologies, than in a general attitude to these implements: specifically that they must be re-situated in their wider technological and material contexts. While archaeologists may specialise in ancient textiles, ceramics, lithics or other materials, ancient people did not. The world in which flint daggers were produced was a world in which most people probably had at least a bit of skill in a variety of technological processes, while a very few people developed specialist knowledge in one or two specific technologies. Thus, cross-craftsmanship, that is the migration of knowledge from one technological or material domain into another, cannot be ignored. Much has been made of the relationship between lithic daggers and metal daggers, but only recently have the lithic and metal industries of this period begun to be compared (Frieman 2012). Similarly, the presence of daggers in materials beyond stone and metal, such as bone, antler and wood (see Shoda, this volume), suggests that the people making daggers were taking part in complex systems of production, value and meaning which a tight focus on flint and/or metal will not allow us to address. In fact, this sort of narrow perspective obstructs our ability to examine these wider networks of material and technological relatedness.

How useful is cross-cultural comparison?

Although I have just suggested that more work needs to be done to draw parallels and contrasts between different assemblages of flint daggers, over national boundaries and across archaeological periods, archaeologists also must not lose sight of the value of the fine-grained approach. As many of the papers in this volume demonstrate, developing an intimate knowledge of a small, regionally bounded set of flint daggers can yield enormous dividends in the form of new data and new insights. In fact, the very granularity of this research has set this volume up as challenge to the broader narrative of the 'dagger idea' as discussed in the introduction. If we accept the variety in flint dagger forms, technologies, social interpretations and physical

functions, we are left with little to no evidence *aside from the widespread production, use and deposition of hand-held, pointed, double-edged blades* that any sort of universal dagger idea even existed. Yet, people did produce daggers in a variety of materials for hundreds of years, largely during the extended and slow transition to metal use. Clearly, we are left looking at a much more complex situation than the development of a display weapon for elites or of a sacrificial tool for new rites. This very complexity can only be resolved through further regional studies focussed on developing a deep understanding of the technology and significance of specific sets of flint daggers through the application of, for example, use-wear analysis, raw material studies, or any other of the approaches discussed above. This volume has, for the first time, brought together a variety of these studies, and the major result is the impression that, while different communities were making use of their flint daggers in vastly different ways, contact between them and other flint-dagger-using groups was, perhaps, more intensive, longer lasting and more complicated than we have previously appreciated.

Certainly worth discussing in this context is the appearance and use of lithic daggers in northeast Asia at the very start of the Metal Ages (Shoda, this volume). Like the central and western European examples, many of these pieces were very finely made of special raw materials and regularly accompanied male burials during the transitional phase between Stone Age and Metal Age. Research into these lithic implements is not as long-standing as it is in Europe and until very recently focussed only on typological classification with little attention paid to production technology or function. The first comprehensive catalogue of lithic daggers from the Russian Far East has only just been published (Yanshina & Shoda 2014). Consequently, it may be too early to begin examining the striking and intriguing parallels between these implements and the flint daggers of Central and Western Europe (Shoda & Frieman 2010). The lack of any obviously similar Central Asian artefact types probably precludes a direct relationship, but broader concepts about metal, metallurgy and the significance of daggers may have influenced their production. Certainly people living in Eurasia in later prehistory were highly mobile, and a variety of archaeological and technological data confirms that ideas, technologies and some individuals travelled very long distances at this time (Kohl 2009).

Perhaps looking for a universal meaning or even a small handful of reasons why people made flint daggers is the wrong tactic. Instead of applying the last hundred years' top down approach to the appearance and use of flint daggers, we need to take the sort of bottom-up approach which this volume seeks to highlight. Working from the data and re-evaluating it as necessary, for example to include broken implements and pieces without contexts or to re-structure older typologies, we have the tools and material to hand to re-write the narrative of each of the different clusters of flint daggers in Europe and beyond and, consequently, to re-write the entire story of dagger production and use in later prehistory. In doing so, we allow regional and chronological differences to shed light on localised practices, technologies and levels of engagement with wider contact networks, while also highlighting those aspects of dagger production, use and deposition which cross periods and regions. Instead of seeking out a dagger idea, we should perhaps spend the next few years seeking out more daggers and attempting to tease out their position in local, regional and continental spheres of technological knowledge and social practice.

References

Adams, W. Y. & Adams, E. W. 1991. *Archaeological Typology and Practical Reality: a dialectical approach to artifact classification and sorting.* Cambridge: Cambridge University Press.

Apel, J. 2012. Tracing pressure-flaked arrowheads in Europe. In: C. Prescott & H. Glørstad (eds.), *Becoming European. The transformation of third millennium Northern and Western Europe.* Oxford: Oxbow Books. 156–164.

Beugnier, V. & Plisson, H. 2004. Les poignards en silex du Grand-Pressigny. Fonction de signe et fonctions d'usage. In: P. Bodu & C. Constantin (eds.), *Approches fonctionnelles en préhistoire: XXVe Congrès préhistorique de France, Nanterre, 24–26 novembre 2000.* Paris: Société Préhistorique Française. 139–154.

Bloemers, J. H. F. 1968. Flintdolche vom Skandinavischen Typus in den Niederlanden. *Berichten van de Rijksdienst voor het Oudheidkundig Bodemonderzoek* 18. 47–110.

Eriksen, B. V. ed. 2010. *Lithic Technology in Metal Using Societies.* Aarhus: Jutland Archaeological Society.

Frieman, C. J. 2012. Flint daggers, copper daggers and technological innovation in Late Neolithic Scandinavia. *European Journal of Archaeology* 15(3): 440–464.

Grace, R. 1990. The limitations and applications of usewear data. *Aun* 14: 9–14.

Green, H. S., Houlder, C. H. & Keeley, L. H. 1982. A flint dagger from Ffair Rhos, Ceredigion, Dyfed, Wales. *Proceedings of the Prehistoric Society* 48: 492–495.

Grimes, W. F. 1932. The Early Bronze Age flint dagger in England and Wales. *Proceedings of the Prehistoric Society of East Anglia* 6(4): 340–355.

Högberg, A. 2010. Two traditions and a hybrid? South Scandinavian Late Bronze Age flint. In: Eriksen 2010: 61–80.

Högberg, A. & Olausson, D. 2007. *Scandinavian Flint – an Archaeological Perspective.* Aarhus: Aarhus University Press.

Hughes, R. E., Högberg, A. & Olausson, D. 2012. The chemical composition of some archaeologically significant flint from Denmark and Sweden. *Archaeometry* 54(5): 779–795.

Kohl, P. L. 2009. *Making Bronze Age Eurasia.* Cambridge: Cambridge University Press.

Kühn, H. J. 1979. *Das Spätneolithikum in Schleswig-Holstein.* Offa-Bücher 40. Neumünster: K. Wachholtz.

Lomborg, E. 1973. *Die Flintdolche Dänemarks: Studien über Chronologie und Kulturbeziehungen des südskandinavischen Spätneolithikums.* Nordiske fortidsminder serie B in quarto 1. København: Universitetsforlaget i kommission hos H.H.J. Lynge.

Mottes, E. 2001. Bell Beakers and beyond: flint daggers of northern Italy between technology and typology. In: F. Nicolis (ed.), *Bell Beakers Today: Pottery, People, Culture, Symbols in Prehistoric Europe. Proceedings of the International Colloquium, Riva del Garda (Trento, Italy) 11–16 May 1998.* Trento, Italy: Provincia Autonoma di Trento Servizio Beni Culturali Ufficio Beni Archeologici. 519–545.

Olausson, D. 2008. Does practice make perfect? Craft expertise as a factor in aggrandizer strategies. *Journal of Archaeological Method and Theory* 15(1): 28–50.

Pétrequin, P., Cassen, S., Errera, M., Klassen, L., Sheridan, A. & Pétrequin, A.-M. eds. 2012. *JADE. Grandes haches alpines du Néolithique européen, Ve au IVe millénaires av. J.-C.* Besançon, France: Presses Universitaires de Franche-Comté.

Read, D. W. 2007. *Artifact Classification: A Conceptual and Methodological Approach.* Walnut Creek, CA: Left Coast Press.

Shoda, S. & Frieman, C. J. 2010. Comparative study of the adoption of metallurgy in northeast Asia and northwest Europe-Focusing on weapon-shaped bronze and stone tools. In: S. Shoda, T. Kishimoto & S. Arai (eds.), *Program and Abstracts of the 3rd International Conference of the Society for the History of Asian Casting Technology.* Tokyo: Society for the History of Asian Casting Technology. [in Japanese]

Van Gijn, A. 2010a. *Flint in Focus: Lithic Biographies in the Neolithic and Bronze Age.* Leiden: Sidestone Press.

Van Gijn, A. 2010b. Not at all obsolete! The use of flint in the Bronze Age Netherlands. In: Eriksen 2010: 45–60.

Vaughan, P. C. & Bocquet, A. 1987. Première étude fonctionelle d'outils lithiques Néolithiques du village de Charavines, Isère. *L'Anthropologie* 91 (2): 399–410.

Whittaker, J. C., Caulkins, D. & Kamp, K. A. 1998. Evaluating consistency in typology and classification. *Journal of Archaeological Method and Theory* 5(2): 129–164.

Yanshina, O. & Shoda, S. 2014. *Weapon-shaped stone tools from the Russian Far East: The Museum Collections.* Nara: Nara National Research Institute for Cultural Properties.